St. Caillin, W. M. Hennessy, D. H. Kelly

The Book of Fenagh in Irish and English

St. Caillin, W. M. Hennessy, D. H. Kelly

The Book of Fenagh in Irish and English

ISBN/EAN: 9783337147730

Printed in Europe, USA, Canada, Australia, Japan

Cover: Foto ©ninafisch / pixelio.de

THE
BOOK OF FENAGH

IN

Irish and English,

ORIGINALLY COMPILED BY

ST. CAILLIN,

ARCHBISHOP, ABBOT, AND FOUNDER OF FENAGH,

ALIAS

DUNBALLY OF MOY-REIN,

TEMPORE ST. PATRICII;

WITH

THE CONTRACTIONS RESOLVED, AND, (AS FAR AS POSSIBLE), THE ORIGINAL TEXT RESTORED.

THE WHOLE CAREFULLY REVISED, INDEXED, AND COPIOUSLY ANNOTATED, BY

W. M. HENNESSY, M.R.I.A.,

AND DONE INTO ENGLISH, BY

D. H. KELLY, M.R.I.A.

DUBLIN:

PRINTED BY ALEXANDER THOM, 87 & 88, ABBEY-STREET.

1875.

DEDICATION

TO THE

LADY LOUISA TENNISSON.

My Dear Lady Louisa,

I consider myself peculiarly fortunate in being permitted to bring out my volume under the auspices of that rare being, a fashionable English woman who does not disdain to take an interest in the history and antiquities of the land of her adoption; and who, a circumstance still more rare, has made herself acquainted with our old Celtic tongue.

This, as a spoken language, is now rapidly dying out; but it is fortunate that it has of late years, especially in Germany, arrested the attention of the ablest philologists of the day.

Much has been done to rescue its ancient records (perhaps the most ancient *written ones* in Europe) from manuscript oblivion; but very much still remains to be done; and as it is most desirable to have this done whilst still the spoken tongue remains to correct the speculations of those who only study it as a dead language, I have imposed upon myself the task of endeavouring to rescue one such ancient tome from MS. oblivion, and present it in print, with a faithful translation into English, with its ancient and sometimes extremely arbitrary contractions *carefully resolved*, and with a text sedulously collated with all existing exemplars, so as to have it as pure and as perfect as possible.

This ancient book contains the history and traditions, from the fifth century, of the Two Breifneys, comprising the counties of Leitrim and Cavan, which are illustrated by copious explanatory notes by my friend Mr. W. M. Hennessy, who has successfully identified many places whose locality had been before unknown; and I trust to present it to your Ladyship in a form which, considering it as the voluntary effort of a mere country Gentleman, may be permitted to pass without much adverse criticism. It is true that some of its legends are wild and fanciful, but they are not one whit more preposterous than those of ancient Greece or Rome; and mixed up with them is much of genuine history, and much that may yield valuable information also to the topographer and philologist. And now thanking you for your interest in our national history, and your kind patronage, and also for the photographs from which the illustrations of this volume are taken,

I beg to subscribe myself,

Your Ladyship's very obliged humble Servant,

D. H. Kelly.

INTRODUCTION.

The text of the following edition of the "Old Book of Caillin," as the Book of Fenagh was anciently called, has been taken, as far as possible, from a very fine transcript[1] most accurately made by the

Illustrations.

At the end of the dialogue between SS. [illegible] infra, p. 291, he says that it was "through metre and extacy

(1) This is referred to as MS. A. in the notes appended to the present work.

(2) This MS., Cott. Vesp. E. VI., is indicated as MS. B. in the following pages.

(3) The late Dr. Todd so thought. "The MS. of the Book of Fenagh," he wrote, "by Maurice O'Mulconry, written in 1517, from which Mr. O'Donovan made his transcript, is in private hands. But the more ancient MS. from which Maurice O'Mulconry's copy was taken, is in the British Museum."—*Ir. Archæol. Miscellany*, Vol. I., p. 113, note f.

Caillin spake the foregoing things to Manchan, *though we have written them in prose.*" Further on we are told, "that it was this Tadhg (O'Roddy) that caused Maurice O'Mulconry to put this Book here in a narrative form . . . for there was *only poetry in the Old Book* (p. 311);" and again the copyist adds, "that the Book was *only in metre* until now; and it is in *stories* and *poems* from henceforth (p. 393)."

If, then, O'Mulconry's statements can be relied on (and there seems no reason to doubt their correctness), it is plain that the British Museum fragment *cannot be a part of the Old Book of St. Caillin.* It would rather appear to be a transcript made from O'Mulconry's copy.

The contents of some of the folios missing from the latter, are also wanting in the British Museum fragment, which, however, supplies(1) the matter of the lost folios 11 and 29 of O'Mulconry's transcript; but unfortunately, between them both, the full text of the Old Book cannot be recovered. As regards the Old Book, it is now impossible to ascertain either the actual date of its composition or its ultimate fate. But it must have been compiled, judging by its contents, about or previous to A.D. 1300. Its transcriber, O'Mulconry, assigns, as one of the reasons for his having copied it, that "the vellum on which Caillin's Old Book was before this time, had grown old and decayed (p. 393)." Professor O'Curry thought that a portion of the work was composed about the year 1430(2); but he was led into this error through mistaking(3) the identity of

(1) Vide infra, p. 111, n. 8, and p. 237, n. 10.

(2) See MS. Materials, 398.

(3) Professor O'Curry's error is the more pardonable, that Tady O'Roddy, who ought to have known the contents of the MS., says of this William Gorm, "ce be he neрсıо," "who he was I know not." See p. 72, n. 5.

the person called "William Gorm," or William de Lasci, referred to at pp. 73, 77, infra.

It could not, however, have been written by St. Caillin; for if it had been, O'Mulconry would surely have said so. It rather seems to have been a work in the composition of which more than one person had assisted; as, in one place, the copyist complains "that the *Old Book of Fenagh had tired him, for it was a cleric that wrote the exemplar of this part of it.*"(1) If the writer in question had been St. Caillin, the complaint would scarcely have been uttered in the presence of Tadhg O'Roddy, St. Caillin's successor, who, through the excess of his devotion to Caillin,(2) had caused the Book to be put "in a narrative form."

We are not able to say what other liberties O'Roddy and his scribe may have taken with the original Book, besides interpolating "the prose summaries," which he caused to be written, probably with the object of enhancing the value of the work, if not of explicitly specifying the extent and nature of the *dues* to which he, as St. Caillin's successor at Fenagh, was entitled; but his learned descendant, Tadhg O'Roddy,(3) who has added several marginal notes in the O'Mulconry copy, naively reproves "the ignorant people" who were perpetually saying, "that Tadhg O'Roddy put many *lies* into this Book of Caillin, which was written in the year of Christ's age, 1516."(4)

Of the family of O'Roddy, hereditary comharbs of Fenagh, or successors of St. Caillin, by whom the Old Book of Fenagh was preserved, with the shrine and the bell of the saint, much might be

(1) Vide p. 330, n. 8.

(2) Vide p. 311.

(3) For some account of this remarkable man, see Dr. Todd's paper in the *Irish Archæological Miscellany*, Vol. 1., p. 112, et seq.

(4) Vide p. 170, n. 2, infra.

written. It is stated in the present work that the "Abbotship or Herenachship of Fenagh" were always filled from one branch of the family called "the sons of the clerech" (¹) or cleric. This cleric, whose name was Alexander, was the grandson of Rodachæ, from whom the name of O'Rodachæ or O'Roddy has been derived, and must have lived about A.D. 800, since Tadhg O'Roddy, who caused the transcription of the work in 1516, was the 25th in descent from him. There is no reason to doubt the statement above quoted, that the succession to the Abbacy of Fenagh was hereditary(²) in his family. The O'Roddys seem to have been distinguished for great zeal in the promotion of Irish literature. Their generous hospitality has often been the subject of laudation by Irish poets.

The last learned representative of the family, Tadgh O'Roddy of Crossfield, near Fenagh (whose annotations on the O'Mulconry MS. are reproduced in the present work), states in his letter to Edward Llwyd, written about A.D. 1690, that he had "as many Irish books of philosophy, physic, poetry, genealogies, mathematics, invasions, law, romances, &c., and as ancient as any in Ireland."(³) Where are they all now? It is only surprising that the O'Mulconry copy has not shared their fate. Its preservation is doubtless owing to the veneration attached to it as a relic of the founder of Fenagh.

The last of the O'Roddys to whom the custody of this ancient Book descended was parish priest of Kilronan, and a man of sadly intemperate habits. He used to eke out his slender dues by sending out the Holy Book for a small gratuity, to be used by any who

(¹) Vide p. 391.

(²) Regarding the hereditary nature of the succession in some Abbacies, see Todd's St. Patrick, p. 155, and Reeves's Adamnan, p. 335.

(³) *Ir. Arch. Miscel.*, p. 122.

wished, by swearing upon it, to clear themselves from any imputation, or to render any agreement especially binding by having its attestation upon it; for the simple peasantry looked upon such an oath or attestation as something *awfully binding*, and its violation sure to be attended with *terrible retribution* to the violators. Notwithstanding, it was alas! very carelessly kept by its reverend custodian; and being in loose folios without binding, several of them have been lost.

At his death it passed, with his other small effects, to his successor, the Rev. Mr. Fitzgerald, who had him respectably interred, and to whose courteous politeness the Translator and Editor is indebted for being permitted to see and examine it, having been brought to his residence at Kilronan for that purpose, by his excellent friend Thomas M'Dermott Roe, with whom he was then on a visit at Alderford the year previous to the terrible potato famine (1845), when that excellent specimen of a true Irish chief was cut off by fever, caught in his benevolent exertions to relieve his suffering countrymen.

The Rev. Mr. Fitzgerald too had these precious folios loose in a drawer along with his wearing apparel; but I believe that none of them have been lost whilst in his custody. From him they passed into the possession of the late Rev. Mr. Slevin, P.P. of Gortlitteragh, County Leitrim, who kindly permitted my friend Mr. W. M. Hennessy to collate the translator's transcript of Dr. J. O'Donovan's copy in the Royal Irish Academy with it, and thus enabled him to certify its exact correctness.

In fact this undoubted ancient volume of Irish literature is in the Editor's opinion a RENTAL of the rents, tributes, privileges, and immunities of St. Caillin's right-royally endowed Abbacy of Fenagh, in the County of Leitrim, consisting of poems and rhapsodies, and legendary historical accounts of their origin and extent; and which were subsequently put together with prose narrative, as its remains have descended to our times. It is, however, an indubitable specimen of very ancient Gælic literature; and neither trouble nor expense has been spared to present it to the public in as complete a state as possible. In this effort the Editor has had the cordial assistance of Mr. W. M. Hennessy, who accompanied him to Fenagh to personally inspect the locality; who kindly went over to London and searched the Irish MSS. in the British Museum, and then went to Oxford and examined the Irish collections there. And here the Editor must express his great obligations to Mr. Hennessy for revising his MS. and correcting its errors; for his valuable annotations, and his inestimable aid in putting the volume through the press; so that if any credit be given to it, it is more due to him than to the Editor—a mere country gentleman, who for love of the ancient literature of his native land, has for nearly thirty years applied himself to its production.

As to what portion of the Old Book of St. Caillin, if any, there may be in the inaccessible library of Lord Ashburnham, we can only refer to Dr. O'Conor's Catalogue of the Stowe Library.

The Editor must also express his obligations to the Very Rev. the Dean of Armagh, Messrs. O'Loony and O'Longan, and other valued friends, who have aided him in fixing localities; and to Miss Stokes for kindly designing the initial letter.

Leabar Fidhnacha.

THE BOOK OF FENAGH.

Ego sitienti dabo de fonte aquae uiuae gratis .i. Inti sandtaigeas ind firinde do berra do indascuid do ṫobar in usci bí.

Qui uicerit possidebit haec .i. Inti chlofeas is do dobertar na netheri.

Et ero illi deus. Ocus is meisi bas dia do.

Et erit ille mihi filius. Ocus is hesium bis mac damsai.

Isu Crist mac De bí, tigernda na huili dulu, dara perso na diadachtu, medonfithaigthid muintiri nime ocus talman, Slainicid in ċinidai daennai. Is he ro raiḋ na briathrasai do inchoiscc in mor maithiusai tidnaices dia noemaib ocus dia firinaib, ocus dond fairinn doberait morgraḋ do isind eclais i fos.

Eoin immorro mac Etcebedei, comarba na hoġi, in dara hapstal déc ro thog Isa, fer ro scrib in soscela comdita, inti rosindiġestair tobar ind fir ecna do huċt int ḟlaithemdai, is he ro scrib na briatḣrasa, ocus forfáccaib i cuimne las in eclais co dered in doṁain; conaraid hisund, Ego sitienti dabo de fonte aquae uiuae gratis. Inti ṡanntaiges ind firinde doberra do innascuiḋ do thobar ind usci bí. Compaint immorro na briathrasa is he leth atoebi la hEoin co du in erbairt Isu remhe, Ego sum alpha et omega, principium et finis .i. is me tosach na huili dulai, is me a forbai. Coimd for slicht na mbriathairsin

The ornamental letter which heads this page was designed by Miss Stokes, drawn by Mr. Connell, and engraved by Mr. George Hanlon.

[1] *freely.*—ind ascuiḋ.—Literally "as a gift." "Without money and without price."—Isaiah, lv. 1.

[2] *possidebit hæc.*—possedebit, A.

[3] *comarb.*—This term, which means "heir" or "successor," being comp. of

EGO sitienti dabo de fonte aquæ vivæ (*sic*) gratis; i.e. He who thirsteth for the Truth, to him will I give from the Well of the Water of Life, freely[1].

Qui vicerit possidebit[2] hæc; i.e. He that conquers, to him shall these things be given.

Et ero illi Deus. And I will be his God.

Et erit ille mihi filius. And he shall be a son to me.

Jesus Christ son of the Living God, Lord of all created things, the Second Person of the Godhead, the intercessor of the people of Heaven and Earth, the Saviour of the Human race—He it is who spake these words to proclaim the great benefits which He bestows upon His saints and Just ones; and upon those that bear Him great love in the Church on Earth.

John, moreover, the son of Zebedee, the Comarb[3] of the Virgin, the twelfth Apostle whom Jesus chose; the man who wrote the Divine Gospel; the person who established the well of true knowledge[4] from the bosom of the Saviour—He it is that wrote these words, and left them as a memorial with the church to the end of the world; when he said here, "Ego sitienti dabo de fonte aquæ vivæ gratis"; i.e. "Whosoever thirsteth for the truth, to him will I give from the Well of the Water of Life *gratis*." The complement of these words, moreover, as used by John, is where Jesus said before "EGO SUM ALPHA ET OMEGA, PRINCIPIUM[5] ET FINIS," i.e. I am the beginning of all things: I am their end. And it is in pursuance of those words John weaves together

com=co, and *arba*=orpe (hæreditas: cf. *an orpe nemde*, gl. hæreditas cœlestis, Zeuss' Gram. Celt. I. 245), seems to be used here with reference to our Lord's expression, "Woman, behold thy son" (John xix. 26), and to indicate John as the successor of His Divine Master in the affection of the Virgin.

4 *knowledge.*—eclma, A.

5 *principium.*—in principium, A.

compuaiges ocus comḋluthas Eoin in aisneissea, conarair for slicht a maigistrech Isu, Ego sitienti dabo de fonte aquae uiuae gratis. INti ṡantuigfes ind firinne dobersa do inascuiḋ do thopar in usci ḃi.

Qui uicerit possidebit haec .i. INti chloisfes is do doberthar na nitheriu.

Et ero illi deus; ocus is me bus dia do.

Et erit ille mihi filius; ocus bid mac herium daṁsa.

Is on tosassa tra .i. o Isa Crist is tosar ind fir ecna ro linait inna huili noeiḃ o rath ecna ocus ḟaitsine, o fertaib ocus mirḃailiḃ, o chumachtu diaisneri oc forcetal na neretecdai, oc traethad ingrinntide na mac mallachtan, amail ro linad inti diata lith ocus foraithm[e]t i tecmaing na rearsa .i. in lassar lainnerdai, ocus in locarn solustu, ocus in puiṫean tatniṁach, ocus in lia loġṁar, ocus in gescai torthach

fol. 1 b. co clanuib[a] subalach .i.

Caillin
Mic Niatach
Mic Dubain
Mic Fraoich
Mic Cumscraiġ
Mic Echta
Mic Eirc
Mic Ercdail
Mic Echta
Mic Duib
Mic Maġnuaiḋ
Mic Nerta
Mic Fornerta
Mic Echta
Mic Uisle
Mic Beire
Mic Beiḋḃi
Mic Doilḃri
Mic Luiġdech Conmaic
Mic Oirbren ṁair
Mic Etheḋoin
Mic Seġda
Mic Airt
Mic Allta
Mic Oġamuin
Mic Fiḋcaire
Mic Doilḃri
Mic Eona

[1] *possidebit.*—possedebit, A.

[2] *indescribable.*—diaiṡneri, A; the stroke over the first s in the word being an error.

[3] *Caillin.*—This pedigree is, to say the least, rather unreliable. Including the first and last names (Caillin and Rudraigo), there are 36 generations in the list; and as in well attested pedigrees 30 years represent a generation, it follows that 36 × 30 (=1080) should indicate the number of years between the age of Caillin

and combines this narrative, when he says, after his Master Jesus, "Ego sitienti dabo de fonte aquæ vivæ (*sic*) gratis." "Whosoever earnestly desires the truth, I will give unto him from the Well of the Water of Life *gratis*."

"Qui vicerit possidebit[1] hæc," i.e. he that conquers, to him shall these things be given.

"Et ero illi Deus;" "and I will be his God."

"Et erit ille mihi filius;" "and he shall be my son."

It is from this fountain, moreover, i.e. from Jesus Christ who is the fountain of true knowledge, that all the saints were filled with the grace of wisdom and prophecy, with [the gift of working] wonders and miracles, with indescribable[2] power in instructing heretics, in overcoming the persecutions of the sons of malediction; as he was filled whose festival and commemoration occur at this time, viz., the brilliant flame, and the shining torch, and the sparkling ray, and the precious stone, and the fruitful branch to children of virtue, viz.:

Caillin,[3]
Son of Niata,
Son of Duban,
Son of Fraech,
Son of Cumscrach,
Son of Echt,
Son of Erc,
Son of Eredal,
Son of Echt,
Son of Dubh,
Son of Moghruadh,
Son of Nert,
Son of Fornert,
Son of Echt,
Son of Uisel,
Son of Beire,
Son of Beidhbhe,
Son of Doilbhre,
Son of Lugaid Conmac,
Son of Oirbsen Mór,
Son of Ethedon,
Son of Seghda,
Son of Art,
Son of Allta,
Son of Oghamun,
Son of Fidhchar,
Son of Doilbhre,
Son of Eon,

and that of Rudraige. But as Rudraige (or Rury) the grandfather of Fergus MacRoy, must have lived about, or shortly before, the beginning of the Christian era, this calculation would refer Caillin's time to the 10th century A.D., which is certainly some centuries too late. It is probable that two separate lines of descent are here jumbled together. There is a pedigree of St. Caillin given in the *Leabhar*

Mic Cetguinc chalurach	Mic Conmaic
Mic Mochta	Mic Fergusa
Mic Meromain	Mic Rosa
Mic Moġad taet	Mic Rudruige.

Is ann dono atfiadar lith ocus sollamain inti noem Chaillin i mi nouimbir int sa[i]nnred; in dara laithe iar feil Martain.

Finntan mac Labrada mic Betha mic Lamiach, qui dicitur mac Bochna (ar Bochna nomen matris eius). Ba he tra in Findtan sin ardsenoir hErend. Is aige do hoiled ocus do lesaiged inti noim Chaillin gur bo slan a .c. bliadan. Is airesin ro ḟorcongair Findtan fair dol do Roiṁ, do ḟoġlaim ecna ocus eolus, gumad gem tsochair ocus gumad eoċair fuaraileti ainḃfis ocus aineolais d'feraiḃ Erenn a ecna sum ocus a eolas iartain.

Da ced bliadain imorro ro anustair Caillin, co tainic Patraicc mac Calpruinn do sil[ad] irsi ocus creidmi, ocus do innarbad idal ocus arracht a hErind.

Inaimsir Laegaire mic Neill imorro tainic Patraicc [in] Erinn. Da bliadain .x. iar tiachtuin Patraicc do riacht Caillin doċom nErend. Ni sochaide do noemuib olchena do ġenadar in foġluim ocus in saethar dorinne Caillin noem. Daig ro b'imċ[i]an itir na ġradaiḃ ocus na cemib rogab naem Chaillin. Fri re Chormaic mic Airt ro gaḃ grada coronta

Breac (p. 16), but it does not carry the line beyond the fifth generation, Cecht, or MacCecht.

[1] *Second day.*—The 11th of November is St. Martin's day; and St. Caillin's festival is commemorated on the 13th of the same month.

[2] *Finntan.*—This is the fabulous character who is said to have survived the Deluge in Ireland, and to have imparted to St. Finnian of Moville, under the name of Tuan Mac Cairill, the colonizations of Ireland from the Flood to St. Finnian's time (*circa* 560). In ancient Irish legends four persons are represented as having been saved from the Flood, besides the inhabitants of the Ark; namely *Fors* in the East, *Farran* in the North, *Finntan* in the West, and *Annoid* in the South. Keating thinks the fable (which he states that he could not find in "any chief book of authority") worthy of refutation. (*Hist. of Ireland*, Haliday's ed., 157). But it is strange that he was not acquainted with the account of these four individuals contained in *Lebor na hUidhri*

Son of Cetguine Calusach,	Son of Conmac,
Son of Mochta,	Son of Fergus,
Son of Mesoman,	Son of Rossa,
Son of Mogh Tacth,	Son of Rudraige.

The time in which is celebrated the festival and solemnity of St. Caillin, moreover, is in the month of November in especial, the second day[1] after the festival of Martin.

Finntan[2] son of Labraid, son of Bith, son of Lamech, who is called Mac Bochna (for Bochna was his mother's name)—This Finntan was, indeed, the arch—senior of Ireland. It is by him St. Caillin was nursed and fostered until his hundredth year was completed.

Then it was that Finntan commanded him to go to Rome, to learn wisdom and knowledge, in order that his wisdom and knowledge might afterwards be, to the men of Ireland, a precious gem, and a key for the unlocking of ignorance and want of knowledge.

Two hundred years, moreover, Caillin remained [in Rome], until Patrick son of Calpurnd came to sow piety and faith, and banish idols and images out of Ireland.

In the time of Laeghaire Mac Neill, however, Patrick came [to] Ireland. Twelve years after Patrick's arrival, Caillin came to Ireland. Not many other saints performed the study[3] and labour that Saint Caillin performed. For much time intervened between the grades and degrees that Saint Caillin received. In the time of Cormac Mac Airt[4] he received the order of Tonsure,

(p. 120, b), although he refers to the MS. (*Hist.*, pref. xcvi., Haliday). The same MS. (*Lebor na hUidhri*) contains also a fragment of the more detailed notice of the colonizations of Ireland, already alluded to, as communicated to St. Finnian of Moville, which is particularly valuable for giving the ancient Irish idea of the subject of the Metempsychosis.

[3] *Study.*—foȝluim, lit. "learning," A.

[4] *Cormac Mac Airt.*—Cormac is believed to have reigned 23 years, or from A.D. 254 to 277. (See O'Flaherty's *Ogygia*, p. 333, sq.) But the Four Masters and the Annalist Tigernach make his reign 40 years, including a period of 17 years, during which he was in forced retirement. This chronology of the life of St. Caillin is a good example of the extravagance of Irish scribes, in exalting the virtues and merits of their favourites. But it may be confidently asserted that

ic altair Petair i Roim Letha. Fri linn Laeġaire mic Neill ro ġaḃ grada espuic. Ceiṫre riġ .x. roġab Erinn fris in re sin cona naṫġabail araen .i.

Cormac ua Cuind .xl. bliadan conerbailt i tig chletig.

Eocha gunnat oen bliadan cotorchair la Cormac.

Corpre lifecair mac Cormaic .uii. mbliadna .x. no a secht fichat, co torchair hi cath Ġabra Life. Fri a re siḋe roġab Caillin grada suibdechain.

Na Fothaid oen bliadian co torchair in Fothad cairpthech lasin Fothad airgtheach. Do cher dana Fothad airgthech i lLine muig, i cath Ollarba, la feine Find .h. Baiscne.

Fiacha sroiptine .xxx.i. no a trichat, co torchair las na tri Colla .i. i cath Dubċomair. Fri ré in Fiachaid sin roġab Caillin graḋa deochain fair.

Muiriḋach tirech .xxx. bliadain, co torchair la Caelbad ri Ulad, mac Cruinn badrui, uas Dabull.

Oen bliadain do Chaelbad co torchair la hEochaid muidmedon.

Eochaid muidmedon .uiii. bliadnai conerbailt do ġalar hi Teṁraiġ.

Crimthand mac Fidaig .xiii. b., conerbailt don digh neiṁ ro dailed la

these extravagant statements found no place in the original Life of St. Caillin.

[1] *Letha.*—Latium. The name *Letha* was also applied by Irish writers to Armorica, or Brittany. But the Latinized form of the name in this case is *Letavia.* Dr. O'Donovan (*Hy Fiachrach*, p. 412) seems to countenance the statements of Patrick Lynch and Lanigan, that the name *Letha* was never applied to Latium. But he was certainly wrong, as the evidences which he himself adduces (loc. cit.) conclusively show. See also O'Curry's *Lectures*, app., p. 502.

[2] *Cormac.*—This is an error. Eochaidh Gunnat, who is not reckoned as a king of Ireland by Tigernach, although he is so called in other Annals, was slain by "Lugaidh Menn, son of Aengus, of the Ulster men." (Four Mast., A.D., 267.)

[3] *Gabhair-Lifè.*—"Gabhair of the Liffey." There were many places in Ireland called *Gabhair* (gen. *Gabhra*). The place here referred to seems to have been in *Lifè*, a plain in the county Kildare through which the *Abhainn Lifè* ("River of the Liffey") flows. It was probably the old name of the hilly country near Ballymore-Eustace, from Bishop Hill to Brittas.

[4] *Fothad Cairpthech.*—"Fothad the Charioteer."

[5] *Airgthech.*—i.e. "the Plunderer."

[6] *Mugh-Linè*, or Moylinny, was the

at the altar of Peter in Rome of Letha.[1] During the reign of Laeghaire Mac Neill he received the degree of bishop. Fourteen kings governed Ireland during that time, including those two, viz. :—

Cormac Ua Cuind, 40 years, until he died in the house of Cleitech.

Eocha Gunnat one year, till slain by Cormac.[2]

Corpre Lifechair, son of Cormac, 17 years, or 27, until he was slain in the battle of Gabhair-Lifè.[3] During his time Caillin received the order of sub-deacon.

The Fothads one year, until Fothad Cairpthech[4] fell by Fothad Airgthech. Fothad Airgthech,[5] moreover, fell in Magh-Linè,[6] in the battle of Ollarba, by the soldiers of Find Ua Baiscne.[7]

Fiacha Sroptinè, 31, or 30 [years], until he was slain by the three Collas, i.e. in the battle of Dubh-Comar.[8] In the time of this Fiacha, Caillin took upon him the grade of deacon.

Muiredach Tirech, 30 years, until he was slain by Caelbad, king of Ulster, son of Crunn Badrai, over the Dabhall.

One year reigned Caelbad, until he fell by Eochaidh Muidmedhon.[9]

Eochaidh Muidmedhon[10] 7 years, until he died of illness in Tara.

Crimthand son of Fidach 16 years, until he died of the poison-drink dealt to him by Mongfind,[11] daughter of Fidach. In the year after the death of

ancient name of a plain nearly co-extensive with the present barony of Upper Antrim, county Antrim. See Reeves' *Down and Connor*, p. 62.

[7] *Find Ua Baiscne.*—Alias, Find Mac Cumhaill.

[8] *Dubh-Comar.*—Lit. the "black confluence." The confluence of the rivers Blackwater and Boyne, near Navan, county Meath.

[9] *Muidmedhon.*—Munbeoan, A.

[10] *Muidmedhon.*—Munbecli, A.

[11] *Mongfind.*—Lit. "Fair hair." This woman, who is a famous character in Irish legend, was the wife of Eochaidh Muidmedhon, and sister of Crimthand, son of Fidach, king of Ireland (ob. A.D. 378, Four Mast.) She is said to have died from tasting—to encourage her victim—the poisoned drink which she gave to her brother Crimthand, whom she wished to replace in the kingship by her own son Brian, ancestor of the Hy-Briuin families of Connacht. She was regarded as a great sorceress; and in a Tract in the Book of Ballymote (fol. 144, b. 1). Allhallow Eve is stated to have been called *Feil Moing*, or "Mong's festival," by the vulgar.

Moingfind ingen Fiduig fair. Isin bliadain iar mbas Echach muigmeḋoin roḃai Caillin ic timṫireċt os altoir ina saccart inRoim Leṫai.

Niall .ix. giallach mac Echach muidmedoin .xx. ui. bliadna conerbailt
* fol. 2, a. do ġuin* Echach mic Enna censealaiġ oc muir Icht, occ insaiġid rigi Lethai. IS fri a linn riḋein do ronad manach don ti noem Chaillin mac Niatach.

Laegaire mac Neill ba ri hErend in tan roġaḃ Caillin grada espuic. IAR tiachtain do in hErinn IS an[n] ro gaḃ gradai ardespuic o laiṁ noim Patraicc mic Calpuirn .i. o ard apstal iarthair Eorpai.

Dorat Patraicc soerċuairt gacha fir ealadan in hErind do Chaillin, ocus ro oesccuin Patraicc gaċ aen dib na riarfad aċomarbai ocus a ċaem cheall .i. Fidnachai. Dorat Patraicc do iaram ardlegoideċt insi hErend ar belaib naom hErend uili, ar ba herium ba sine dib; ocus robai ced bliadna illegoideċt hErend iarsin.

Tri ced uinge don or derg dron ised tucc Finntan do noem Chaillin in tan ro ḟoid co Roim he dia foglaim air tus. Dobert imorro Caillin taisi ocus reilci imda lais don fechtsin ic tuiḋecht o Róim, do metugad imorro onora ocus chadais ocus chomairce a chatrach ocus a choem ċille .i. Fidnacha moiġe fein.

Ba hiat dono na taisi remraite tuc Caillin lais o Roim .i. taisi ind aon

[1] *Letha.*—See note [1], p. 8.

[2] *Muir-Icht.*—"The sea of Icht;" supposed to have taken its name from the *Portus Iccius* of Cæsar. Irish writers use the term to express the British Channel. (See Reeves' *Adamnan*, 145, 149). But some place on the French coast, probably near Boulogne, is here referred to. See Dr. O'Donovan's note, regarding the expedition of King Niall, *Annals F. M.*, under the year 405.

[3] *Letha.*—This is Letavia, or Armorica, as distinguished from the other *Letha*, or Latium. In the lower margin of fol. 1 b. occurs a note stating that "Deighe, daughter of Trian, son of Dubhthach Mac Ui Lughair, chief poet of King Laeghaire Mac Neill" (who stood up to do reverence to St. Patrick, in Tara, to the dishonouring of the king), was Caillin's mother. If this is correct, we could safely refer Caillin's era to the latter half of the 6th century, which is probably the real time; for Dubhthach Mac Ui Lughair was certainly a contemporary of St. Patrick, and his great grandson might have lived about the year 600.

[4] *Neill.*—nel, A. Although St. Caillin is generally called a bishop in the Irish Records, his name is not found in any

Eochaidh Muidmedhon, Caillin was ministering over the altar of the priests in Rome of Letha.[1]

Niall the Nine-hostage-taker, son of Eochaidh Muidmedhon, 26 years, until he died of the wound [inflicted] by Eochaidh, son of Enna Cennselach, at Muir-Icht,[2] when invading the kingdom of Letha.[3] It is during his time that Caillin, son of Niata, was made a monk.

Laeghaire Mac Neill[4] was king of Ireland when Caillin received the grade of bishop. After he came to Ireland, it was there he received the degree of archbishop from the hand of St. Patrick, son of Calpurn, to wit, from the chief apostle of the west of Europe.

Patrick gave the tribute of every man of learning in Ireland to Caillin; and Patrick cursed every one of them who would not obey his successors, and his fair church, i.e. Fidhnacha. Patrick afterwards gave him the arch-legateship of the isle of Ireland, in presence of all the saints of Ireland, for he was the eldest[5] of them; and he was 100 years in the legateship of Ireland after that.

Three hundred ounces of solid red gold was what Finntan gave to Saint Caillin, when he sent him to Rome to study at first.[6] Caillin also brought with him numerous remains and relics[7] on that occasion, when coming from Rome; to increase, moreover, the honour, and respect, and right of protection of his See and fair church, i.e. Fidnacha of Magh-Rein.

The aforesaid relics, therefore,[8] which Caillin brought with him from

list of the bishops alleged to have been ordained by St. Patrick, whose contemporary he undoubtedly was not.

[5] *eldest.*—He certainly was, if the preposterous account above given of him be true. St. Ciaran of Saighir is gravely stated to have lived to the age of 360 years. But this is a moderate age compared to that of St. Caillin, according to his biographers, who would have him eclipse all other saints.

[6] *first.*—Here commences the Fragment of the Book of Fenagh in the British Museum, Cott. Vesp., E. 11, indicated by the letter B in these notes.

[7] *relics.*—St. Patrick is also stated to have brought relics from Rome, which he obtained by a "pious fraud or theft ('pio astu furtove;' *Trias Thaum.*, Colgan, p. 164), whilst the keepers of the sacred places were asleep." It is strange that Caillin's biographer did not make him emulate the example of the great missionary in this respect. See Todd's *St. Patrick*, p. 481.

[8] *therefore.*—ᴅō, A; ᴅonn, B.

apsdail .x. ocus taisi Martain, ocus taisi Lurint, ocus Stefain martir. ISed ba coimed ocus ba comrair taisceda do fo na taisibh sin .i. bret do roine Muire oiġ dia lamaiḃ féin. IS he no bith itimchell Isa ica biathad ina noiḋin.

ISiat sin na taisi ro fulairsium do chumdach iartain, ocus scrin do iaḋad impa. Acus ro fagaib (.i. Caillin) coṁairle ic Manchan iartain fri dered a ḃetha .i. a aḋlacad irrelicc Mochoemocc, ocus in tan ro bad imlan da bliaḋain decc iar mbas noim Chaillin, a thaisi do thogbail, ocus a ċur in aon scrinn fris na taisib sin. Do riġne Manchan amail adobairt Caillín fein; ro thogaib a thaisi, ocus ro ḟoslaicc in scrin; cona in oen scrinn fri taisi in ain apsdail decc, ocus fri taisi Stefain ocus Lurint, ocus fris in mbreitt ro bai itimchell Isa Crist ata taisi noem Chaillin ṁic Niatach.

Ocus ro ḟagaiḃ dia chaṫraig ocus dia congḃail, comad ard nemed ocus ardeclais os hErinn huili hi; ocus ro ḟaguibh fos gumad termand laech ocus clerech go dered domain in scrinn hisin.

IS fodeirc follus do chach chena onoir ocus airmitin in ard ḟenoir ocus in ard noim huasail irrisin ḟirchraibdig sin fiad Dia .i. Caillin caid craibdech, ar is chuige ro chuir Dia a thechtaire ocus a aingeal fein, dia ḟaisneis acus dia innisin do gach riġ ocus gaċ flaith roġab hErinn o thainig Cesair innti coa haimsir Patraicc ocus Laogaire mic Neill; ocus Germanus ba habad Roma in tan sin, ocus Amatho ba ri Roman

[1] *cloth.*—bret. This word now signifies frieze, or coarse woollen material; but formerly it meant a veil, or linen cloth. In the lists of relics mentioned in the Lives of Irish Saints, there is none more curious than this "dribble-cloth."

[2] *ordered.*—fulair, by metathesis for furail, "to command," "to order."

[3] *word.*—coṁairle; lit. advice,

[4] *Manchan.*—St. Manchan of Moethail, or Mohill, county Leitrim, where his festival is kept on the 14th February, on which day a fair is held, called "Monahan fair." The local explanation of this name, as communicated to the editor, during a recent visit to the place, by his excellent friend the Rev. F. Hunt, Rector of Mohill, is that it was so called because "buyers from the county Monaghan frequented it"! *But they don't.* "Monahan's" (or St. Manchan's) Well is still shown there.

[5] *Relig-Mochaemhog.*—The "Cemetery of Mochaemhog." This must have been

Rome, were the relics of the eleven Apostles, and the relics of Martin, and of Laurence, and of Stephen the Martyr. The guard and protecting cover which he had about those relics was a cloth[1] which the Virgin Mary made with her own hands. It is it that used to be around Jesus when He was being fed in His infancy.

Those are the relics which he subsequently ordered[2] to be covered, and inclosed in a shrine. And he (i.e. Caillin) left word[3] with Manchan[4] afterwards, towards the close of his life, to inter him in Relig-Mochaemhog;[5] and when twelve years after the death of St. Caillin would be completed, to take up his relics, and put them in the same shrine with the other relics.

Manchan did as Caillin himself commanded. He disinterred his [Caillin's] relics, and opened the shrine; so that in the same shrine with the relics of the eleven Apostles, and with the relics of Stephen and Laurence, and with the cloth that was about Jesus Christ, are the relics of St. Caillin, son of Niata.[6]

And he left [the privilege] to his city and habitation, that it should be a chief sanctuary and high church over all Ireland. And he also ordained[7] that the shrine should be a protection to laics and clerics to the end of the world.

Plain, manifest, to everyone, is the honour and reverence before God of that illustrious, pious, truly devout arch-senior, and arch-saint, the chaste, devout Caillin; for it was to him God sent His own messenger and angel, to recount and relate to him every king and every lord[8] that possessed Ireland since Cesair came into it, to the time of Patrick and Laeghaire Mac Neill. (And Germanus[9] was Abbot of Rome then; and Amatho[10] was King of the Romans

St. Mochaemhog, founder of Liath-mor-Mochaemhog (now Lemokevoge, bar. of Eliogarty, county Tipperary), who was descended, by the father's side, from Conmac, the ancestor of the Conmaicne, and therefore related to St. Caillin. His death is recorded in the Chron. Scotorum under the year 646; and it may be inferred from the context that he predeceased St. Caillin.

[6] *son of Niata.*—Omitted in B.

[7] *ordained.*—ꞃoꝼaꝫuıbh; lit. "he left."

[8] *Every lord.*—ꝫaċ ꝼlaıṫh, B. ꝫaċa ꝼlaṫhaı, A.

[9] *Germanus.*—There was no "Abbot of Rome" bearing this name. It is probably a mistake, for "Celestinus," the first Pope of the name, by whom Germanus, Bishop of Auxerre, was sent to Britain to suppress the Pelagian heresy. See Todd's *St. Patrick*, 269–70.

[10] *Amatho.*—This is also an error of

fri a linn. Ni luga imorro ro ḟaillsig int angel do tria forchongra Crist gach rí no ticfad ina diaid co brath for Erinn.

Gabail Cessra hic prima.

Roġab em ol int aingel fri Caillin cetamus, Cesair ingean Bethaḃ mic Noi, int oilen iarsech ainglıḃeri .i. Eri. L. ben umorro do riachtatar imaraon fria; triar fer imorro tancatar le .i. Finntan mac Labradai mic Bethaḃ mic Lamiach. Bith mac Noi mic Lamiach on ainmnigthear Sliaḃ Betha. Ladru luam on ainmnigther ard Ladrand. IS heside cetna marḃ hErenn rian dilind; atbath do ḟurail banaich.

Da fichet la rian dilind do rochtatar. Fuaratar huili bas rian dilind aċt Findtan nama, bai ina ċoḃlad fri ré na dilend. Oin bliadain dec air tri ced bliadan bai Findtan ic aṫrib hErenn co tainic Parthalon.

Gabail Parthaloin secunda.

Ba fas tra hEriu .ccc. bliadan iar ndilind, ar int aingel fri Caillín, co torocht Parthalon mac Sera mic Sru mic Esru do Gregaiḃ. Boi side tri ced bliadan in hErind gur bo marb do tham iartoin .ix. mile fri

course, as there was no such "King of the Romans." The writer was probably thinking of Amator, the predecessor of St. Germanus in the See of Auxerre, who is also called "King of the Romans" in the Tripartite Life of St. Patrick. *See* Todd's *St. Patrick*, 317, note [2].

The following note, the first three lines of which represent a quatrain, in Tadhg O'Rody's handwriting, is added in the lower margin of the orig. MS., col. 2, a :—

"Ocht .xx. sruḃan sa nai, fer Chaillin faṫ gan ġai, Triur fa gaċ sruḃan diḃsin, do lucht ċanta celeabraiḋ. .i. Mile, ceiṫre ced ocus daḟiċet sruḃan, ocus ceṫre Mile tri ced, ocus ḟiċe fer do gnaṫ muintir d'eglais ag Caillín, maille gaċ naoiḋeḋ oile ḋa ttiġ os a ċionn sin, ocus le serḃḟoġantaiġ ocus araile. Mise Taḋg O Róḋaiġe, mac Geroid oig, mic Taiḋg, mic Geroid, mic Taiḋg, mic Taiḋg, mac Uilliam, 7c. Anno Domini, 1688."

"Eight score cakes, nine times, was Caillin's feast, fact without falsehood. Three persons to each cake of these, of the band of Celebration-chanting, viz.: — 1,440 cakes; and the usual number of Church people with Caillin was 4,320 men, together with all other guests who might come besides, and servants and others. I am Tadhg O'Rodaighe, son of Garrett junior, son of Tadhg, son of Garrett, son of Tadhg, son of Tadhg, son of William, &c. Anno Domini, 1688."

during his time). Not less also did the Angel manifest to him, at the command of Christ, every king who would come after him for ever over Ireland.[1]

The Colonization of Cesair here, first.

"Cesair, then," said the Angel to Caillin, "the daughter of Bith, son of Noah, first occupied this religious angelic island, i.e. Ireland. Fifty women, moreover, came with her. Three men came with her likewise, to wit, Finntan, son of Labraid, son of Bith, son of Lamech; Bith, son of Noah, son of Lamech, from whom Sliabh-Betha[2] is named; and Ladru the pilot, from whom Ard-Ladrand[3] is named. He [Ladru] was the first that died in Ireland before the Deluge. He died of female persecution.[4]

Forty days before the Deluge they came. They all died before the Deluge, except Finntan alone, who was asleep during the Flood. Three hundred and eleven years was Finntan inhabiting Ireland, until Parthalon came."

The Colonization of Parthalon, secunda.

"Ireland was waste for 300 years after the Flood," said the Angel to Caillin, "until Parthalon, son of Sera, son of Sru, son of Esru, of the Greeks, arrived. He was 300 years[5] in Ireland, until he died of a plague afterwards, with

[1] *over Ireland.*—ḟ. eṙ. for ḟoṙ eṙinn, B. A. has ḟaiṫ ſonn, "a prophecy here." The MS. B is defective here, the next entry in it being the line beginning "in Cu ſin bid tochal cell," given at p. 76, *infra.*

[2] *Sliabh-Betha.*—Now Slieve-Beagh, or Slieve Baugh, a mountain on the confines of the counties of Monaghan and Tyrone. The cairn in which Bith is supposed to have been buried still exists. See O'Donovan's ed. of the Four Mast. A.M. 2242, note [s].

[3] *Ard-Ladrand.* — Supposed by Dr. O'Donovan to be identical with Ardamine, county Wexford. But though it appears from the Life of St. Moedhog to have been a place on the coast of that county (Colgan's *Acta Sanctorum*, pp. 210, 217), sufficient evidence has not yet appeared to identify it with Ardamine.

[4] *female Persecution.*—ḟuṙail banaich. In some accounts it is stated that he was hunted about by his wives, from whom he vainly sought safety in flight.

[5] 300 *years.*—Parthalon's posterity is probably meant; for it is not pretended in any of the more reliable ancient accounts that Parthalon himself lived so long after his arrival in Ireland. See Keating's *Ireland* (Haliday's ed. p. 171), where 30 years only are allowed to him.

hoin sech[t]main .i. fir mnai meic ocus ingena; .xxx. bliadain bai Eriu fas iarsin.

Gabail Nemiḋ hi sechtsa.

Doriacht iarsin Nemid mac Agnomain mic Phaim mic Tait mic Sera mic Sru mic Esru, iar trichait bliadain tares Parthaloin. Starn, Fergus, Iartan, Ainnind a chethri meic. Oin bliaḋain deg air da cet ro chaiṫetur in Erinn co togail tuir Conaing.

Conaing mac Faebair d'Fomorchaib, is lais do ronad in tor sin, do chor daerchisa for chlannaib Nemiḋ.

IS aire sin do riachtatar clanna Nemid do ṫogail in tuir sin, do dingḃail a ndochraitti diḃ. Tri fiċet mili dolotar fir hErenn don togail sin. Ro chomraicset Fomoraig ocus fir Erenn i farrad tuir Conaing, ocus ni ro airiġ nechtar dib la duire in chathaigthi co toracht in lan mara ṫairribh diblinaiḃ, co nach terno diḃ acht oen barc imbatar .xxx. trenfer d'feraiḃ hErenn.

Do gabail bFer mBolg innso.

Ba fas trau hEri fri re .cc. bliaḋan, amail atfet int aingel don ḟir naom huasal isiriuch, do Chaillin mac Niatach .i. co tancatar clanna Stairn ṁic Nemid asin Gréicc .i. Fir Bolgc, ar teiched in chisai do ratsat Gregaig forra .i. tarrud huire for lecaib loma comtar moiġe ro

[1] *Tat*, or Thoth, is said to have been the brother of Parthalon, and the son of Sera, son of Sru, son of Esru, son of Bramant, son of Fathacht, son of Magog, son of Japhet. Some accounts make Fathacht the son of Riphat, son of Gomer, son of Magog.

[2] *Iartan.*—This name is more correctly written "Iarbhanel" in other authorities.

[3] *Conang's Tower.*—This tower is alleged to have stood on *Tor-inis*, "Tower-Island" (otherwise Tory Island), off the northern coast of Donegal. It is supposed to have been a vitreous tower. See Todd's *Irish Nennius*, p. 47, *n.**

[4] *Fomorians.*—The ancient popular idea as to the origin of the Fomorians is thus given by O'Flaherty. "Hos Historici nostri *Fomhoraigh* nuncupant; qua voce Nostrates transmarinos omnes adversus Colonias primas Hiberniam infestantes denotant; Chamoque ex Africa omnes satos asserunt; exceptis his primis Fomoriis, queis nullam aliam sedem nec originem assignant."—*Ogygia*, p. 5.

[5] *men of Ireland.*—By "men of Ireland," Nemed's descendants are meant.

9,000 in one week, viz., men, women, sons, and daughters. Thirty years was Ireland waste afterwards.

The Colonization of Nemed this time.

After that came Nemed, son of Agnoman, son of Pamp, son of Tat,[1] son of Sera, son of Sru, son of Esru; at the end of thirty years after Parthalon. Starn, Fergus, Iartan,[2] Ainnind, were his four sons. They spent 211 years in Ireland, until the demolition of Conang's Tower.[3]

Conang, son of Faebar, of the Fomorians—by him that tower was built, in order to impose tribute on the children of Nemed.

On that account the children of Nemed went to demolish the tower, to avert from them their oppressions. Three score thousand strong the men of Ireland went to that demolition. The Fomorians[4] and the men of Ireland[5] met in the vicinity of the Tower, and neither of them perceived, owing to the obstinacy of the fighting, until the full tide came over both parties, so that there escaped of them only one bark in which were 30 warriors of the men of Ireland.

Of the Colonization of the Fir-Bolg here.

Ireland was uninhabited during the space of 200 years, as the Angel announced to the noble, pious, true Saint—to Caillin, son of Niata—until the sons of Starn, son of Nemed, to wit, the Fir-Bolg, came out of Greece, escaping from the exaction which the Greeks[6] imposed on them, viz., the placing of clay upon bare rocks until they were flowery plains. These men made for

[6] *Greeks.*—Gregaig. This is the last word of the text of fol. 2, b, MS. A. In the lower margin occur the lines—

Nocha mmanachad aoibe neach da fiadachad feine.
Is ferr foigdi tre aille má gairbe ocus geire.
Cleith an uilc do gni co taoi maith do breith cuirp o dail Dé;
Cen co hadma in ti dogni, cuici ni na hagra e.

This may be translated:—

"It does not increase respect, for one to extol himself.
Humility, with gentleness, is better than roughness and sharpness.
Silently to hide the evil one does, is a good way for taking bodies from God's presence;
Though he who commits does not admit it, to him 'twill not be forgotten."

scothaiḃ. Do ronsat na fir sin sithchurcha doib dona bolgaib imbertis in úir. Tancatar dochom nErenn .i. trian in inber Slainge im Slangi mac nDela mic Loith, mili do dáiniḃ allín. In trian aili in inber Dubglaisi im Gann ocus im Sengand; da mile allinside. Genand ocus Ruḋraige co trian int sluaiġ in inber Doṁnann. Is airi asberar Fir Doṁnann diḃ. Is iatsin Fir Bolg ocus Fir Domnan ocus Galeoin.

Slange ri Galian, is he a chinged o inbiur Cholptha co comar tri nusce. Gann on chomar co beluċ Conglais. Sengan o belaċ Conglais co Luimnech .i. for da ċoicced Muman. Genann for ċoicced Medba ocus Oilella. Rudraige dana for coicceḋ Conchobair. Da mili beus allinsiḋe. Tugatar in rigraid sin eli riġ[e] nErenn do Slainge dono.

Ro airneid imorro Caillin iarsin amail do innis int aingel do amail do rachtatar dochom nErenn cetamus in triar iarcairi .i. Capa, Laiġne, Luasat an anmann. Bliadain ri an dilind do rachtatar, gur ṫriallsatar ar cenn amban affuthiri, gu ro baided ic Tuaiġ inber. Ised adbert Caillin ica airneis so. IS aire naċ doiḃso do ratus túr airiṁe riasna gaḃalaibsi eli, ar daig ni ruccsat do lonn leo ina luing actmad teora glacu glassfeoir nama. IS aire ro airiṁus anois iat, ar Caillin, fodaiġ na beṫ nech agam inchrechad.

[1] *Inbher-Slainge.*—The estuary of the river Slaney, at Wexford.

[2] *Inbher-Dubhglaisi.*—Various conjectures have been made regarding this locality, the name of which signifies the "Inver (or Estuary) of the Black Stream," and might be Anglicised Inver-Douglas. But the account of the first battle of Magh-Tuiredh, in the Trin. Coll. MS. H. 2. 17, states (p. 91, b) that Gann and Sengann landed at a place called Ard-na-Caerach, on *Inbher-Dubhglaisi*, "the boundary between Corcomroe and Corco-Bhaiscind," in the county Clare; which would seem to point to the mouth of the river Enny, that falls into Liscannor Bay.

[3] *Inbher-Domhnann.*—This was the ancient name of Malahide Bay according to some authorities. But it was most certainly applied to Broadhaven, in the barony of Erris (county Mayo), which was formerly called Irrus-Domhnann, or Erris of the Damnonii.

[4] *Inbher-Colptha.*—The estuary of the Boyne.

[5] *Comar-tri-nusce.*—The "comar" (or confluence) of three waters, viz., of the Suir, Nore, and Barrow, opposite Cheek-Point, near Waterford.

[6] *Belach-Conglais.*—"The pass of Glas's hound." This was the name of a place near Cork. The ancient name of Baltin-

themselves long coracles of the bags in which they used to transport the clay. They came to Ireland; viz., one-third in Inbher-Slainge,[1] along with Slainge, son of Dela, son of Loth, their number being 1,000 men; another third in Inbher-Dubhglaisi,[2] along with Gann and Sengand, their number being 2,000. Genand and Rudhraige, with a third of the host, arrived in Inbher-Domhnann:[3] hence it is that they are called Fir-Domhnann. These are the Fir-Bolg, and Fir-Domhnann, and Gaileon.

Slainge, king of the Gaileon—his province is from Inbher-Colptha[4] to Comar-tri-nusce;[5] Gann's from the *Comar* to Belach-Conglais;[6] Sengann's from Belach-Conglais to Luimnech,[7] i.e., over the two provinces of Munster. Genann was over the province of Medhbh and Ailill.[8] Rudhraighe, however, was over the province of Conchobhar.[9] Two thousand, also, was the number of his people. All these chieftains, moreover, gave the kingship of Ireland to Slainge.

Caillin also related after that, as the Angel told him, how the three fishermen arrived first in Ireland, whose names were Capa, Laighne, and Luasad. A year before the Flood they arrived; and they set out to return for their wives, but were drowned at Tuagh-Inbher.[10]

Thus said Caillin in relating this: "The reason why I did not give them the first place in the enumeration, before those other Colonizations, is because they took no provisions with them in their ship, but three handfuls of green grass only. The reason why I have reckoned them now," said Caillin, "is that no one should be reproaching me."

glas, county Wicklow, is similarly written.

7 *Luimnech;* i.e. Limerick.

8 *province of Medhbh and Ailill*, i.e. Connacht; of which M. and A. were Queen and King (Consort), in the first century of the present Era.

9 *Conchobhar.*—Conor Mac Nessa was king of Ulster at the time that Medhbh and Ailill governed Connacht; for which reason Ulster is frequently called *Cuiged* Conchobhair, i.e. Conor's Province; lit. Conor's fifth (of Ireland).

10 *Tuagh-Inbher.*—This was the name of the mouth of the River Bann, and was derived, according to the Dinnsenchus, from Tuag, daughter of Conall Collamhrach [king of Ireland, A. M., 4876], who was drowned there. See Reeves's *Down and Connor*, p. 341, n [h].

Mad ail a ḟir tra, ar Caillin, in lín bliadan fil o thosach domain go Slange mac nDela, do berra em a ḟir uaim feb fuarus on aingel:

Ui bliadna caecat air se chet air ṁili o tosach domain co dilind.

Da bliadain L. ar x.c. o dilind co riġe Slange.

Moisset duib in ḟeċtsa, ar Caillin, in lin riġ cona nanmannaib ro ġaḃ hErind o Slange co Diarmait mac Cerbaill.

Do rigaib fer mBolg.

Ro gab cetamus Slange mac Dela mic Loich oin bliadain.
Rudraige a braṫair da bliadain.
Gand ocus Genann .iiii. bliadna.
Sengann .u. anno[s].
Fiachra cendfindan u. anno[s].
Rinnal .ui. bliadna.
[F]odbgein .iiii. bliadna.
Eoċo mac eirc .x.

Do rigaib tuath de Danand, amal ro aisnes Caillin.

Nuada airgetlam ceiṫre bliadna ria tiachtain in Erind, gur benad a laiṁ de i ced chath Muiġe tuired.
Bres mac Elathain .uii. mbliadna, go ro hicad lam Nuadat.
Nuaḋa argatlaṁ aris .xx. bliadain.
Lug lamfada .xl. bliadain.
In Daġda .lxxx. bliadain.
Delbaeth .x. bliadna.
Fiachna mac Delbaeth .x. bliadna.
MacCuill, MacCecht, MacGreine .ix. mbliadna .xx.

[1] *Six.*—The number looks like iii., but is meant for ui., as the computation is according to the chronology of the Hebrews, which gives 1656 years as the age of the World at the time of the Flood. See Petavius, *Rationarium Temporum* (Lugd. Batav. 1745), par. I., p. 5.

[2] *Cendfindan.*—The Etymologists, to

"If it is desired also to know," said Caillin, "the number of years from the beginning of the World to Slainge son of Dela, I will impart the knowledge as I obtained it from the Angel.

Six[1] years, fifty, six hundred, and a thousand, from the beginning of the world to the Flood.

Two years, fifty, and ten hundred, from the Flood to the reign of Slainge."

"I will tell you now," said Caillin, "the number of kings, with their names, who governed Ireland from Slainge to Diarmat Mac Cerbhaill."

Of the Kings of the Fir-Bolg.

Slainge, son of Dela, son of Loth, first occupied [Ireland] one year.
Rudraighe, his brother, two years.
Gand and Genann, 4 years.
Sengann, 5 years.
Fiachra Cendfindan,[2] 5 years.
Rinnal, 6 years.
[F]odbgen, 4 years.
Eocho, son of Erc, 10 [years].

Of the kings of the Tuatha De Danann, as Caillin related.

Nuada Airgetlam, four years before coming to Ireland, until his hand was cut off him in the first battle of Magh-Tuiredh.
Bres Mac Elathan, 7 years, until Nuada's hand was healed.
Nuada Airgetlam again, 20 years.
Lug Lamhfada, 40 years.
The Daghda, 80 years.
Delbhaeth, 10 years.
Fiachna, son of Delbhaeth, 10 years.
Mac Cuill, Mac Cecht, and Mac Greine, 29 years.

account for the name, have invented a ridiculous story about the men of Ireland having "white heads" (*cenda finda*) during the reign of this Fiachra. See Keating's *Ireland* (Haliday's ed.), p. 191.

Do rigaib mac Milid amail ro airimh Caillin.

* fol. 3 b. Heremon ocus Eber bliaḋuin hi comrc, gur bo marb hEber i cath Argatrois la hEremon.

Erimon mac Milid coic bliadna déc.

Muimne ocus Luiġne ocus Laiġne, co ro ecsat a triur.

Ceṫri meic Eber .i. Er, Orba, Feron, Fergna, leṫ bliadain.

Hirial faith mac Erimoin .x. bliadna.

Ethriel mac Irial mí ocus .xxx. bliadain.

Conmael mac Ebir (ced ri Erend a Mumain), re coecat bliadain, no a secht .x.

Tigernmas mac Follaich mic Ethereoil. Ced mbliadan do irriġe.

Eochaid (.i. ethgothach) mac Conmail .xxx.

Cermna ocus Soḃairċi da .xx. bliadain; ced riga Erenn a hUltoiḃ.

Eochaidh faebarglas fiċi .b.

Eber mac Conmail.

Fiacha labraind mac Smirgaill .xx.iiii. b.

Eocha mumo .xx. bliadain, no bliadain ar fichit.

Oengus ollmuchaiḋ mac Fiachach labrainde ocht mbliadna déc.

Enna airgdech mac Echach (.i. mumo) .xl. bliadain.

[1] *was slain.*—gur bo marb: lit. "until was dead." With these words concludes fol. 3, a in A., in the lower margin of which occur the lines :—

Onoir [ ] maṫ in moḋ, a oigreir a oirfiteod;
Gid be dalta diamba bes, atetha fein a coibes.
S[c con]airi roictear nem; lubair leigion, tetaidhecht,
Fogail maine, monar ngle, almsa, áine urnaiġṫe.

"Honour [ ], custom good; his obedience, his delight;
Whatever foster-son observes this, shall himself receive its equivalent.
In six ways is heaven reached: by book-reading, music-playing;
Distributing treasures in profusion; alms, abstinence, and prayer."

[2] *Argatros.*—"Silver Wood." The ancient name of a wood, on the Nore, in the parish of Rathbeagh, bar. of Galmoy, co. Kilkenny. The fort from which the parish derives its name (Rath-Beothaigh, now Rathbeagh) is stated to have been constructed by Heremon. Some antiquaries, however (and among them the Four Masters, at A.M. 3501) represent the battle as fought in the neighbourhood of Geshill, in the King's County.

[3] *one hundred.*—The reign of Tighern-

Of the kings of the sons of Miled, as Caillin reckoned them.

Heremon and Heber, one year in joint sovereignty, until Heber was slain[1] in the battle of Argartros,[2] by Heremon.

Heremon, son of Miled, fifteen years.

Muimne, and Luighne, and Laighne, until the three died.

Heber's four sons, viz., Er, Orba, Feron, Fergna, one half-year.

Irial the Prophet, son of Heremon, 10 years.

Ethriel son of Irial, a month and 30 years.

Conmael son of Heber (first king of Ireland from Munster), during 50 years, or 27.

Tighernmas, son of Follach, son of Ethriel; one hundred[3] years was he in sovereignty.

Eochaidh (i.e. Ethgothach), son of Conmael, 30 [years].

Cermna and Sobhairche,[4] 40 years. The first kings of Ireland of the Ultonians.

Eochaidh Faebharglas, twenty years.

Eber[5] son of Conmael.

Fiacha Labraind,[6] son of Smirgall, 24 years.

Eocho Mumho,[7] 20 years, or 21 years.

Oengus Ollmuchaidh, son of Fiacha Labraind, eighteen years.

Enna Airgtech,[8] son of Eocho, (.i. Mumho), 40 years.

mas is variously fixed at 100, 70, and 50 years.

[4] *Cermna and Sobhairche.*—These are represented as having been slain in the battle of Dun-Cermna (or Dun-mic-Phatrick, as it was called in Keating's time; Haliday's ed. of Keating, p. 125), a fort on the Old Head of Kinsale, co. Cork. From Sobhairce was named Dun-Sobhairce now Dunseverick, in the barony of Cary, co. Antrim. The date of the battle is given as A.M. 3707.

[5] *Eber.*—Some critic, probably Thady O'Rody, has added the marginal note, ni fagbaim int Eber si isin gabaltus: "I do not find this Eber in the [Book of] Occupation." His name does not occur in the ordinary lists of the Kings of Ireland.

[6] *Fiacha Labraind.*—Slain in the battle of Belgadan (now Bulgadan), near Kilmallock, co. Limerick, A.M. 3751.

[7] *Eocho Mumho* (a quo Mumha, i.e. Momonia, or Munster).—Slain in the battle of Clin (or Cliach), a territory lying around Knockany, co. Limerick, A.M. 3772.

[8] *Airgtech.*—A cognomen derived from

Roṫechtaiḋ mac Main mic Aongusa olmucaiḋ
Setna art mac Airt mic Ebir mic Ir.
Fiacha finnscothach, a mac.
Muinemon mac Cais clothaig.
Aildergdoit a mac iarum.
Ollam fotla mac Fiachach finnscothaig.
Findachta mac Ollaman fotla.
Slanoll mac Ollaman cetna.
Gede ollgothach mac Ollaman fotla.
Fiaċ[a] findoilces mac Findaċta.
Berngal mac Gede.
Oilill mac Slanuill.
Sirna mac Dein mic Roṫeaċtaiġ.
Rothechtaig.
Elim ollfinachta.
Giallchad mac Oilella olchain.
Art imlig iarsin.
Nuada findfail mac Giallchada.
Bresrige mac Airt imlig.
Eochu apthach do ċorco Luigdech, mac Lugdach, no mac Airt mic Ebir bric mic Lugdach cail.
Find mac Blatha.
Setna innarraid mac Bres.

the silver shields which he is stated to have given away. *Airgtech* = argenteus, from *airget* = argentum. Enna Airgtech was slain in the battle of Raighne (or Magh-Raighne), in Ossory, A.M. 3842.

[1] *Finnscothach.*—The Irish etymologists have explained this epithet as derived from *finn* (wine), and *scotha* (flowers), adding that in the reign of this Fiacha Finnscothach, there were flowers bearing wine, which was pressed into cups See *Keating* (Haliday's ed.), p. 329.

[2] *Aildergdoit.*—In some ancient authorities the name is written Faildergdoit, and explained as signifying "red handring"; for in his reign, it is added, "gold rings were worn around the hand." *Book of Leinster*, fol. 9, b 2.

[3] *son of Rothechtach.*—More correctly, "son of Demal son of Rothechtach." See *Book of Leinster*, fol. 10, a 1.

[4] *Ollfinachta.*—He was the son of Rothechtach, his predecessor in the monarchy, and was slain by his successor, A.M. 4177,

Rothechtadh, son of Maen, son of Oengus Ollmuchaidh.

Setna-art, son of Art, son of Eber, son of Ir.

Fiacha Finnscothach,[1] his son.

Muinemon, son of Cas-clothach.

Aildergdoit,[2] his son, afterwards.

Ollamh Fotla, son of Fiacha Finnscothach.

Finnachta, son of Ollamh Fotla.

Slanoll, son of the same Ollamh.

Gede Oll-gothach, son of Ollamh Fotla.

Fiacha Findoilces, son of Finnachta.

Berngal, son of Gede.

Oilill, son of Slanoll.

Sirna, son of Dian, son of Rothechtach.[3]

Rothechtach.

Elim Ollfinachta.[4]

Giallchad, son of Oilill Olchan.

Art of Imlech afterwards.

Nuada Findfail, son of Giallchad.

Bresrige, son of Art of Imlech.

Eocho Apthach,[5] of the Corco-Luigdech,[6] son of Lugaid; or son of Art, son of Eber Brec, son of Lugaid Cail.[7]

Find, son of Blaith.

Setna Innarraidh,[8] son of Bres.

according to the chronology of the Four Masters, or A.M. 3389, according to O'Flaherty's computation. *Ogygia*, pars iii. cap. xxxii.

[5] *Apthach.*—The etymologists say that Eocho was so called from the great number of persons who died in his reign (A.M. 3301, *Keating*; 3432, *O'Flaherty*). *Apthach* is an adj. deriv. from *aptu* (exitium); acc. sg. *apthin* (perniciem), Ebel's *Zeuss*, 266.

[6] *Corco-Luigdech*; or "sept of Lugaid."—This tribe, which derived its name from Lugaid Laighde, the 8th in descent from Lugaid son of Ith (the nephew of Milesius), was settled in the S.W. of the present county of Cork. See the Tract on the history of this sept, published by Dr. O'Donovan, from the *Book of Lecan*, Celtic Society's *Miscellany*, 1849, pp. 1-144. The O'Driscolls were its chiefs.

[7] *Lugaid Cail.*—Brother to Lugaid Laighde, referred to in last note.

[8] *Innarraidh.*—So called from having been the first person who gave pay to

Simon brec mac Aedain glais.

Duach find mac Setna indarraid.

Muiredach mac Simoin.

Enna derg mac Duac̄ find.

Lugaid iardonn mac Enna.

Sirlaim mac find.

Eochu uarches mac Lugdach.

Eochu (.i. fiadmuine), ocus Conaing (.i. bec iacla), da mac Conmail mic Lugdach cail (ii. bliadna i comḟlaithius). No is da mac Congail mic Lugdach do chorco Luiġde. Atberat araile is mac do Congal Eocha, ocus is mac Duach mic Muiredaiġ mic Simoin in Conaing bec iacla; ocus is inan mathair doib ocus int Eocha uairches mac Congail. Lugaid mac Echach uarches, is lais ro tuit Eochaid fiadmuine.

Lugaid iarsin .uii. mbliadna, co torchair la Conuing mbec iacla (.i. bec a egla).

Conaing bec ecla iarsin.

Art mac Lugdach mic Echach uarches.

Eochaid mac Airt; Ac̄t in airim in gabaltus sin manab he Oilill find mac Airt.

* fol. 4 a, 1. Eocha mac Oilella find.[a]

Argatmar.

soldiers in Ireland. The epithet *innar-raidh* seems comp. of *inn*, or *ind*, the Irish def. art., and *araidh*, a word cognate with the Latin æs, æris.

[1] *Fiadhmuine.*—Latinized "Venator," or the "hunter," by O'Flaherty, who probably considered the word to be comp. of *fiadh*, a deer, and *muine*, a brake.

[2] *Bec-iacla.*—See note [5].

[3] *Carco-Luighde*, or *Corco-Luigdech.*—See note [6], p. 25.

[4] *Congal.*—Lugaid (Iardonn?) is indicated above as the father of Eocho Uarches.

[5] *bec a ecla;* lit. "little his fear"; *iacla*=*ecla* ("fear").—In the *Book of Leinster* (fol. 10, b. 1) Conaing is called *bec fhiaclach* (or "little-toothed"); and also *bec-eclach*, or "little fearing," because "he never felt fear or terror."

[6] *reckon him.*—The name of "Eochaidh" is doubtless a mistake for that of Oilill Finn, or Oilill the "Fair," who reigned from A.M. 3542 to 3551, according to O'Flaherty's chronology. In Keating and the Four Mast. the name of Fiacha Tolgrach is given as the predecessor of this Oilill Finn; but it does not appear in O'Flaherty's list, nor in the more ancient list in the *Bk. of Leinster*,

Simon Brec, son of Aedan Glas.

Duach Find, son of Setna Innarraidh.

Muiredhach, son of Simon.

Enna Derg, son of Duach Find.

Lugaid Iardonn, son of Enna.

Sirlamh, son of Find.

Eocho Uarches, son of Lugaid.

Eocho (.i. Fiadhmuine),[1] and Conaing (.i. Bec-iacla),[2] two sons of Connal son of Lugaid Cail, were five years in co-sovereignty. Or they were two sons of Congal son of Lugaid, of the Corco-Luighde.[3] Some say that Eocho was son to Congal, and that Conaing Bec-iacla was the son of Duach, son of Muiredach, son of Simon; and the same mother had they and Eocho Uarches, son of Congal.[4]

Lugaid, son of Eocho Uarches—by him fell Eochaidh Fiadhmuine. Lugaid reigned afterwards seven years, until he was slain by Conaing Bec-iacla (i.e. *bec a ecla*):[5]

Conaing Bec-ecla afterwards.

Art, son of Lugaid, son of Eocho Uarches.

Eochaidh son of Art. But the [Book of] Colonization does not reckon him,[6] unless he is Oilill Find, son of Art.

Eocha, son of Oilill Find.[7]

Argatmar.

as that of one who actually reigned. St. Caillin was therefore right in omitting Fiacha Tolgrach from his list of kings.

[7] This concludes fol. 3 b, in the lower marg. of which is written the following notes:—

Aiġiḋ Isa sa croich siar, soir cen cisa cul an uain
In cle bodes leṫ le gréin enaireid a ḋes buḋ tuaiġ.

"The face of Jesus on the Cross was to the west; to the east the back of the stainless Lamb.
The left side to the south, towards the . . . . . sun; His right towards the north."

And also the further note:—

Dena maiṫ for degduine dobeir dot réir;
Maiṫ for droċ duine mad sua dobud forruaill beiṫ gan ċéill.

"Doing good to a good man, makes him obedient to thee.
Act well to a bad man, if thou'rt wise; it were senseless to be proud."

Duach laḋrach mac Fiachaċ tolgraich.

Luġaiḋ laidech.

Aeḋ ruaḋ mac Badoirn mic Argatṁair, ocus Dithorba mac Dimain a hUisniuch Miḋe, Cimbaeth mac Findtain mic Argatmair .i. [a] Findabair muigi inis.

Macha ingen Aeda ruaid.

Rechtaid rigderg mac Luiġdech mic Echach mic Oilella find mic Airt mic Luigdech-laimderg mic Echach uarches.

Ugaine mor mac Echach buadaig; gabuis rigi hErenn ocus Alban ocus co muir nIcht.

Laegaire lorc mac Ugaine moir.

Cobthach cael Breg.

Labraid loingsech mac Oilella aine mic Laegaire luirc.

Melgi molbthach mac Cobthaiġ cail Breg.

MocCorb mac Rechtada a Mumain.

Oengus ollam oa Labrada.

Iarero fathach mac Melgi molbthaich.

Fercorb mac Moġa cuirb.

Conlaed caeṁ mac Iarero.

Oilill casfiaclach mac Conlai.

Amadair mac Firċuirb.

Echaid altlethan mac Ailella.

Fergus fortamail.

Oengus tuirmech mac Echach.

Conall collamrach.

Nia segamain mac Aḋamair foltchain.

Enna airgthech mac Aengasa tuirmiġ.

Crimthand coscarach .iiii. bliadna, co torchair do laim Ruḋraiġe.[5]

[1] *of Magh-Inis.*—Muigis̄, A.

[2] *Muir-Icht.*—See note [2], p. 10, *supra.*

[3] *Amadair.*—So written in A. But the name is Adamair in all ancient documents; and it is even so written five lines lower down.

[4] *Altlethan.*—"Of the broad joints." He is called "Foltlethan," or "Foltlebhar" ("of the flowing hair"), in other authorities.

[5] *Foltchain.*—"Of the fair hair." A. reads Foilt, which is corrupt. The epithet

Duach Ladhrach, son of Fiacha Tolgrach.

Lughaidh Laidech.

Aedh Ruadh, son of Badurn, son of Argatmar; and Dithorba, son of Diman, from Uisnech-Midhe; [and] Cimbaeth, son of Finntan, son of Argatmar, i.e. [from] Finnabhair of Magh-Inis.[1]

Macha, daughter of Aedh Ruadh.

Rechtaid Rig-derg, son of Lugaid, son of Eochaidh, son of Oilill Find, son of Art, son of Lugaidh Laimhderg, son of Eochaidh Uarches.

Ugaine Mor, son of Eochaidh Buadach, obtained the kingship of Ireland, and Alba, and as far as Muir-Icht.[2]

Laeghaire Lorc, son of Ugaine Mor.

Cobthach Cael Breg.

Labraid Loingsech, son of Oilill Aine, son of Laeghaire Lorc.

Melgi Molbthach, son of Cobthach Cael Breg.

Mog-Corp, son of Rechtaid, from Munster.

Oengus Ollamh, grandson of Labraid.

Iarero Fathach, son of Melgi Molbthach.

Fercorp, son of Mog-Corp.

Conlaed Caemh, son of Iarero.

Oilill Casfiaclach, son of Conla.

Amadair,[3] son of Fercorp.

Echaidh Altlethan,[4] son of Ailill.

Fergus Fortamhail.

Oengus Tuirmech, son of Eochaidh.

Conall Collamrach.

Nia Segamain, son of Adamair Foltchain.[5]

Enna Airgthech,[6] son of Oengus Tuirmech.

Crimthand Coscrach, 4 years,[7] until he fell by the hand of Rudhraighe.

is differently written *foltchain*, and *folt-lebhar* ("fair-haired" and "long-haired") in other accounts. The Adamair here mentioned is the individual referred to in note [3].

[6] *Airgthech*; lit. "the plundering."

[7] *4 years.* The numerals IIII of MS. A. probably represent UII (7), the number of years which Crimthand is generally understood to have reigned; for it is not always easy to distinguish between the numbers U (5) and II (2) in Irish MSS.

Rudraige tra mac Sithriġe imorro, is uad Dal nAraide, ar is iatside fir Ulaid Emna .i. clanna Olloman fodlu mic [Fiachach] finnscothaiġ. Ro gaḃsat .xx.u. dib riġi hErenn; daig isiat tri sair hErenn Cond, Araide, Eogan, ut Eochaid cecinit:

Tri sair hErenn arcanar,
Slu[a]ig Araḋ co naib Ulaḋ,
Cond dian ceolaḋart coḋal,
Ocus Eoganacht Muman.

Rudraige tra mac Siṫride, sen athair Conaill chernaig mic Aimirgin, ocus Fergussa mic Roiġ. Gach roi ro reraig Rudraige for Erind ro suidig Fergus a ċloinn foraiḃ a murt chatha .i. Ciarc ocus Ciarraiġe ocus Conmaicne. Ro bris fiċi cath ic cosnaṁ ċirt Rudraige for Erinn, amail atbert lebar gabala.

Bai rudraige .lxx. bliadain isriġi nErenn, conerbailt do tham in Argatglind.

[1] *Dal-Araidhe*—The Dal-Araidhe, who derived their tribe-name from Fiacha Araidhe, king of Ulster in the third century, occupied the greater part of the present co. Antrim. See *Ogygia*, pt. iii. cap. 18; and Reeves's Eccles. Antiqq. p. 334, sq.

[2] *Emhain*—The royal residence (near Armagh) of the kings of Ulster, until A.D. 332, when the place was demolished by the Brothers Colla, progenitors of the Oirghialla, and the Rudrician septs were driven into the district of Ulidia proper, or the present counties of Down and Antrim.

[3] *Eochaidh*, i.e. Eochaidh Ua Floinn, a famous Irish poet, who died about A.D. 984; for an account of whom see O'Reilly's *Irish Writers*, p. lxiv. O'Clery's copy of the *Leabhar Gabhala* (MS. R. I. Acad.) contains (fol. 134) a poem ascribed to Eochaidh, in which the descendants of the three chieftains, Conn, Araidhe, and Eoghan, are thus referred to:—

Conn, Eoghan, Araiḋe án.
Até cinnudh na ttri mál;
Araiḋe ino Emain cen áil;
Conn ced chathach i Temair.
Eoghan i Caisiol na riogh;
As ann tarrusair a síol.

"Conn, Eoghan, noble Araidhe—
The descendants of the three chieftains are:
[The] Araidhe in Emhain without stain,
Conn ced-chathach in Temhair;
Eoghan in Caisel of the kings—
There his seed resided."

Rudhraighe, also, the son of Sithridh. From him, moreover, are the Dal-Araidhe;[1] for they are the true Ulidians of Emhain,[2] viz., the descendants of Ollamh Fodla, son [of Fiacha] Finnscothach. Twenty-five of them obtained the sovereignty of Ireland, for the three free [septs] of Ireland were Cond, Araide, Eoghan, as Eochaidh[3] sang:

The three free [septs] of Ireland, it is sung,
Are the hosts of the Araide[4] with the pride of Ulster;
Cond[5] to whom assemblies were dear,
And the Eoganacht[6] of Munster.

Rudhraighe, son of Sithridh, moreover, was the ancestor of Conall Cernach, son of Amergin, and of Fergus Mac Roigh. Every place which Rudhraighe governed throughout Ireland, upon them Fergus established his descendants through dint of battle, viz., Corca,[7] and Ciarraidhe,[8] and Conmaicni[9] He gained twenty battles defending Rudhraighe's right over Ireland, as the *Lebar Gabhala* says. Rudhraighe was 70 years in the sovereignty of Ireland, until he died of a plague in Argat-glend.[10]

4 *Araide.*—See note 1.

5 *Cond*, or *Conn*, i.e. the race of Conn of the hundred battles.

6 *Eoganacht.* — This was the tribe name of the descendants of Eoghan Mór, son of Oilill Olum, king of Munster in the second century.

7 *Corca.*—By *Corca* would seem to be meant the Corca-Modhruadh, or ancient inhabitants of Corcumroe, co. Clare, viz., the O'Loghlens and O'Conors, descended from Corc Ferdoid, alleged to have been a son of Fergus Mac Roigh and Medhbh (or Mab) queen of Connacht, the Cleopatra of Irish history.

8 *Ciarraidhe.*—These are stated to have been the descendants of Ciar, another son of Fergus Mac Roigh, by the same Medbbh. The principal branch of this family was settled in *Ciarraidhe-Luachra*, the ancient name of the county of Kerry (although Ciarraidhe only represented the northern division of the present county). Other sections of the tribe have given name to districts in the counties of Roscommon and Mayo.—See O'Flaherty's *Ogygia*, part iii. cap. 46.

9 *Conmaicni.*—For the various septs of Conmaicni, descended from Conmac, son of Fergus Mac Roigh and Queen Medhbh of Connacht, see *Ogygia*, part iii. cap. 46.

10 *Argat-glend.* Lit. Silver-glen. O'Donovan says (note to Four Mast., A.M. 4981 of the Four Masters' reckoning) that this was the "name of a glen in the barony of Farney, Co. Monaghan." But he offers no authority in support of the statement, which is questionable.

Gabair Findatmar mac Niad segamain.

Bresal bodibaid mac Rudraige.

Lugaid luaigne mac Findatmair; ocus nir airim Caillin in Lugaid sin ina duain.

Congall claringnech mac Rudraige.

Duach dallta Degaḋ.

Fachtna fathaċ mac Cais mic Rudraige.

Eochaid fedlech mac Find.

Eochaid oirem, brathair e d' Eochaidh Fedlech.

* fol. 4 b, 1. Etirscel mor mac .h. Iair, di Ernaib.[a]

IS ri so [bliadain] ingenair Crist mac De bi i mBeṫil Iuda, do teroncain in ċiniuda daeno.

Na coicedaig iarsin .i. Conchobar mac Fachtna fathaig, Coirpre niafer, Tigernaċ tetbannaċ, Curái mac Dari, Ailill mac Mataċ.

Nuaḋa necht do Laignib: iarsin

Conaire mor. Combad iar Conaire mor nobetis coicedaig ut alii aiunt.

Lugaiḋ riabnderg. IS he in Lugaid sin do ronsat na tri findemna fria a siar, fria Clothrund ingen Echach fedliġ dana. Do rinde in Lugaid mac fria a ṁathair .i. Crimthand mac Luigdech. Ba ri Erenn in Crimthand sin.

[1] *Segamain.*—A. reads Iſ̄, indicating that the letter s, being "infected," is to be pronounced like *h*.

[2] *Bodibaid.*—"Cow-destruction;" so called from a "rinderpest" that occurred in his time.

[3] *poem;* i.e. the poem which follows, beginning Eriu oll oilen aingeal.

[4] *Claringnech;* "flat-nailed."—He is otherwise called *Clar-eineach*, or "flat-faced."—Ob. circa, A.M. 3889; O'Flaherty.

[5] *Erna.*—There were two septs of this name in Munster; one located in the north of the co. Limerick, and descended from Cathair, the son of Etirscel; and the other settled near Kinsale, descended from Corc Duibhne, son of the same Cathair. See *Ogygia*, part iii. c. 44. The tribe-name (*Erna*) is stated to have been derived from Oilill Erann, from whom Etirscel was the 14th in lineal descent.

[6] *born.*—This entry is misplaced, and should come in under the reign of Crimthann Nianair. See note [1], p. 34.

[7] *Pentarchs.*—coicedaig; from coiced, a fifth; Ireland being at this time divided into five kingdoms. On the lower marg. of A., fol. 4, b, occur the lines:—

Findatmar, son of Nia Segamain,[1] reigned.

Bresal Bodibaid,[2] son of Rudhraighe.

Lugaid Luaigne, son of Findatmar; (and Caillin did not reckon this Lugaid in his poem).[3]

Congall Claringnech,[4] son of Rudhraighe.

Duach Dalta-Degadh.

Fachtna Fathach, son of Cas, son of Rudhraighe.

Eochaidh Fedlech, son of Find.

Eochaidh Oiremh; brother to Eochaidh Fedlech.

Etirscel Mór, great-grandson of Iar, of the Erna.[5]

This is [the year] in which Christ son of the Living God was born[6] in Bethlehem of Judea, to save the human race.

The Pentarchs[7] afterwards, viz., Conchobhar son of Fachtna Fathach, Corpre Niafer, Tigernach Tetbannach, Curoi Mac Dari, Ailill Mac Matach.

Nuada Necht of the Leinstermen; after him

Conaire Mor. Perhaps the Pentarchs should be after Conaire Mor, ut alii aiunt.

Lugaidh Riabhnderg.[8] It is this Lugaid the three Findemnas begot by their sister, by Clothru, daughter of Eochaidh Fedlech. The same Lugaidh begot a son by his mother, to wit, Crimthand son of Lugaidh. This Crimthand was king of Ireland.

Mairg cuinges ni ar a ċaraid,
Muna lonn leis a tabairt;
Is e dede nosbia de,
Miscais ocus oirbire.

Is saoith lem int aos leigind
Do dul an ifern pianach,
Is inti nach leġ egna
Do ḋul a partus grianach.

Which may be rendered—

"Woe be to him that asketh of a friend,
Unless that friend to giving be inclined.
Of all such asking two things are the end,
Bitter reproaches, and an hateful mind.

"Is't not sad that learned men should go
To Hell's dire pains and everlasting woe!
And simple unlearned dullards should rejoice
In all the joys of sunny Paradise!"

[8] *Riabhnderg.*—Properly "Sriabhnderg, "of the red stripe." So called from two red stripes with which he is alleged to have been born (round his neck and middle), in token of his incestuous origin.

Conchobar abratruad, bliadain.
[Crimthand mac Luigdech.]
Cairpre caitċenn d'feraib bolg.
Feradach fechtnach mac Crimthainn.
Fiatach find, a quo dal Fiatach.
Fiacha findolaid.
Ellim mac Conrach.
Tuathal techtṁar mac Fiachach findolaid.
Mal mac Rocraide.
Fedlimid rechtṁar mac Bane.
Catair mor.
Conn cetchaṫach .xx. bliadain.
Conaire caem, cliamuin Cuinn.
Art mac Cuinn .xxx. bliadain.
Lugaid mac Con.
Fergus dubdeṫach.
Cormac O Cuind.
Eochaiḋ gunnat.
Corpre Lifechair.[6]
Ua tri Fothaid.
Fiacha sraiptine.

[1] *Crimthand.*—Omitted in his proper sequence in the list of kings in A. This is the Crimthand Nianair who led the famous expedition into Britain in the time of Agricola, for an account of which see Keating's *Hist. of Ireland* (Haliday's ed.), p. 409; and *Ogygia*, iii., 52. It is said that Our Lord was born in the 12th year of his reign. See note [6], p. 32.

[2] *Caitchenn.* "Cat-head."—He was chief of the rebel "Aithech-Tuatha," or plebeians (misnamed Attacotti), who overturned the legitimate monarchy, and slew the Milesian nobility. See a detailed account of this transaction, extracted from O'Clery's copy of the *Leabhar Gabhala*, in O'Donovan's note to the entry in the Four Mast., A.D. 10.

[3] *Feradach.*—Fadach, A.; the sign of abbrev. over F being omitted.

[4] *Banè.*—This was the name of Fedhlimidh's mother, who is said to have been daughter of Scal-Balbh (lit. "dumb-shadow"), king of Finland. His father was Tuathal Techtmar.—*Ogygia*, pp. 303, 306.

[5] *grandson of Conn.*—Better known as Cormac Mac Airt, or "Cormac son of Art," one of the most illustrious of the

Conchobhar Abratruad, a year.
[Crimthand[1] son of Lugaidh].
Cairpre Caitchenn,[2] of the Fir-Bolg.
Feradach[3] Fechtnach, son of Crimthand.
Fiatach Find, a quo Dal Fiatach.
Fiacha Findolaidh.
Ellim Mac Conrach.
Tuathal Techtmhar, son of Fiacha Findolaidh.
Mal Mac Rochraide.
Fedlimidh Rechtmhar, son of Banè.[4]
Cathair Mor.
Conn Cet-chathach, 20 years.
Conaire Caemh, son-in-law of Conn.
Art son of Conn, 30 years.
Lugaid Mac Con.
Fergus Dubhdetach.
Cormac, grandson of Conn.[5]
Eochaidh Gunnat.
Corpre Lifechair.[6]
The three[7] Fothads.
Fiacha Sraiptine.[8]

Irish kings. He died in 266 (A.D.) according to the Four Masters; and is said to have been buried in Rosnaree, on the southern bank of the Boyne, nearly opposite Newgrange. The mound which is supposed to have been raised over his grave was ruthlessly levelled by a farmer named Tiernan a few years ago, when some human bones were uncovered. The site of the mound is still pointed out.

[6] *Lifechair.*—Keating states that this epithet was owing to Corpre, who was the son of Cormac, having been fostered near the Liffey.

[7] *three.*—In some authorities only two Fothads are mentioned, namely Fothad Airgthech (F. the plunderer), and Fothad Cairpthech (F. the charioteer), alias Fothad Canand, two sons of Mac Con; but in the *Book of Lecan*, fol. 122, b. 1, it is said that there were three, the third being named Fothad Dolus. They were the sons of Mac Con, son of Maeniadh. The statement in the *Book of Lecan* is prefaced by the expression "sic invenitur hi Saltair Caisil," i.e. "*sic invenitur in the Psalter of Cashel.*"

[8] *Sraiptine.*—Fiacha was so called from

Colla uais.
Muiredach tirech.
Caelbad mac Cruind badrai.
Eochaid muidmedhon.
Crimthan mac Fidaig.
Niall .ix. giallach mac Echach muidmedoin.
Daṫi mac Fiaċrach.

Laegaire mac Neill. Is fri a lindside tainicc Patraic in hErind. Da bliadain decc iar tichtain Patraic in hErind do riacht Caillin mac Niataċ dochom nErenn, la techta Conmaicne, dia fuasalgud ón ḟingail ocus on brisiuḋ braithrerai ro thriallsat, co rois Dia deg coṁairle doib .i. Caillin do ṫabairt ċuca o Roim, amail atfet in lebar inar ndiaid, acht in an oin inad ocus na rigsi.

Oilill molt mac Naṫi.

c. n. Lugaiḋ mac Loegaire. Patricius episcopus scotorum quievit.

c. n. Muircertach mac Erca ocus Muiredaich.

Tuathal maelgarḃ mac Cormaic caich mic Cairpre mic Neill.

Diarmait mac Cerbaill .i. Diarmait mac Fergusa cerrbaill mic Conaill cirrbreg mic Neill.

having been fostered at Dun-Sraiptinè, in Connacht. He was son to Corpre Lifechair.

[1] *Colla Uais*, or "Colla the Noble."—One of three brothers called "the Collas" (sons to Eochaidh Doimhlen, son of Corpre Lifechair), by whom the ancient residence of the Rudrician kings at Emania, near Armagh, was demolished in the year 332; the Rudrician tribes, the ancient Ulstermen, or Clann-Rury, being at the same time driven to the east of the Bann and Lough Neagh. The territory to which they were thus confined, comprising the present counties of Antrim and Down, was afterwards known as Ulidia proper.

These Collas were the progenitors of the principal families of Oirghiall, or Oriel, and several other districts not only in Ireland, but also in Scotland. From Colla Uais, the eldest of the three, are descended the Mac Donnells, Mac Alisters, and Mac Dugalds of Scotland; and from Colla Dacrich, the O'Kellys of Hy-Maine derive their well-authenticated descent.

[2] *Muidmedhon.*—muinbethan, A. But the word is written muidmedoin (gen. of muidmedon) in the second line following.

[3] *at the request.*—la techta; lit. "with the messages," A.

[4] *these things.*—The meaning is that the statement anticipated here is not contained

Colla Uais.[1]

Muiredach Tirech.

Caelbad, son of Crund Badrai.

Eochaidh Muidmedhon.[2]

Crimthand Mac Fidaig.

Niall Nine-Hostage, son of Eochaidh Muidmedhon.

Dathi son of Fiachra.

Laeghaire son of Niall. It is during his time Patrick came into Ireland. Twelve years after the coming of Patrick to Ireland Caillin arrived in Ireland, at the request[3] of the Conmacni, to rescue them from the fratricide and breach of brotherhood they practised, until God gave them good advice, viz., to bring home Caillin from Rome, as the following book relates, but not in the same place as these things.[4]

Oilill Molt, son of Dathi.[5]

Lugaidh[6] son of Laeghaire. Patrick bishop of the Scoti went to his rest.

Muirchertach, son of Erc and Muiredach [7]

Tuathal Maelgarbh, son of Cormac Caech, son of Corpre, son of Niall.

Diarmait Mac Cerbhaill, i.e. Diarmait, son of Fergus Cerbhaill, son of Conall Errbreg, son of Niall.

in the part of the following poem which speaks of the regal succession.

[5] *Dathi.*—nati, A.; a change produced by the assimilation of the *d* of Dathi to the final letter of some preposition or governing word preceding it in a sentence. Thus *ren Dathi* (before D.) would be pronounced nearly *re Nathi.*

[6] *Lugaidh.*—The letters c. n. are prefixed to signify that this king was of the Clann-Neill, or descendants of Niall of the Nine Hostages.

[7] *son of Erc and Muiredach.*—Erc, usually a man's name, was the name of Muirchertach's mother. She was the daughter of Loarn, king of Alba (or Scotland). His father was Muiredach, son of Eoghan, son of Niall of the Nine Hostages. (See the account of Muirchertach and his mother, printed from *Mac Firbis's Genealogies*, in Todd's *Irish Nennius*, App. pp. ci.–civ). A remarkable tract descriptive of the life and death of Muirchertach Mac Erca is contained in the *Yellow Book of Lecan*, from which it would appear that through the wiles of a fairy or sorceress named Sin (pron. *Sheen*), for whom he had abandoned his own wife, he was drowned in a vat of wine, and subsequently burned in the "house of Cleitech over the Boyne." The Four Masters refer this catastrophe to A.D. 527. The letters c. n. in the mar-

Bai Caillin dana fria linn Diarmata; ocus ro gell feisin comindisfed ainm gach rig rogab hErinn o flaith co Diarmait. Oin rig air

ª fol. 5 a, 1. seacht fichtib ri etursa,ª amail forglius Caillin noib feisin, iar nairem na rig anuas isin duain inar ndiaid .i. Eriu oll oilen aingeal, ut dixit:

Oen ri ar secht fichtib rig,
Adrimm rib gan imsnim,
O flaith co Diarmaid ngrinn,
In lin rig ro gab hErinn.

Is iarsuidiu atbert Caillin .i. o haithle na rig sin do chomairim, amail fuair on aingeal a foillsiugadh do, o ro airmius imorro, arse, gach ri rogab hErinn oflaith conicci so .i. co Diarmaitt mac Cerbaill, dogensa umorro, arse, ni fechtsa ni is doidnge ocus is duaithnighthi inas sin .i. aisnedfed anmma gach rig gebus Erinn onu co brath .i. o Diarmait co brath, ar an ti noem Chaillin. Gid diamair ocus gid duaithnid ar daimib in domain in ni na cluinit ocus na faicit, ocus na nethe airdhalta bis a cinded ocus andan doib, nir ba hurfa ocus nir ba soillsi do Chaillin na righa tainig fri a re fesin ocus reme for Erinn, inait na riga ticfaitis tar a es, iar na foillsiugad do on aingel, dianad fola ocus dianad rochma gach ret.

Ro aisneid iarsin do na rigaib ro biad for Erinn o Diarmait co brath .i.

Diarmait mac Cerbaill cetumus.

c. n. Domnall ocus Fergus, da mac Muircertaig mic Erca; oin bliadain,

ᵇ fol. 5 a, 2. no tri bliadna. Ecc atbatatar.ᵇ

c. n. Baetan mac Muircertaig, ocus Eocha mac Domnaill, tri bliadna.

gin signify that Muirchertach was of the Clann-Neill.

[1] *between them.*—etursa. These are the last words of the text on fol. 4, b., in the lower margin of which occurs a *rann*, or stanza, not worth reproduction.

[2] *more difficult.*—doidnge; compar. of dodaing, "difficult." Cf. *ar a doidngi*, ob ejus difficultatem, Nigra's *Reliq. Celt.* p. 31.

[3] *Saint Caillin.*—an ti noem chaillin; lit. "the person Saint Caillin."

[4] *doom.*—*brath;* lit. "judgment."

[5] *three years.*—According to the Annals of the Four Masters, the joint reign of Fer-

Caillin lived, then, during the time of Diarmait; and he himself promised that he would tell the name of every king that obtained Ireland from Slainge to Diarmait. One king and seven score between them,[1] as Saint Caillin himself explains, after enumerating the foregoing kings, in the poem which follows, i.e. "Noble Ireland, island of Angels," ut dixit:

"One king, and seven score kings,
I tell you, without difficulty,
From Slainge to jovial Diarmait,
Is the number of kings that possessed Ireland."

It was after that Caillin said, (i.e. after enumerating those kings, according as he had received from the Angel the gift of explanation): "Since I have therefore reckoned," said he, "every king that possessed Ireland from Slainge to this time, i.e. to Diarmait Mac Cerbhaill, I will do further," said he, "on this occasion, a thing more difficult[2] and incomprehensible than that—to wit, I will relate the name of every king who will possess Ireland from this day until doom, i.e. from Diarmait until doom," said Saint Caillin.[3] However obscure and incomprehensible to the men of the world may be the thing which they hear not, and see not, and the certain things that are fated and in store for them; not more easy, and not more plain, was it for Caillin [to enumerate] the kings who came over Ireland during his own time, and before it, than the kings who would come after him, when they had been explained to him by the Angel, to whom every thing is possible and easy.

He spoke after that of the kings who would be over Ireland from Diarmait until doom,[4] viz.,

Diarmait Mac Cerbhaill, firstly.

Domhnall and Fergus, two sons of Muirchertach Mac Erca, one year; or three years.[5] They died.[6]

Bactan, son of Muirchertach, and Eochaidh, son of Domhnall, three years.[7]

gus and Domhnall, two sons of Muirchertach, son of Muiredach, son of Eoghan, son of Niall of the Nine Hostages, lasted three years. Other authorities allow them only one year. See note [7].

[6] *died.*—ecc atbatatar; lit. "death they died," A.

[7] *years.*—The letters c. n, prefixed, indicate that the kings mentioned were of the Clann-Neill, or descendants of Niall.

Ainmire mac Setnai, tri bliadna.

c. ɔ. Baetan mac Ninneda.

c. ɔ. Aod mac Ainmirech,

c. n. s. a. s. Aed Slaine ocus Colman rimid.

c. n. Aed Uairidneach.

c. ɔ. Maelcoba clerech.

c. n. Suibne mend.

c. ɔ. Domnall mac Aedai.

c. ɔ. Conall (.i. cael mac Mailicoba), ocus Cellach mac Mailecoba.

c. n. Blathmac ocus Diarmait, da mac Aeda Slaine.

s. a. s. Sechnusach mac Blathmaic.

Cendfaelad mac Blathmaic.

s. a. s. Findachta fledach.

c. ɔ. Loingsech mac Aengussa.

Congal cindmagair.

c. n. Fergal mac Mailedúin.

Fogartach mac Neill.

Cinaed mac Irgalaig.

Flaithbertach mac Loingsig.

[1] *Baetan.—Aedh.* The characters c. ɔ. signify that they were of the Cinel-Conaill, or descendants of Conall Gulban, son of Niall of the Nine Hostages.

[2] *Aedh Slaine.*—The characters c. n, and s. a. s., prefixed in the margin, are to indicate that Aedh Slaine was of the Clann-Neill, and the progenitor of the "Slicht-Aedha-Slaine" ("posterity of Aedh Slaine"), signified by s. a. s.

[3] *Aedh Uairidnech.*—Also of the Clann-Neill, as the letters c. n. indicate.

[4] *Cleric.*—So called from having embraced a monastic life, as is stated by some writers; although the Annalists assert that he was slain, A.D. 615, by his successor, after a short reign of three years. See *Cambrensis Eversus* (Kelly's ed.), vol. ii. p. 19; and Reeves's *Adamnan*, p. 37, note [e]. The characters prefixed to his name signify that he was of the Cenel-Conaill, or descended from Conall Gulban, son of Niall.

[5] *Mend*; i.e. "dumb."—Of the c. n., or Clann-Neill.

[6] *Aedh*; i.e. the Aedh referred to in note [1]; of the c. ɔ., or Cinel-Conaill.

[7] *Cael.*—"Slender."

[8] *son.* mic, A.—Conall and Cellach were of the direct line of Conall Gulban, son of Niall, as the characters c. ɔ. indicate.

Ainmire, son of Setna, three years.
Baetan,[1] son of Ninnid.
Aedh,[1] son of Ainmire.
Aedh Slainè[2], and Colman Rimid.
Aedh Uairidnech.[3]
Maelcobha Cleric.[4]
Suibhne Mend.[5]
Domhnall, son of Aedh.[6]
Conall (i.e. Cael[7]), son of Maelcobha, and Cellach, son[8] of Maelcobha.
Blathmac and Diarmait, two sons of Aedh Slaine.
Sechnusach,[9] son of Blathmac.
Cennfaeladh, son of Blathmac.
Finnachta Fledach.[10]
Loingsech,[11] son of Aengus.
Congal of Cenn-Maghair.[12]
Fergal,[13] son of Maelduin.
Fogartach, son of Niall.
Cinaed, son of Irgalach.[14]
Flaithbertach, son of Loingsech.

[9] *Sechnusach.*—The letters ꞅ. α. ꞅ. signify that he was of *Slicht Aedha Slaine*, or sept of Aedh Slaine, before referred to. See note [2], p. 40.

[10] *Fledach;* "The festive."—Of the sept of Aedh Slaine, as the letters ꞅ. α. ꞅ. imply. This king is said to have remitted, at the intercession of St. Moling (A.D. 680), the Boromean Tribute imposed on the Leinstermen by King Tuathal Techtmar in the second century. For a curious account of the means by which the Saint obtained this concession, see *Frag. of Irish Annals*, p. 77, sq.

[11] *Loingsech.*—One of the Cenel-Conaill, as indicated by the characters c. ɔ.

[12] *Cenn-Maghair.*—Kinnaweer, in the bar. of Kilmacrenan, co. Donegal.

[13] *Fergal.*—The letters c. n. are prefixed, to signify that Fergal was of the Clann-Neill, or direct descendants of Niall of the Nine Hostages. He was the contemporary and rival of Cathal Mac Finghuine, king of Munster (ob. A.D. 737), the subject of the remarkable story published from the *Leabhar Breac*, by Mr. Hennessy, in Fraser's Magazine for Sept., 1873.

[14] *Irgalach.*—See an amusing account of a contest between this person and Adamnan, in the *Three Fragments of Annals*, published by the Irish Arch. and Celt. Soc., Dublin, 1860, pp. 101–5.

Aod allan mac Fergaile.
Domnall mac Murchada
c. n. Niall Frosach mac Fergaile
c. col. Donnchad mac Doṁnaill.
Aoḋ ordniḋe.
Conchobar mac Donnchada.
Niall Caille mac Aoda.
* fol. 5, b. 1. Maelsechnaill mac Maelruanaig
Aedh Findliath mac Nell Chaille.[a]
c. ċ. Fland mac Moilsechnaill.
c. n. Niall glundub mac Aoda.
c. ċ. Dondchad mac Floind mic Maelsechnaill.
r. a. r. Congalach mac Maelmithid mic Falannagain mic Cellaig mic Congalaig mic Amalgada mic Congalaig mic Conaing mic Aoda Slane.
c. n. Doṁnall mac Muircertaiġ ṁic Neill glunduib.
Maelsechlainn mor mac Domnaill mic floind sinnda mic Maoilsechnail mic Mailruanaig.
Brian mac Cennetig.

[1] *Domhnall.*—A marg. note adds that he was ced rig ċloinne Colmain, or the "first king of Clann-Colman," a sept descended from Colman (sl. A.D. 558, *Chron. Scotorum*), son of Diarmait, son of Fergus Cerrbheoil, son of Conall Cremthainn, son of Niall of the Nine Hostages. "Clann-Colman" was the tribe name of the powerful family of the O'Melaghlins of Meath and Westmeath. The chronicles mention 17 Irish monarchs of the Clann-Colman sept.

[2] *Frosach:* "the showery."—So designated, because three remarkable showers (of silver, blood, and honey), are stated to have fallen in Ireland in the year of his birth, A.D. 716; and three more (of silver, wheat, and honey) are recorded as having fallen in Inishowen, co. Donegal, in the first year of his sovereignty (A.D. 763, *Four Mast.*) He was of the Clann-Neill, as the letters c. n. attest.

[3] *Donnchad.*—Of the Clann-Colman (c. col.) See note [1].

[4] *Caille.*—This should probably be Caillne, as the epithet is derived from the name of a river (Callann) in which Niall is recorded to have been drowned, A.D. 844. See *Four Mast.* ad an. O'Donovan (loc. cit.) wrongly supposes it to be the King's River, in the co. Kilkenny.

This entry concludes fol. 4, a. 2, on the lower margin of which is a stanza addressed to a person named Guaire, a specimen of pedantry not worth reproducing here.

Aedh Allan, son of Fergal.

Domhnall,[1] son of Murchadh.

Niall Frosach,[2] son of Fergal.

Donnchad,[3] son of Domhnall

Aedh Ordnidhe

Conchobhar, son of Donnchad.

Niall Caille,[4] son of Aedh.

Maelsechnaill, son of Maelruanaigh.

Aedh Finnliath, son of Niall Caille.

Flann,[5] son of Maelsechnaill.

Niall Glundubh, son of Aedh.

Donnchad, son of Flann, son of Maelsechnaill.

Congalach,[6] son of Maelmithidh, son of Flannagan, son of Cellach, son of Congalach, son of Amhalgaidh, son of Congalach, son of Conaing, son of Aedh Slainè.

Domhnall,[7] son of Muirchertach, son of Niall Glundubh.

Maelsechlainn[8] the Great, son of Domhnall, son of Flann Sinna, son of Maelsechlainn, son of Maelruanaigh.

Brian,[9] son of Cennedigh.

[5] *Flann.*—Called Flann Sinna, or "Flann of the Shannon." Of the Clann-Colman (c. ċ.), or descendants of Colman the Great.

[6] *Congalach.*—The letters ꞅ. a. ꞅ. are meant to express that he was of *Slicht Aedha Slaine* (or sept of Aedh Slainè), as the descent above given testifies.

[7] *Domnall.*—Of the Clann-Neill (c. n.)

[8] *Maelsechlainn.*—This name is comp. of *Mael* (calvus) and *Sechlainn*, the genit. of Sechlann, a metathesis for *Sechnall*, or St. Sechnall, founder of the Church of Dunshaughlin, co. Meath, and means "Servant of Sechlann." The name was pronounced Melaghlin; and is now Anglicised Malachy, as a Christian name, and M'Laughlin or Loghlin, as a surname. The M'Laughlins, or O'Melaghlins, were the senior branch of the Southern Hy-Neill, who inhabited the present counties of Meath and Westmeath, with part of the co. Dublin.

[9] *Brian:* i.e.—Brian Borumha, who deposed his predecessor, Maelsechlainn the Great, in the year 1001. He seems to have attempted to depose him in the previous year, for the Chron. Scotorum records, under the year 998=1000, the "first turning of Brian and the Connacht-men against Maelsechlainn." See Todd's *Cogadh Gaedhel re Gallaibh*, introd., cliv.-v.

Maelsechluind iterum.

Toirrdelbach O Conchobair (ri con fresabra)

Muirchertach mac Neill.

Ruaidri mor O Conchobbair, ri gan fresabra.

Ro airim iarain Caillin ni na tainic ocus nat fettatar senchaidhe nait fileda .i. na riga do ġebad hErind ó Ruaidri O Conchobair co brath; ocus ni nama ba baile ocus ba faistine do Chaillin na riġasa na tainig fós, aċt chena ba tria ḟis ocus ba tria ḟáistine in aingil do ro tharngair Caillin gach ri fogebad hErind o Diarmait mac Cerbaill

[a] fol. 5, b. co brath, ar is a comre fria Diarmait do roine Caillin in duan[a] .i.

2.

hEri oll oilen aingeal.

Nói riga coicat ro airim Caillin do gabail hErend o Diarmait co braṫ; tria ḟaistine ocus baile na riga sin huile.

Oin ri air ṡecht ḟiċtiḃ riġ o ṡlainge co Diarmaid ro airneid Caillin

[1] *again*; i.e.—after Brian's death, at the battle of Clontarf, in 1014.

[2] *with opposition.* — fresabra (from fris, "against him," and abraḋ, "to speak"), i.e. not generally acknowledged. The order of the succession to the throne of Ireland, from the death of Maelsechlainn II. (or the Great), to the accession of Ruaidhri O'Conor, is rather uncertain. The historians of Munster and Connacht maintain that Turlogh O'Conor was undoubtedly king of Ireland; but the northern writers deny him that dignity. Keating states that Donnchad, son of Brian; Turlogh, son of Tadhg, and Muirchertach, son of Turlogh, reigned in turn after Maelsechlinn II., but he adds "only in the kingship of Leth-Mogha (or the southern half of Ireland), and the greater part of Ireland." Muirchertach is indeed styled the "glorious king of Ireland" by Anselm; and Dr. Lynch contends that at least Turlogh and Muirchertach are entitled to rank amongst the supreme monarchs of Ireland. See *Cambr. Evers.* vol. II. Dublin, 1850; pp. 45-9. The historians of Leinster assert that Diarmaid Mac Maelnambo, great grandfather of Diarmait Mac Murrough, was king of Ireland after Donnchad, son of Brian. His claims are thus put forward in the *Book of Leinster*, a 12th cent. MS. in Trinity College, Dublin: Speaking of "Kings with opposition," the writer says, "thus are 'kings with opposition' reckoned in the regal list; if the king be of Leth-Chuind (the northern half of Ireland), and that he has *all Leth-Chuind, and one province of Leth-Mogha* (the southern half), that man is king of Tara and of Ireland, 'with opposition.' If he is of Leth-Mogha, however, he is not called king of Ireland unless he have *all Leth-*

Maelsechlainn again.[1]

Toirdhelbhach O'Conchobhair, (king with opposition).[2]

Muirchertach, son of Niall.[3]

Ruaidhri the Great O'Conchobhair, (king without opposition).

Caillin afterwards enumerated what had not yet come to pass, and what neither historians nor poets know—to wit, the kings that would possess Ireland from Ruaidhri O'Conchobhair until doom. And not alone[4] was it a prophesy and prediction on the part of Caillin [to indicate] these kings that had not yet come, but it was also through the knowledge and prediction of the Angel that Caillin foretold each king who would possess Ireland from Diarmait Mac Cerbhaill until doom; for it was in the time of Diarmait Mac Cerbhail that Caillin composed the lay:—

"Noble Ireland, Isle of Angels."

Fifty-nine kings, Caillin reckoned, would reign in Ireland from Diarmait until doom. Through prophecy and ecstasy [he enumerated] all those kings.

One king over seven score[5] kings, from Slainge to Diarmait, Caillin

Mogha, and Tara with its territories, and the second province of Leth-Chuind added thereto. Mac Maelnambo was thus king of Ireland, for he had all Leth-Mogha, and Connacht, and the men of Meath, and the Ulidians and Airghialla. And it is by him Donnchad, son of Brian, was expelled beyond the seas." Fol. 13, a. 2. See *Cambr. Eversus*, Vol. II., p. 39.

[3] *of Niall;* i.e.—of Niall Mac Lochlainn, one of the northern Hy-Neill.

[4] *alone.* nama.—More correctly nammá (tantum, solum), which Ebel would resolve into *na-n-má*, "ut non sit magis," (Zeuss, 2nd. ed., 614.) It is now obsolete as an adverb, its place being supplied by amain, which O'Donovan considers its actual equivalent (Irish Grammar, pp. 263, 268). He probably regarded *amain* (though he does not say so) as formed from *nama*, by the process which Cormac characterizes as *delidin*, or "inversion of letters"—a process by which *fer* is converted into *ref*. But the ancient form *namma* (in which the *m* is doubled) is opposed to this; and Herr Ebel's suggestion seems more likely to be correct, especially as he gives an instance (loc. cit.) where the form is *nammá*.

[5] *one king over seven score.*—This agrees with O'Flaherty's calculation. Of the whole list, 136 were Pagan. See O'Flaherty's curious classification of the various modes in which they lost their lives; *Ogygia*, p. 420. Only 17 of them died a natural death.

ina duain. Noi fichit ri ocus a noí dec sin huile can aṫgabail ḟlainge, amail adubairt Caillin ina duain .i.

.IX. fichit ri sa .ix. deg,
O ḟlange co brath ni breg,
Ised ro airmius co grinn,
In lin riġ ro ġaḃ (sic) Erinn.

Maḋ ail a ḟis tra, cid imo ro airim Caillin na rigasa, Ishe imorro in fath fodera .i. do medugaḋ onóra ocus cadais ocus comairci dia chatraig ocus dia ċongḃail, ocus dia eclais ocus dia ard nemed, co dered doṁain .i. Fidnacha muiġe rein. Fodaig ni uil ri na tairech na ngrada flata, na brugaid na biataċ, na ollam na ardfileḋ in Erinn na beṫ for slicht rig dib sud, ocus combetis huili ic onoragad a chaṫrach dia es .i. Fiḋnacha muiġe rein.

Atat dono neṫe eli labrus in duansa do rinde Caillin mac Niatach, dianad adbar na neṫeri anuas .i. in gaḃaltus sa anuas, ocus in rem riġraide o ḟlange mac Dela mic Loich co Diarmait mac Cerbaill; ocus ro tharngair iarsin gach ri ro gebad Erinn co braṫ.

* fol. 6, a. 1. Is emilt linde tra anad fri gach ní labras in duan, aċt aisnedfem in mad eli is in lebar inar ndiaid. Isi so duan.

Eriu oll oilen aingeal,
Port cadais na prim chaingen;

[1] *without including.* can aṫgabail. aṫgabail, as a law term, means "distraint," "reprisal," *withernam.* But in the text it is certainly used in the sense of "including."

[2] *habitation.* congḃail=con-gabail, "co-occupation," "co-possession;" from *con,* "together," and *gabail,* "taking." Wrongly explained by some glossarists as =Convallis. With the adj. *nua* prefixed, it forms, as *Nuachongbhail* (*Anglice,* Nohoval, or Noghoval) the name of several places in Ireland.

[3] *sanctuary.*—The word nemed is glossed "sacellum," in the 8th cent. MS. cited by Zeuss (Gram. Celt., p. 11, where he gives the Gaulish forms *nemeton, vernemetis* gl. fanum ingens). Dr. O'Donovan (suppl. to O'Reilly, *voce* nemeaḋ) gives, from Irish MSS. several apocryphal meanings of the word, in which it is used to signify "musician," "carpenter," "smith," "cow," &c.; but in these cases the idea of protection seems involved.

[4] *brughaidh;* i.e. "landholder," or "farmer."

announced in his Lay. Nine score kings and nineteen altogether, without including[1] Slainge, as Caillin said in his Lay, i.e.

Nine score kings and nineteen,
From Slainge to doom—no lie;
It is, as I have diligently reckoned,
The number of kings who shall possess Ireland.

If it is desired to know, therefore, why Caillin enumerated those kings, this is truly the reason why, viz., to the increasing of honour, respect, and protection for his city and habitation,[2] and for his church and high sanctuary,[3] to the end of the world, i.e. Fidhnacha of Magh-Rein. Because there is neither king, nor chief, nor any of princely degree, no *brughaidh*,[4] nor *biatach*,[5] nor *ollamh*,[6] nor eminent poet in Ireland, that should not be of the race of some king of those; and [he wished] that they should all be honouring his city after him, to wit, Fidhnacha of Magh-Rein.

There are also other things spoken of in this poem, which Caillin son of Niata composed, the subject of which is these foregoing[7] affairs, i.e. the *gabhaltus*[8] down to this, and the roll of kings from Slainge, son of Dela, son of Loth, to Diarmait Mac Cerbhaill. And he afterwards foretold every king who would possess Ireland until doom.

We think it tedious, however, to dwell here on every thing of which the poem speaks; but we shall relate them in another place in the book *infra*.[9] This is the Poem.

Noble Ireland,[10] Isle of Angels,
Honoured home of prime actions;

[5] *biatach*; lit. "victualler."—A person who supplied biaḋ (food, refection) to kings, guests, and pilgrims, under certain conditions laid down in the Brehon Laws.

[6] *ollamh*, pron. *ollave*.—The chief professor of any science, was called an *ollamh* of that science.

[7] *foregoing*. anuaſ; lit. "from above."

[8] *gabhaltus*.—"Occupation," "invasion," "colonization." The word is a derivative from *gabhail*, taking, assuming.

[9] *infra*. inar nDiaiḋ, lit. "after us." Two unimportant stanzas are added in the lower marg. of fol. 5 b., in A.

[10] *Ireland*.—The form in the text, eriu (*Eriu*), is the proper nomin., gen. erenn; dat. erinn; from which latter the popular form *Erin* is incorrectly taken. In the

A gabala uili anall
Innesat duit i caitchend.
Findtan is Bith is Ladra.
Gabsat ar tus in banba;
Is ccoiggad ingen ngel ngrind,
Da fichet la re ndilind.
Ni lucht sin huili ba marb,
Re ndilind, ba mor in plag,
Achtmad Findtan in fer seng,
Na cadlad re re ndileand.
Ares dilend do ni brecc,
Oin bliadain decc is tri chet,
Ic aitreb Erend cen brón,
Go ticc anoir Partholon.
Partholon in gregach grind,
Tri cet bliadan bai ind Erind,
Gur marb ri sechtmain do tham,
Ocus nói mili imlan.
Tricha bliadan d'Erind oig
Aress Partholoin int sroill,
Co tainic Nemed anoir,
Ogus a meic na fochair.
Se bliadna decc, ced ua ḋo,
Re nairem ni himargo,
Do chaith Nemeḋ sa ċlann grind,
No gur legad tor Conaing.
Da chet bliadain go cert grind,
On maidm sin chaṫraig Conaing,

present translation the name is printed "Ireland," for no other reason than to avoid misconception.

[1] *Ladhra.*—See *ante*, p. 15.

[2] *Banba.*—A bardic name for Ireland; said to have been applied to it at the request of Banba, wife of Mac Cuill, one of the Tuatha De Danaun kings of Ireland on the arrival of the Milesian Colony.

[3] *died.* ba marb; lit. "was dead."—A.

[4] *slept.*—See note,[1] p. 6, *ante*.

All its colonizations, hitherto,
I shall tell thee in general.
Finntan, and Bith, and Ladhra,[1]
Occupied Banba[2] at first,
With fifty fair, sprightly maidens,
Forty days before the Flood.
All that band died,[3]
Before the Flood—great the plague—
Except Finntan, the subtile man,
Who slept[4] during the period of the Deluge.
After the Deluge was he[5]—it is no lie—
Eleven years and three hundred,
Inhabiting Ireland, without grief,
'Till Partholan came from the East.
Partholan, the joyous Greek,
Was three hundred years in Ireland,
Until in one week, of a plague,
Died he and full nine thousand more.
Thirty years was virgin Ireland
[Waste], after the brilliant Parthalon;[6]
Until Nemed came from the East,
And his sons along with him.
Sixteen years, and twice an hundred,
(Tis no falsehood[7] to be reckoned),
Nemed and his joyous clan spent
Until Tor-Conaing[8] was razed.
Two hundred pleasant years, exactly,
From that breach of Conang's city,

[5] *was he.* ᴅo; lit. "for him." A. A well known idiom.

[6] *brilliant Parthalon.* Paꞃꞇholoın ınꞇ ſꞃoıll. ꞅꞃoll is explained ꞅollꞅı, "light," "brightness," in Cormac's Glossary. It also means satin, or any cloth with a shining surface.

[7] *falsehood.* ᵹo.—The MS. (A) has bꞃeᵹ, ⁊ ᵹo; but as ᵹo rhymes with the last word in the preceding line, it has been adopted as the correct reading.

[8] *Tor-Conaing.*—See note [3], p. 16, *ante.*

Co ticc clann in miled Sdairn,
Asin Greg uallaċ ngairb.
Coicc rioġa teagait anoir,
I tri loingsib tar glas moir;
Gur roindset etarrai tra,
Eri i cuig ranna certa.
Rudraige ba ri fer mBolg,
Slange for nGalion na nord;
Rigraid fer nDomnann gan ḟell,
Gann, Genann, ocus Sengann.
Sengann, Genann ocus Gann,
Ocus Rudraige na lann,
Tugatar sin imalle
Rige nErend do ṡlange.
Gaḃala Erend mini,
No gur gab Slainge riġi,
Do indiser daib gan acht,
Acht Capa is Laiġne is Luasat.
IS uime nar airmes tuas
Gabail an trir co firchruais,
Oir ni rucsat na luing loir
Achtmad tri glaca glaisḟeoir.
Uime airmim duib anois
In gabail sin ro ḟagbos,
Nach lamad nech air doman
Int ugdar do cronogad.
Airium na mbliadan dogen,
O thosach doṁain can len,

[1] *Fir-Bolg.*—According to O'Flaherty, the Fir-Bolg were a branch of the Belgæ of Britain, who, emigrating from Belgium, or the inferior parts of Germany, occupied the country in and about Somersetshire, Wiltshire, and the interior of Hampshire, in England. *Ogygia*, p. 14.

[2] *Galion.*—This was the name of the primitive inhabitants of Leinster, which was anciently called *Coiced-Galion*, or the Fifth (or province) of Galián.

[3] *Fir-Domnann.*—O'Flaherty endeav-

Until the sons of the hero Starn
Came from the proud, rugged Greece.
Five kings come they from the East,
In three ships, across the blue sea;
And they between them, moreover, divided
Ireland into five equal portions.
Rudhraighe was king of the Fir-Bolg[1]
Slainge was over Galion[2] of the weapons;
The chieftains of the Fir-Domnann[3] without guile,
Were Gann, Genann, and Sengann.
Sengann, Genann, and Gann,
And Rudhraighe of the lances—
They all with one accord gave
The kingship of Ireland to Slainge.
The 'Occupations' of smooth Ireland,
Until Slainge assumed kingship,
I have told you, without doubt,
Except [that of] Capa, Laighne, and Luasat.
The reason why I have not above reckoned
The 'Occupation' of the hardy trio, is
Because they carried not off in their good ship
But three handfulls of green grass.[4]
Why I reckon for you now
That 'Occupation' which I omitted,
Is, that no one on earth should dare
To reprove the author.
The enumeration of the years will I perform,
From the beginning of the world without woe,

ours (*Ogygia*, p. 14), to prove that the Irish Fir-Domnann were the same as the Damnonii placed by Ptolemy in Cornwall and Devonshire, which latter name he derives from "Damnonii." The Irish etymologists explain the name otherwise. See *Keating* (Haliday's ed.) p. 189.

[4] *green grass.*—In some of the bardic accounts of the Colonizations of Ireland, the fishermen Capa, Laigne, and Luasad, are stated to have carried away with them

Ares na ngabal malle,
No cur gab Slange rige.
Se bliadna coicait gen char,
Se ced is mili bliadan,
O thosach domain anall,
No gur ḟer flechad dilend.
Da bliadain coicait .x. ced,
O dilind co becht ni brecc,
Gur gab Slange rige tend
Air tur re feraib Erend. E.
Eirtid foderta re rim,
conndirsur gan imsnim
O ṡlange co Diarmaid ngrind
Ainm gach rig ro gab hErind. Eri oll.
Slange, Rudraige nar gann,
Gann, Genann ocus Sengann;
Fiaċa ocus Rinnail don rind,
Ocus [F]odbgein mac Sengaind.
Eocha is Nuada is Bres[3] is Lug;
Eochaid ollath[ar] iarum,
Fris aderthi in Dagda tend,
A eolcha aill Erenn.
Delbaiṫ is Fiachna combuaid;
Tri meic Cermada conuaill;

a *sod* cut from the soil of Ireland, as if in token of a right of possession.

[1] *Six.* ui.—A.

[2] *down.* anall, i.e. hither (lit. "from beyond").—A.

[3] *Slainge.*—The first king of the Fir-Bolg, or Damnonian Race; and the first absolute king of all Ireland, according to the bardic accounts. The capital letter E at the end of the stanza is a repetition of that with which the poem begins. The practice of repeating, at the *end* of a poem, the initial letter or line, was generally observed by Irish scribes, but the repetition here noted is rather irregular.

[4] *Ireland.*—The two first words of the poem, Eri oll, are added at the end of this stanza.

[5] *of the point.*—It is stated in Irish legendary history, that there were no

After the 'Occupations,' all summed up,
Until Slainge assumed sovranty.
Six[1] years and fifty, without stain,
Six hundred and a thousand years,
From the beginning of the world, down,[2]
Until the waters of the Flood descended.
Two years, fifty, ten hundred,
From the Flood exactly—'tis no lie—
'Till Slainge[3] assumed firm sway,
At first, before the men of Ireland.
Listen henceforth awhile to me,
That I may relate, without perplexity,
From Slainge down to jovial Diarmaid,
The name of each king who possessed Ireland.[4]
Slainge, Rudhraighe who was not mean,
Gann, Genann, and Sengann;
Fiacha, and Rinnail 'of the point';[5]
And [F]odbgen son of Sengann.
Eocha, and Nuadha, and Bres, and Lug;[6]
Afterwards Eochaidh Ollathar,
Who was called the stout Dagda,
You splendid sages of Ireland.[7]
Delbhaeth and Fiachna the triumphant;
The three proud sons[8] of Cermaid;

points on spears until the time of Rinnail, who was so called from having introduced pointed weapons. ꞃinn, in Irish, signifies "point."

[6] *Lug*. Lugaidh lamh-fada; or Lugadius Longimanus, as the name is Latinized by O'Flaherty, who refers his accession to A.M. 2764. In the lower margin of fol. 6 a, in A, the scribe has added two distichs, not worth printing.

[7] *Ireland*.—The original of this line A cotcha ailli Eꞃenn, is like the first line of another well-known chronological poem.

[8] *sons*.—These were Mac Cuill, Mac Cecht, and Mac Greine. They had other names, viz., Ethor, Tethor, and Cethor. Ethor is said to have been called Mac Cuill ('son of *Coll*'), from having worshipped *Coll*, or the hazel-tree. Tethor

Epemon, Ebep nap cle;
Muimni, Luigni ip Laigni.
Cethpi meic Ebip na plog;
Ep, Opba, Fepgna, Fepon;
Ipial, Ethepel gan oil,
Ogup Conmal mac Ebip.
Tigepnmap ba loeč calma;
Eochaidh etgothach ampa;
Cepmna, Sobaipche nap bpap
Ogup Eocha faebapglap.
Ebep mac Conmail na nech;
Fiacha labpainde laigthech;
Eochoid mumo pi gan oil,
Ocup Oengup ollmucaiḋ.
Enna, Roṫechtach, Setna;
Fiačna, Muinemon detla;
Aildepgdoid, Ollam na long;
Findachta ogup Slanoll.
Gede, Fiac, Bepndgal co ngoil,
Oilill, Sipna, Rothechtaig;
Elim, Giallchad, Apt gu mbloid,
Nuada ip Bpep ip Eochaid.
Mac Blatha (.i. Find), Setna na cpech,
Simon, Duach, ip Muipedach;
Enna depg, Lugaid na clep;
Siplam ip Eoča uaipcheap.

was called Mac Cecht, "son of plough," from having deified the plough; and the name of "Mac Greine" was given to Cethor, from the sun (*grian*), which was his God. In their reign, circa A.M. 2934, the Milesian colony arrived in Ireland, according to Irish legendary history.

[1] *Eremon.*—Epennon, A.

[2] *and.* 7, A.—This is the usual abbrev. for ocup or ogup ('and') throughout the MS. A.; but the exigencies of metre oftentimes led the poet to use the shortened form of ocup (viz. ip), which the scribe not unfrequently represented by the sign "7."

[3] *Eber.*—The name of this king is not

Eremon,[1] Eber who was not unjust;
Muimhne, Luighne and[2] Laighne.
The four sons of Eber of the hosts—
Er, Orba, Fergna, Feron—
Irial, Etherel without stain;
And Conmal son of Eber.
Tigernmas, who was a puissant hero;
The illustrious Eochaidh Etgothach;
Cermna, Sobhairke not false,
And Eocha Faebharglas.
Eber,[3] son of Conmal of the steeds;
Fiacha Labrainde the Lessener;[4]
Eochaidh Mumo, a stainless king;
And Oengus Ollmucaidh.
Enna, Rothechtach, Setna;
Fiachna, Muinemon the bold;
Aildergdoid, Ollamh[5] of the ships;
Finnachta, and Slanoll.
Gede, Fiacha, Berngal the brave;
Oilill, Sirna, Rothechtach;
Elim, Giallchad, Art the famous;
Nuada, and[6] Bres, and Eochaidh.
The son of Blaith (i.e. Find); Setna of the preys;
Simon, Duach,[7] and Muiredach;
Enna the Red; Lugaid of the games;[8]
Sirlamh, and Eocha Uairches.

in any of the ordinary lists of Irish kings.

[4] *the Lessener.* laıᵹᴛhech.—So called, perhaps, from having subdued his enemies in several battles. See *Keating* (Haliday's ed.), p. 327.

[5] *Ollamh.*—The word "Fotla" is written as a gloss over this name, to signify that the person intended was Ollamh Fotla.

[6] *and.* 7, A. See note [2].

[7] *Duach.*—ᴅuaċ., A.

[8] *of the games.*—Lugaidh was nicknamed *iardhonn*, which Keating explains as equivalent in meaning to *dubh-dhonn*, "black-brown," from the colour of his hair. Haliday's ed., p. 337.

Eocha, Conaing, maith a nert;
Lugaid, Conaing ocus Art;
Eoċa mac Airt, Eocha mac Oil;
Argetṁar, Duaċ, is Lugaid,
Oeḋ, Diṫorb, Cimbaeṫ na celg;
Macha in bean, Rechtaid rig derg;
Ugaine is Laegaire gel;
Cobthach is Labraid loingsech.*
* fol. 6, b. 2.
Melgi, MocCorb, Oengus raiṫ;
Iarero, Fercorb, Conla daiṫ;
Oilill Adamair co ngus;
Eochaidh, Fergus is Oengus.
Conall, Nia, Enna cen bron;
Crimthan, Rudraige ro mor;
Findatmar Bresal caing[n]ech;
Ocus Congal clairingneach.
Duaċ, Faċtna, Eochaiḋ feḋlech;
Oirium (.i. Eochaid); Etirscel nemnech;
Nuada, Conaire cin cron;
Lugaid ocus Conchobar.
Crimthand is Cairpre cinn cait;
Feradach, Fiatach lan baile;
Fiachna, Elim, Tuathal co noeb
Mal, Fedlimid is Caṫair.
Cond, Conaire, Art, Lugaid lond;
Fergus, Cormac, Eoċa donn;

[1] *Eocha*. Eocha Fiadhmuine.—See note [1], p. 26, *ante*.

[2] *Conaing*.—This is the Conaing mentioned in the line preceding. He reigned jointly with Eochaidh Fiadhmuine from A.M. 3520 to 3525; and by himself from 3529 to 3536. O'Flaherty; *Ogygia*, p. 265.

[3] *Eocha*.—This should be Oilill Find. See note [6], p. 26, *supra*. Some authorities, among them Keating, give him a predecessor named Fiacha Tolgrach. O'Flaherty, following the Annals of Clonmacnois, denies him the title of king. *Ogygia*, p. 100.

Oil.—A shortened form of Oilill.

Eocha,[1] Conaing—good their might—
Lugaid, Conaing,[2] and Art;
Eocha[3] son of Art; Eocha son of Oil;[4]
Argatmar, Duach, and Lugaid.
Aedh, Dithorba, Cimbaeth of the wiles;
Macha[5] the woman; Rechtaidh Rigderg;
Ugaine, and Laeghaire the Fair;
Cobthach, and Labraid Loingsech.
Melgi, Mog-Corb,[6] Aengus the lucky;
Iarero, Fercorb, active Connla;
Oilill, Adamair[7] the valorous;
Eochaidh, Fergus, and Aengus.
Conall, Nia, Enna without sorrow;
Crimthand; the mighty Rudhraighe;
Findatmar; Breasal of the compacts,[8]
And Congal Claringnech.
Duach, Fachtna, Eochaidh Fedhlech;
Oirium (i.e. Eochaidh); venomous Etirscel;
Nuada; Conaire without fault;
Lugaid, and Conchobhar.
Crimthand, and Cairpre Cat-head;
Feradach; the full-strong Fiatach;
Fiachna, Elim, the courteous Tuathal;
Mal, Fedhlimidh, and Cathair.
Conn, Conaire, Art, fierce Lugaidh;
Fergus, Cormac, Eocha the brown;

[5] *Macha.* This woman is remarkable, as being the only one of her sex recognised by Irish historians as having occupied the throne of Ireland.

[6] *Mog-Corb.*—ɱc copb, A.

[7] *Adamair.*—amaꝺaıp, A.

[8] *compacts.*—In the prose list, *supra*, p. 32, Breasal is nicknamed *Bo-dibaid*, or "cow destruction," from a great murrain that happened in his time. The name of Lugaidh Luaighne, which occurs after that of Breasal in the lists of Irish kings generally, is omitted in its proper place in the poem.

Cairbre, na Fothaid co ngal;
Fiacha, Colla is Muiredach.
Caolbad, Eochaid, Crimthan nar;
Niall, Dati, Laoghaire slan;
Oilill molt, Lugaid ria la;
Is Muircertach mac Erca.
Tuathal maelgarb, ri gan gait;
Ba lan ri Erenn Diarmait;
Go Diarmait do gellad lem
Aınm gach rig d'feraib Erenn. E. oll.
Oen ri air secht fichtib rig,
Aderim rib gan imsnim,
O Slange co Diarmait ngrinn,
In lin rig rogab hErind. E. o. o. a.
Ildesaid misi anos tres,
Is ni luga d'eolus,
Ainm gach rig gebus go grind
Oniu amach air Erind. E. o.
Diarmait, Domnall, Fergus na fled,
Baetan is Eochaid uchtgel;
Ainmire is Baetan na fled,
* fol. 7 a. 1. Ocus Aod mac Ainmirech.*
Aed slane, Colman is Aed;
Maelcoba 7 Suibne araen;

[1] *Fothads.* See p. 35, note [7], *supra.*

[2] *Colla.* Surnamed *Uais*, or "Noble." See note [1], p. 36, *supra.*

[3] *Diarmait;* i. e. Diarmait Mac Cerbhaill, king of Ireland from A.D. 544 to 563.

[4] *Ireland.* The characters E. oll, added at the end of the original text of this stanza, represent the two first words of the poem, Eriu oll, and should indicate the conclusion of the poem, according to the practice of Irish scribes. But the transcriber of the present poem has unmeaningly added these characters in several places.

[5] *kings.* This agrees with the computation of O'Flaherty, who counts 136 kings from Slainge, the first Belgic monarch, to Dathi, the last pagan king. His curious enumeration of the various ways in which they were disposed of is worth quoting. "Of these 136 kings," he says, "100 died

Cairbre; the valorous Fothads;[1]
Fiacha, Colla,[2] and Muiredach.
Caelbad, Eochaidh, noble Crimthand;
Niall, Dathi, perfect Laeghaire;
Oilill Molt; Lugaidh in his day;
And Muirchertach Mac Erca.
Tuathal Maelgarbh, a stainless king;
Full king of Ireland was Diarmait.[3]
Down to Diarmait, by me was promised
The name of every king of the men of Ireland.[4]
One king and seven score kings,[5]
I say unto you, without difficulty,
From Slainge to joyous Diarmait,
Is the number of kings who ruled Ireland.
I will relate now, meanwhile,
(And it is no lesser knowledge),
Each king's name who shall merrily rule,
From this day forth, over Ireland.
Diarmait, Domhnall, Fergus of the feasts;
Baetan, and fair-bosomed Eochaidh;
Ainmirè, and Baetan of the banquets;
And Aedh son of Ainmirè.[6]
Aedh Slanè, Colman, and Aedh;
Maelcobha and Suibhne both;[7]

by the sword; 17 died a natural death; the plague carried off six; 3 were killed by lightning; ten departed this life by different casualties; one devoted himself to idolatry; another died by the most excruciating tortures; another was crucified; another expired without any external cause, or change of colour; one was drowned; another burned to death; one died of grief; another was killed by his horse; one was choked by a fish-bone; and another was poisoned:

'Mille modis Lethi miseros mors una fatigat.' Statius; *Thebaid*: lib. ix., vers. 280." *Ogygia*, p. 420.

[6] *Ainmirè*. The scribe has written some poetical memoranda in the lower margin of fol. 6, b., which are not worth the trouble of transcribing; much less of printing.

[7] *both*. apaen. The lit. meaning is

Domnall is Conall cin traitt;[1]
Cellach, Bladmac is Diarmait.
Sechnusach, Cennfaelad cin feall;
Findachta, Loingsech, Congal;
Fergal, Fagartaċ, Cinaed and;[2]
Flaithbertach, Oed is Domnall.
Niall, Donnchad, Aed, Conchobar cas;
Fedlim,[3] Niall, Maelsechnuil dear;
Oed findliaṫ, Flann, Niall nar gann;
Donnchadh, Congalach, Domnall.
Maelseċluinn[4] is Brian Banba;[5]
Maelsechnaill[6] cetna calma;
Toirdelbaċ, Muircertaċ tenn;
Ocus Ruaidri flaith Erenn.
Derg donn, Aed foltlebair cas,
In lam fada 'san cliab glas;
Crissalach, Spartine naill;
Orgamuin donn oineċ Dabaill.

"together;" but as Maelcobha and Suibhne reigned separately, the word has been rendered by "both."

[1] *without quarrel.* cin traitt. cin is for cen, "without;" and traitt = traid, a quarrel, or conflict. Conall is usually called Conall *Cael*, or C. "the slender." He reigned conjointly with his brother Cellach, from A.D. 642 to 654, and singly from 654 to 658.

[2] *also.* and; lit. "there." A.

[3] *Fedhlim.* A marg. note, most probably added by Thady O'Rody, adds "ni uil in fer sin in atgabalaib na rig, acht o Chaillin nama;" i.e. "that man is not in the 'assumptions' of the kings, except from Caillin alone." The Fedhlim in question was Fedhlim Mac Crimthainn, king of Munster (ob. A.D. 847), whom the Munster historians assert to have been monarch of Ireland. But the Northern writers deny him this honour. See O'Donovan's observations on the subject; *Leabhar na g-ceart*, Introd. p. xvi., note f.

[4] *Maelsechlainn.* See note [6].

[5] *Brian of Banba.* Brian Borumha. Called Brian of Banba, or "Brian of Ireland;" *Banba* being a bardic name for Ireland.

[6] *Maelsechnaill.* This is the person called "Maelsechlainn" (by metathesis) in the preceding line. Displaced by Brian Borumha in A.D. 1002, he re-ascended the

Domhnall, and Conall without quarrel;[1]
Cellach, Blathmac, and Diarmait.
Sechnasach; Cennfaeladh without guile;
Finnachta, Loingsech, Congal;
Ferghal, Fogartach, Cinaed also;[2]
Flaithbertach, Aedh, and Domhnall.
Niall, Donnchadh, Aedh, Conchobhar the mild;
Fedhlim,[3] Niall, the handsome Maelsechnaill;
Aedh Findliath, Flann, Niall who was no niggard;
Donnchadh, Congalach, Domhnall.
Maelsechlainn,[4] and Brian of Banba;[5]
The same mighty Maelsechnaill;[6]
Toirdelbhach, stout Muirchertach,
And Ruaidhri, lord of Ireland.
Derg-donn;[7] comely Aedh of the long hair;
The Long Hand,[8] and the Gray-chest;[9]
Crissalach;[10] another Sraptinè;[11]
The brown-faced Osgamuin of Dabhall.[12]

throne in 1014, after Brian's death at the battle of Clontarf, and held it until his own death in the year 1022.

[7] *Derg-donn.* This and the ten names that follow are fanciful. A marginal note describes them as "do na ṙigaib na fetatur caċ cenmoṫa toimdiu na suad nama;" i.e. "of the kings whom nobody knows, save the conjecture of the sages only." *Derg-donn* means "Red-brown." There is a prophetic poem in the *Yellow Book of Lecan*, col. 908, attributed to Finnachta, a king of Connacht in the 9th cent., in which *Donn-derg* ("Brown-red") is mentioned in a list of future kings of Connacht.

[8] *Long Hand.* lam fada. The individual indicated by this title has not been identified. It may be an epithet for the Aedh mentioned in the preceding line.

[9] *Gray-chest.* cliab glas. This may also be an epithet for Aedh.

[10] *Crissalach.* This name signifies "dirty girdle." It is doubtless apocryphal.

[11] *another Sraptinè.* The son of Corpre Lifechair, son of Cormac Mac Airt, was called Fiacha Sraiptinè. See note [8] p. 35, *ante*.

[12] *Dabhall.* This was the ancient name of the river Blackwater, which flows between the counties Armagh and Tyrone, and falls into Lough Neagh.

Osnadaċ Uisnig cen gai;
Iarthu Ailig ar aon chai;
Foltgarb, is Fland cithach seng;
Ard ri degenach Erenn. E.

Do airmius daibsi co huain,
Mar do gellus, im deg duain,
Ainm gach rig o Diarmait tend,
Co la braṫa na mbemend.
O Diarmait co brath na mbemend,
Insim duib i coitċend,
Coicait is nonbar go clu,
Is he lin gebus hErinn. Eri oll. o.
Noi fichet ri 'sa noi deg,
O ḟlange co brath ni brég,
Amail ro airmeass go grind,
In lin rig forbiad Erind. E.
Mile 7 a ceṫair deg,
O gein Crist, coir a ċoimet,
Go marbat genti co nim
Brian uasal mac Cennetig.[a]
Na gulla sin muirbfes Brian,
Is a mac Murchad lanfial,
Is ait lem cridi nach dub
Marbad na ngall 'sa mbathud.

[a] fol. 7 a. 2.

[1] *Osnadach.* Lit. the "Sigher;" from osnad, "a sigh."

[2] *Uisnech.* Now the Hill of Usney, in the co. Westmeath, 6 miles to the west of Mullingar, on the Moate road.

[3] *Ailech.* This was the residence of the ancient kings of the Northern Ui Neill. Its remains are still pointed out at Elly, or Greenan-Elly, in the parish of Killygarvan, bar. of Kilmacrenan, co. Donegal. But the size of the ruins, only 77 feet in diameter, give a very poor idea of the extent of an ancient Irish regal abode.

[4] *FlannCithach.* "Flann the Showery." Called also, in other accounts, "Flann Ginach," or "Flann the Voracious." This character plays a conspicuous part in old Irish prophecies, in several of which he is

Osnadach[1] of Uisnech,[2] without falsehood;
Iartru of Ailech[3] in the same track;
Foltgarb, and Flann Cithach[4] the slender,
The last arch-king of Ireland.

I have leisurely recounted for you,
As I promised,[5] in my good lay,
Each king's name, from stout Diarmait,[6]
'Till Doomsday of the blows.
From Diarmait 'till Doom of the blows—[7]
I tell you all in general—
Fifty and nine famous [kings]
Is the number that will possess Ireland.[8]
Nine score[9] kings, and nineteen,
From Slaingè to Doom—'tis no lie—
As I have cheerfully reckoned,
Is the number of kings who'll rule Ireland.
One thousand and fourteen [years],
From Christ's birth—fit it should be remembered—
Until gentiles shall venomously[10] slay
The noble Brian, son of Cennedigh.[11]
Those Foreigners who will slay Brian,
And his full-generous son Murchadh—
Joyful to my heart, which is not black,
Is the killing and drowning of the Foreigners.

described as the last king of Ireland, in whose reign Antichrist will appear. He is mentioned in the *Baile Moling*, or Rhapsody of (St.) Moling, a copy of which is contained in the Yellow Book of Lecan (a 15th cent. MS. in the Library of Trin. Coll. Dublin), col. 340.

[5] *promised*. See *ante*, p. 59.

[6] *Diarmait*. Diarmait MacCerbhaill.

[7] *of the blows.* na mbend, for na mbemend, A.

[8] *Ireland.* hEriu. The words Eriu oll o., the commencing words of the poem, are here repeated in the text.

[9] *Nine score.* 9. 20., A.

[10] *Venomously.* co nim. co nem, A.

[11] *Cennedigh.* This was the name of Brian Borumha's father. From him has

Aitreba na ngall iarsin,
Nocha bia in Erinn ettir,
Co ti chuca longes trean
Tre bithin mna Tigernain.
Ben Tigernain gu met nglonn,
Daersus gaċ criċ rogab Conn,
Mairg neċ atcluinfe a dala,
Ar ndenum di a fagbala.
Tresin bfagbail sin dobeir
Ardriġan uallach Uisniġ,
Air O Ruairc go caime cnis,
Cuirfiḋ ri Laigen tairis.
Le Diarmait ticfaid anair
Loinges mor do saxanaib,
Do gabail Laigen re la,
Do digail a indarbta.
In loinges sin tic anair,
Mo criḋea ni ḟed a ċleith,
Nert Erenn ni gab co han,
No go marbait Tigernan.
I Tlaċtga marbthar in riġ,
Tigernan, gid imda a ċoim;

been derived the family name of O'Kennedy of Ormond, a sept thus entitled to be considered as senior to the family of O'Brien.

[1] *Tighernan's wife.* The famous Derbforgaill, daughter of O'Melaghlin, king of Meath, whose alleged abduction by Diarmait Mac Murchadha, king of Leinster, is asserted to have led to his expulsion from his kingdom of Leinster, and to the subsequent invasion of Ireland by the Anglo-Normans in his interest. Thady O'Rody adds the marg. note: "An cuis dia ttainic diberrt Erenn .i. Diarmuid na nGall ocus Derbforgaill ingen riġ Miḋe, ben Tigernain ċaoiċ Ui Ruairc ri breifne;" i.e. "the cause from which came the destruction of Ireland, viz., Diarmait na nGall [Dermot of the Foreigners], and Derbhorgaill, daughter of the king of Meath, wife of blind Tighernan O'Ruairc, king of Breifne." The writer signs his name Taḋg ó Rodaiġe, and adds the date, Aug. 8°. 1693.

The habitations of the Foreigners, after that,
Will not be in Ireland at all,
'Till comes to them a mighty fleet
On account of Tighernan's wife.[1]
Tighernan's wife of many crimes
Shall enslave each land that Conn[2] ruled;
Woe to him who hears her proceedings
After having committed her elopement.
Through this abandonment, which
The proud arch-queen of Uisnech[3] commits
Against O'Ruairc of fairest skin,
He will send Leinster's king[4] across [the sea].
With Diarmait will come, from the East,
A great fleet of Saxons,
To seize Leinster in his time;
To avenge his banishment.
This fleet that comes from the East,
(My heart cannot conceal it),
Shall not firmly possess the power of Ireland
Until they slay Tighernan.
In Tlachtga[5] will be slain the king,
Tighernan, tho' numerous his companions;

O'Rody was right in describing Tighernan O'Ruairc as *Caech*, or "one-eyed." Giraldus Cambrensis also calls him "Monoculus" (*Hib. Expugnata*, lib. 1, cap. 1). Queen Derbhorgaill died in Mellifont Abbey, A.D. 1193, in the 85th year of her age; so that at the date of her alleged elopement with Dermot Mac Murrough, in 1152, she was 44 years of age, the profligate Dermot being 62!

[2] *Conn.* Conn of the Hundred Battles, slain by Tibraide Tirech, A.D. 212.

[3] *Uisnech.* See note [2], p. 62, *ante*. Derbhorgaill is here called Queen of Uisnech, in accordance with a well-known practice observed by Irish writers, of designating princes by the names of famous places within their territories.

[4] *Leinster's king.* Diarmait Mac Murchadha.

[5] *Tlachtga.* This was the ancient name of the Hill of Ward, near Athboy, co. Meath, on which is a remarkable earthen fort, said to have been erected by King

Iſ loſgaḋ lem cꞃoiḋe anoſ,
  A ċoſgaꞃ ꞃiſin longuſ.
IS goiꞃt lem cꞃoiḋe iſ aſ cꞃeach,
  In ꞃi ſin in eꞃblib ech,[1]
  'Sa cꞃochaḋ ic Ath Cliath[2] taiꞃ,
  Iſ loſgaḋ ḋo bꞃeꝼnechaib.[3]
Ni loingeſ oſin co beacht,
  Ga mbet ꝼiꞃ Eꞃenn ina ſmacht,
  Biḋ imḋa a naiꞃgne gaꞃba,
  Iſ a caingne allmaꞃḋa.
Biḋ imḋa a nuilc aſ gaċ muḋ;
  Biḋ imḋa a ꝼell 'ſa mebul;
  Biḋ imḋa a celga tenna;
  A ngemli 'ſa ngebenḋa.
IMḋa a netheaċ 'ſa cꞃoċtha,
  'Sa toigi ḋaingne cloċḋa;
  Biḋ imḋa a mbꞃeg 'ſa mbꞃeṫa;
  Biḋ minic a ciꞃꞃꝼeḋa.
Giḋ imḋa nemeḋ iſ cell
  Aiꞃgthеꞃ leoſin i coitcenn;
  Gombia a neꞃt i tuaiṫ ſa cill,
  Ni ḟaġbait itiꞃ Eꞃinn.
Ge maḋ moꞃ liḃ gꞃain na ngall.
  A ꝼiꞃa aille Eꞃeann;
  Aḋeꞃ ꞃim int aingell an,
  Ḋiglait bꞃeiꝼnig Tigeꞃnán.
Bennacht aꞃ in lucht go mbloiḋ
  Ḋiġlaſ an ꞃiġ aꞃ Galloib;

Tuathal Teachtmar, in the 2nd cent., where the Druids lighted their sacred fires on the eve of Samhain (Hallow-een).

[1] *horses' tails.* This is the only account, as far as the Editor is aware, in which O'Ruairc is stated to have been "drawn" at horses' tails, after his murder.

[2] *Ath-cliath.* Dublin.

[3] *to Brefnians.* ḋo bꞃetnecħ., for ḋo bꞃeꝼnecħ., A.

A burning to my heart now is
His slaughter by the invaders.
Bitter to my heart, and woe, is
That king at horses' tails;[1]
And his gibbeting at Ath-cliath[2] in the East
Is a burning to Brefnians.[3]
The invaders[4] thenceforth, truly,
Who will have Irishmen in their power—
Many will be their fierce plunders,
And their piratical exactions.
Many will be their evil deeds in every form;
Many their deceits and treacheries;
Numerous will be their powerful wiles,
Their fetters, and their manacles.[5]
Numerous their lies, and executions,
And their secure stone houses;
Many their falsehoods and judgments;
Frequent will be their lacerations.
However numerous the sanctuaries and churches
That may be all plundered by them;
Till their power is over state and church,
They shall in no wise obtain[6] Ireland.
Though great you deem the success of the Foreigners,
You noble men of Ireland;
The glorious Angel tells me
That the Brefnians will avenge Tighernan.
A blessing on the famous band
That avenges the king on the Foreigners

[4] *invaders.* loingeṡ, lit. "fleet," A.

[5] *manacles.* Some poetical memoranda, of no literary value, are added in the lower margin of fol. 7, a.

[6] *obtain.* The meaning is that, until the Galls (English) should place the whole of Ireland under subjection, their rule would not be acknowledged.

Is he diġlas in dus garg,
Mac a derḃrathar, Ualgarg.
Brisfid int Ualgarg go hán
Na da maidm isin oen trath;
Maidm sleibi Cairbre co nem,
Maidm Cranċa na cert dreng.
Bid mor maidm osin amaċ
Brisfes int Ualgarg reḃaċ,
Ag gabail nirt ṫiar is tair,
Air Galloib is air Gaidelaiḃ.
Deich mbliadna fichet gan mairg,
Bidh i trenrigi in Ualgarg;
Biḋ i in rigi taile menmnach;
Bid toirthech, bid etallach.
Ar a namdaib bid crechach;
Bid oirdeirc, bid tindlaicthech;
Biḋ soḃanach, bid fledach;
Bid marcsluaġach fiḋchellach.
Mongenar do Ualgarg tend,
Bid oiliṫrech med remend;
Gid imda a uile siar is soir,
D'iarann ni marbthar etir.

[1] *Ualgarg.* Ualgarg O'Ruairc, son of Cathal, who was brother to Tighernan. From this name Ualgarg (*Anglicè* Ulrick), now obsolete as a Christian name, is derived the surname Magolrick (=Mac-Ualgairg), borne by a collateral branch of the O'Ruaircs, whose representatives are now very numerous in Leitrim and Cavan.

[2] *Win.* brisfid; lit. "will break."

[3] *Sliabh-Cairbre.* The ancient name of the wild, mountainous, district on the northern boundary of the present county of Longford.

[4] *Crannagh.* See notes [6], [7], p. 77.

[5] *thirty years.* 10. mbliadna 20, A.

[6] *fruitful.* The ancient Irish considered that the produce of both land and sea, together with the condition of the seasons, was regulated by the character of their princes. The same belief prevailed among the Eastern nations. See O'Donovan's ed. of the *Battle of Magh-Ratha*, p. 100.

[7] *foes.* A marginal note reprehends

He that avenges the fierce hero is
His brother's son, Ualgarg.[1]
This Ualgarg will nobly win[2]
Two victories on the same day;
The breach of Sliabh-Cairbre,[3] venomously;
The breach of Crannagh[4] of the true contests.
Many will be the victories, from thenceforth,
Which the active Ualgarg shall gain,
In assuming power, West and East,
Over Galls, and over Gaedhil.
Thirty years,[5] without sorrow,
Will Ualgarg be in strong sovranty.
'Twill be the firm, spirited reign;
'Twill be fruitful,[6] profitable.
Against his foes[7] he will be a plunderer,
He will be illustrious, bountiful;
He will be joyful, will be festive;
Will be rich in cavalry;[8] fond of chess.[9]
Happy is it for stout Ualgarg,
That he will be a famous pilgrim;[10]
Though many his offences, West and East,
With iron, still, he'll not be slain.

Caillin for a fault in his metre. Is camrann sin a Chaillin. Naċ mor an naire Caillin aḃeiṫ cionntach a gcamrann marso. Laiṁ mo ċairdes Crist ni maiṫ lem e, gidh naċ bfuil araċ air. "That is a crooked stanza, Caillin. Is it not a great shame that Caillin should be guilty of a crooked stanza? By my gossip's hand, I don't like it. However, there is no help for it." The critic was Thady O'Rody, who probably could not decipher the first word of the stanza, owing to the form of the initial letter, and therefore accused Caillin unjustly.

[8] *rich in cavalry.* marcsluaġach; lit. "horse—multitudinous."

[9] *fond of chess.* fíchellach. This is properly an adjective, derived from fíchell, "chess;" but it is not easy to render it by one word, unless one could say "chessy."

[10] *pilgrim.* The Four Mast. record that Ualgarg O'Ruairc, lord of Breifne, died in 1231, on his way to the River Jordan.

Ocht mbliadna do rigi in ḟir
Do ḟagbus gan imsin,
Ic gaḃail gaċa tire,
[a] fol. 7, b. Etir rige is aiṫrige.[a]
2. Bid Art athrighfus he artus,
Is im eolach na imthus;
Tan ḟaraigfes mo chell ċain,
Art ni chomollfa a bliadain.
Gebaid Ualgarggg sel iarsin
Riġe tenn air Brefnechaib;
Gu naithrighthar he ua do
Ri Oed fa tren tromsluaġo.
Gebaid Ualgarg mac Cathail
In riġe arus re hathaig,
Gu naiṫrig he in Caṫal an,
Ua Domnaill mic Tigernain.
Gebaiḋ in Cathal iarsin
Rigi d'es Ualgairg athaiġ;
Conaċrig he in Pilip tren
Cuigeḋ Connacht fa a chomthren.
Foecfid in Breifne gan fell
In Pilip sin co lin ngall;
Aderim rib as gach muḋ
Foecfid in tir ic Cathal.
No co tí ant Aod aniar,
In tres fecht do gaḃail giall,

[1] *Occupying.* ic gaḃail. The prep. iarsin is written over ic, as a various reading, signifying "after occupying." At the end of this stanza Thady O'Rody adds the note, ni maiṫ ra bu leir dam in rann soin; "that stanza was not very plain to me." Nevertheless, in a letter addressed by him to Edward Lhuyd, and published in the *Miscellany* of the Irish Arch. Soc. pp. 119–125, he represents himself to be able to read Irish MSS. "as well at least as any now (1690) in Ireland."

[2] *Art.* Under the year 1208, the Four Masters state that Ualgarg was "deprived of the Lordship of Breifne," and that "Art, son of Domhnall, son of Ferghal

Eight years of the man's reign
    Have I left without relating,
    Occupying[1] every country,
    Between regnancy and dethronement.
'Tis Art[2] that will dethrone him at first.
    I am learned in his history.
    When he profanes my holy church,
    Art will not complete his year.[3]
Ualgarg will afterwards, for a while, obtain
    Firm sovranty over the Brefnians;
    Until he is a second time dethroned,
    By Aedh[4] whose strong hosts are mighty.
Ualgarg, son of Cathal, will obtain
    The kingship again, for a time,
    'Till dethrones him the noble Cathal,
    Grandson of Domhnall, son of Tighernan.
Cathal[5] will subsequently obtain
    The kingship, for a while, after Ualgarg.
    Until the stout Philip[6] dethrones him,
    The province of Connacht[7] will be under his sway.
He will leave Breifne, without guile—
    This Philip—with his force of Foreigners.
    I tell you, in every way,
    He will leave the land to Cathal.
Until Aedh comes from the West,
    The third time, to take pledges,

(O'Ruairc), assumed his place, through the influence of the English."

[3] *year.* Art was slain 1209, after which Ualgarg resumed his authority.

[4] *Aedh.* Aedh (or Hugh), son of Domhnall, son of Ferghal O'Ruairc, and therefore brother of the Art referred to in the preceding stanza.

[5] *Cathal.* This would seem to be Cathal Reagh, son of Gilla-Brude O'Ruairc, "lord of Breifne," who died in 1236, according to the Four Masters, and the Annals of Loch Cé.

[6] *Philip.* Philip de Braosa.

[7] *Connacht.* This is a boast; as the whole of Connacht was certainly not in

Ni atrugthar Cathal donn,
Derbaimsi daib gan forbond.
Dil in Aeda sin arsin,
Inderat duib co demin;
Marbthar in rig gan gainde
I bfeall ar Loch Aillinde.
Isin aimsir sin gan feall
Millfit na Goill mo chaim cheall;
Indiaid Chathail find co mblaidh
Muirfer int Aod i mebail.
Digelaid misi co tenn
Ar Galloib Erenn mo chell;
Oir is lorgad lemsa aniug
Uilliam Gorm dom sarochud.
Do bera misi gan fell,
Ocus naim uaisli Erenn,
Nach geba Uilliam arsein
Nert go brath ar Gaidelaib.[a]

[a] fol. 8 a, 1.

subjection to the chiefs of Breifne during, or after, the 13th cent.

[1] *extravagance.* forbond (fbond, A). forbann is explained as "bad or false law," by O'Donovan. Supplt. to O'Reilly, *in voce.* But it seems to mean "excess," "extravagance," being comp. of for, "super," and *band*, "saltus."

[2] *Loch-Aillinne.* Lough Allen, in Leitrim. The murder of Aedh, son of Domhnall, son of Ferghal O'Ruairc, is recorded in the Annals of the Four Masters, under the year 1226.

[3] *Cathal.* This Cathal was not an O'Ruairc, but an O'Reilly. See Four Mast., A.D. 1226.

[4] *church;* i.e. Fidhnacha, or Fenagh, co. Leitrim.

[5] *William Gorm.* Lit. "Blue William." Ce be he nescio, "who he was I know not," adds Thady O'Rody, in the margin. William Gorm was son to Hugo de Lasci, or De Lacy, by his second wife, the daughter of Ruaidhri O'Conor, the last monarch of Ireland; for marrying whom, without the licence of Henry II., De Lasci was dismissed from the office of Viceroy in 1181. He is called fer mad an rig (or Viceroy) *infra.* But he never was Viceroy.

[6] *doom.* In the lower margin of fol. 7 b (continued in the corresponding marg. of fol. 8 a), some poetical memoranda are

Brown Cathal will not be deposed—
I certify to you, without extravagance.[1]
The fate of that Aedh afterwards,
I shall certainly tell you :
The opulent king will be slain
In treachery, on Loch-Aillinne.[2]
In that time, without falsehood,
The Foreigners will ruin my fair church,
After the fair famous Cathal,[3]
Who will slay Aedh in treachery.
Stoutly will I avenge
My church[4] upon the Foreigners ;
For 'tis a burning to me this day
That William Gorm[5] should profane me.
I will grant, without deceit,
And the noble saints of Ireland also,
That William Gorm shall not obtain, thereafter,
Power over the Gaedhil, until doom.[6]

written. One note gives the writer's view of an enemy's love :—

Serc mbidba innsa duit
dianestithea limsa beg ;
sech ni rogenairim let
is ni. hadnaicfer maille let.

" An enemy's love here for thee,
If thou wouldst listen to me a little :
Neither have we been born with thee,
Nor shall we be buried with thee."

Another is a copy of the verses about Cucumni, printed in Todd's ed. of the Book of Hymns, part II., pp. 139, 144, 155.

Cuicimni [Cuicimni],
ro leg suithe co druimni ;
a leth aill hi aratha
ro lega for caillecha.

An do Coincuimni rombúi,
is ni rualad de conad súi ;
ro leig a caillecha i faill,
ro leġ araill aratmbúi.

" Cuchuimne [Cuchuimne],
Read learnèd works half way ;
The other half of his task
He abandoned for hags.

" Happy was it for Cuchuimne,
That he ceased not, till he was a sage ;
He abandoned his hags ;
He read the rest whilst he lived."

L

Bid andsin in cuigeḋ fecht
    Dangeba Ualgarg a nert;
    Nert da esi sin ni geb.
    Uair ni fettfa re hsuilib.
Secht mbliadna ocus da deich,
    Ocus da ced do bliadnuib,
    O marbaḋ Briain, mor in mairg,
    No gur sguir rigi Ualgairg.
Da rig dec do ṡil in ḟir,
    Ualgairg U Ruairc a Cruaċain,
    Gebus ardrigi go tend
    Ar Bresnechaib i coitchend.
Gid rand don tir gaḃus nech,
    Adersim rib gu haiṫnech,
    Ni coir a airium go tend
    I reim rigraiḋe hErend.
Gebaid rigi arsin go grind
    Conchobar mac mic Domnaill,
    Con athriġan he arsoin
    In Cathal find mac Annaid.
Cathal ni gabann rigi,
    Adersim bid scel fire,
    Acht nert Bresnech tiar is toir
    Aigi in fat biar na bethaid.

There are four copies of this distich, including the present copy. Of the other three, one occurs in the scholium to Cuchuimne's Hymn in praise of the Blessed Virgin (Book of Hymns, ed. Todd, part II., p. 139); another in the marg. of the Dublin Copy of the Annals of Ulster, at A.D. 746; and the third in the Annals of the Four Mast., A.D. 742. They are all very corrupt as to text. Little is known of this Cuchuimne, besides the record of his death, which is variously entered in the Annals under 742, 746, and 747.

[1] *on account of his eyes.* re hsuilib, for re ṡuilib. This may mean that Ualgarg became blind, and resigned the chieftainship of his clan, with the object of proceeding on the pilgrimage to the Holy Land, on which he died. See next note.

[2] *twice ten.* ocus da deich. This enumeration of 227 years from the death of Brian Borumha in 1014, would refer

Then will be the fifth occasion
On which Ualgarg will assume his rule.
Power after that he'll not obtain;
For he could not, on account of his eyes.[1]
Seven years, and twice ten,[2]
And two hundred years,
From the killing of Brian—great the woe—
Until ceased Ualgarg's reign.
Twelve kings of the seed of the man,
Of Ualgarg O'Ruairc from Cruachan,[3]
Will stoutly obtain chief sovereignty
Over the Breifnians in general.
Whatever part of the land each one gets,
I say to you, knowingly,
'Tis not right firmly to reckon him,
In the regal roll of Ireland.
After that, Conchobhar, grandson of Domhnall,
Will joyously obtain the kingship;
Until dethrones him, subsequently,
Cathal Find,[4] son of Annad.
Cathal obtains not sovereignty,
(I say that 'twill be a true story);
But the power of the Breifnians, West and East,[5]
Shall be his as long as he lives.

the end of Ualgarg's reign to the year 1241. But his death is entered in the Annals of the Four Masters under 1231, as already noticed (*supra*, p. 69, note [10]). Probably instead of ocuṡ ḋa ḋeich we should read ocuṡ a ḋeich, "and ten;" which would make the calculation right.

[3] *Cruachan.* Not Cruachan, or Rathcroghan, in the co. Roscommon, the ancient seat of the kings of Connacht; but probably Croghan, in the bar. of Tullyhunco, co. Cavan, adjoining Leitrim.

[4] *Cathal Find.* "Cathal the Fair." This man seems to have been an O'Reilly, and the same person above referred to (p. 73) as having slain Aedh, son of Domhnall O'Ruairc, on Loch-Allen, in the year 1226. Annad, the name of Cathal's father, was a common Christian name in the family of O'Reilly, but not in that of O'Ruairc.

[5] *West and East.* In other words, on

Athrigṫar Conchobar leis
  In Cathal finn gan eisleis;
  Is na re ticfa go grinn
  Cuairt Chonaill do mo choim chill.
I Re in Conchobair sin fein,
  Ocus Domnaill in rois ḟéil,
  Dober Cathal finn co mbloid
  Rigi don Choin, da brathair.
Bid i re in Coin sin cin tar
  Ticfa arir Uilliam tar sal;
  Ge dobera Goill is tir
  Brister air maidm i Crandchain.
Uimi ṫarngirim aniuġ
  Crandchain do ġairim don mad,
  On ċrannaig doberthar and
  On mona cum na haḃann.
* fol. 8, a 2. D'Uilliam gorm on maidm arsin,*
  Sechtmain fo tri co demin,
  I Mide do nem a chned,
  Go traoṫar nert in miled.
Mi Cu sin bid tocbail cell,
  Inneraid duib a ferann;

both sides of the mountains of Slieve-an-Iarainn, co. Leitrim.

[1] See note [4], p. 75.

[2] *tribute of Conall*; i.e. the dues, or visitation fees, of the Cinel-Conaill, or descendants of Conall Gulban, son of Niall of the Nine Hostages, whose possessions included Tir-Conaill ("the land of Conall"), the present county of Donegal.

[3] *Ross.* There are two places named Ross in the barony of Dromahaire, co. Leitrim; one of which is probably here meant.

[4] *the Cu.* Lit. "the Hound;" a word frequently employed in the composition of Irish proper names, as Cu-Chonnacht, "Hound of Connacht;" Cu-Ulad, "hound of Ulster," &c.

[5] *William.* The William Gorm, or William de Lasci, mentioned above (p. 73), and also in the 2nd next stanza. Professor O'Curry mistook the identity of this William, whom he considered to have been the same as William Ruadh O'Ruairc who died in 1430; about which time the Professor thought that this poem (or "very glaring forgery," as he calls it) had

Conchobhar will be deposed
By Cathal Find,[1] without delay.
In his time will merrily come
The tribute of Conall[2] to my fair church.
In the time of that same Conchobhar,
And of the generous Domhnall of Ross,[3]
The famous Cathal Find will give
The sovereignty to the Cu[4] his brother.
'Tis in the time of this stainless Cu,
That William[5] will come again across the sea:
But though he brings Foreigners into the country,
He will be defeated in Crandchain.[6]
The reason why I prophesy this day,
That the place shall be called Crandchain,
Is from the *crannagh*[7] that will be given there,
From the bog unto the river.
To William Gorm, after that defeat,
Three weeks exactly [I allow]
In Meath, until from the poison of his wounds
The knight's strength is subdued.
That Cu[8] will be an erector of churches.
I will tell you[9] his territory:

been concocted. See O'Curry's *Lectures*, p. 398. But O'Donovan was more correct in referring its composition to about the year 1300. *Brefny Letters, Ordn. Survey Correspondence*, R. Ir. Acad., p. 194.

[6] *Crandchain*. This battle is recorded by the Four Mast. under the year 1233, the name of the site being written "Moin-Crandchain," which was somewhere in the co. Cavan, not far from the Meath border. The account represents De Lasci as having been wounded by the O'Reillys, and having died from the effects of his wounds. The battle is also recorded under the same year in the Annals of Clonmacnois, in which William de Lasci is said to have been "the chiefest champion in these parts of Europe; and the hardiest and strongest hand of any Englishman from the Nicene seas to this place, or Irishman."

[7] *crannagh*. A figurative expression for "slaughter," or "crashing;" deriv. from *crann*, a tree.

[8] *That Cu*. The text of the poem, from this down to p. 86 is contained in MS. B. (Brit. Mus.; Cott. Vesp., E. II.)

[9] ꝺuıb, B. ꝺuıτ ⁊ ꝺuıb (to thee, or to you), A.

Gebaid in Cu celtach cain
O Bun Lainne co Lemain.
1 Re in Con sin, truaġ in gnim,
Bid imda nech in imsnim;
Bid imda thiar thair ga chrud
Mes ocus blicht is torud.
Bid terc flaiṫi na ṫirṫe
In Chon ga tu tharngaire,
Mana derna tri traisge
Gum sgrinn ar lar m'ecalsi.
Des a traiscṫi gum chill ċaidh
Tabraid in ri dam mo chain;
Doberra do is ri na rend
Flaithi is mes na ferann.
Indesaid mesi co grind
In chain sin fein mar dligim;
Is a fath ma tugad dam
Indesaid me na ḟarrad.
Indesaid me don Choin ḟel
Fath mar thairngires he fein,
Is an faṫ ma tucus lem
Ard rigraid uasal Erenn.
Isi mo chainsi dom ṫoig,
O ṡil Aeda find fledaig,
Screpall gach carċig go fir,
Is cath erred gach ardrig.

[1] *Bun-Lainne to Lemain* (Leamuin, B.) In a note to his ed. of the Four Mast. A.D. 1172, Dr. O'Donovan remarks:—"It is stated in the Book of Fenagh that Tigherman acquired dominion over the entire region . . . . . . from the sea at the borders of Ulster and Connaught to Drogheda." But there is nothing in the MS. to support this statement, except the limits here prescribed to the "Cú's" possessions, or those fixed further on (p. 87) as the limits ("from Drogheda to Sligo") of the area out of which Caillin's dues were payable. But Bun-Lainne seems to be the place called Bunluiny, in the Down Surv. for the par. of St. John's, co. Sligo; and Lemain, alias Magh-Lemhna, alias the Closagh, was the name of a district com-

The mild, belted Cu will possess
From Bun-Lainne to Lemain.[1]
In the time of that Cu—woeful the fact—
Many will there be in trouble;
In the West and East, many will be the exactions,
In fruit, and milk, and produce.
Lords will be scarce in the lands
Of this Cu, whom I am foretelling,
Unless he performs three fasts
At my shrine in the middle of my church.[2]
After his fasting at my holy church,
The king will give me my tribute;
I, and the King of the Stars, will give him
Lords and produce in his land.
I will cheerfully relate[3]
That same tribute as 'tis due to me;
And the reason why to me 'twas granted,
I will tell besides.
I will relate to the generous Cu,
Why I have foretold himself;
And the reason why I've brought with me[4]
The noble arch-kings of Ireland.
My tribute[5] to my house is,
From the race of festive Aedh Find,
A *screpall*,[6] truly, out of every sheepfold,
And the battle-dress[7] of each arch-king.

prising part of the parishes of Clogher and Errigal-Keeroge, co. Tyrone. See Reeves's *Colton's Visitation*, p. 126.

[2] *my church.* mechalri, A.

[3] *I will . . . relate.* meraid, A.

[4] *brought with me.* tucur lem. This should probably be rendered "enumerated;" the meaning being that the writer had brought the succession of the kings before the attention of his readers.

[5] *tribute.* The words cain ril Aoda finn ("the tribute of the race of Aedh Find") are written in the margin.

[6] *screpall.* A screpall was equal to a *siclus*, a small coin of the value of three *pingins*, or pennies. See Petrie's Eccl. Archit., pp. 214, sq.

[7] *battle-dress.* It was a common prac-

Edach ech gech toirig chaid,
    Etir chend is chois is laim;
Serrech maiṫ on rig co rath,
    'Sa tabairt illaim ṁabaḋ.
Dligim don rigain co raṫ,
    A heċ ocus a hetach;
Dligim don Bantairiġ ḟeil
    Edach is each dum oġreir.
Do gach biataig oin baili,
* fol. 8, b 1. O Ath Droiċit go Sligech;*
    Do gabala do gaċ creich
    O gaċ mac rig is toiseich.
An dalta sa mac ḟethar,
    Dligimsi dib co trebar,
    Mad ail leo a nduṫchus co daith,
    Tabrat a cuart dom catraig.
Gid cuiċ naċ tibre mo chain,
    Mar aderim, dom chill chaiḋ,
    A nduṫchus ni geba a clann,
    Agus de gebat ifernn.
Gid cuiċ dobera mo ċain
    Mar aderim dom chill ċaiḋ,
    Saerfad a cined sa clann;
    Ni gebat Goill a ferann.

tice among the Irish princes to give ornamental dresses to ecclesiastics, probably in order that they might be converted into vestments. The same practice obtained also in other countries. Harold Harefoot bestowed his coronation mantle on the abbey of Croyland. Lappenberg's *England*, vol. II., p. 227.

[1] *cavalry-dress.* edach ech. This would also mean horse-cloths, or horse trappings; but the descriptive references to "head, and leg, and hand," seems to point to a horseman's dress.

[2] *my abbot's hand*; i.e. into the hand of the abbot of Fenagh, St. Caillin's successor.

[3] *one-bally Biatagh;* i.e. a Biatagh, possessed of one ballybetagh. The Biatagh was a farmer who held his land under certain conditions involving the supply of food (*biad*) to the chief and his

The cavalry dress[1] of each noble chief,
  Between head, and leg, and hand;
  A good team from the prosperous king—
  And they to be given into my abbot's hand.[2]
I claim as my due from the gracious queen,
  Her steed and her dress;
  I claim from each generous chieftainess,
  A dress and a steed, at my demand.
A cow from every one-bally Biatagh,[3]
  From Ath-Droichit[4] to Sligo;[5]
  A fat cow out of every prey,
  From each son of a king and chieftain.
The foster-son, and the sister's son—
  I exact from them, discreetly,
  If they desire their inheritance quickly,
  That they bring their tribute to my city.[6]
Whosoever[7] furnishes not my tribute,
  As I say, to my holy church—
  His children shall not obtain their inheritance;
  And they shall obtain Hell.
But whosoever[8] furnishes my tribute,
  As I say, to my holy church—
  I will save his kin and his children:
  Foreigners shall not possess their land.

retainers, as well to other classes of guests. The extent of a Ballybetagh was 1,440 acres, according to ancient Irish enumeration. (See Reeves's Paper on the *Townland Distrib. of Ireland;* Proceed. R. I. Acad., vol. vii., p. 474. But Ware makes a Ballybetagh=16 Tates, and a Tate=60 acres; or 960 acres altogether. Harris's *Ware,* vol. ii., p. 227.

[4] *Ath-Droichit,* alias *Droichet-atha,* the "Bridge of the Ford;" now Drogheda.

[5] *Sligo.* ꞅliᵹcech, A.

[6] *to my city.* ꝺom caꞇhꞃaiꝺh, B. Over the word caꞇhꞃaiꝺh, the scribe has added .1. ꝼı. ꝺñ (i.e. Fidhnacha).

[7] *whosoever.* cuıċ. The characters ⁊ n (or "n") are added over the last letter of the word in B., to signify that the word should probably be cum, "when."

[8] *whosoever.* cuıċ. cum, "when," B.

Gairged glasraige do ṡir
    Aed dub mac Fergna in milid;
    Is delb Riocc ba find daṫ
    Do ṫabairt ar na bairteaḋ.
Aed ger dub in caṫṁilid,
    Do bairdes he gan timi;
    Is misi dorinne de,
    Aoḋ findglan ḟa lor finde.
Me dorat, is nir mérte,
    Deṫbir ar delb na deiri;
    Coroin i cind Rioicc gil,
    Aod find gan ċoroin itir.
Agso in faṫ ma tucad dam,
    In cuairtt mor sin dom ḟognam,
    'Sar a corp do breṫ dom chill,
    Gid c'ait bud marb in Erind.
O da bairtius Aed combloiḋ,
    Gur adlaices he im durṫoiġ,
    Eaḋ ro ċaiṫ in ri cen gaitt
    Da bliadain dec tri fichit.
Uime airmim in Cu tenn
    Irrem rigraide Erenn,

[1] *Glasraige*; i.e. the tribe of Glas. The Glasraige were descended from Cairbre, son of Niall of the Nine Hostages, and were not therefore of the same stock as the Breifnians.

[2] *Aedh Dubh*. "Black Aedh (or Hugh)." Subsequently known as "Aedh Find." From him was derived the tribe name of a division of the Breifnians, "Sil-Aedha-Find," or the race of A. F.

[3] *Fergna*. The great ancestor of all the Breifnians.

[4] *Riocc*, or St. Mo-Riocc, of Inis-Mic-Ualaing (or Inis-bo-finde, now Inishboffin) in Loch-Ree; whose festival is set down at the 1st Aug. in the *Martyrology of Donegal*.

[5] *whiteness*. The note, amail do rinde Caillin Aed find don Aed dub mac Fergna ("how Caillin made Fair Aedh of the Black Aedh son of Fergna"), is added in the margin. The power of changing the complexion of persons was not confined to St. Caillin; for in the lives of St. Maedhoc of Ferns, and of St. Finnchu of Brigown, a similar power is re-

The championship of the Glasraige[1] he sought—
  Aedh Dubh[2] son of Fergna,[3] the knight—
  And the form of Riocc[4] of fairest hue,
  To be given to him after his baptism.
Though black was the warrior Aedh,
  I baptized him, without fear.
  It was I that made of him
  Pure-fair Aedh of ample whiteness.[5]
'Twas I that made, and it was no harm,
  A distinction 'twixt th'appearance of both;
  A crown[6] on the head of fair Riocc;
  Aedh Find without a crown at all.[7]
This is the reason why to me was given
  That great tribute,[8] for my use;
  And for bringing his body to my church,
  Wheresoever in Ireland he might die.
From the period in which I baptized Aedh the Famous,
  Until I buried him in my oratory,[9]
  The time[10] the guileless king spent
  Was twelve years[11] and three score.[12]
The reason why I reckon the stout Cu
  In the regal roll of Ireland, [is,

corded. St. Finnchu so changed the face of Cairbre Crom, a Munster Prince (father of Aedh Caemh, K. of Munster, 571–601), that he was afterwards called Cairbre *Caemh*, or "Cairbre the *Handsome*." See *Book of Lismore*, fol. 72, 1.

[6] *crown*. This refers to the coronal tonsure. But Riocc, the son of Darerca, St. Patrick's sister, must have been tonsured in the old Irish fashion, "in front from ear to ear," for the coronal (or Roman) tonsure was not used in Ireland before A.D. 718. See Todd's *St. Patrick*, p. 487; and Reeves's *Adamnan*, p. 350.

[7] *at all*. itir. etir. B.

[8] *tribute*. cuairt. Properly a visitation fee, or dues received on a cuairt, a visit, or (lit.) circuit.

[9] *in my oratory*. im durṫoiġ; nom. durtech; lit. "stern house," or "house of penitence."

[10] *The time*. ead. Omitted in B.

[11] *twelve years*. da bliadain x. A. B.

[12] *score*. xx^it. A. B.

Les is na diaid tic gu grind
A ċuairt ar tus dom chaom chill.
A dala in Con sin gan tlas,
Derb limm do geba dian bas,*
Is truag lem in faṫ da fuil
A tuitim ina naiḃid.
Derbaim duit a Chu oebda,
Genfid neċ do sil Aeda;
Is he chumdaigfes gan ċol
Mo scrinn ocus mo ṫempol.
Cathal, Conchobar arsin,
Sitrec is Art na deagaid;
Domnall ocus Oed combloiḋ;
Brian is Niall is Lugaid.
Tigernan is Donnchad gel,
Ocus a brathair Fergal;
Isse in Fergail bus maith clu
Faicfaidit gulla Eriu. hEri o.
Ni gamanraid osin amaċ,
No co tora in braṫ breṫaċ
Bid he int ardport caḋair grind,
Mo cheall fodeoid in Erind.

* fol. 8, b 2.

[1] See note [8], p. 83.

[2] *as regards the fate.* a dala, A. B. reads a dalta, which would mean "the *protégé.*"

[3] *Cathal.* The Four Mast., under A.D. 1236, record the death of Cathal Riabhach O'Ruairc, Lord of Ui-Briuin.

[4] *Conchobhar.* Conchobair, A. B. The same annalists state, under the year 1257, that Conchobhar, son Tighernan O'Ruairc, was displaced from the chieftainship of his tribe, by Aedh O'Conor, son of Fedhlim, King of Connacht, in favor of Sitric O'Ruairc; who was slain in the same year, however, by Domhnall son of Conchobhar.

[5] *Sitric.* See last note.

[6] *Art.* See next note.

[7] *Domhnall.* Son of Conchobhar. (See note [4].) He was appointed chief of Breifne in 1258; but was displaced in the same year, and Art, son of Cathal Riabhach O'Ruairc appointed in his stead.

[8] *Aedh.* Not identified.

[9] *Brian and Niall.* The Four Mast.,

That] with him, and after him, will merrily come
His tribute,[1] at first, to my fair church.
As regards the fate[2] of this fearless Cu—
I am certain he'll meet a violent death.
Grievous to me is the cause whence comes
His fall in his youth.
I assure thee, O handsome Cu,
That one shall be born of the seed of Aedh,
Who will cover, without transgression,
My shrine and my temple.
Cathal,[3] Conchobhar[4] afterwards ;
Sitric,[5] and Art after him ;[6]
Domhnall[7] and the famous Aedh ;[8]
Brian, and Niall,[9] and Lughaidh.[10]
Tighernan,[11] and Donnchadh[12] the fair,
And his brother Ferghal.[12]
In the time of Ferghal, of good repute,
The Foreigners will leave Ireland.
The Gamhanraidh[13] from thenceforth,
Until the judging judgment comes.
The joyous, honoured, arch-abode,
My church shall at last in Ireland be.

under the year 1259, mention that Niall son of Donough O'Ruairc, and Brian son of Niall, were blinded by Hugh O'Conor, in whose hands they had been placed as hostages by Domhnall O'Ruairc. But they are not stated to have held the chieftainship of Breifne.

[10] *Lughaidh.* There is no mention of this man in the ordinary lists of the chieftains of Breifne.

[11] *Tighernan.* The death of a Tighernan, son of Aedh O'Ruairc, Lord of Breifne, is entered in the Ann. F. Mast. under the year 1275. He was probably the person here referred to.

[12] *Donnchadh—Ferghal.* No names answering to these are found in the ordinary lists of the chieftains of Breifne.

[13] *Gamhanraidh.* ᵹubanꞃaıḋ, A. This was the name of the third principal family of Connacht of the Firbolg race. "Tres præcipuæ fuerunt familiæ, viz., Gamanradii, Fir Craibii et Tuatha Taidhen ; a quibus Connactia in ternas Connactias distincta." O'Flaherty's *Ogygia*, pars III. cap. xi. The meaning of the text is, pro-

Is me Caillin Duin baile;
  Mor in fir tarla ar m'aire;
  Fir na nGaideal is na nGall,
  Ag gabail neirt na hErenn. e.
Ni derais me anos go gar
  In fir eli tarrfas dam;
  Mar genit ar tus go grinn
  Ard rigrad ḟinnrois alainn.
Genit a Findros, gan brecc,
  Ri dan tosach anma Eicc;
  Bid maiṫ a rem ri na ngiall,
  No co tuit do gaib Oirgiall.
Gebaid a mac na degaid
  Domnall Findrois feramail;
  Ar Conall bid tren a ċert,
  Fri re deich mbliaḋna fichet.
Cath Craibe, cath Camlinne,
  Cuirfid Domnall ria dar;
  Daimim duib a tharngaire,
  Bid garb in scel re scarad.
Ge gontair e i cath Droma,
  Domnall Finnrois no toga;

bably, that Breifne-O'Ruairc (or Leitrim) would thenceforward share the fortunes of Connacht, and be ruled by its rulers.

[1] *Dun-baile.* The ancient name of Fidhnacha, or Fenagh.

[2] *Ireland.* With this line the poem breaks off in B, the hiatus in which extends to the prose account, p. 110, *infra.*

[3] *relate.* The note do rigaib Connacht isechtra ro ṫircain Caillin; i.e. "Of the kings of Connacht Caillin prophesied this time." But this is an error; as the kings spoken of were kings of Tirconnell.

[4] *Finnros.* This was the ancient name of the district now called the "Rosses," barony of Boylagh, co. Donegal. But, although the chief of the sept of O'Donnell was styled "Lord of Finnross," it would appear that Finnross was the patrimony of O'Furadhran (or O'Farran) in 1370, when O'Dugan wrote his Topogr. Poem.

[5] *Eicc.* Eignechan O'Donnell, Lord of Tirconnell, slain by the people of Fermanagh (who were of the race of the Oirghialla), in 1207. See Four Mast., and Annals of Loch-Cé.

I am Caillin of Dun-baile.[1]
Great the knowledge that has come under my notice;
Knowledge of the Gaedhil and of the Foreigners,
Assuming the power of Ireland.[2]
I shall now briefly relate[3]
The other vision manifested to me:
How first will happily be born,
The high chiefs of beautiful Finnros.[4]
At Finnros will be born, without falsehood,
A king the beginning of whose name shall be Eicc.[5]
Good will be his career, the king of the hostages,
Until he falls by the darts of the Oirghialla.
His son will rule after him—
The manly Domhnall[6] of Finnros—
Strong will be his power over Conall[7]
During the space of thirty[8] years.
The battle of Craebh;[9] the battle of Camlinn,[10]
Domhnall will fight with vigour.[11]
I prophesy it unto you,
'Twill be fierce news to spread.
Tho' he be wounded in the battle of Druim—[12]
Domhnall of Finnros, of the darts—

[6] *Domhnall.* Called Domhnall Mór, or Donnell the Great. He died in the habit of a monk, in the Cistercian Monastery of Assaroe, co. Donegal, in 1241.

[7] *Conall.* A conventional name for the Cinel-Conaill, or people of Tir-Conaill (Tirconnell; or co. Donegal), who were descended from Conall Gulban, son of Niall of the Nine Hostages.

[8] *thirty.* The *Annals of Loch-Ce* (A.D. 1241) state that Domhnall Mór O'Donnell had only been 14 years in the government of his principality.

[9] *Craebh.* Probably Creeve, on the banks of Lough Swilly, to the north of Rathmullen, co. Donegal.

[10] *Camlinn.* There is a place called Camlin in the barony of Tirhugh, co. Donegal. But these battles are not recorded in the Irish Annals.

[11] *with vigour.* ꞃıa ꝺaꞃ, A. The translation is merely conjectural, the text being evidently corrupt. What word is represented by ꝺaꞃ, the Editor is unable to say; but it should be a dissyllable, to agree with the last word of the stanza.

[12] *Druim.* The place here referred to

Bed aige, is bid go cialla,
Conall, Eogan, Oirgialla.*

* fol. 9, a 1.

Is mor maidm dober da ċois,
In ri sin Domnall Finnrois;
Go ngabann leṫ Cuinn go han
Tri bliadna deg co himlan.
Gid mor sires sair is siar,
In Domnall sa ag gabail giall;
Fagbuimsi do is ri nime,
A ecsan an oilithri.
Mo bennacht ort, a Domnaill;
Tairngirim tu gan dograing,
Tabair dam mo ċuairt gech tan,
Mar douc Conall gulban.
Conall ba ced ri Temra,
Do cloinn Nell gan [f]rerabra;
Gur marbad he i Moig Rein raiṫ,
Se bliadna dec ro ċaeiṁ chaiṫ.
Marraige do ċuatar soir,
Fect ar mor crech co Temraig,
Co tic Conall gulban becht
Co Mag Rein nan iarmoracht.
Ga retha do marb in ri,
Don chuairtsin gan imargai,

is probably Druim-thuama, or Drum-home, in the bar. of Tirhugh, co. Donegal.

[1] *Conall.* See note [7], p. 87.

[2] *Eoghan;* i.e. the Cinel-Eoghain, or descendants of Eoghan, son of Niall of the Nine Hostages, who have given name to the present county of Tyrone (Tir-Eoghain).

[3] *Oirghialla.* In the time of Domhnall Mór O'Donnell, the territorial name "Oirghialla" was applied to the district comprising the present counties of Armagh, Louth, and Monaghan. In the 5th cent., the Oirghialla (who were the descendants of the three Collas), included the greater part of Ulster to the west of the Upper and Lower Bann. In recording the death of Domhnall Mór, the Four Mast. state (A.D. 1241), that he was "Lord of Tirconnell, Fermanagh, and Lower Connacht as far as the Curlew Mountains, and of Oirghiall from the plain (i.e. the level part of the co. Louth), northwards." On the lower marg. of fol. 8 b, some rhymes are written, which are not worth printing.

He shall have, and justly have,
Conall,[1] Eoghan,[2] and the Oirghialla.[3]
Many a defeat besides will he inflict—
That King Domhnall of Finnros—
Until he nobly[4] obtains Leth-Chuinn,
For fully thirteen[5] years.
Though much he seeks, east and west—
This Domhnall—taking pledges;
I, and the King of Heaven, decree him,
That he shall die[6] in pilgrimage.[7]
My blessing on thee, Domhnall;
I prophesy thee, without anguish.
Give me my tribute every time,
As Conall Gulban gave it.
Conall was the first king of Tara,[8]
Of the Clann-Neill, without dispute.
'Till he was slain in prosperous Magh-Rein,[9]
Sixteen years he happily spent.
The Masraighe[10] went to the East
Once, on a great foray to Tara;
Whereupon Conall quickly came,
To Magh-Rein, in pursuit of them.
A flying spear killed the king,[11]
On that journey, without falsehood,

[4] *nobly.* ᵹo han̄, A.

[5] *thirteen.* See note [8], p. 87.

[6] *shall die.* a echꞃan, for a ecꞃan, A.

[7] *pilgrimage.* See note [6], p. 87.

[8] *Tara.* This is certainly an error, as Conall Gulban was never king of Tara (i.e. monarch of Ireland).

[9] *Magh-Rein.* The ancient name of the district in which Fenagh is situated. The origin of the name is related further on.

[10] *Masraighe.* This was a Firbolg tribe, seated in Magh-Slecht ("Campus adorationis"), a plain adjoining Magh-Rein, to the east, and remarkable for containing the great gold-and-silver pagan idol Crom-Cruach, which, with its 12 attendant images of bronze, St. Patrick is stated to have sent under the ground. (See Miss Cusack's Life of St. Patrick, p. 399.) Dallan Forgaill, the composer of the Amhra Choluim Chille, was of the Masraighe of Magh-Slecht. (*Lebor na hUidhre*, p. 5 a).

[11] *King.* The words oıᵭeᵭ Conaıll

Aꝛ Mag Ren iꞅ Dun baile,
  Ꞡuꝛ chommaiꝺꞅeꞇ Maꞅꞅaiꞡe.
Ro haꝺnachꞇ Conall innuꝛ,
  Iꞇiꝛ in loċ iꞅ an ꝺun;
Coic bliaꝺna co leċ bai annꞅoin,
  No ꞡo ꞇanaꞡꞅa in caꞇhꞅuiꞡ.
Bliaꝺain co leċ ꝺam co huain,
  Ꞡo ꞇuꞡaꞅ a ċlann aꞇuaiꝺ,
  Ocuꞅ noeim Eꞅenn aille
  Do ꝺenam a ꞇꞅanꞅlaiꝺe.
Do ꞇꞅaiꞅꞡeꞅ ꞅe ꞅiꞡ na ꞅenꝺ,
  Ocuꞅ naim uaiꞅli Eꞅenꝺ;
  D'aiꞇhbeoaꞡuꝺ Conaill moiꞅ,
  Ꞡumaꝺ ꞇꞅeꞅi ꝺe m'onoiꞅ.
Do chuiꞅ chuꞡam ꞅi nime
  A aingil im ꞇꞅocꞅaiꝺe,
  Ꞡuꞅ ꝺuiꞅꞡeꞅ Conall ꞡan ḟeall,
[a] fol. 9, a 2. I bꞅiaꝺnaiꞅi ḃꞅeꞅ nEꞅeann.[a]
Conall ꞡulban ꞇicc ꝺa ċoiꞅ,
  On uaiꞡ connice in eccloiꞅ;
  Ꞡuꞅ benaiꞡeꞅ he 'ꞅa chlann,
  Maille ꞅe noemaib Eꞅeann.
An[n]ꞅin ꝺo uꞡuꞅa ꝺaib,
  Do ċinel Conuill mic Nell,
  Ꞅꞅi ꝺeꞅeꝺ ꝺomain co ꞡꞅinꝺ
  Combiaꝺ a neꞅꞇ aꞅ Eꞅinꝺ. E.
An[n]ꞅin ꝺo uꞡuꞅa ꝺaib,
  Do ċinel Conaill in aiꞡ,

ꞡulbain, "death of Conall Gulban," are added in the margin.

[1] *boasted.* ꞡuꞅ chommaiꝺꞅeꞇ; lit. "so that they boasted." The letters ꞇ ꞅi are added over the conclusion of the word, as if to indicate that the reading should be ꞡuꞅ chommaiꝺ ꞅi Maꞅꞅaiꞡe, "so that he was hacked by the Masraighe."

[2] *Lake.* Loch-Rein, or Loch-Saloch, at Fenagh.

[3] *Dun.* Dun-baile; the ancient name of Fenagh.

[4] *to the city;* i.e. to Fenagh. caꞇh-

THE CROMLEC AT FENAGH.

On Magh-Rein, at Dun-baile,
Of which the Masraighe boasted.[1]
Conall was interred in the earth,
Between the Lake[2] and the Dun.[3]
Five years and a half was he there,
Until I came to the city.[4]
A year and a half was I there, leisurely,
Until I brought his children from the North,
Along with the glorious Saints of Ireland,
To effect his translation.[5]
I fasted before the King of the Stars,
And the noble saints of Ireland [fasted also],
For the resuscitation of great Conall—
That my honour might be the greater therefor.
The King of Heaven sent to me
His Angels to my assembly;
And I awakened Conall, without deceit,
In the presence of the men of Ireland.
Conall Gulban came on foot
From the grave to the church,
Where I, along with the saints of Ireland,
Blessed him and his race.
Then[6] I granted to them—
To the descendants of Conall son of Niall—
That towards the end of the world, joyously,
Their power should be over Ireland.
Then[6] I granted to them—
To the race of valorous Conall—

ruig (*rectè* cathraig), dat. of cathair, a city, Bishop's See, or residence.

[5] *translation.* translaide=Lat. translatio. From what follows, it would appear that Conall's resuscitation was St. Caillin's object.

[6] *Then.* ansin, A. A marg. note reads na fagbala ro fagaib Caillin do ċinel Conaill mic Nell; "the gifts Callin left to the race of Conall son of Niall."

Rath cagaid 's cloinde naċ dir
Rath rigi, raṫ noirechuir.
Rath biḋ, is raṫ coṁairli;
Rath garmac ocus dalta;
Rath ban, rath clerech is ceall;
Rath noirfideċ, rath gabann.
Grain chatha ar gaċ aen nonbar,
Do fagbus daib condruinne;
Is gabail daib airdrigi,
Grain nonbair ar gaċ nduine.
Tugus for da ċloind co tend,
Acht go riaraitis mo ċell,
Clann ocus tagadh malle;
Focraice is fat naimsire.
Arsin da ongus in ri,
Conall gulban na mor gnim;
Is annsin do ordaig dun
Cuairt a chloinde dom chaem Dun.
ISsi cuairt do ordaig dam,
O tharnicc lium a ongad,
Unga oir no fiaċ co tenn
O gach toisech na ḟerann.
Ech gach rig 's gach rigdamna,
'S gach bantairsgi gribḋa;
Do gach mactoisig combloid;
Ocus scerepall gaċ cairchig.
Amlaid tuc dam Conall gel
In chuart sin, gach tres bliadan

[1] *of warfare.* caḡ, A.

[2] *nephews.* garmac. gormac is explained by mac seaṫar, "a sister's son," in O'Clery's Glossary.

[3] *of women.* baṅ, A.

[4] *success of battle.* The words grain chatha sometimes mean this. But they have also another signification. In a MS. Ir. Glossary in Trin. College, Dublin (H. 2.15, p. 126) they are explained as "seeds of battle," or "spikes" which are fixed in fords and passes to obstruct the enemy—

Luck of warfare,[1] and of children not mean
Luck of kingship ; luck of supremacy ;
Luck of food ; and luck of counsel ;
Luck of nephews,[2] and of foster-children.
Luck of women ;[3] luck of clerics and churches ;
Luck of minstrels ; luck of smiths.
Success of battle[4] on every ennead,[5]
I left to them firmly,
And when assuming arch-kingship,
The power of nine in each man.
I also firmly gave to his children,
Provided that they obeyed my church,
Descendants, and prosperity[6] besides,
[Heavenly] reward, and length of days.
Afterwards I anointed the king—
Conall Gulban of the mighty deeds.
It was then he ordained for us,
His clann's tribute to my fair Dun.[7]
The tribute he ordained for me,
When I had done anointing him,
Was an ounce of gold, or its strict value,
From every chieftain in his land ;
A steed from each king, and royal heir,[8]
And from each stately chieftainess ;
A cow from each famous son of a chief ;
And a *screpall* out of every sheepfold.
Thus did fair Conall give to me
This tribute, every third year

See Todd's *Irish Nennius*, App. pp. 11, 12.

[5] *on every ennead.* This means that any nine of the descendants of Conall Gulban might gain a battle.

[6] *prosperity.* ταξαδh=ταccαό, which O'Donovan translates "support" (Four Mast., A.D. 1222). O'Reilly explains ταcαό by "prosperity."

[7] *Dun.* The writer has added, by way of gloss, .ι. δun mbαιlι, nomen ꝼιδnαchα ceδúꞅ ; i.e. "Dun-baile, the name of Fenagh at first."

[8] *royal heir.* ꞃιξδαmnα ; lit. "materies

Da eri ar gaċ nech da chloind
Itir Albain is Erinn.* (* fol. 9, b 1.)
Ro escain Conall gan ell,
Ocus naim uaisli Erend,
A chlann 'sa ċined malle,
Mana icdais in chainse.
Ainsin ro thairngiser sen,
Do Chonall gulban mac Nell,
Congeinfed uad nech go clu
Damad lan Alba is Eriu.
Ainsin da iarfaid sium dim,
Conall gulban na mor gniṁ,
Ga hainm do beri ar in bfer
Genfes as mo corp comgel.
Ised adubartsa ris,
Colam Cille aderthar ris;
Robad lor d'Erind huile
A ḟerta sa ṁirḃuile.
Ni nech eli genfeas huait,
Adamnan bid maith a chuairt.
Bid me oide na deri,
Aderim bar fiadnuise.
Is annsin tarrnig saegal
Conaill gulban gan baegal,
Iar nordagad dam go tend
Cuarta Alban is hErend.

regis," or "timber of a king," as it is conventionally expressed.

[1] *Alba.* Scotland. With this line concludes the text of fol. 9, a., on the lower margin of which are written some poetical memoranda, the purport of which is that "every hill is not a Tara; every water not a Shannon;" that "every one who refuses is not a sage, and every man not a Donough." It is also stated that Aengus was another name for Cairbre Musc; Eochaidh a name for Cairbre Riada, and Oilill for Cairbre Baschain.

[2] *Conall.* The text has Caillin no Conall ("Caillin, or Conall"), as if the scribe was uncertain who uttered the

After him, on each of his children
Both in Alba[1] and Ireland.
Conall[2] cursed, without deceit,
And the noble saints of Ireland [cursed],
His children and his race together,
If they did not pay this tribute.
Then I myself foretold
To Conall Gulban, son of Niall,
That a renowned one should be born from him,
Of whom Alba and Ireland would be full.
Thereupon he asked of me—
Did Conall Gulban of the mighty deeds—
'What name do you give to the man
Who'll be descended from my fair body ?'
This is what I said to him :
'Collum Cille[3] will he be called ;
Sufficient for all Ireland would be
His wonders, and his miracles.
The other person who shall be descended from thee—
Adamnan[4]—good will his tribute be.
I shall be the tutor of both—
I assert it in your presence.'
It was then ended the life
Of Conall Gulban, without peril,
After firmly ordaining for me,
The tributes of Alba and Ireland.

curse. But it would appear from the context that Conall must have been the agent.

[3] *Colum Cille.* First Abbot and founder of Hy, or Iona. He was the great grandson of Conall Gulban (slain A.D. 464), and died in the year 597.

[4] *Adamnan.* Ninth Abbot of Iona, and writer of the celebrated *Vita Sancti Columbæ*, which Dr. Reeves has edited, with singular ability, for the *Irish Arch. and Celtic Soc.* He was descended in the 7th generation from Conall Gulban ; and died in 704. Saint Caillin could not, therefore, have been his tutor, as the poem asserts, if SS. Caillin and Colum Cille were

Adlaicim Conall co fir,
  Im doirṫaigh fein gan imṡnim.
  Tabairsi in chuairt sin dom chill,
  Iaruimsi ort a Domnaill.
Comairle duit, a Domnuill;
  Tabair in chuairt dom chaem ċill,
  Ocus saer ṫu fein gan fell
  Ar esccaine noem Erenn. E.
Nidirim duit co tuaimda,
  A Domnaill Droma Tuama,
  Congenfe in trear fer co fir,
  Tall a Finnros nan ardris.
Bid he sin dirrumaċ dori,
  Biar itir ainglib nime;
  Do berra do is Colam na cell,
* fol. 9, b 2. Gumad ri tuaiscert hErend. h. oll.*
Nonbar rig osin amach,
  A Conall, gebus Oilech;
  Da rig dibsin fen gan feall
  Gebus ardrigi hErend. E. O.
Bid mor ri nan ingnais sin,
  Aderim gan imresain,
  Gambia, do ṡil Conuill duind,
  O Doire co clar Coruind.

contemporaries, of which there is little doubt.

[1] *interred.* adlaicī, for adlaicim; lit. "I inter."

[2] *In my . . . . penitentiary.* im doirṫaigh. The form doirṫaigh is the abl. case of doirtech=durtech; for the meaning of which, see note [9], p. 83, *ante.* As in a previous passage of this poem (see line 4, p. 90) Conal Gulban is stated to have been buried in a spot between the *Loch* and the *Dun*, the place of his interment must have been between the Lake immediately to the south of Fenagh, and the Church which occupies the site of the old Dun.

[3] *Druim-thuama.* Drumhome, in the bar. of Tirhugh, co. Donegal.

[4] *Finnros.* See note [4], p. 86.

[5] *'man of multitudes' of Derry.* The

I interred[1] Conall, truly,
  In my own penitentiary,[2] without anguish.
  Give thou that tribute to my church;
  I entreat of thee, Domhnall.
A counsel to thee, Domhnall:
  Give the tribute to my fair church;
  And save thyself, without deceit,
  From the curse of the saints of Ireland.
I tell thee, solemnly,
  O, Domhnall of Druim-thuama,[3]
  That the third man will be born, truly,
  Yonder in Finnros[4] of the high kings;
Who will be the 'man of multitude' of Derry,[5]
  Who shall be amidst Heaven's angels.
  I, and Colum of the Cells,[6] will grant him,
  That he shall be king of the North of Ireland.
Nine kings from that time forth,
  [Descended] from Conall, will possess Ailech.[7]
  Two of these kings, without falsehood,
  Shall obtain the arch-kingship of Ireland.
Many shall be the kings besides these,
  I say, without dispute,
  Of the seed of brown Conall, who will have
  From Derry to the plain of Corann.[8]

Editor does not know how otherwise to render the words dirrumaċ (dirrīaċ, MS.) dori, which is probably corrupt. Dirrumaċ has been considered as a deriv. from dirim (di-rim, "without number"), and dori as for dairi, gen. of daire, or daire calgaig, the Irish name of Derry, or Londonderry.

[6] *Colum of the Cells*; i.e. Colum Cille.

[7] *Ailech.* The ancient seat of the kings of Ulster. See note [3], p. 62, *ante*.

[8] *Corann.* Now represented by the bar. of Corran, co. Sligo. But the limits of the ancient Corann would seem to have also embraced the present baronies of Gallen, co. Mayo, and Leyny, co. Sligo. See O'Flaherty's *Ogygia*, pars. iii., cap. lxix.

Gach Ḃreḟnech, gaċ Conall tend,
Mo bennacht daib i coitċend,
Fri dereḋ in domain den,
Aċt condernat mo ċaoimreir.
Naċ mithig dam, a Crist caid,
In tir i fil[im] d'ḟagbail;
Uair d'ḟoillsiġer gan ḟell,
Ainm gaċ riġ d'ḟeraib Erend. e.
Naċ mithig dam, a Crist ċaid,
In tir i bfilim d'ḟagbail,
Ocus dol d'iaraid nime
Ar mac Moire mingloine.
Naċ mithig dam, a Crist ċaid,
In tir i bfilim d'ḟagbail,
Uair d'ordaig m'oide coir,
M'annlacad in uir aineoil.
Sai frecra, sai feichemnais;
Soi gacha dala ar doman;
Sai legind, sai breṫemnais;
Sai gaċ dana gan oman;
Sai crabaid, sai tredenais;
Gaċa aine gan longod;
Sai fesa, sai bfaitsine;
M'oidesi Finntan ollom.
Naċ mithig dam, a Chrisṫ ċaid,
In tir i bfilim d'ḟagbail,
Uair atchimsi fen aniu,
Gach dil biar ort a Eriu. e.
A Eriu, is duit bas doraid
ecce episcopos (sic). Epscuip deirid in domain;
Noċo lenfat riagail cert,
a fol. 10, a 1. Noċondignet acht escert.[a]

[1] *Conallian;* i.e. every native of Tir-Conaill, or descendant of Conall Gulban.

[2] *tutor.* This was, of course, Finntan, whose praises are sounded in the three

Every Breifnian; every stout Conallian[1]—
My blessing on them in general,
Towards the end of the stern world,
If they fulfil my mild commands.
Is't not time for me, O Holy Christ,
To leave the land in which I am;
For I have explained, without guile,
The name of each king of the men of Ireland.
Is't not time for me, O Holy Christ,
To leave the land in which I am,
And go to seek Heaven
From sweet-pure Mary's Son.
Is't not time for me, O Holy Christ,
To leave the land in which I am;
Since my just tutor[2] has ordained,
That I should be buried in unknown clay.
A sage in answering; a sage in advocacy;
A sage in all affairs on earth;
A sage in reading; a sage in brehonship;
A fearless sage in every art;
A sage in devotion; a sage in fasting—
(Every Friday eating nothing)—
A sage in knowledge; a sage in prophecy,
Was my tutor, the Ollamh Finntan.[3]
Is't not time for me, O Holy Christ,
To leave the land in which I am,
For I myself behold this day,
Every fate which shall come upon thee, Ireland
O, Ireland, unhappy for thee will be
BEHOLD THE BISHOPS! The bishops of the end of the world;[4]
They will not follow just rules;
They will only do injustice.[5]

stanzas that follow.

[3] *Finntan.* See p. 7, *supra.*

[4] *end of the world*; i.e. of later times.

[5] *injustice.* egcept (*recte* eceirt). With

A hEriu, is duit bas dorais,
Escuip deirid in domain;
Bi[d] imdai a coin 'sa ngille;
Ni comaillfeat firinde.
A hEriu, is duit bas dorais
Escuip derid in domain;
Na ceallaib ni dingned coir;
Bis essidan os altoir.
A hEriu is duit bas dorais
Escuip derid in domain;
Bettitt aca mna taide,
Ach do phlaig in chomchainthe.
A hEriu is duit bas dorais,
Escuip derid in domhuin;
Bid gortach beacc a toige;
Marg nech thairna ga toige.
Na espuicc sin, truag ind lus,
Mana dichrat a nuabur;
Daib fein ni fogain co becht,
Beag na mor da timtirecht.
Na sagairt ac lot a ngrad,
Uch, a Crist, as truag in plag;
Ar slicht nan escop co grind,
Sailechdait uili Erind. E. o.
Na drochrig, na droch esscuip,
Cagendait cella is tuatha;

Ecce sacerdotes.

this word ends the text of fol. 9, b, in the lower margin of which are some poetical notes, only one of which is worth reproducing:—

Tar uibh Neill aonachta, fodes la
taoib na hEchta,
Reilgi mic Ui Crimhtannain, berar
co hinis Celtra.

"Across the united Ui-Neill, southwards by the side of Echtga,
The relics of the son of O'Crimthannan are borne to Inis-Celtra."
Echtga is Slieve Aughty, between Clare and Galway; and Inis-Celtra is in Loch-Derg. The son of O'Crimthannan (or, the "son of the descendant of Crimthan-

O, Ireland, unhappy for thee will be
The bishops of the end of the world.
Numerous will be their hounds, and servants;
They will not uphold the truth.
O, Ireland, unhappy for thee will be
The bishops of the end of the world.
In their churches they'll not do right;
They will be impure over the altar.
O, Ireland, unhappy for thee will be
The bishops of the end of the world;
They will have concubines,
Alas! as a plague to the virtuous.[1]
O, Ireland, unhappy for thee will be
The bishops of the end of the world;
Their houses will be stingy and small;
Woe to him who visits their abodes.
Those bishops—woeful the sentence—
Unless they shake off their pride,
Their ministrations,[2] whether great or small,
Shall not be of service to themselves.
The Priests, violating their orders—
BEHOLD THE PRIESTS!
Alas, O Christ, woeful the plague—
Joyously emulating[3] the Bishops,
Will pollute all Ireland.
The bad kings, the bad bishops,
Who will waste[4] churches and territories—

nan") was probably St. Cammin of Inis-Celtra, who was the sixth in descent from Crimthann, son of Enna Cennselach, king of Leinster *circa* A.D. 400.

[1] *virtuous.* comchainthe. This line is rather corrupt; and the translation, therefore, only conjectural. If the poet has not exaggerated the conduct of the bishops in his time, the prototypes of those of the "end of the world," the Irish Church must have been in a sad state at the end of the 13th century.

[2] *ministrations.* timtirecht. The first t is incorrectly marked with the aspirate sign in A.

[3] *emulating.* ar slicht; lit. "upon the track (of)."

[4] *waste.* cagendait. This has been

Bid he an mac dorcha tinn,
Lecaċ fuar ichtair iffinn.
Drochriga derid domain,
ecce reges. Bid utmall lat gach conair;
Bid imda a nethech 'sa mbrat;
Cairdes Crist ni ċomaillfet.
D'Erinn bid mor in digal,
ecce rusticorum proles, etc. Meic nam bachlach do rigad;
Meic na rig 'sna ruireċ tend
Do dichur ar fat Erend. E. o. o. a.
Brethem is cerd is gaba,
Tic ri dered in beṫa,
Ar andenait d'ulc re lind,
* fol. 10, a 2. A cur i tenid iffind.*
Oirfideċ is fer dana,
Sudaire sgingetoir geanna,
Meni threget brecc gan ḟell,
Cuirfider iat in ifernn.
Mairg atchluin, a ri nime,
Oirchindech tuata cilli,
'Sna clerich do ċor on ċill,
Biḋ digal uili d'Erind. E.

taken as the third pl. fut. of the verb cagnaim, "I chew, masticate." It should therefore more properly be rendered "eat," or "consume;" but it should be understood that the substance, or stock, of the churches and territories was meant.

[1] *cold.* fuar. A curious word to apply to Hell, unless the text is corrupt.

[2] *rustics.* bachlach, nom. sg., and gen. pl. The marginal note is valuable as fixing the actual meaning of bachlach, which O'Donovan translates "shepherds" (Four Mast., A.D. 565), and Dr. O'Conor "custos boum," in his ed. of the same Annals in the same passage; although in his ed. of Tighernach (A.D. 566) O'Conor renders the words bachlachaib bairrne (lit. "by the rustics of Bairrin") by "trabibus tecti ruentibus."

[3] *Stingy embellishers.* This is a conjectural translation. The word translated 'stingy,' geanna, should apparently be ganna, to rhyme with the last word of the

Their dark, fast abode shall be
The cold[1] flagged floor of lowermost h—l.
The bad kings of the end of the world
BEHOLD THE KINGS! Will be unquiet in every way.
Many will be their lies and treacheries;
The friendship of Christ they'll not retain.
To Ireland great the retribution will be, for
BEHOLD THE SPAWN OF RUSTICS, &c.! The crowning of the sons of rustics,[2]
And the banishment of the sons of kings,
And of stout chieftains, throughout Ireland.
Judges, and Artizans, and Smiths
Who will come towards the end of time—
For the evils they do in their day,
Shall be put into h—l fire.
The Musician, and the Poet,
The tanner, and the stingy embellisher—[3]
Unless they honestly forsake falsehood,
They shall be sent to h—l.
Woe to him that hears, O King of Heaven,
Of a lay Herenach[4] of a church.
And the expulsion of the clerics from the church
Will be utter woe to Ireland.

preceding line; and sgingetoir[e] seems a deriv. from sging (*recte* scing), which means both a bed (see Stokes's ed. of *Cormac's Glossary*, p. 37, note [c]), and an ornament (*Leabar Breac*, 6, a).

[4] *Herenach.* This word, in Irish airchinnech, or oirchinnech, anciently signified "princeps," or "præpositus;" but in later times it seems to have been put for "archdeacon." (See Stokes's *Three Irish Glosses*, p. 75.) Before the complete establishment in Ireland of the diocesan system, in the 12th century, the Herenachs, who were the stewards, or farmers, of the church lands, were frequently laymen. But for some time after the 12th cent., these officers were generally ecclesiastics. The foregoing lament would indicate that the lay element was again intruding itself at the date of the composition of the present poem, which may be referred to about the year 1300. See Todd's *St. Patrick*, pp. 160–162, on the duties, &c., of Herenachs.

San aimsir sin, is truag lind,
  Fairid saerchlann re daerċloind,
  'San cuan cumaisg sin o aniu,
  Milsius do raṫ, a Eriu. E. o.
O da innisius co druim
  Sgela derid in domain,
  Inderaid me fein anois
  Sgela rochair don neglois.
Ba he Findtan m'oide coir
  Do chuir meri sair do Roiṁ;
  Eaḋ tuc m'oide dam do lon,
  Tri ced uinge do ḋearg or.
Uime docuired me sair,
  D'foglaim ecna is crabaid;
  Is co tugainn lium co tenn
  Fis coitchenn d'feraib Erenn.
Eaḋ ro ba slan dam annsin,
  Nocha 'sa deich do bliadnaib,
  In tan romcuir Findtan grind
  Gu Roim ainglidi a hErind. E.
Noċa tainig meri anair
  Fri re da ced do bliadnaib,
  No gur aitrib Patraicc bind
  Da bliadain dec in Erind. E. o.
And ro gabus coroin ċoir,
  Ic altoir Petair 'san roim,
  In aimsir Cormaic ui Ċuinn,
  Mac suilig suntach d'Erinn.

[1] *slaves.* The note pósaḋ nan uasal ris na hanuaislib, "marriage of the nobles with the ignoble," is added in the margin in A.

[2] *of later times.* derid in domain; lit. "of the end of the world."

[3] This would be about A.D. 444.

[4] *tonsure.* coroin = corona. The note amail ro ġab Caillin grado i Ruaim letha taitnigther nunc; "how Caillin received *gradus* in Rome of Letha is now explained," is added in the margin. Re-

In that time—it is grievous to us—
Freemen shall wed with slaves;[1]
And that mixed brood from this day forth,
Will destroy thy prosperity, O Ireland.
As I have diligently told
The history of later times;[2]
I myself shall now relate
Happy tidings for the church.
'Twas Finntan, my upright tutor,
That sent me eastwards to Rome;
The provision my tutor gave me
Was 300 ounces of red gold.
The object for which I was sent to the East
Was, to learn wisdom and devotion;
And that I might firmly bring back
Universal knowledge to the men of Ireland.
The time I had completed then
Was ninety years and ten,
When pleasant Finntan sent me
To angelic Rome from Ireland.
I did not come from the East
During a period of two hundred years,
Until sweet Patrick had lived
Twelve years[3] in Ireland.
There I received proper tonsure,[4]
At the altar of Peter in Rome,
In the time of Cormac[5] grandson[6] of Conn—
An efficient, active son of Ireland.

garding the name "Letha," see note [1], p. 8, *supra*. The words coꞃoin ċoiꞃ, "proper tonsure," would appear to indicate that this portion of Caillin's alleged *prophecy* must have been composed after the period of the dispute between the Irish and English ecclesiastics respecting the "anterior" and the "coronal" tonsure; the latter form having only been adopted by the Irish Church about A.D. 718. See Reeves's *Adamnan*, p. 350.

[5] *Cormac.* obiit, A.D. 266.

[6] *grandson.* ua, in A. The genit. sg. form is ui.

Ann bam ruibdeochain comblaid,
Isse Cairpre Lifeċair;
Is ann bam deochuin bene
Fria re Fiachaidh sraiptene.*

*fol. 10, b 1.

Is ann bam sacart san Roim,
Ic timtirecht os altoir,
Isin bliaduin co cert coir
Ar eis Echach muigmedoin.
And doriuned dim manaċ
In aimsir Nell mic Echach;
Fri re Laegaire nar glic
Ro gabus grada escuip.
Arsin tanacsa in Erind,
D'indsaigid Patraicc glebind,
Gur ro ordaig dam gomblaid
Grada airdescuip idain.
Cuairt gaċ fir eladain grind,
Tucc dam Patraicc mac Calpruind;
Is ra escuinn he gan ḟell,
Mana riarad mo chaoṁ ċell,
Tuc dam imarcraid oile,
seċ naemaib hErend uile,
Uair is me ba sindser ann;
Legoidecht insi hErend. e.
Ced bliadain dam amlaid sin,
Im legoid ar Ġaidelaiḃ,

[1] *Cairbre Lifechair.* Son of Cormac. Slain A.D. 284.

[2] *Fiacha Sraptene.* Slain A.D. 322.

[3] *over.* ós, written like os̄, A.

[4] *Eochaidh Muidhmedhoin.* obiit A.D. 365. The following rhymes are added in the lower marg. of fol. 10 a, in A.:—

Procept do borb, ceol do bodur,
cruit do muileann iarmotha,
Is i sin samail do ċuala,
duana do gabail riaḋ mna.

"Preaching to the ignorant, music to the deaf;
A harp to a mill also;

When I was a famous sub-deacon was
In the reign of Cairbre Lifechair;[1]
The time I was a deacon *bene*,
Was in the reign of Fiacha Sraptene.[2]
The time when I was a priest in Rome,
Ministering over[3] the altar,
Was right exactly in the year
After Eochaidh Muidhmedhoin.[4]
'Twas there that I was made a monk,
In the time of Niall, son of Eochaidh;
In the reign of Laeghaire[5] the unskilful
I received the grade of bishop.
After that, I came to Ireland,
To meet the candid Patrick,
When he ordered for me, with fame,
The degree of a pure archbishop.[6]
The tribute of every active man of science
Patrick, son of Calpurn, gave me;
And he cursed them, without guile,
Unless they obeyed my fair church.
He gave me another superiority
Above the saints of Ireland all,
(Because I was the senior[7] there)—
The Legateship of the Isle of Ireland.
A hundred years thus was I
A legate over the Gaidhel,

This is the simile I have heard [compared]
To singing songs before women."

"Any one who desires it, may traduce me;
If false, why should it move me; if true why should it pain me."

M'egnachra ir ceaᴅ ᴅo neoch noᴛραιᴅe;
Maᴅ ɡo ciᴅ aρ nomluaiᴅe, maᴅ ϝιρ ciᴅ aρ nomcραιᴅe.

[5] *Laeghaire.* Monarch of Ireland from A.D. 429 to 458.

[6] *archbishop.* See note [4], p. 10, *supra.*

[7] *senior.* ϝinᴅϝeρ. ϝinᴅϝaeρ, A.

Cussin mbliadainsi rem la,
Ic denum na duainisea.
Aingeal De roḟoillsig dam
In fiss morsa do denam,
Do morad cadais mo ċille
Re firdereḋ aimsire.
Mo chellsa Fionaċa reid,
Is i is annsa lium fa grein;
Bid hi in chomairchi glan grinn
Bias fa dereḋ in Erinn. e.
Mo bennaċt dom ṫsamud grind,
Gebus Fionacha aluinn,
Acht na tregett do duine
A n-eneċ na a comairge.
Me Caillin Fionaċa fir,
Luigimsi fa laim mo riġ
Neoċ dorаid me im duain comblaid,
a fol. 10, b Firfar fri dereḋ domain.[a]
2. Gid cuiċ foillsigfes cen chair
Mo duansa an dered domain,
Dobersa do is ri nime,
Rath cloinde, buaid naiṫrigi.
IS beg nach tarnig mo duan;
Coraide comrad go luath,
Rit a Manchain com binde,
Anos ar lar m'ecailsi.
He mo ċomrad a noim choir;
Na hisi tugar o roim,
Scrinn do iaḃad impa anois,
Ar cenn troċair dom eglois.
Tairsi ind aon apstal decc
Faoicfet im chill ga commet,

[1] *of my age.* rem la; lit. "with my day," A.

[2] *to impart.* do denam; lit. "to make."

[3] *To increase.* do morad. A. has

Until this year of my age[1]
[In which I am] composing this poem.
An angel of God that explained to me
How to impart[2] this great knowledge;
To increase[3] the honour of my church
Unto the true end of time.
My church is smooth Fidhnacha;
'Tis the dearest to me under the sun;
'Twill be the pure, pleasant sanctuary,
That shall be at the last in Ireland.
My blessing to my cheerful community
That will obtain beautiful Fidhnacha,
If they abandon not for any man
Their protection, or their guarantee.
I am true Caillin of Fidhnacha.
I swear by the hand of my King,
That everything I have said in my famous poem
Will be verified towards the world's end.
To whoever explains, without blemish,
My poem at the end of the world,
I, and the King of Heaven, will give
Luck of children, and victory of penitence.
My poem is almost finished;
Fit therefore 'tis that I converse quickly
With thee, O sweet Manchan,[4]
Now in the middle of my church.
'Tis my request, O just saint,
That a shrine be now closed about
Those things which I brought from Rome,
For sake of advantage to my church.
The relics of the Eleven Apostles
I will leave to be preserved in my church;

an alias reading moḃfaḋ, which means "would increase."

[4] *Manchan.* See note [4], p. 12, *supra.*

Is tairi Martain co han,
Tairi Luirint is Sdephan.
Bret dorinde Moire glan,
Is do bi im Crist 'ga biathad;
Is he in breit ata comblaid
I cengal ua na tairib.
Hi cind cet bliadan o nocht,
Delechas m'anam rem ċorp;
Ic lia Moċaeṁog comblad,
Is tu dogena m'ongad.
Da tecmad nech do iarrad,
Ort a Manchain, mo ḟaegal;
Ceiṫre cet bliadan he co grind,
Itir Roim ogus hErind. h.
Adluic meri a Manchain grind,
Ar eis oilithre in domain,
Irrelicc Mochoemog thall,
Ar es oilithri Ereann.
IS uime anaim abos,
In Erinn con imat cross,
Uair ni aca cus anniu,
Tir bud naime ina Eriu. h. o. o. a. p.
O lo m'adluicṫi co becht,
Bid da bliadain decc co cert,
Tan dobera co mairi
D'ḟidnacha mo chaoṁthairi.

Doriacht imorro Caillin mac Niatach docum nErend iar forcongra Dé ocus in aingil, iar mbith da ced bliadain do irRóim Leatha ic

[1] *cloth.* See note [1], p. 12, *supra.*

[2] *Lia.* *Lia* means a flag, or stone. "*Mochaemhog's Lia.*" Lia- (or Liath-) Mochaemhog, now Lemakevoge, co. Tipperary. See note [5], p. 12, *supra.*

[3] *four hundred.* ceiṫre cet. 400, A.

[4] *dear.* grind. This word has various meanings, all expressive of joy or pleasure. The MS. A. has an alias reading gil, i.e. bright; but grind seems the more correct reading.

[5] *Relig-Mochaemhog.* See note [6], p. 12, *supra.*

[6] *Till.* The word tan would be more

And the relics of Martin the Noble,
The relics of Laurence and Stephen.
A cloth[1] which pure Mary made,
And which was round Christ when being fed—
This is the famous cloth that is
Tied about the relics.
Before the end of 100 years from to-night,
My soul will depart from my body.
At Mochaemhog's famous *Lia*[2]
'Tis thou that shalt anoint me.
If any one should chance to ask thee
My age, O Manchan—
It is exactly four hundred[3] years,
Between Rome and Ireland.
Bury me, O dear[4] Manchan,
After the world's pilgrimage,
Yonder in Relig-Mochaemhog,[5]
After the pilgrimage of Ireland.
The reason why I remain here,
In Ireland of many crosses, is,
Because I saw not, unto this day,
A land more saintly than Ireland.
From the day of my burial, exactly,
'Twill be just twelve years,
'Till[6] thou shalt gloriously bear
My fair relics to Fidhnacha.[7]

Caillin[8] son of Niata came to Ireland, moreover, according to the command of God and the Angel, after he had been 200 years in Rome of Letha, learning

correctly rendered by "when;" but the sense is better expressed by "'till."

[7] *Fidhnacha.* With this line concludes the text of fol. 10, b. 2, in A., on the lower margin of which is a couplet not worth printing.

The text from this to the first word of the last line, p. 114, which is wanting in A., has been supplied from B., in which it occupies fol. 107.

[8] *Letha.* See note [1], p. 8, *ante.*

foġluim ecna ocus crabaiḋ, iar na cur sair d'Finntann mac Boċrau, dia oide fesin. Ni roleig imorro int aingel fuirech na furnaiḋe do i maiġin eile co riacht Maġ Rein i mBrefne Connacht, co dun mBaile intinnraiṫ .i. áit i fil Fidnacha aniu. Oir is ann robúi i tarngaire do aitreab a ċille ocus a congbala iar forcetal Dé.

Is cian már ém o ro tharrnġair Cathfad caomdrai co ticfad Caillin isin lucc sin .i. fri re Echach feidliġ do bith i riġe nErend. Cid fil ann tra, arsed dorriacht Caillin co dun mBaile i Maġ Rein.

Ciḋ dianebraḋ dun mBaile cedamus fris in n-inadsin. Ni annsa son. Ri uasal oirbidnech ro gab hErinnd fecht naill .i. Conaing mac Congail. Is ann imorro robui domgnas ocus dunaras in rig sin ar Mag Rein intsainred. Do ronad imorra daingen ocus caisil cloch lais indusin i farrad Locha salach. Salach mac Samail do Troiannaib is he ba drai don Conaing sin mac Congail, ocus is uada ainmnigther Loch Salach.

Baile binn berlach mac Buain .i. mac rig hUlaḋ atuaiḋ. Dalta sen do Conaing mac Congail, do rig hErend. Is uada din ro hainmniged dun mBaile. Ticcis chena riga ocus flaithe Ereand ocus a lathgaile, ocus cach archena, cus in dun sin do denam a caingen ocus a coda ocus a cairdine, ocus do erneaḋ a cana ocus a cisa ocus a mbesa. Ro len iarum dun mBaile don n-inad sin o aimsir Conaing mic Congaile, ocus Baile mic Buain a daltai, co haimsir Patraicc mic Calpuirnn, ocus co haimsir Fergna mic Fergusa mic Muiredaig mail mic Eogain sreim mic Duach galaiġ mic Briain mic Echach muiġmedon.

1 *Cathbad.* A famous druid in the time of King Conor Mac Nessa, who died *circa* A.D. 50.

2 *Eochaidh Feidlech.* King of Ireland, and father of the famous Queen Medbh of Connacht. He died in the year of the world 3934 (of the Hebrew calculation), or 18 years before the Incarnation, according to O'Flaherty's chronology. *Ogygia*, pars III., cap. xliii.

3 *Conaing.* Conaing Bec-ecla, or "Conangus Impavidus," as the name is Latinized by O'Flaherty, who refers his reign to the year of the world 3529 accord. to the Hebrew chronology, or 423 years before the Incarnation. See p. 27, *ante*, and *Ogygia*, p. 256.

4 *stone inclosure.* caisil cloch. The remains of a stone inclosure, or cashel (Lat. "maceria") are still visible at Fenagh, the old church of which stands within its circle.

5 *Baile.* See a curious legend regarding this individual in O'Curry's *MS. Materials*

wisdom and piety, after having been sent to the East by Finntan son of Bochra, his own preceptor. The Angel, moreover, did not permit him to rest or remain in any other place until he came to Magh-Rein, in Briefne of Connacht, to Dun-Baile particularly, to wit, the place where Fidhnacha is this day; for it was prophesied that there the site of his church and habitation should be, according to the instructions of God.

It is a long time, truly, since the fair druid Cathbad[1] foretold that Caillin would come to that place—to wit, in the time that Eochaidh Feidlech[2] was in the sovereignty of Ireland. Howsoever, where Caillin came to, was to Dun-Baile in Magh-Rein.

Why, firstly, is that place called Dun-Baile? Not difficult [to tell], truly. A noble, illustrious, king one time possessed Ireland, viz., Conaing[3] son of Congal. The place, moreover, where the habitation and residence of that king was situated, was in Magh-Rein precisely. A fastness and stone inclosure[4] was likewise made by him there, near Loch-Salach. Salach, son of Samal, of the Trojans, was druid to that Conaing son of Congal; and it is from him that Loch-Salach is named.

Baile[5] the sweet-speaking, son of Buan, i.e. son of the king of Ulidia from the North, was foster-son to Conaing son of Congal, king of Ireland. From him, therefore, Dun-Baile was so called.

The kings and lords of Ireland, its warriors, and all others besides, were wont to go to that *dun*, to make their compacts, and their covenants, and their treaties, and to pay their tributes, and their rents, and their customs. [The name of] Dun-Baile attached itself afterwards to that place, from the time of Conaing son of Congal, and his foster-son Baile son of Buan, to the time of Patrick son of Calpurnius; and of Fergna, son of Fergus, son of Muiredach Mal, son of Eoghan Sremh, son of Duach Galach, son of Brian, son of Eochaidh Muidhmedhon.[6]

(Dublin, 1861), pp. 465–7, and 472–8. As Baile was the sixth in descent from Rudhraidhe, monarch of Ireland, who died *circa* 212 B.C., he could not have been the contemporary of Conaing. See note [3].

[6] *Eochaidh Muidhmedhon.* "Eochaidh moyst-middle," as the name is explained in the Annals of Clonmacnois, was king of Ireland, and died A.D. 371, according to the Chron. Scotorum. Fergna, the sixth in descent from him, must therefore have flourished about the year 550.

Is he in Fergna sin ba ri indurin in tan do riacht Caillin co dun mḃaile. Do riacht co hairm araibe Fergna do furail creidme fair. Ní ro faemsam in ni sin o Chaillin na o naoṁuiḃ. Targaiḋ imorro Caillin ocus a naeiṁ coṁaḋa maithe don tí Fergna .i. saoġal fada in deaġbeathaiḋ ocus flaithius nime tria bithu sir ma dia creideḋ doiḃ. Obair Fergna na comaḋa soin, ar nir bo hail do creideṁ ecin. Is o na comaiḃ sin ainmnigther Fan choba remper.

Ar a haiṫle sin iaram ro forċongair Fergna for a mac .i. for Aod nduḃ dol do athċor Caillin ocus na clerech olchena arin mendat sin. Is iarsin do riacht Aoḋ duḃ mac Fergna, in cuingiḋ ocus in cathmiliḋ calma, cona ṡluaġaiḃ do dichur Chaillin ocus a ċlereċ. Ot chonnairc iarum Aodh Caillin cona ṡalmcetluiḃ ocus cona chlerchaib ag urnaiġthi ocus ag slechtanaib, ro ċreid Aodh cona muintir fochetoir Larodain do Dia ocus do Chaillin, ocus ro slechtsat do; ocus do bais[t]eḋ Aeḋ duḃ iarsuidiu. Ro edbair dno dun mḃaile do Chaillin feb ro tairngired do.

Is iarsuidiu doratad Fidnacha d'ainm ar dun mḃaile .i. ón fednach ocus on imfedain ocus on tarruḋ do bert Caillin docum in baile, unde Fidnacha nominatur.

Ot ċonnairc Fergna gu ro creit a mac ocus a muintir do Dia ocus do Chaillin, ro fergaiġeḋ he co mór iarum, ocus atbert re druidib dol do indarbad na clerech. Ro ergetar na druithe Larodain co hathlam fo cedoir. Focertat a tona ocus saorcal a mbronnann an airde suas iarsin frisin aer. Ro oslaicset a ngnuba ocus a ngin-chraesa, ocus ro glamsat ocus ro grisatar ocus ro chainetar co hindliġthech[*] egcoir ar Chaillin ocus ar a naom chlerchib. Ba decair,

[*] fol. 12, a 1.

[1] *Fan-choba;* "the slope (or declivity) of conditions;" from fan, "a slope," and coba (*rectè* coma) "a condition," or "consideration." The name of the place is more correctly written *Fan-Chomha*, p. 117, *infra*.

[2] *in.* The Irish is do, equivalent to the preposition "to," and "for." But the sense is correctly rendered by "in."

[3] *to him;* i.e. to Caillin. See last page.

[4] *teams—traction.* fednach. imfedain. These words seem derived from fedain, which is variously explained as "labour," a "team," "a yoke," "drawing," &c. See *O'Donovan's* suppl. to *O'Reilly's* Dictionary, v. feaḋain. The derivation of "Fidnacha" from fedain is

It is this Fergna that was king there, when Caillin came to Dun-Baile. He went to the place where Fergna was, to persuade him to receive the faith. He did not accept it from Caillin or his saints. Caillin and his saints, moreover, offered good conditions to Fergna, to wit, long life in a good state, and the kingdom of Heaven for all eternity, if he would believe for them. Fergna refused these conditions, for it liked him not to believe at all. It is from these conditions Fan-Choba[1] is named *semper*.

Immediately afterwards Fergna commanded his son, i.e. Aedh Dubh, to go and expel Caillin and the other clerics from the place. Thereupon Aedh Dubh, son of Fergna, the mighty hero and warrior, came with his hosts, to expel Caillin and his clerics. But when Aedh subsequently beheld Caillin, with his psalmodists and clerics, engaged in prayer and prostrations, Aedh with his people forthwith believed thereat in[2] God, and in[2] Caillin; and they knelt to him. And Aedh Dubh was afterwards baptized. He also presented Dun-Baile to Caillin, as it was foretold to him.[3]

It was after this that the name "Fidhnacha" was given to Dun-Baile, to wit, from the teams,[4] and from the traction,[4] and from the draughting, that brought Caillin to the place. Unde Fidnacha nominatur.

When Fergna saw that his son and his people believed in God and Caillin, he was greatly enraged thereat; and he told his druids to go and banish the clerics. The druids thereupon arose actively at once. They turned up their podices, and the *faoscal*[5] of their *bronnann*,[5] against the air. They opened their jaws and gluttonous mouths, and shouted, and uttered provocation,[6] and reproaches, unlawfully and unjustly,[7] against Caillin and his holy clerics.

a silly guess. It is more probable that the name (by which other places in Ireland were formerly known) was derived from ꞅıᴅh, "a wood;" for it appears that as late as the year 1688 Fidhnacha was beautifully wooded. See O'Donovan's *Breifne Letters*, Ord. Surv. Correspondence, R. I. Academy, p. 185.

[5] *faoscal—bronnann.* These words would hardly bear translation.

[6] *uttered provocation.* The verb ꞃo ᵹꞃıꞅaꞇaꞃ, thus translated, is really an active verb (3 pl. pret. ind.), signifying "they incited;" but the context, which implies that the action was "at," or "against" Caillin (aꞃ Chaıllın), necessitated the liberty that has been taken in rendering it by the words in question.

[7] *unjustly.* eᵹcoıꞃ. The text of A. recommences, after the hiatus left by the loss of fol. 11, with this word. The foregoing text from the second last line

em, imchaimed ocus athair ar an ti noem Chaillin mac Niatach, Uair is he ba caile ocus ba craibdige do noemaib a chomaimsiri, ba hoiġi ocus ba hindraco. Ba he in tene lasamain do leoṁ ocus do lorgad ingrentid De ocus na hecclaisi; ocus ba he in brath tar a bidbadaib ri borbdigail ar gaċ neċ notuillfed. Ba he in leoman londchrechtaċ sir naċ fulangṫi imguin. Ba he in muir gan traġad i fertaib ocus i mirbailib, ocus i sailmċetluib i sirmolad in Chomded.

Ot chuala Aod dub tra na draithe ocus na cainte ag sindad ocus ag sraiṫissiuġad na clerech, ro aiṫin ocus ro forconġair for a ṡluagaibh na draithe d'fobairt ocus d'indsoigid dia coscc don abairt sin. Nato ar Caillin, ni imeram cumachta daenna forra; acht chena is cet liumsa, mara chet lem Dia nime ocus talman, gu ro ṡoa na draithe i clochuib ittraitte.[4] Iarsdain ro chetoir ro soaḋ na draithe in delbaib cloch la breṫir in ti Caillin i fiadnuise na slog. Ro morad em ainm De ocus Caillin tresin firt sin et triasan mor mirbail.

Mar tan imorro do connaic Fergna na nethisi .i. a mac cona ṡluaig ocus cona ṡochraide do creidem do Dia ocus do Chaillin, ocus a ḋraithe do chor a ndelbaib ċolaman cloch, Ro linad he o ferg ocus o oman ocus o ancretem. Ised do roine fesin; ro ḟagaib a ṡloġa gan ḟis gan airiugad do neoch dib, ar imgabail (.i. seaċanta) creidmiu do Chaillin. Isi conair ro gab co san ċoiṁa. Is andsin ro maiḋ in talam foi indusin, ocus ni ro soad aigned do. Ot connairc Dia fesin nar bo menmarc la Fergna cretem tre bithu, ro delig a anam fria a ċorp do.

on p. 110 to this has been supplied from B.

[1] *practice.* abairt. abairtt, B. The more ancient form of the word is abairt, which literally means "game," "amusement." Cf. ingnad em reb ocus abairt ocus adabair dogni; "wonderful, truly, the play, and game, and sport he performed." *Book of Leinster*, 54, b 1.

[2] *it is my will.* The Irish is cet liumsa, literally translated, would be "est permissio apud me."

[3] *if it be.* mara, A. ocus mara, "and if it be," B.

[4] *turned into forms of stone at Caillin's word.* la breṫir in ti Caillin; lit. "at the word (or prayer) of the person Caillin." O'Donovan writes, in his *Breifne Letters* (Ord. Surv. Papers, R. I. Acad.); "In the townland of Longstones, in the parish of Oughteragh, to the N.E. of Fenagh, are several standing stones which, unquestionably, are the very stones here referred to; for Maurice O'Mulconry, who lived

It would be hard, truly, [to cast] reproach and contempt on Saint Caillin son of Niata, for he was the best reputed, and the most devout, of the saints of his time—the purest and most worthy. He was the blazing fire to destroy and burn the persecutors of God and the Church. He was the doom over his enemies, for enacting stern vengeance on every one who would deserve it. He was the fierce-wounding lion, with whom no conflict could be maintained. He was the unebbing sea in prodigies and miracles, and in psalm-singing in perpetual praise of the Lord.

When, therefore, Aedh Dubh heard the druids and satirists reviling and continually disparaging the clerics, he ordered and commanded his hosts to attack and encounter the druids, to restrain them from that practice.[1] "No," said Caillin; "we will not exercise human power upon them; but it is my will,[2] if it be[3] the will of my God of Heaven and Earth, that the druids may be changed into stones forthwith." Thereupon the druids were immediately turned into forms of stone, at Caillin's word,[4] in presence of the multitude. The name of God and of Caillin was magnified, verily, through that miracle and great marvel.[5]

When Fergna, however, observed these things, to wit, that his son, with his host and army, believed in God and Caillin, and that his druids were transformed into the shape of stone columns, he was filled with fury, and with fear, and with[6] unbelief. What he did himself was: he quitted his armies, unknown to, and unobserved by, any one of them, to avoid believing for Caillin. The road he took was to Fan-Chomha.[7] Then it was that the ground sundered under him there;[8] but his mind changed not.[9] When God Himself saw that Fergna was not inclined[10] to believe through life, He separated his soul from his body.

at Fenagh, stated in his prose preface to this poem (i.e. the poem beginning at p. 124, *infra*), that the stones into which the druids were turned stood to the N.E. of Fenagh."

[5] *marvel.* mıṗbaıl=mirabilia. The MSS. have mıṗbaılı, the plural form; but the comp. preposition, *triasan*, is sing.

[6] *with.* The preposition o (which properly signifies "from," but could not be so translated here, without altering the sense of the narrative) is omitted in B.

[7] *Fan-Chomha.* See note [1], p. 114, *ante.*

[8] *there.* ımᴅuṗın. ınᴅuıṗı, A.

[9] *his mind changed not.* nı ṗo ṗoaᴅ aıgneᴅ ᴅo, A. B. reads nı ṗo ṗoaᴅ an aıgnaᴅ ᴅo, "it changed not in mind to him."

[10] *inclined.* naṗ bo menmaṗc la Fergna. Lit. "that it was not desired by Fergna."

Larodain do riacht int aingel co Caillin ocus ro indis co follus firmaith do na mirbaili sin do rinned for Fergna .i. a slugad fon
[a] fol. 12, b 1. talmain. Ro morad ainm De ocus Caillin treisin firt sin.[a]

Ro forchongair iaram int aingeal for Chaillin na sloga do thinol fa Aod ndub mac Fergna, ocus in rigi do thabairt do, fodaigin is do ro is Dia fein hi ar a umla ocus ar a airmitin do naom Chaillin. Do roine Caillin in ni sin.

Ro thaircomlaid na sloig ma Aed, ocus do ratad in rigi do iarum. Atbert iarum Aod fris in aingel; atchimsi tusa in ainm De, a fag-bail ó Chaillin ocus o Dia claechlod mo delbai, ar ni comtig lium in delb rig ata orm d'follamnugad os rigaib ocus os flaithib olchena, ar na tugthar frim mo duibe ocus mo dodelba. Atbert int aingel fri Caillin: tabairsi d'Aed dub in ni connaigess .i. a roga dealba ocus denmasa fair. Delb imorro Riocc Indsi bo finde ro thog Aed fair fein.

Ro throisce imorro Caillin cona chlerchib in oidche sin imon caingin sin. Iar nergi imorro do na slogaib iar na barach, Ni raibe deochair na dealugad delba itir Aed ndub ocus Riocc Indsi bo finni, acht nama coroin i cind Riocc, ocus ni raibe i cind Aeda.

[b] fol. 12, b 2. Amail[b] forfuair Eogan mac Nell o Patraic, ar airin ba hinan dealb do Aod dub mac Fergna ocus d'Eogan mac Nell, ar is i dealb Riocc bui la cechtar nae.

[1] *around.* fa, B. uad, A.

[2] *it.* hi. Omitted in B.

[3] *given.* The note in rigi do radad d'Aod dub, "the kingship given to Aedh Dubh," is added in the margin in A.

[4] *Riocc of Inis-bo-finde.* Riog, or Moriog, of Inishbofin in Lough-Ree, is stated in an ancient Tract on the Mothers of the Saints (*Book of Lecan*, fol. 89[b]; *Book of Ballymote*, p. 249) to have been the son of Darerca, one of St. Patrick's sisters. See Colgan's *AA. Sanctorum*, pp. 716–17. Dr. Lanigan denies the relationship (Eccl. Hist., vol. i., p. 419). If Riocc was the contemporary of St. Caillin and Aedh Find, as above implied, Dr. Lanigan was probably right. It appears from the *Litany of Aengus*, however, that Riocc was a foreigner. See Petrie's Round Towers, p. 137.

[5] *moreover.* imorro. After this word, which concludes the 20th line of MS. B., fol. 118 b, there is a blank space of two lines, with the exception of the query ci

Thereupon the Angel came to Caillin, and told him plainly and truly the miracles that had been wrought on Fergna, to wit, that he had been swallowed under the ground. The name of God, and [the name] of Caillin, were magnified through that miracle.

The Angel afterwards commanded Caillin to assemble the armies around[1] Aedh Dubh son of Fergna, and to give him the kingship, because it was to him God Himself had granted it,[2] on account of his humility and reverence towards Saint Caillin.

Caillin did so. The armies were assembled around Aedh, and the kingship was afterwards given[3] to him.

Aedh then said to the Angel: "I beseech thee, in the name of God, to obtain from Caillin, and from God, the transformation of my visage; for I do not deem the kingly form that I have fit to rule over other kings and princes, lest my blackness and ugliness should be brought against me." The Angel said to Caillin: "Grant to Aedh Dubh that which he requests—to wit, that he may have his choice of features and of form." The form of Riocc, of Inis-bo-finde,[4] moreover,[5] was that which Aedh chose for himself.

Caillin, along with his clerics, fasted that night regarding the affair; and after the hosts had risen on the morrow, there was neither distinction nor difference[6] of visage between Aedh Dubh and Riocc of Inis-bo-finde,[4] except only that there was a corona[7] on the head of Riocc, and none on Aedh's head. As Eoghan Mac Neill[8] had obtained [a similar request] from Patrick, the visage[9] of Aedh Dubh son of Fergna was therefore identical with that of Eoghan Mac Neill, for it was the likeness of Riocc each of them had.[10]

ar ata in da line so, "why are these two lines (   )?"

[6] *nor difference.* na dealugad, omitted in A.

[7] *corona;* i.e. coronal tonsure. Vid. *ante*, p. 104, *n.* [4].

[8] *Eoghan Mac Neill.* See the curious account of the manner in which St. Patrick gratified the wish of Eoghan Mac Neill, to be made as handsome as St. Riocc, in the *Tripart. Life of St. Patrick*, Miss Cusack's ed. p. 436. The note Aodh dubh na Aodh find, i.e. "Black Aedh changed into Fair Aedh," is added in the margin.

[9] *visage.* dealb; more correctly "image," or "form."

[10] *each of them had.* ro bui (bae, A.) la cechtar nae; lit. "that was with each."

Ba Aed find a ainm on huairsin. Is uada ro genetar cath Aeda find .i. in tres rigraide Connacht co brat̄.

AS a haithle sin do riacht Aed find cus in cartí a primdoras na catrach ocus na congbala. Ro edbair ferann dia anmcharait .i. do Chaillin, ocus dia comarba co brath, do medagad a chathrach ocus d'onoragad a ecailsi co dered domain.

Is annsin ro ordaig Aed find cuairt ocus circhanachus a cinid co brat̄ do Chaillin ocus dia chomarba. Ised atbert Caillin, nem doitsi ocus dot ciniud iadiaid, acht co togatt im chillsi ocus im chongbail. Togaimsi agat chena bar Aod, cidbe dom chiniud na hicfa do chain nar gaba rath na rigi. Da bliadain lxx. ro bai Aed find i flaithes iarsin.

Rugadsom .i. Aed iarum iar na bas la Caillin co Fidnacha maige Rein. Ro adlaicc he iarum ic ibar na rig ro leic nan aingel intsainred .i. ar lár relgi duin Baili .i. Fidnacha in tan so.*

*fol. 13, a 1.

Isi so in chain ro ordaig Aed find mac Fergna do Chaillin mac Niatach for cath Aeda find co brath.

Each gabail gach rig do sil Aeda find, ocus a eirred cuirp itir cend ocus cois ocus lamh. Mar in cetna o gac̄ toisech do sil Aeda find do Chaillin ocus dia chomarba co brath.

Each gach rigna ocus a hetach amail ata o'n rig. Mar in cetnai o gac̄ mnai thoisig mar ata ó na toisechaib.

[1] *sept.* cath. This properly means "battle;" but like "battle," it is also used to signify "battalion," and in a wider sense "kindred," "followers," and "tribe."

[2] *pillar-stone.* cartí. A large stone, in the form of a pillar, or flag-stone. O'Donovan asks (*Breifne Letters*, R. Ir. Acad., p. 187), "Was this to close the door of the *Cathair* (Cahir), like the flag of the Cyclops Polyphemus?" Stones of this kind are still standing in the middle of several ancient *raths*. In the *Brudin Da Derga*, it is stated that pillar-stones were erected to celebrate victories, and cairns heaped to commemorate slaughters. (*Lebor na hUidhre*, p. 86 b.)

[3] *and.* ocus. et, A., B.

[4] *that they choose.* co togatt. co togad, A.

[5] *in my abode.* im chongbail. im congsbail, A.

[6] *with thee.* This means that Aedh Find made choice of Fenagh as his place of sepulture. The note toga Fidnacha

Aedh Find was his name from that hour. From him descended the sept[1] of Aedh Find, i.e. the third regal family of Connacht for ever.

Aedh Find arrived immediately afterwards at the pillar-stone[2] in the principal door of the city and abode ; and he granted land to his soul-friend, i.e. to Caillin, and to his successors for ever, to magnify his city, and to honour his church, to the end of the world.

It was then that Aedh Find ordered the dues and[3] tribute-rents of his kindred [to be paid] for ever to Caillin and his successors. What Caillin said was "Heaven for thee, and for thy race after thee, provided that they choose[4] [to be buried in] my church, and in my abode."[5] "I make my choice with thee,"[6] said Aedh. "Whosoever of my race shall not pay thy tribute, may he not obtain grace or sovereignty."[7]

Seventy-two years was Aedh Find in the sovereignty after that.

He, to wit Aedh, was afterwards, after his death, taken to Fidh-nacha of Magh-Rein, by Caillin, who subsequently buried him at the "yew of the kings,"[8] exactly under the "flag of the Angels,"[9] i.e. in the middle of the cemetery of Dun-baile, now Fidhnacha.

This is the tribute which Aedh Find, son of Fergna, ordained for Caillin, son of Niata, from[10] the race of Aedh Find for ever.

The riding steed[11] of every king of the seed of Aedh Find, and his body raiment[12] between head, and foot, and hand. The like from every chieftain of the seed of Aedh Find, to Caillin and his successor for ever.

The steed and dress of every queen, in like manner as from the king. In the same way, from each chieftain's wife as from the chieftains.

d Aoḋ fionn ocus da sliocht ⁊c ; "selection of Fenagh by Aedh Find and his race, &c.," is added in the margin.

[7] *sovereignty.* riġi. riga, A. A marginal note has cain Chaillin for caṫ Aoda finn ; "Caillin's tribute upon the race (*cath*) of Aedh Find."

[8] "*yew of the kings.*" ibar na rig. ibar na na rig, A. There is no trace or tradition of this celebrated tree at present.

[9] *flag of the Angels.* The precise position of this flag, in the cemetery of Fenagh, is not at present known.

[10] *from.* for, lit. upon, A. B.

[11] *riding steed.* ech gabail. In the poem printed above (see line 3, p. 80), this is represented by serrech (or serrech) maiṫ, "a good team," or "colt."

[12] *body raiment.* eirred cuirp. The poem referred to has caṫ erred, "battle

Do gaċ biataig ocus gaċa cind baili o Ath droiċit go Sligech.

Screapall gacha cairchigh. Do gabala ar gach creich o gaċ mac riġ ocus toisiġ.

In chuairt sin o gach dalta ocus o gaċ mac seċar dambe ag sil Aeḋa find.

In neach dib na tibri in chain sin co nach gaba a duthaid, ocus ni geba raṫ na riġi. Gach tres bliadnai dlegar in chain sin do íc.

Isi loiġiḋecht na cana sain o Chaillin do chath Aeḋa Find, Nocha
fol. 13, a 2. gebatt goill a ferann ar air na air eccin in cein icfait in chain siu. Rath ocus toicthi doib fós.

Gibe nach tibre in chain siu, mallacht Chaillin ocus noem hErend do, ocus co nach gebat a mic a ferann dia és, ocus bid ifern a iar-taiġe dono.

Is do dinnsenchus duin Baili, ocus Fidnacha, ocus Loċa Salac, ocus Fain coba, ocus do na draithib do chor a ndelbaib cloċ do Dia, ocus di Chaillin soirċuaid o Fidnacha .i. corrguinecht fognitis na draithi sin, ocus do bas Fergna, ocus don ni dia tug Aeḋ find Fidnacha do Chaillin, ocus in faṫ ima tug in chain sin ar a chineḋ co brath do Chaillin ocus dia choṁarba ocus dia ḟamad ro chán in sui senchusa .i. Fland mac Floind in duansa, edon.

"Dun mBaili righbaile caith ⁊c."

dress," which is probably the more correct. (See last line, p. 78.)

[1] *Biatagh.* See note [3], p. 80, *supra.*

[2] *Ath-droichit.* See note [4], p. 81.

[3] *screpall.* See note [6], p. 79.

[4] *whosoever.* In neach. In each, A.

[5] *in addition.* fos. foss, A. A somewhat similar tribute over the Cinel-Conaill, payable also every third year, was granted to St. Caillin by Conall Gulban, according to the poem. See p. 93, *supra.*

[6] *dinnsenchus.* This word is usually translated "history of celebrated places." But it really signifies "history of fortresses," being comp. of *dinn* (gen. *denna*), a hill, fortified hill, or residence; and *senchus*, history.

[7] *corrguinecht.* Some kind of druidical incantation, as O'Davoran explains in his Glossary (Stokes's *Old Irish Glosses*, p.

A cow from every Biatagh,[1] and from every chief of a bally, from Athdroichit[2] to Sligo.

A screpall[3] from every sheep-owner. A fat cow out of every prey from every son of a king and chieftain.

This tribute [also] from every foster-son, and from every sister's son, whom the race of Aedh Find may have.

Whosoever[4] of them does not furnish this tribute shall not obtain his inheritance, and shall not obtain grace or kingship.

Every third year this tribute is required to be paid.

The reward for this tribute given by Caillin to the descendants of Aedh Find, was that Foreigners should not obtain their land by consent, or by force, as long as they paid this tribute. Prosperity and luck should be theirs in addition.[5]

Whoever will not give this tribute, may he have the malediction of Caillin and the saints of Ireland; and may his sons not possess his land after him; and may h—l be his final inheritance also.

It is regarding the *dinnsenchus*[6] of Dun-baile and Fidhnacha, and of Loch-Salach and Fan-cobha, and the turning of the druids (which druids used to perform *corrguinecht*[7]) into forms of stone, by God and Caillin, to the north-east of Fidhnacha; and regarding the death of Fergna, and the reason why Aedh Find gave Fidhnacha to Caillin, and the cause why he gave that tribute upon his race for ever to Caillin, and to his successor, and to his community, the sage of history, i.e., Flann son of Flann,[8] sang this poem, to wit, "Dun-Baile, holy, regal place,[9] &c."

63), in uttering which the person rested on one foot, and one hand; and had one eye closed. The formula used was a *Glaim dichind*, or extempore lampoon. It is further explained in the same authority (*Old Irish Glosses*, p. 66) as a trick done by sleight of hand. The manner of performance described in the following poem is rather coarse.

[8] *Flann son of Flann.* Better known as Flann Mainistrech, or Flann of the Monastery, Lector of Monasterboice. He died in 1056. The present poem is not attributed to him by any other authority than the writer of the foregoing Introduction to the poem, and the composer of the poem, as far as the Editor is aware.

[9] The words from "to wit," to the end of the sentence, are added from B., from which the poem itself is missing.

Dun mbaili rigbailea caiġ,
  Port cur tigdir flaṫa ḟail,
  Tan ba ri croḋa crechach
  Conuing beoḋa beg eglach.
Conaing mac Conguil calma,
  Is tren ro thecht in Banba,
  Condernà carul caem cloch
fol. 13, b 1. Ar Mag Rein ic loċ Saloċ.
Salaċ mac Samail co mbloid,
  Mac in druaġ do Troianaib,
  Is he ba drai tairrpthech tenn
  Ac Conuing ac rig Erenn.
IS huada adeirthor Mag rein
  O rian mac Echada trein,
  Ocus on reidiuġaḋ glan
  Tugatar goill ri a mbalan.
Dalta do bi ag Conuing ḟial,
  Mac rig hUlad na mor giall,
  Baile mac Buain, rigda a run,
  O'n ainmnigther in caem dun.
Dun mBaili ainm don chatraig,
  Ocus nir gerr in athuig
  O re in Conaing mett ngosa,
  Co Fergna mac Fergusa.
Mic Muiredaig mic Eogain co mblad
  Mic Duach mic Briain mic Echach,

[1] *Fal.* A bardic name for Ireland.

[2] *Conaing Beg-eglach.* See p. 27, *ante.*

[3] *Congal.* *ib.*

[4] *cashel.* This cashel, or stone wall, can still be traced around the church of Fenagh. It consists of large blocks of stone, regularly laid, without cement; but it is in many places levelled to the ground.

[5] *Was.* The Irish, is he ba, literally rendered, would be "'tis he that was."

[6] *To.* ac, lit. "apud."

[7] *This is why.* The words thus rendered, IS huada, actually mean "it is from it," i.e., from the rian, or track, mentioned in the line following. The derivation given is one of those silly in-

Dun-Baile, holy, regal place;
Mansion to which the lords of Fal[1] were wont to come,
When a valiant, predatory king
Was vigorous Conaing Beg-eglach.[2]
Conaing, son of mighty Congal,[3]
Powerfully possessed Banba.
He built a fair *cashel*[4] of stone
On Magh-Rein, at Loch-Salach.
Salach, son of Samal of fame,
Son of the druid of the Trojans,
Was[5] a grand and mighty druid
To[6] Conaing king of Ireland.
This is why[7] Magh-Rein is so called:
From the track[8] of the sons of valiant Eochaidh;
And from the clear levelling
The Foreigners made with their fighting.
The generous Conaing had a *dalta*,[9]
Son to the king of Ulad of great hostages;
Baile mac Buain,[10] regal his mind,
From whom the fair *Dun* is named.
Dun-Baile was the name of the *cahir*[11]
(And not for a short period)
From the time of the powerful Conaing,
To Fergna, son of Fergus,
Son of Muiredach, son of famous Eoghan,
Son of Duach, son of Brian, son of Eochaidh,

ventions in which Irish etymologists were too fond of indulging, to account for names of places.

[8] *track.* ruan (gen. rein), a track or passage.

[9] *dalta*, a foster-child. Generally a male foster-child, or foster-son. But in old Irish tales a girl is sometimes called a *dalta.* The word is still used as a term of endearment (to boys) by the Irish-speaking people.

[10] *Baile mac Buain.* Baile, son of Buan. See note [5], p. 112. The Irish name of Dundalk strand, *Traigh-Bhaile-mhic-Buain*, was derived from this person.

[11] *cahir.* cathair (gen. cathrach, dat.

Mic Muireḋaig mic Ḟiacra sraip
Mic Cairpre mic Cormaic culglais.
Mic Airt ocus mic Chuind tra;
Rugus genealach Fergna;
O ré in Fergna sin comblaid
Ro claechlo ainm don chatraig.
Ag so daib in soḃ anma
Tugad ar chatraig Fergna,
Fidnacha on ḟednach ur
Tucc Caillin les na ċoem dun.
Andsin tig Caillin 'sa naim
Inagaid Fergna foltchain,
Co targaid do coma caid,
Saegul fada in ndegḃethaid.
IS ann adubairt Fergna
Re hAed ndub, re mac calma,
Erig is cuir arin tir
[a] fol. 13, b 2. Na clerig ud co hanmin.[a]
Andsin do erig colluath
Aed cirdub cona ṁarcsluag,
Do chur na clerech ar cul,
Is da ndichur on caeṁdun.
O't connairc Aed cirdub cain
Caillin 'sa naim ag slechtain,
Ro cred doib 's a sluaig co gur,
Ro tindlaic doiḃ in caem dun.
O't connairc Fergna co reid
Fellad air da maccaib féin
Ro chan re draithib co nim,
Ergid, dingbaid na clerig.

cathraig), a city, and also a *cahir*, or stone fort=Brit. *Caer*.

[1] *Sraip*[*tene*]. The *tene* is suppressed in the original, to avoid a false measure, about which the Irish poets were very exact.

[2] *Culglas;* "of the grey locks." This word has been added for the sake of metre.

Son of Muiredach, son of Fiacha Sraip[tene],[1]
Son of Cairpre, son of Cormac Culglas,[2]
Son of Art, who was son of Conn, to whom
I have traced the pedigree of Fergna.
From that famous Fergna's time
The name of the *cahir*[3] was changed.
Here's for you the change of name
That was given to Fergna's *cahir*:[3]
"Fidhnacha;" from the noble *fednach*[4]
Which Caillin brought to his fair Dun.
Then Caillin and his saints came
Against Fergna of the fair hair,
And offered him a noble consideration:
A long life in good existence.[5]
'Twas then that Fergna said
To Aedh Dubh, his mighty son;
"Arise, and fiercely expel
Those clerics from out the land."
Thereupon quickly arose
The jet-black Aedh, with his cavalry,
To send the clerics back again,
And to expel them from the fair Dun.
When the mild, jet-black Aedh
Saw Caillin and his saints a-kneeling,
He and his host bravely believed for them;
And he presented to them the fair Dun.
As soon as Fergna plainly saw
That he had been betrayed by his own sons,
He venomously[6] sang out to his druids,
"Go ye, and repel the clerics."

[3] *cahir*. See note [11], p. 125.

[4] *fednach*. See note , p. 114, *ante*. This derivation is very far-fetched.

[5] *in good existence*. The original, ın ndegbethaıd, means in "good life." "In good estate" would give the sense.

[6] *Venomously*. co nım; lit. "with poison." co nem, A.

Ergid na draithi co luas,
  Is cuirid a tona suas,
  Is gluaisit a nguib con grain;
  Tainic na naimh co hegair.
O't connairc Aed mac Fergna
  Na draithi ag techt co ferda,
  Ro chan re a muintir comblaith,
  Ergid dingbaid in trom daim.
Ni rachat ar Caillin uain
  Do marbad nan druth co cruaid,
  Acht mirbaile De do nim
  Do chor nan druth i clochaibh.
O da connairc Fergna in sguir
  Na druith do chor i g-clochaib
  Ro fhagaib a slogh co gur
  Co Fan coba tre mirun.
Ge do tuit in talam trean
  Mo Fergna is he a aenaran,
  Ni móide do chred Dia dil
  Gur sgar a chorrp re a anmain.
IArsin tig int aingel coim
  In onoir Chaillin 'sa noimh;
  Atfet co solus andsin
  Fergna do dul fon talmuin.
Andsin do raid int aingel
  In onóir Chaillin credhuil,[a]
  Tabraid in rigi d'Aed dub,
  Gairmther a slois na fharrud.

[a] fol. 14, a 1.

[1] *backs.* tona; lit. "podices." O'Donovan translates "tunics." (*Breifny Letters*, R. I. Acad., p. 186.) See the curious account of the "Races of Feradach" in Todd's edition of *Cogadh Gaedhel re Gallaibh*, p. 83, where captive women were driven along on all fours. And see also his note on the subject; Introd. cxxii., note [2].

[2] *into stones.* See note [4], p. 116, *supra.*

[3] *of the steeds;* or rather "of the stud." in sguir. sgor, of which sguir (recte

The druids arise quickly,
And turn up their backs;[1]
And their jaws move angrily,
As they unjustly revile the clerics.
When Aedh son of Fergna saw
The druids advancing boldly,
He said to his renowned people,
"Arise; and repel the great company."
"They shall not go from us," said Caillin,
"To slay the druids rigorously;
But the miracles of God from Heaven
Shall change the druids into stones."[2]
When Fergna of the steeds[3] beheld
The druids changed into stones,
He furiously left his army,
[And went] to Fan-Cobha, through evil mind.
And although the mighty earth sank
Under Fergna, and he all alone,
Not the more did he believe the loving God,
Until his soul departed from his body.[4]
After that came the mild Angel,
In honour of Caillin and his saints,
And then plainly[5] related
That Fergna[6] had gone under the ground.
Then the Angel said,
In honour of devout Caillin:
"Give ye the kingship to Aedh Dubh;
Let his army be summoned unto him."

scuir) is the gen., signifies a stud of horses, and also a tent.

[4] *body*. The literal translation of this line is "until his body separated from his soul," rather a peculiar manner of expressing the action of dying.

[5] *plainly*. co ꞅoluꞅ, lit., "with light." It is probably an error for co ꝼoluꞅ (*recte* co ꝼolluꞅ), plainly.

[6] *Fergna*. Ꝼeꞃᵹnai, A.

Arsin do atuig Aed dub
  Int aingel caem ba bind guth,
  Abair re Caillin nemda
  Gan laech dub na tigerna.
Epair for re Crist nemda,
  Tabrad dam roga ndelba,
  Mad ail les mo beṫ abus
  Ar ḟlaithuṡ i tigernus.
Do raid int aingel annso
  Re Caillin uasal idon,
  Tabair mar sud d'Aeḋ a breṫ
  Aṁail do ṡir gan eteċ.
Caillin is a noiṁ iarsoin
  Troisgit re Dia co madoin,
  Gur bo hAed findgel Aed dub
  Iar nergi do as a ċollud.
Tig Aed cus in cairṫi amaċ,
  I primdorus na caṫrach,
  Co tug annsin ferand tra
  Do Chaillin, da anmchara.
Annsin do raid Caillin fein,
  Re hAed mac Fergna co ceill,
  Nem duit is dot chloinn gan fell,
  Acht co togat mo ċaeṁ ċell.
Gach Brefnech toġus mo chell,
  Ar Caillin re hAed na lenn,
  Gobḟagu nem as gach muġ,
  Is gombe a cland na inuḃ.

[1] *holy.* nemda, lit. "heavenly," A.

[2] *wish.* The original is breṫ, which properly means "award," or "judgment."

[3] *black Aedh.* Aed dubh (Aedh Dubh).

[4] *fair-white Aedh.* Aed findgel. The last syllable (gel) is added for the sake of metre. Aedh Find (fair Aedh) is the name by which the former "black" Aedh is called henceforward in this work.

[5] *pillar-stone.* See note [2], p. 120.

[6] *cahir.* See note [11], p. 125.

[7] *soul's friend.* anmchara; from anm

Aedh Dubh after that besought
The pure Angel of sweetest voice:
"Say to holy[1] Caillin,
That a black warrior should not be Lord."
"Say, moreover, to Heavenly Christ,
That He grant me my choice of features,
If He wishes that I should be here,
In sovereignty over princes."
Hereupon spake the Angel,
To pure, illustrious Caillin:
"Grant so his wish[2] to Aedh,
As he has sought, without refusal."
Caillin and his saints, afterwards,
Fasted before the Lord until morning,
So that black Aedh[3] was fair-white Aedh[4]
When he from his slumber rose.
Aedh came out to the pillar-stone[5]
In the principal door of the *cahir*[6];
And he then, moreover, presented land
To Caillin, his soul's friend.[7]
Then Caillin himself said
To the wise Aedh son of Fergna:
"Heaven for thee, and for thy guileless race,
Provided they select[8] my fair church."
"May every Breifnian that selects my church,"
Said Caillin to Aedh of the spears,
"Obtain Heaven in every way,[9]
And may his children be in his place."[10]

(*recte* anam)=anima, and cara, "a friend" (cf. Lat. *carus*). The word is generally used in the sense of "confessor," or "spiritual adviser." See Reeves *On the Culdees*, Trans. R. I. Acad., vol. xxiv., p. 88.

[8] *select*; i.e. as a place of sepulture.

[9] *in every way*. ar gach mug. The word mug is by mistake for mud=modus. The expression is equal to Lat. omnimodo.

[10] *be in his place*; i.e. succeed him.

Togaimsi tu a Chaillin chaith,
Ar Aed mac Fergna co blaith;
Nem is rath dot chloind gan gai,
Acht co togat dun mbaili.

*fol. 14, a 2.

On huair sin ar bairted Aed,
Adeirim rib ni rad saeb,
Ised ro chaith Aed na n-agh,
Da bliadain ar sechtmogat.
Ac ibar na rig arsin
Ro hadhnacht Aed go deimhin,
Fa leic na naingel gan gai,
Ar lar relgi Dunn Baili. D. mb.
IS me Flann mac Flaind ro chan
In senchussa co huasal,
Do Chaillin ont sen mag ur
Do sil Aedha sa chaoimh dun. D. mbaili. r.b.c.

IS don chuairt sin dliges Caillin do sil Aedha find, ocus amail ro thuill a fagbhail, ro labair Caillin fein isin duain remain .i. "Eri oll oilen aingel"; ocus cuirfemni drong dona rannaibsin annso, ar is usaide a cuimniugad.

Caillin dixit:

IS hi mo chainsi dom thigh,
O sil Aedha find fledhaigh,
Screpall gach cairchigh co sir,
Ech is erred gach ardrig.

[1] *Heaven.* This line and the following are supposed to be spoken by St. Caillin.

[2] *of the battles.* na nogh, for na nagh, A.

[3] *seventy.* lxx. at, A.

[4] *Relig*; i.e. cemetery.

[5] *Flann, son of Flann.* See note [8], p. 123, *supra.* The foregoing poem, which is not in B., was certainly not composed by "Flann of the Monastery," who died A.D. 1056. It is not mentioned in the authentic lists of Flann's compositions. See O'Curry's *Manners and Customs*, ii. 149, sq. The copy in this *Book of Fenagh* is the only one known.

[6] *Dun.* The characters representing the first line of the poem are added at the close in A., according to the practice of Irish scribes, as already alluded to.

"Thee, holy Caillin, do I choose,"
Quoth Aedh son of Fergna, the renowned.
"Heaven[1] and prosperity be to thy race,
Provided that they choose Dun-Baile."
From that hour in which Aedh was baptized,
(I tell you, 'tis no false assertion),
The time that Aedh of the battles[2] lived
Was two years and seventy.[3]
At the yew of the kings, afterwards,
Aedh was certainly buried;
Under the flag of the Angels, truly,
In the middle of the *Relig*[4] of Dun-Baile.
I am Flann, son of Flann,[5] who sang
This narrative most noble,
Of Caillin from the old green plain,
For the race of Aedh, and his fair Dun.[6]

It is of that tribute to which Caillin is entitled from the descendants of Aedh Find, and the way he deserved to obtain it, that Caillin himself spoke in the poem above,[7] to wit,

"Noble Ireland, Isle of Angels";

and we shall set down here a number of the stanzas, that they may be the more easily remembered.

CAILLIN dixit:[8]

My tribute to my house is,
From the race of festive Aedh Find,
A *screpall*,[9] truly, out of every sheepfold,
The steed and battle dress of each arch-king.

[7] *above.* ꞃemαın; lit. "before us," A.

[8] *dixit.* The text in B. recommences, on fol. 115 b, with this fragment. The stanzas here repeated are those printed above, viz., from the last stanza on p. 78, to the last stanza on p. 82, inclusive. On fol. 115 a, in B. however, a pedigree of St. Caillin is given, which it is not necessary to reproduce here, as it agrees with the pedigree printed *supra*, pp. 4–6.

[9] *screpall.* See note [6], p. 79, *supra*. The note cáın αꞃ ꞅıol Ccoḋα ꝼínꝺ etc.

Edaċ ech gaċ toisiġ caiḋ,
Etir chend is ċois is laiṁ,
Séirraċ maiṫ on riġ co raṫ
'Sa tabairt a laiṁ ṁabaḋ.
Dligim don rigan co raṫ
A heċ ocus a hetaċ.
Dligim don bantoisiġ feil,
Etaċ is eċ dom ogreir.
Do gach biatuig oin baili,
O Aṫ droiċit co Sligeċ,
Do gaḃála da gaċ creiċ
O gach mac rig is taiseċ.[a]
An dalta 'sa mic fethar,
Dligimsi dib go trebar,
Mad ail leo a ndutchus co daith,
Tabrad a cuairt dom cathraig.
ISsi sin mo ċain gan [f]ell
O sil Aeda na ferann;
Amenci dligim in chain
Gaċ tres bliadain co comlan.
Gid cuiċ naċ tibri mo ċain,
Mar aderim dom chill ċaiḋ,
A ndutċus ni geḃa a clann,
Ocus do gebat ifernn.
Gid cuich dobera mo ċain,
Mar aderim dom chill ċaiḋ,
Saerfad a cined 'sa clann,
Naċ gebat goill a ferann.
Gairsed glassaige do sir,
Aed dub mac Fergna in milid,
Is delb Rioc ba find dath,
Do tabairt do ar na bairted.

[a] fol. 14, b 1.

ó ḋroiċet aṫa co Sligioċ .i. an breifne; "The tribute on the Race of Aedh Find, &c., from Drogheda to Sligo, i.e. the Breifne," is added in the margin in A.

[1] *coll.* seirraċ, B. A. has seissec, "team," as in line 3, p. 80.

The cavalry dress of each noble chief,
    Between head, and leg, and hand ;
    A good colt[1] from the prosperous king—
    And they to be given into my abbot's hand.
I claim as my due from the gracious queen,
    Her steed and her dress ;
    I claim from the generous chieftainess,
    A dress and a steed, at my demand.
A cow from every one-bally Biatagh,[2]
    From Drogheda to Sligo ;
    A fat cow out of every prey,
    From each son of a king and chieftain.
The foster-son, and the sisters' sons—
    I exact from them, discreetly,
    If they desire their inheritance quickly,
    That they bring their tribute to my city.
This is my tribute, without guile,[3]
    From Aedh's descendants in their land ;
    The tribute is due to me as often as
    Every third year fully.
Whosoever furnishes not my tribute,
    As I say, to my holy church—
    His children shall not obtain their inheritance ;
    And they shall obtain Hell.
But whosoever furnishes my tribute,
    As I say, to my holy church—
    I will save his kin, and his children ;
    Foreigners shall not possess their land.
The championship of the Glasraige[4] he sought—
    Aedh Dubh son of Fergna, the knight—
    And the form of Riocc[5] of fairest hue ;
    To be given to him after his baptism.

[2] *Biatagh.* See note [3], p. 80, *supra.*

[3] *guile.* This stanza is not in the poem above printed, p. 80.

[4] *Glasraige.* See note [1], p. 82, *supra.*

[5] *Riocc.* See note [4], *ib.*

Oed ger dub in cathmilid,
Do bairter he gan time;
Is miri do rinde de
Aed findglan is lor finde.
Me do rat is nir merte,
Dethbir ar deilb na deiri;
Coroin i cind Rioicc gil,
Aed finn gan choroin itir.
Uime sin do ratad dam
In chuairt mor sin dom fognam;
'S ar a chorp do breċ dom chill,
Cid c'ait bud marb in Erinn.
O da bairtius Aed comblaid
Gur adluicer he im doirċoiġ,
Eaḋ ro chaith in ri gan gaitt,
Da bliadain ar sechtmogaitt.

Ni beag sin do sgribad isin inadsa, oir ata ní is mo ina sin ar ċlainn Fergna isin duain moir .i. Eri oll oilen aingel.[a]

[a] fol. 14, b 2.

Mad ail a fis tra amail' fuair naem Chaillin mac Niataċ in ċuairt dliges do chlan[n]aib Conaill mic Neill .i. dona secht maccaib oiregdae batar aige, ocus da fil co brath, gurab do derbad na cloinde sin, ocus dia n-anman[n]aib, adubrad in rannsa,

Fergus, Aengus, Eochaid, Enna,
Nati, Ruaman, dluigdis fuilt;
Itiat sin fri sithblad soḋaing
Secht mic Conaill gulbain guirt.

1 *whiteness.* See note 5, p. 82.

2 *crown.* The coronal tonsure. See note 6, p. 83.

3 *tribute.* cuairt. See note 8, *ib.*

4 *seventy.* lx. aitt, A. B.; which is incorrect.

5 *that is enough.* Ni beag sin; lit. "that is not little."

6 *in this place.* desin, "of that," B.

7 *more than that.* moran, "much," B.

8 *Fergna.* The remainder of the sentence is represented by the words inar ndiaid tuas, "after us above," in B.; in which follows the poem beginning cotlad sind imdairiu (see *infra*, p. 154).

9 *If.* This portion of the text in B. follows after the introduction to the poem beginning "Dun-Baile, &c.," p. 123, *supra.*

Though black was the warrior Aedh,
I baptized him, without fear.
It was I that made of him
Pure-fair Aedh of ample whiteness.[1]
'Twas I that made, and it was no harm,
A distinction 'twixt the appearance of both;
A crown[2] on the head of fair Riocc;
Aedh Find without a crown[2] at all.
This is the reason why to me was given
That great tribute,[3] for my use;
And for bringing his body to my church,
Wheresoever in Ireland he might die.
From the hour I baptized Aedh the Famous,
Until I buried him in my oratory,
The time the guileless king spent
Was two years and seventy.[4]

That is enough[5] to write in this place;[6] for there is more than that[7] regarding the clan of Fergna[8] in the great poem, to wit, "Noble Ireland, Isle of Angels."

If[9] it is desired to know how St. Caillin, son of Niata, obtained the tribute to which he is entitled from the children of Conall son of Niall, to wit, from the seven illustrious sons he had,[10] and from their descendants, for ever, [be it known] that it was in proof of those sons, and of their names,[11] this *rann* was spoken:—

Fergus, Aengus,[12] Eochaidh, Enna;
Nathi, Ruamann—who cleft heads—
These were, with enduring fame,
The seven[13] sons of stern Conall Gulban.

[10] *he had.* bacaṗ aige. Transposed in A.

[11] *and of their names.* The corresponding words in the text, omitted in B., are transposed in A.

[12] *Aengus.* The sobriquet "Boguine" is added over this name in A.; but it belonged to Enna.

[13] *seven.* Only six are mentioned in the stanza.

Isiat so sila na mac sin neoch da ndliġend Caillin a ċis .i. clann Dalaig[1] in rigraid cetus, ocus cinel mBogaine,[2] ocus cinel Lugdech,[3] ocus cinel Móildoraig,[4] ocus hI Chanannan, ocus mic Gilli Findein, ocus sil Chonaill archena.

Ba he Conall ba cet ri Teṁra do ċlan[n]aib Neill co taratt fein do Laegaire iaraċt na rigi; ocus ba cloch in inaḋ uiġi sin; Uair ba he Conall ro bris caeca cath ic cosnaṁ Erenn, ocus ni ro brised cath na comlan fair riam. Ni dernad olc na ecraitte fri nech dia braithrib nach fri Conall do ċoraitfed; ocus ni gabad Conall crod

[a] fol. 15, a 1.

na coma tar a eiss, acht cenn curaid no caṫmilid dia ic.[a]

Ro bai imorro nert ocus niadachus Cuind cetchathaig ina athairsium .i. Niall naigiallach, ocus bai nert Neill i Conall fein.

Ishe do roind forba dia ḃraiṫrib, ocus dobert leth n-Ulaḋ do fein a aenar, ocus alleṫ naill dia braithrib, daig is he fein ro chosain in cuigeḋ sin doib.

Fecht naen dia n-dechatar Marraigca Moigi slecht ar creich go Temraig, go tarttsat leo echraid anair. Doracht Conall fo na heghmib cussin uathaid sloig bai ina ḟarrad in tan sin, ocus ni ro an dib co riacht co dun Conaing ar Muig rein .i. Fidnacha [h]odie, go rogonsat sen tuaṫa slecht he, ar ba diairm sium, ocus ni bad lam ar airgṫi doibrium sin mana deonaiged in toichṫi; no is ga reṫa ro marb he. Acht chena gid be dib a bas isiat Marraide ro maiḋset int echt.

[1] *Clann-Dalaigh*, or "descendants of Dalach." This was the tribe name of the great sept from which the O'Donnells of Tirconnell, and their correlatives, have sprung. Dalach died in 868. From his grandson, Domhnall, the O'Donnells derive their hereditary surname.

[2] *Cinel-Boghaine.* The descendants of Enna Boghaine, son of Conall Gulban, who have given name to the barony of Bannagh, co. Donegal.

[3] *Cinel-Luigdech.* This would seem to have been the original tribe name of the O'Donnell sept, before the time of Dalach (ob. 868), who was the first person of the O'Donnell race that obtained entire sway over the territory of Tirconnell, or Donegal. Dalach was fifth in descent from Lughaid (*a quo* "Cinel-Luigdech"), great-grandson of Conall Gulban.

[4] *Cinel-Maeldoraidh.* The family of Muldory, or O'Muldory, descended from Maeldoraidh, fourth in descent from Flaithbertach, king of Ireland 727–734, were chiefs of Tirconnell, alternately with the

These are the descendants of those sons, from whom Caillin is entitled to his tribute, viz., the Clann-Dalaigh,[1] the kingly sept, firstly; and the Cinel-Boghaine;[2] and Cinel-Luigdech;[3] and Cinel-Macldoraidh;[4] and the Ui-Canannain, and Mec Gilla-Finnein,[5] and the race of Conall besides.

It was Conall that was the first king of Temhair[6] of the sons of Niall, until he himself gave the loan of the kingship to Laeghaire. And that was "a stone in the place of a egg;"[7] for it was Conall that broke fifty battles contending for Ireland; and neither battle nor combat was ever broken upon him. No injury or injustice was done to any of his brethren, that would not be complained of to Conall; and Conall would not accept cattle or considerations therefor, but the head of a knight or warrior should pay for it. Moreover, the strength and valour of Hundred-battle Conn was in his [Conall's] father Niall Nine-hostage; and the strength of Niall was in Conall himself.

It was he that distributed land to his brothers. And he gave the half of Uladh to himself alone, and the other half to his brothers; for it was he himself that defended that province for them.

One time the Masraidhe[8] of Magh-Slecht went on a predatory expedition to Tara, when they brought a prey of horses with them from the east. Conall, on hearing the shoutings, proceeded with the small number that was near him at the time; and he ceased not from [pursuing] them until he came to Dun-Conaing on Magh-Rein, to wit, Fidhnacha at this day. And the old Tuatha-Slecht[9] slew him, because he was unarmed; and that would not have been an occasion of slaughter[10] to them, if luck had not willed. Or it is a flying spear that killed him. But whichever of them was his [manner of] death, it was the Masraidhe that committed the deed.

O'Canannans, before the Clann-Dalaigh (see notes [1],[3]) rose to power.

[5] *Mec Gilla-Finnein.* This name is now generally Anglicised Leonard.

[6] *Temhair.* Tara. This statement is not found in any other authority; and is a mere flourish on the part of the writer, who wished to magnify, as much as possible, the character of Conall-Gulban, whose descendants paid dues to the Abbots of Fenagh.

[7] *egg.* This is a proverbial saying frequently used by Irish writers.

[8] *Masraidhe.* See note [10], p. 89, *supra.*

[9] *old Tuatha-Slecht;* or old tribes of Magh-Slecht, i.e. the Masraidhe.

[10] *an occasion of slaughter.* The expression lam ar airgṫi is rather obscure, and would seem to be some proverbial form of observation.

Cid tra acht ro ladh a lia ocus a lecht in ti Conaill ar Muig fein icc Dun mbaili.

Coicc bliadna ocus leth bliadhuin imorro, iar mbas Conaill, doriacht Caillin cussin inad sin, ocus bai ic tabairt chuarta in choem ferainn sin co fuair lecht Conaill chathchalmae,[a] gu ro foillrighed do amail fuair Conall bas, ocus a beth i fen iarum.

Ba trog thra ocus ba tuirsech la Caillin in ní sin. Iarsin ro tinoil Caillin naim Erend huili d'forglai, ocus clanna Conaill atuaid. Ro throisce Caillin ocus naim Erend ma thodhusgadh Conaill. ACCsruidiu ro thodiusgad Conall a bas ocus a fein do. Do riacht leo comicce an eclais. Ro morad ainm De ocus Caillin tritt sin. Ro baisteadh he iarum a clug na righ. Oen anosin dia raibe dosom a ainm. Ro Bendaig Caillin ocus naeim hErend Conall iarsin, ocus ro hongad Conall iarsin dono.

ACCRsuidiu ro ordaigh Conall cain for a chloind do Chaillin ocus da chomarba ocus da famuid co brath. Isi so in chain ro gealladh ann a fiadhnaisi naem Erend .i. Ech gabail ocus sliasta gach rig ocus a dechelt dathai, ocus cendaige Conallach co brath. Each gach ban-toisighi. Uingi d'or no a fiach gach toisigh. ACCgh tri nglac o gach baili biathur ri. Screpall gach cairchig. A hic gach tres bliadain co brath.

Bennacht naem hErend ocus Conaill, ocus bithbennacht Chaillin, do chloind nDalaigh[b] ocus do chined Conaill archena ar chomallad na

[a] fol. 15, a 2.

[b] fol. 15, b 1.

[1] *grave.* The place where Conall Gulban was first interred is not now known to tradition, unless the remarkable Dolmen at Fenagh, represented in the illustration to this volume, may mark the site. The words fath na cana for cinel cconuill gulban; "the reason of the tribute on the descendants of Conall Gulban," are added in the margin.

[2] *Clog-na-Righ.* The "Bell of the Kings," so called from the number of kings baptized out of it. This bell still exists, and is preserved in the R. C. Church at Foxfield, near Fenagh, where it is regarded as a sacred relic. See an account of it by the Rev. W. Reeves, D.D.; *Proceedings* R. I. Acad., vol. 8, p. 445. It is stated further on that St. Patrick gave Clog-na-Righ to St. Caillin. Dr. Reeves describes it as circular in form, and resembling an inverted globe; being very unlike other bells in shape and

Howsoever, the stone and grave[1] of Conall were placed on Magh-Rein, at Dun-Baile.

Five years and a half, moreover, after Conall's death, Caillin came to that place; and he was making a circuit of that fair land, until he found the grave[1] of battle-strong Conall, when it was manifested to him how Conall died, and that he was afterwards in torment. This was sad and grievous to Caillin.

Caillin afterwards assembled the greater number of the saints of all Ireland, and the children of Conall from the north. Caillin and the saints of Ireland fasted regarding the resuscitation of Conall. Thereupon, Conall was resuscitated from death and pain by him; and came along with them as far as the church. The name of God, and [the name] of Caillin, were magnified thereby.

He [Conall] was afterwards baptized out of Clog-na-Righ;[2] and he was one of those from whom its name was derived. Caillin and the saints of Ireland blessed Conall after that; and Conall was subsequently anointed also.

After these things Conall ordained a tribute from his children to Caillin, and to his *comarb*[3] and congregation, for ever. This is the tribute that was promised there, in the presence of the saints of Ireland, viz., the yoke and riding horse of every king, and his coloured mantle, and the *cendaige*[4] of the Conallachs for ever. A steed from every chieftainess. An ounce of gold, or its value, from every chieftain. An *agh tri nglac*[5] from every *bally* that supplies[6] a king. A *screpall* from every sheepfold. All to be paid every third year for ever.

The blessing of the saints of Ireland, and of Conall; and the everlasting blessing of Caillin, be upon the Clann-Dalaigh and the race of Conall besides,

pattern, wherefore it might be considered of modern date, if it were not mentioned in old authorities.

[3] *comarb*, i.e. successor. The note ᴀn ċᴀın ꝼoꞃ ċınel conᴀıll ᵹulbᴀn, ⁊c; "the tribute on the race of Conall Gulban, &c.," is added in the margin.

[4] *cendaige*. The meaning of this word is not clear; but it probably signifies "customs," or "donations."

[5] *agh tri nglac*; lit. a "cow of three hands;" i.e. in which the flesh should be three hands in thickness, or width, in some part.

[6] *that supplies*. bıᴀꞇhuꞅ; i.e. that furnishes food-tribute.

cana sa. Bithmallacht ocus trist ocus anorait naem hErend doibrium mana chomallat.

Is iat raṫa na cana sin Patraicc apstal Erend cona noemaib, ocus Michel con ainglib nime. Adamnan iarsin in tan tainig.

Is iat buada ro ḟaġaib Caillin i fagbalaib doib ar a comall .i. buaḋ catha rompa; buad n-indscne ocus n-ergna ocus n-irlabra; buad forba ocus tindscetail; buad n-dealba ocus buad n-denmasa. Buad ngormac ocus gilla ocus dalta; buad rig ocus rigna; buad n-amus ocus n-ardoglach, ocus firgaisgedaiġ. Buad clainni ocus buad comairli; buad cell ocus clerech; buad n-oirfitech; buad gaband. Buad toicti ocus trom conaig. Fot saegail ocus fochraic tre bitha do chinel Conaill ar chomallad na cana sa. Grain chatha air gach nonbar dib, ocus grain nonbair air gach n-en duine aca ag a n-egraitte.

Ro tharngir umorro do Chonall Caillin iarsin congenfed gein n-airegda uaḋ, ocus combad lan Albai ocus Eri dia chlu .i. Collam cilli; ocus ro tharngir for Adamnan iarsin; ocus atbert dono comad e fein oide na deiri sin.

[a] fol. 15, b 2. Is iarsin fuair Conall bas.[a] Ro adluic iarum Caillin Conall gulpan iarsin co n-onóir ocus co n-airmitin moir, co torruma chlerech ocus naem, in doirthaig Chaillin fein; ocus ro daingnig Colum cilli iarum in chain sin for chloind Conuill.

Is do ḃas ocus do aiṫbeoagad Conuill, ocus do tharngire na rig ticfaitis huada, adubrad in duan sa.

C. cc.

Eta sunn lecht Conaill chruaid;
Mor fecht rig buaid ar gaċ leth;

[1] *reprobation.* anorait, "evil prayer;" from an (a negat. particle), and orait= oratio.

[2] *virtues.* buada, nom. pl. of buaid, glossed "victoria," Zeuss, 27; and "palma," ib. 262.

[3] *of form.* denmasa. denma, A.

[4] *nephews.* gormac. See note [2], p. 92.

[5] *success of battle.* See note [4], p. 92.

[6] *against.* ag; lit. "with." There is a note in the margin, apparently referring to this preposition, which is rather obscure.

if they observe this tribute. The perpetual malediction, and curse, and reprobation[1] of the saints upon them, unless they observe it.

The guarantees of that tribute are Patrick, apostle of Ireland, with his saints; and Michael with the Angels of Heaven; and Adamnan, afterwards, when he came.

The virtues[2] which Caillin left to them as gifts, for observing the tribute, are victory in battle before them; the palm of learning, and wisdom, and eloquence. The palm of ending and of beginning. The palm of features, and the palm of form.[3] Luck of nephews,[4] and of *gillas*, and foster-children. Luck of kings and queens. Luck of soldiers, and of noble heroes and true warriors. Luck of children, and luck of counsel. Luck of churches and clerics. Luck of minstrels. Luck of smiths. The palm of prosperity and great wealth. Length of life, and eternal reward, to the Cenel-Conaill for observing this tribute. Success of battle[5] on each ennead of them; and the puissance of nine in each man of them, against[6] their enemies.

Caillin also prophesied to Conall, afterwards, that an illustrious offspring should be born from him, and that Alba and Ireland would be full of his renown, to wit, Colum Cille. And he further prophesied Adamnan after that. And he also said that he himself would be the tutor of that pair.[7]

It was after this that Conall died. Thereupon Caillin buried Conall Gulban, subsequently, with great honour and reverence, with the attendance of clerics and saints, in Caillin's own oratory. And Colum Cille afterwards confirmed that tribute on Conall's children.

It is regarding the death and resuscitation of Conall, and to foretell the kings who would descend from him, this poem was composed.[8]

CAILLIN[9] cecinit.

Behold here the grave of hardy Conall,
Who often achieved victory on every side;

It is .i. a chlaen, no comad delidín .g. is ferr an inad an duir thuas, iar nurd Ogma mic elathain; "its oblique [case]; or perhaps the inversion of g [scil. ga for ag] is better, instead of the *dur* (d) above, according to the arrangement of Ogma son of Elathan." What *d* is referred to does not plainly appear.

[7] *pair*. See note [4], p. 95.

[8] *was composed*. adubrad, lit. "was said."

[9] CAILLIN. C., A. In B. it is stated

Sochaide do chuir in eg,
Mor cuire, mor ced, mor chrech.
Ba ruathar rig techtad treoin,
In leoman lond re nert niad;
Ni bai cineḋ ar nar chlai,
Re gai, re chlaidib, re sciaṫ.
A chathreim mar Tuathal techt,
In fer sa 'sa lecht os tu;
A gaisced amail Choin Cuailnge,
Ag breth buaide os gach du.
Mac Nell naigiallaig na nert,
Is laeċda a leċt air muig fein;
Ar chomairċi in rig soscairim,
Go tuca a ainim a pein.
Dun Conaing so cur aniu,
Re reimess sescat rig raiṫ,
No cor taeṫ Conall mac Nell
Re cloind in leṫ os bern braiṫ.
Bernn in braiṫ cus in la aniu,
O braṫ Conaill ċinn in chuain;
Fionachai Caillin mic Net;
A ainm gan breg go lá in luain.
fol. 16, a 1. Indiaid eċ tainic co tren
Anoir o Themraig na tret;
In uaite sloig, ba toirg baeth,
Mar ṫaeth re sen Tuathaib Slecht.

that "Colam Cille cecinit hoc carmen," But it appears from the poem that Caillin should be regarded as the author. A marginal note, nevertheless, has tomti son, "a conjecture, truly."

[1] *Tuathal Techtmar.* Tuathḟ techt in A.; (the word techt being put for Techtmar, to avoid a metrical error. B. has tuathaib techt, which is wrong, as the intention of the poet plainly was to compare Conall with Tuathal Techtmar, monarch of Ireland in the first cent., from whom Conall was descended in the tenth generation.

[2] *Cu of Cuailnge;* i.e. Cuchulaind.

[3] *sixty.* sescat. lx., A., B.

Multitudes to death he sent—
Great bands, great hundreds, great armies.
Regal his onslaught subduing the strong—
The furious lion of heroic might;
No sept was there over which he did not triumph,
With spear, with sword, with shield.
Like Tuathal Techtmar's[1] was the battle-career
Of this man over whose grave I stand;
His valour like that of Cu of Cuailnge,[2]
Triumphing over every land.
The son of mighty Niall Nine-Hostage—
Heroic his grave on Magh-Rein.
May the King whom I love, in mercy,
Deliver his soul from pain.
Dun-Conaing was this place [called], till to day,
During the time of sixty[3] prosperous kings,
Until Conall son of Niall fell,
By the sons of the Liath,[4] over the gap of treachery.
Berna-in-braith[5] was its name[6] until this day,
From the betrayal of Conall, the head of the host;
Fidhnacha of Caillin son of Niata[7]
Shall be its name, without falsehood, to the day of doom.[8]
In pursuit of horses he stoutly came,
From the east, from Tara of the flocks,
With a small company; 'twas a foolish journey,
For he was slain by the old Tuatha-Slecht.[9]

[4] *Liath.* gen. Leth. This person has not been identified.

[5] *Berna-in-braith*; lit. "gap of treachery."

[6] *its name*; i.e. another name for Fenagh.

[7] *Niata.* The gen. sg. is written net, to avoid a metrical error; but it is niatach where it occurs in the text generally.

[8] *day of doom.* lá in luain; lit., the "day of the Monday," A. B. furnishes an alias reading, lá in luaig, "the day of the reward." *La in Luain* is an expression still used for the "day of judgment." See the use made by St. Moling of the ambiguous meaning of the expression, Reeves's *Adamnan*, p. xlix.

[9] *old Tuatha-Slecht.* See note [9], p. 139.

A gae cro do ṫuill don triaṫ
  Beṫ gan sciath re saitib sleg;
  Imatt fer is imat airm
  Fuaratar i faill in fer.
Bettra ag suiḋi riġ na rend,
  Is gabail psalm os a leic,
  Malle rem trichaitt fer ngraid,
  Uair is baig leam mar do cred.
Ar mo chomairche do chuaid,
  Ic techt atuaid dar leacht dam,
  Do gell condingned mo riar
  Fo mo mian gemad cian gar.
Gach gein buaḋa co ti brath
  Genfes uada 'sin tir tuaid,
  Cach oin dib nach craid mo ruiri,
  Daib uile faicfiut gach buaid.
Bennaiġim Fergus co fir,
  Combia rem rig ar a slicht;
  Bennaigim Setna na sruan,
  Combia co cian ina ċirt.
Ainmire is Lugaid na long;
  Bennaigim da glond na cath;
  Uaithib in flaithes co fir,
  Imat rig ar ambia rath.
Gebthar uada fo do dec
  Eri na ba breg in breth;
  Is cethrar do sil in duind
  Gebtaitt co tuind luim aleṫ.

1 *Being.* beṫ. agus beith, "and being," B.

2 *will.* mian. miad, "respect," A. and B.

3 *Fergus*, surnamed *Cenn-fota*, or "long-head," son of Conall Gulban.

4 *Setna.* Son of Fergus called *Cenn-fota.* Sennta, B.

5 *Ainmire.* Anmiri, A. Grandson of Fergus Cenn-fota, son of Conall Gulban, and monarch of Ireland, A.D. 568–571.

6 *Lugaid.* Brother of Ainmire, and

Being[1] without a shield against lance-thrusts
Was what caused the king his mortal wound.
Too many men, and too many weapons,
Found the man at a disadvantage.
I shall be entreating the King of the stars,
And singing psalms over his grave,
Along with my thirty men of grade;
For 'tis a joy to me how he believed.
Under my protection he went,
As I was coming from the north past his tomb;
He promised that he would obey my commands,
According to my will,[2] whether long [or] short.
Every fortunate offspring descended from him,
Until doom comes, in the northern land—
Each one of them that vexes not my Lord,
To them all will I leave every virtue.
I bless Fergus,[3] truly,
That a race of kings may be of his family;
I bless Setna[4] of the bridles,
That he may be a long time in his right.
Ainmire[5] and Lugaid[6] of the ships,
Two battle champions, I bless.
From them, in truth, in the sovereignty
Shall be many kings who will have luck.
Twelve times by his descendants[7]
Shall Ireland be possessed—the judgments 's no lie.
And four of the seed of the Donn[8]
Shall obtain hither to Tond-Luim.[9]

ancestor of the Cenel-Luighdech, who occupied a district now comprised in the barony of Kilmacrenan, co. Donegal.

[7] *by his descendants.* uaᴅa, lit. "from him," (i.e. Conall Gulban).

[8] *Donn.* This seems to be an epithet applied to Conall, signifying a "king," or "prince," like Don. But the epithet is also applied to Domhnall Mór O'Donnell, chief of Tirconnell, ob. 1241. See note [11], p. 151.

[9] *Tond-Luim.* The "Wave of Lom." Probably the name of some place on the N.W. coast of Sligo.

Tan naċ biat os hErind uill
Ni gebatt cuiged acht i cath;
Ni biat gan mal dib fodein;
Ni craid mo ċell reim co raṫ.
Gaċa tres bliadna co Flann
[a]fol. 16, a 2. Dlegait ṫall[a] mo reir co daiṫ;
Nith ifos da fuirmett faill,
Dith tall mana tuirmet maiṫ.
Dechelt datha gaċ rig reil,
A ech gabail fen ro fer;
Cendaige Conaill in chuain,
Ar in tir tuaid bid he a lear.
Ag tri nglac dligim co fir
Ar gaċ baili biatur rig,
Da tucat brisit gach bern;
Noċo ticfa teidm na tir.
Cuig airdriġ naċ feallann orm,
Do sil Setna soirb in slicht;
Cuiciur naċ dingni mo riar,
Do gebat pian fir in firt.
Ainmiri Domnall nan dam;
Aed gan crad bid cara dam,
Flaithbertach firen is Moel
Dias do rer na noim gaċ tan.
Ticfa nonbar do sil Gairb,
Bid mor a tairm is tir tuaid;
Curi naċ craidend mo ċell
Bedit dom rer cid cian uaim.

[1] *obtain.* gebatt. gebuid, B.
[2] *Flann.* The Flann Cithach referred to in note [4], p. 62, *supra.*
[3] *yonder.* ṫall; i.e. within their territory of Tirconnell.
[4] *here*; i.e. in this world.
[5] *yonder.* In the world to come.
[6] *cendaige.* See note [4], p. 141.
[7] *agh-tri-nglac.* See note [5], p. 141.
[8] *break every gap.* In other words, overcome every opposition.
[9] *Setna.* enda, B.
[10] *five.* cuiciur. cuicer, B.
[11] *Ainmirè.* See note [5], p. 146.

When they are not over Noble Ireland,
They'll not obtain[1] a province, save by battle.
They'll not be without a chief of their own;
Nor will they annoy my church—a happy thing.
Every third year, 'till [the time of] Flann,[2]
They are bound yonder[3] to obey me readily.
Contention here[4] [shall be theirs], if they practise deceit;
Ruin yonder,[5] unless they practise good.
The coloured mantle of each manifest king;
His own yoke-steed, it is known;
The *cendaige*[6] of Conall of the host,
Out of the northern land, will be for his good.
An *agh-tri-nglac*[7] I truly exact
From every *bally* that victuals a king.
If they 'give it, they 'll break every gap;[8]
And pestilence shall not come into their land.
Five arch-kings will not deceive me,
Of the seed of Setna,[9] a proud race.
The five[10] who'll not obey my commands,
Shall suffer pain—true is the miracle.
Ainmire,[11] Domhnall[12] of the bands,
The tormentless Aedh,[13] shall be my friends;
Flaithbertach[14] the faithful, and Mael[15]—
Two after the manner of the saints at all times.
Nine shall come of the seed of Garbh,[16]
Whose fame will be great in the northern land;
Heroes who will not annoy my church,
Who'll be submissive to me, though a long time from me.

[12] *Domhnall.* Son of Aedh, son of Ainmirè, and k. of Ireland; ob. A.D. 642.

[13] *Aedh.* Father of the Domhnall mentioned in the last note, and king of Ireland. He was slain in A.D. 598, by Brandubh, k. of Leinster, in the battle of Dun-Bolg, near Dunlavin, co. Wicklow.

[14] *Flaithbhertach.* King of Ireland, A.D. 727–734. He was the grandson of Domhnall, referred to in note [12].

[15] *Mael*; i.e., Maelcobha, king of Ireland, 608–611, and brother of the Domhnall just referred to.

[16] *Garbh.* This chieftain was the grand-

Ecnechan Esa na rig,
Dam bid cara fir ro ferr;
Da es tresfear tall mo ċill
No co ti in mal co cliab nglas.
Cliab glas claitigi na cliab—
Domnall naċ dian ainm in fir;
Nocho gairit uaim acht cian
Tan do ni mo riar iartain.
Assin ticfa in feoċair fial,
Is gebaid gialla re gail;
Biaid icon ath tuaid a lecht,
Co becht resin sluag anair.
Ticfa o raiṫ ruaid in derg daith,
Bid flaith co cath in rois reid;
[a] fol. 16, b 1. Mebaiss[a] reme lam ri tuind;
Gebaid mac in duinn na deig.
Mac in duinn dirmaig na rend;
Bid ri tend Domnall naċ dis,
No congairthear ma mael mara,
Terc aicci cara ar nach clis.
Resechaid me ma caċ dail,
Mac in mail Bernais da benn;

son of Lughaidh, *a quo* the Cenel-Luigdech. See note [3], p. 138.

[1] *Ecnechan.* See note [5], p. 86, *supra.*

[2] *Es-na-righ.* The "Cataract of the kings"; now Assaroe, near Ballyshannon, co. Donegal.

[3] *Cliabh-glas.* Lit., "grey-chest."

[4] *Domhnall.* Domhnall Mór O'Donnell. See note [6], p. 87, *supra.*

[5] *warrior.* The warrior here referred to was evidently Melaghlin O'Donnell, successor of Domhnall Mór, who was slain by an army under Maurice FitzGerald, in A.D. 1247, at Ath-Senaigh (the "Ford of Senach"), now the ford at Ballyshannon, co. Donegal.

[6] *Ford in the North.* See last note.

[7] *the host from the East*; i.e. the English army. See note [5].

[8] *Rath-ruadh*; lit. "Red-rath." Possibly the place now called Rarooey, in the parish of Donegal, barony of Tirhugh, co. Donegal.

[9] *Derg-daith.* "Red colour." A nickname. The person alluded to was doubtless Godfrey O'Donnell, chief of Tirconnell, who died in 1258, from the effects of a wound received in a battle fought by

Ecnechan[1] of Es-na-righ.[2]
To me, 'tis known, will be a true friend.
After him, my church yonder will be abandoned,
Till comes the prince with the *cliabh-glas*.[3]
Cliabh-glas,[3] cleaver of bosoms—
Domhnall[4] not violent is the man's name.
Not a short, but a long while from me,
The time that he obeys me afterwards.
After that will come the generous warrior,[5]
Who will obtain hostages by valour.
His grave shall be at the Ford in the North,[6]
Prepared by the host from the East.[7]
From Rath-ruadh[8] will come the Derg-daith,[9]
Who'll be lord till the battle of smooth Ros;[10]
He will triumph onwards, along the sea.
The son of the Donn[11] will rule after him.
The son of the Donn of the armèd host
Will be a stout king, this Domhnall[12] not mean;
Till he is summoned unto Maelmara,[13]
Few his friends over whom he prevails not.[14]
He will obey me in all things—
The hero's son from two-peaked Bernas;[15]

him at Credran-Cille, in Ross-Cede, barony of Carbury, co. Sligo, against an English army commanded by Maurice FitzGerald, Justiciary of Ireland. The Four Mast. (A.D. 1258) relate that when almost about to expire, he had himself borne on his bier before his followers, during a conflict in which the Cenel-Eoghain (O'Neills) engaged them.

[10] *Ros. Ros-Cede* (pron. Roskedy). Now the Rosses, in the parish of Drumcliff, barony of Carbury, co. Sligo. See last note.

[11] *Donn.* A sobriquet for Domhnall Mor O'Donnell, whose son, Domhnall Og, was inaugurated chief of Tirconnell in 1258, in succession to Godfrey O'Donnell. See note [9].

[12] *Domhnall.* Called Domhnall Og, or young Donnell. See last note.

[13] *Maelmara.* The sense of this line is obscure.

[14] *prevails not.* At the end of this line in B. (fol 111, b.) the scribe adds the note aſum tꞃuamuin gan ſeiꞃe [h]oꝺic; "I am weary, without food to-day."

[15] *Bernas.* Barnismore, or Barnas, a

Nucu n-niɼlechtaɲ a ɲath
Ʒo tuca caṫ ʒuiɲt oɼ ʒlenn.
Ɗobeɲa cath 'con benn ɲuaiɗ,
Ach[t] biɗ ɗith ɼluaiʒ aɲ ʒaċ leth;
Biɗ olc biaɼ Eɲi ɗa eɼ;
Biaiɗ Ʒaeiɗul ɼo ċeɼ iɼ cɲech.
Rachait ɼiɲṫi ɗaɲ eɼ ɲuaiɗ;
Biaiɗ in tiɲ tuaiɗ ʒan ɲaṫ ɲiʒ,
No coneɲiʒ oc neit cɲo
In ɼeɲ ʒan ʒo ɗo ni a n-ɗin.
Ʒebaiɗ leṫ Banba ʒan ḃɲeic,
In la téiɗ o Aɲɗ in caiɲn;
Bliaɗain ɗa eiɼ iɼ a ɼecht
Co becht ni tɲoethɼaɲ a ṫaiɲm.
Ticɼa ʒotnech Eɼɼa ɲuaiɗ;
Baʒim comba tɲen a tɲeaɼ;
Ticɼa ɗibaɲtach na ɗiaiɗ,
Ni biaiɗ co cian ic cloɗ cleaɼ.
Ticɼa ɼeɲ in n-oen ʒae aiɲɗ,
Ɗobeɲ ʒolmaiɲʒ in ʒaċ tiɲ;
Aɲɼin ticɼa in Ɗonn ɗiaɗa,
Iɼ biaɗ .ix. mbliaɗna na ɲiʒ.
Ticɼa in Ḟinɗ ɼanat ɼoɗeoiɗ;
Biaiɗ a thɲeoiɲ co cɲich tɲi ɲoɼ;

gapped mountain, in the barony of Tirhugh, co. Donegal.

[1] *Gort.* There are several places of this name in Donegal; but the place referred to in the text was probably in Glenswilly (the valley of the Swilly), bar. of Kilmacrenan. Domhnall Og O'Donnell, the person evidently alluded to in the text, was engaged in many battles; but the names of the places in which they were fought are not specified in the Annals.

[2] *Benn-ruadh.* "Red Point." This is probably the place now called Binroe, barony of Bannagh, co. Donegal.

[3] *Gaedhil.* ʒul, B.

[4] *Net-cro.* An alias name for Ailech, or Ailech-Neit. See note [3], p. 62.

[5] *Banba.* A bardic name for Ireland.

[6] *Ard-in-Cairn.* The "height of the Cairn." This name would be Anglicised Carn-height, or Carnhill, or Ardcarn. There is a townland called Carnhigh, and

His fortunes shall not be humbled,
Till he fights the battle of Gort[1] over the glen.
He'll fight a battle at Benn-ruadh;[2]
But there will be a ruin of hosts on either side.
Unfortunate shall Ireland be after him.
The Gaedhil[3] will suffer persecution and plunder.
Scouts will pass over Es-Ruaidh;
The northern land will be without luck of kings,
Until arises, at Net-cro,[4]
The man, without falsehood, who'll them protect.
He'll possess half Banba,[5] without falsehood,
The day he goes from Ard-in-Cairn;[6]
During a year thereafter, and seven,
His fame will not be entirely subdued.
Gotnech[7] of Es-Ruaidh[8] will come,
Whose combat will be mighty, I proclaim.
An exile[9] shall come after him,
Who'll not be long putting down pranks.
The man of the one long[10] spear will come,
Who'll raise a cry of woe in every land.
After him will come the God-like Donn,[11]
Who shall be nine years a king.
The Find[12] of Fanat[13] will finally come,
(Whose power will extend to Crich-tri-Ros),[14]

another called Carnhill, in the barony of Kilmacrenan, co. Donegal, one of which was probably meant.

[7] *Gotnech.* This is a sobriquet, signifying a "man of darts," from *goth*, a dart. The person alluded to was probably Aedh O'Donnell, who succeeded his father, Domhnall Og, A.D. 1281.

[8] *Es-Ruaidh.* Assaroe, co. Donegal.

[9] *exile.* ᴅıbaɲᴛach. This person's identity has not been ascertained.

[10] *long.* aıɲᴅ; lit. "high." The Editor is unable to say who was this "one-long-spear" man.

[11] *Donn.* This is also a fanciful name, signifying "brown."

[12] *Find;* i.e., "Fair."

[13] *Fanat.* A well known district in the N. E. of the barony of Kilmacrenan, co. Donegal; anciently the patrimony of the O'Breslans, but in later times of their expulsors, the Mac Swineys.

[14] *Crich-tri-Ros.* The "territory of the

In oen aimsir ocus Fland;[1]
Ni chraidend cell imbi cross.
Ni ticfa nech co rath riġ
As tír tuaid ar es[3] in Find.
Achtmad coir[2] corcrach in ċuain,
Is mac in ruaid[4] as in glind.[5]
Ticfa ar m'eisi Colam caiḋ,
Faicfeas daib briaṫra is buaid;
Is he sin oin fer is ferr
Genfeas tall co ti la in luain.
Ar grad Conaill ro ṫag ṁo
Bennechat a ṡil gach la;
Uair geinfitit uad gan brais
Rigraid gan tairi mar ta. Ata s.

[*fol. 16, b 2.]

Ro aisneid Caillin fein tra aigeḋ ocus aṫbeogaḋ Conaill, ocus med na cana dliges dia ċloind ocus dia chined co braṫh, isin duain ṁoir ro scribamar tuas .i.

Eri oll oilen aingeal;

ocus ro aisned fos Caillin don aingeal fecht oili in dia dliged for chloind Conaill, amail adubairt feisin iar na ḟiarfaigid de don aingeal. Caillin cecinit hoc; angelus dixit:—

Aingel.

Cotlad sind imdairiu,
Dun mind oir uirdnidi,
Don mergi lasamain,
Du Chaillin cháid.
Don muir dar minlochuib,
Don grein uas minnrennib,
Don brethir bláith.

three Rosses." A wild district in the barony of Boylagh, co. Donegal.

[1] *Flann.* The apocryphal last king of Ireland. See note [4], p. 62, *supra.*

[2] *Coir.* An apocryphal name, signifying "just."

[3] *harbour* ; i.e. of Lough-Swilly, or Lough-Foyle.

[4] *the Ruadh.* The "Red man." Not known.

[5] *the Glen.* Probably Glenswilly, or the valley of the Swilly, co. Donegal.

In the same time as Flann.[1]
He'll not harass a church in which is a cross.
No one with kingly luck shall come
Out of the northern land, after Find,
Except the victorious Coir[2] of the harbour,[3]
And the son of the Ruadh[4] from the Glen.[5]
After me will come holy Colum,
Who will leave[6] them counsels and victory.
He is the very best man[7]
That will be born yonder until doom.
For love of Conall, who chose me,
I will bless his seed every day;
For from him shall be born, without fail,
Chieftains without weakness, as it is.

Caillin himself also related the death and resuscitation of Conall, and the extent of the tribute due from his children and his sept for ever, in the great poem which we have written above, viz.,

"Noble Ireland, Isle of Angels," &c.,

and Caillin, moreover, related to the Angel, on another occasion, what were his rights over Conall's children, as he himself said, after he had been questioned by the Angel. Caillin cecinit hoc. Angelus dixit.[8]

Sleeping in this bed,[9]
Is the splendid[10] gold diadem,
Is the flaming standard,
The holy Caillin?
Is the sea beyond small lakes,
Is the sun beyond small stars,
He of the blithe speech?

[6] *will leave.* faicfeas. faicbeaiss, A.

[7] *man.* The literal translation of the orig. of this line is "he is the one man that is best."

[8] *dixit.* This poem which follows is in the metre called *Bruilingecht*, for the characteristics of which see O'Donovan's *Irish Grammar*, p. 426.

[9] *in this bed.* sind imdairiu. sind imdaidriu, A.

[10] *splendid.* uirdonidi. uirnidi, B. uirdonige, A.

Caıllın. Cneꝺ tae ꝺom ꝺurgaꝺra,
Ꮳ aıngıl uırꝺnıꝺe,
Ꮟa ꝺenb ın ꝺal.
Cneꝺ ın rır rırınꝺe
Ꝺamra nor ḟaıllrıġtı
Ꮟan cetlaıb clán.

Sıl Conaıll chathchalma,
Oır maıꝺım orra ran,
Ꝺenat mo réր.
Ir maıth ro aıthbeoaıġer
In calma curata,
Conall a n-athaırrıum;
Ꮳ anam tucurra,
Fır ror a pén.[a]

[a] fol. 17, a 1.

Ꮳıngel ꝺıxıt. Cneꝺ ꝺuıt ro gellratar,
Ꮳ ḟınꝺrır ḟenorꝺa,
Ꮳ U chaıḃ Chaıreꝺaı
Ir mor ꝺu neart.
Inꝺır ꝺam rırınꝺı,
Rıam nucha n-ebartaır
Ꮳchtmaꝺ guth ceart.

Caıllın recıt. Screpall gach aen chaırchıġ,
Ireꝺ ꝺlıgım ꝺıḃrıum,
Ꝺaıg ır rcel rír.
Cacha trer cert blıaꝺaın,
Se ṁıncı ꝺlıġımrı,
Ech raıth ın ríg.

[1] *what.* cneꝺ. cnet, A.

[2] *said.* "The words respondit Angelus," are added both in A and B.

[3] *Cuireda.* The gen. is Chaıreꝺaıḋ in B., which is wrong. As this name does not occur in the geneal. of Caillin in the male line, as above given (pp. 4–6), it would seem that the saint's descent from

Caillin.

Why art thou awaking me,
Thou glorious Angel?
The event were sure.
What's[1] the vision truthful,
Unto me manifested,
By your chaunting bands.

The seed of Conall battle-strong,
Since I proclaim it o'er them,
Will my command obey.
Well did I resuscitate,
The mighty warrior,
Their father Conall;
Whose soul I moreover brought,
'Tis true, from pain.

The Angel said.[2]

What[1] did they promise thee,
Thou Elder, thou senior,
Thou holy O' of Caireda?[3]
Great is thy might.
Tell[4] unto me the truth,
For never hast thou said
Save rightful words.

Caillin fecit.

A *screpall*[5] from each sheep-owner,
Is what is due to me from them;
True is the tale.
Every third just year—
So often is due to me,
The king's goodly steed.

Caireda was in the female line. If this Caireda was the son of Finnchaemh, son of Cumscradh (see p. 4 *supra*), as is probable, then he was the maternal grandfather of St. Caillin. See M'Firbis's *Geneal.* MS., 237.

[4] *Tell.* ınnoıɼ. ınnoıSS, A.

[5] *screpall.* See note [6], p. 79.

Aingel. In chain mana tucatsum
Bid digail doiḃsium,
Is demin lem.
Bid sar a tellaigi,
Bid fann a fineda,
Bid beg a dend.

Caillin. Misi da riaratsom,
Biaid ardrath orrasom,
Oir bid scel fir.
Bid calma a cath ingal,
Bib mor a n-uirdnedsom,
Maith rath a rig.

Ro labair for do Conmaicnib iar na fiarfaigeḋ de don aingel isin imagallaim chetna. Acht chena legfem sechaind coleicc go ro labraimm do Conmaicnib fein in inad heli inar ndiaid.

IS do na neiṫib sin ro ḟoillsig Caillin an inad eli .i. dia chanaib for chloind Conaill, ocus do thodiusgad Conaill fein a bas, ocus dia mbuadaib ar chomall na cana sin, ocus dia ndimbuaḋaib mana icat in chain, ocus do na slanaib ocus do na rathaib do radad do Chaillin fria a comall, ro chan Caillin fein isin tairngiri si.*

* fol. 17, a 2.

Caillin cecinit hoc.

Gebaid crith in talam tend,
Gach tir salam iar mbrath nglonn;
Ba demin do chaċ in brath;
Faiċlet ticfa in muir dar chach.
Me Caillin Fidnacha fir;
Traethfaid misi nert gach rig;
Faiċled cach, is demin leam
Mar do aithbeoḋus Conall.

[1] *Angel.* A., B. Om. in A.
[2] *will follow them.* bid (bud, A) . . . . doiḃsium; lit. "will be to them."
[3] *certain.* demin. deimen, B.
[4] *earth.* talam. tallam, A.
[5] *doom.* The original of this line is

Angel.[1]

The tribute unless they give,
Vengeance will follow them,[2]
'Tis certain[3] to me.
Waste shall their firesides be,
Powerless their tribes shall be,
Small be their might.

Caillin.

If they will me obey,
Great luck shall on them come—
'Twill be a true tale.
Brave in battle will they be,
Great shall be their dignity,
Their king's fortune good.

He spoke further of the Conmaicni, on having been questioned by the Angel, in the same dialogue; but we will let that pass at present, until we speak of the Conmaicni themselves in another place further on.

It is of those things which Caillin explained in another place, to wit, of his tributes on Conall's children, and of Conall's own resuscitation from death; and of their successes if they observe the tribute, and their misfortunes unless they pay the tribute; and of the sureties and guarantees given to Caillin regarding its observance, Caillin himself sang in this prophecy.

CAILLIN cecinit hoc:—

Trembling will seize the firm earth,[4]
Every land [will be] waste after the awful doom.[5]
Certain to[6] all will be the judgment.
Beware! The sea will come over all.
I am true Caillin of Fidhnacha.
I will subdue the strength of every king.
Let each beware;[7] certain I am,
How I resuscitated Conall.

rather obscure; and the translation is therefore, perhaps, not strictly accurate, although preserving the sense.

[6] *to*. ꝺo. Omitted, B.

[7] *beware*. ꝼaiċleꝺ. ꝼachleꝺ, A.

Leċ bliadain is cuic bliadna,
Amail tic do reir riagla,
Misi co tanac mo ċell,
Bai Conall gan anmuin ann.
Tathbeoġus Conall na cet,
Ger bo fada ro bai in ég;
Ni hoir a athbeogud thra,
Gid fada go tanacsa.
Do geall dam Conall mo chain;
Do gell go luiġfed mom laim.
Dlegait a chlanna da es,
Cain adbail dam re hairneis.
Secht meic ro bai ag caem Conall,
Geallsat mo chana huli;
Ag so in chain ro gellsatar,
Itir riġ ocus ruiri.
Screpall gacha aon chairchiġ,
Dligim dib gach trear bliadnai;
Eċ in rig bias orrosan,
Da mbet do reir mo riaglai.
Patraicc morglan mor Macha,
Aingil uili dib bathaib,
Ri tabairt na cana sin,
Siat tucad rim irraiṫib.
Int og uasal Adomnan,
Maṫ[i] uili du dib bathaib;
Se fen 'sa clog[a] tugussa,[*]
Do ratad rim irraṫuib.

[*] fol. 17, b 1.

[1] *revived.* tathbeoġus, for do-athbeoġus.

[2] *he obtained not.* ni hoir, a very incorrect form of ni ḟuair, in which the infected (or aspirated) ḟ is not sounded in pronunciation.

[3] *seven.* See note [13], p. 137.

[4] *screpall.* See note [6], p. 79, *supra.*

[5] *sheep owner.* cairchiġ, gen. sg. of cairchech; a deriv. from caire, "a sheep," gen. cairech, accus. cairig. Cf. cáirchuide, gl. ovinus, Zeuss, *Gram. Celt.*, 9.

Half a year and five years,
As it accords with rules,
Until I came to my church,
Was Conall without life.
I revived[1] Conall of the hundreds,
Though long he had lain in death;
His revival he obtained not,[2] moreover,
However long until I came.
Conall promised me my tribute;
He promised he 'd swear by my hand.
His children after him owe me
A tribute prodigious to be told.
The mild Conall had seven[3] sons,
Who promised all my dues.
This is the tribute they promised,
Both kings and chieftains.
A *screpall*[4] from every sheep-owner[5]
Is due to me every third year,
And the steed of the king who is over them,
If they would be according to my rule.
Great pure Patrick of great Macha,[6]
The Angels all of both worlds,[7]
For the payment of that tribute
Were given[8] to me, as sureties.
The exalted, perfect Adamnan,
The nobles all of both worlds;[7]
Himself and his bell, which I gave him,
Were given to me as sureties.

[6] *Macha.* Ard-Macha ("Macha's height"), or Armagh.

[7] *of both worlds.* ꝺıb baċhaıb. baċhaıb is probably written for beċhaıb (dat. and abl. plur. of bıċh, *mundus*), merely to rhyme with the concluding word of the stanza, ꞃaıċıb (*rectè* ꞃaċaıb). In the prose account given above (p. 143), also, among the sureties named are the Archangel Michael, with the saints of Heaven.

[8] *given.* ꞇucaꝺ. ꞇuc, A.

Tri traisgi, con dub regles,
Mini tugat mo chuarta;
Da leget na traisgi sin,
Co brath bid lor a n-duarca.
Da tucaid mo chanara
Buaid a sochar go sluagda;
Fuicfid misi orrasan
No co toir in braṫ buada.
Cathmaidm catha rompa san,
Buaid n-indsene is buaid n-ergna;
Buaid forba, buaid tindscetail,
Buaid n-delba is buaid n-denma;
Buaid ngormac, buaid nglan gilla,
Buaid rig ocus buaid rigna;
Buaid n-amuis, buaid n-ard oglaig,
Buaid firgaisgedaig gribdaig.
Roga agam doibsin,
Amraṫ orra no raṫa;
Uair bid iatso a n-dimbuada,
Dimbuaid creċi is catha;
Dimbuaid rig is rigdaṁna;
Dimbuaid fir, dimbuaid flatha;
Dimbuaid rigi ar Gaidelaib;
Maraen re dimbuaid catha. Ge.

Ata tuille elle dna isin eladuin sin labrus air Conmaicnib, ocus ni beimis do sin i feċt sa, co ro thriallaiṁ tuille eli forro.

Ro mol, imorro, ocus ro daingnig ocus ro ḟaguiḃ Colam cilli mac Fedlimid mic Fergusa cenfoda mic Conaill gulbain .i. primfaiḃ nimhi

[1] *Dubh-Regles.* "Black Regles" (or Church). Possibly another name for St. Caillin's *Duirtech*, or Oratory, at Fenagh. One of St. Columkille's churches at Derry was also called Dubh-Regles.

[2] *virtues.* In the margin in A. is the note buaḋa ċineoil cConaill ar ioc na cana, ocus a ndiombuada muna n-iocad í; "the profits of the Cenel-Conaill if they pay the tribute, and their misfortunes if they do not pay it."

[3] *battle.* The first two letters of the

Three fasts [shall be performed] at the Dubh-Regles,[1]
Unless they give my tributes.
If they omit these fasts,
Their woes shall be, for ever, many.
If they furnish my tributes,
Their profits shall be numerous.
I will leave unto them,
'Till comes the doom, virtues:[2]
Success of battle before them;
The palm of knowledge and of wisdom;
The palm of ending, and of beginning;
The palm of figure, and of form;
Luck of nephews; luck of fair servants;
Luck of kings, and luck of queens;
Luck of soldiers, luck of arch-heroes;
Luck of true, fierce warriors.
A choice I give to them;
They may have ill luck, or graces;
For their misfortunes shall be these:
Ill luck of foray and battle;
Ill luck of Kings and Royal heirs;
Ill luck of men and princes;
Ill luck of kingship over the Gaidhel,
Along with ill luck of battle.[3]

There[4] is also more in that composition which speaks of the Conmaicni; but I will not touch upon it now, until we attempt something further regarding them.

Colum[5] Cille, moreover, the son of Fedlimidh, son of Fergus Cennfoda, son of Conall Gulban (i.e. the chief prophet of Heaven and Earth), awarded, and

poem are added, at the end of this line in the original, in token of conclusion. O'Rody has added in a marg. note, ꝺo ċım naꞃ lıocaꝺ an ċáın oıꞃ ꝺo ṫaınıꝼ na ꝺıombuaꝺa ocuꞅ na mıoꞃaṫa. Nı ḃeanann na naoıṁ bꞃeaꝼ. "I see that the tribute was not paid; for the ill-luck and misfortunes have come. The saints do not commit falsehood."

[4] *There.* This paragraph is omitted in B.

[5] *Colum.* Collam, A.

ocus talman, in chain sin for chlandaib Conaill co brath, do Chail-
[a] fol. 17, b 2. lin ocus dia chomarba.[a]

IS amlaid forcoemnaccair in ni sin. Fecht n-aen dia tainic Columb cilli go Caillin .i. iar mbrisid chathai do, air robris Colam tri catha in Erinn .i. catha na tri cul, ut poeta[1] dixit.

Cath cula Dremni[2] nan drenn,
Ro chualatar fir Erenn;
Cath chuili Feada[3] is fir soin,
Ocus cath chuili Raṫain.

Tainig imorro Colam iar cur chaṫa egin dib sin co hairm i raibi in lia logmar ocus in fir naom forglide, ocus in loċarn laramuin o fertaib ocus mirbailib, ocus in teni bithbeo congmis n-goirtiġe .i. Caillin mac Niatach, co Fiḋnacha Muige rein, do chuinngid dilgada dia anmain. IS aigi ba doig lais a fuaslagad o a thargabalaib ocus dimas. Ba himairgide ocus ba himchubaid dosom sin, uair ba he Caillin sinnser noem hErenn, ocus ba hardlegoid ocus ba hairdepscop Erenn he fos; ocus ba he rob oidi ocus ro ba anmchara do Cholam fein. Ro indis iarum a thargabala do Chaillin, co tart dilgad ocus maithem do.

IS iarsin do rat Colam cilli cuairt ocus caithem a manach ocus a oglach itir Albain ocus Erinn, ocus trian cuarta Coluim cille fein lais sin itir Erinn ocus Albain; ocus ro ordaig ferand gaċa cille
[b] fol. 18, b 1. do Chaillin o Cholam cille;[b] ocus ro ordaig ocus ro fagaib Colum cille do Chaillin na deg comada ocus na cana adubramar romaind,

[1] *poeta.* posta, A.

[2] *Cul-Dremne.* The name (now obsolete) of some place in the barony of Carbury, co. Sligo—between Sligo and Drumcliff. The battle was fought A.D. 561.

[3] *Cul-Feada.* Dr. Reeves (*Adamnan*, p. 254), identifies this place with a Bealach-Dathi, where a battle was fought in 587, between the Northern and Southern Hy-Neill. Tuath-Dathi was the name of a district in Bregia, or Meath (see *Lebor na hUidhre*, p. 42 a), with which the name of *Bealach-Dathi* may be connected. But as St. Colum Cille was not in Ireland in 587, he could hardly have taken part in the battle of Bealach-Dathi. In the authority which Dr. Reeves quotes (ib. p. 253), namely the Preface to the *Altus Prosator* in the *Lebar Brecc*, Cul-Feadha (or Bealach-Feadha, as it is there

confirmed, and left that tribute on Conall's clanns for ever, to Caillin and his successor.

This is the way it happened. One time Colum Cille came to Caillin, to wit, after he had gained three battles; for Colum gained three battles in Ireland, viz., the battles of the three *Culs*, ut poeta[1] dixit.

> The battle of Cul-Dremne[2] of the conflicts
> The men of Ireland have heard;
> The battle of Cul-Feada,[3] this is true,
> And the battle of Cul-Rathain.[4]

Colum came, therefore, after fighting some battle of these, to the place in which was the precious stone, the true manifest saint, the lamp shining with wonders and miracles, and the perpetual fire with vivifying heat, to wit, Caillin[5] son of Niata, to Fidhnacha of Magh-Rein, to implore forgiveness for his soul. 'Twas with him (Caillin) lay, he thought, his absolution from his transgressions and pride. This was right and becoming in him, for Caillin was the senior of the saints of Ireland; and he was also arch-legate and archbishop of Ireland; and 'tis he that was tutor and soul-friend to Colum himself. He afterwards told his transgressions to Caillin, who gave him pardon and forgiveness.

It was thereafter Colum Cille gave [Caillin] the fees[6] and entertainment[7] of his monks and youths both in Alba and Ireland, and the third of Colum Cille's own fees[6] therewith, both in Ireland and Alba. And he ordered land for every church [to be given] to Caillin, from Colum Cille. And Colum Cille ordained, and left to Caillin, the good conditions and tributes we

called) is said to be near Cluain-Iraird, or Clonard, in Meath. The battle of Cul-Feadha was evidently fought before 563, the date of St. Colum Cille's departure from Ireland, since it is assigned as one of the causes of his leaving.

[4] *Cul-Rathain.* Coleraine, co. Londonderry.

[5] *Caillin.* Other authorities say that St. Molaise of Inishmurry, off the coast of Sligo (or St. Molaise of Devenish, as O'Donnell states in his Irish life of the patron Saint of his sept), was the person to whom St. Colum Cille applied for counsel.

[6] *fees.* cuaiꞃꞇ; lit. "circuit, or visitation; and, in a secondary sense, the fees or dues received during the visitation.

[7] *entertainment.* caiꞇhem; lit. "spending."

ar clannaib Conaill gulbain, ocus leṫ orra gaċa tigi oil, ocus cuibrend cach cuigir ria caċ corn gach circaill.

Do bert iaram Colam cille do Chaillin in cethir leabar, ocus in chaṫach ro scrib dia laim fein, ocus ro gell gomad mergi buadaigṫi ocus coscair do manchaib ocus do muintir Chaillin co brath na minda sin .i. in ċathach ocus in cethir lebor; ocus ro fagaib Colum cille co naċ gebad tuat na fine in nech do chlaind Conaill no ṫicfad inagaid na cana sin.

Ro ḟagaib Colam cille fagbala maithi do Chaillin ocus dia chomarbaib, ocus dia ṡamad ocus dia chatraig .i. buaid n-abad, buaid tanaisi, buaid comais ocus comairċi, buaid crabad ocus creidmi, buaid n-enig et n-oededchairi ocus biataċais, buaid sonais ocus sobarthain, buaid caingne ocus comairli ocus gach dala archena. Ro ġeall Colam cille nem do gach neoċ do genad rer Chaillin. Ro gell ifern ocus gar secli do gaċ duine no ṡarechad Fidnacha Chaillin co braṫ.

Ro thairngir Colam co ticfad ab a Fidnacha do thogaibfed in chairsi. Cecinit in duairsi hoc.

Des in ċaṫa ticimsi
Cugut, a Chaillin fertuig.
Agso ort mo chomairci
[a] fol. 18, a 2. Re demna in domuin decraid.[a]

[1] *Gulban.* MS. B. is defective from this (fol. 117 a) to the fourteenth line on p. 236 *infra.* A few sentences in a more recent handwriting on fol. 117 b, are illegible, with the exception of one in which "William Gorm, the Viceroy" is mentioned. But William Gorm (De Lasci) was never Viceroy. See note [5], p. 72.

[2] *door-post.* This is an idiomatic way of signifying free entrance.

[3] *couch.* circaill. This word has many meanings; for it not only signifies a circle (being, indeed, a loan from the Lat. *circulus*), but is also applied to articles which are round, such as a bolster, pillow, &c. It likewise means, in a secondary sense, a bed or couch. This sentence is rather obscurely worded in the original.

[4] *Cethir-lebor.* The Four Gospels, or "quatuor libri." They are sometimes called merely *Cetar* (quatuor) by Irish writers.

[5] *Cathach.* This is the famous MS., containing a copy of the Psalms supposed to have been transcribed by St. Colum Cille, now in the Royal Irish Academy. It is the property of Sir Richard O'Donel, Bart. The battle of Cul-Dreimne, referred to above (see note [8], p. 164) is said to have

have mentioned before, on the children of Conall Gulban;[1] and the door-post[2] of every drinking house, and the portion of any five [to be placed] before each; and a goblet before every couch.[3]

Colum Cille afterwards gave to Caillin the *Cethir-lebor*,[4] and the *Cathach*[5] which he wrote with his own hand; and promised him that those relics would be ensigns of victory and triumph to the monks and people of Caillin until doom, to wit, the *Cathach*, and the *Cethir-lebor*.[4] And Colum Cille declared that whosoever of Conall's children should oppose that tribute would obtain neither territory nor tribe.

Colum Cille beqeathed good gifts[6] to Caillin, and to his successors, and to his community and city, to wit, the palm of abbots; the palm of tanists;[7] the palm of power and protection; the palm of devotion and faith; the palm of generosity, guest-ship, and hospitality; the palm of happiness and prosperity; the palm of covenant and counsel, and of every affair besides. Colum Cille promised Heaven to every one who would do Caillin's bidding. He promised hell and shortness of life[8] to every man who would profane Fidnacha-Chaillin for ever.

Colum Cille foretold that an abbot would come in Fidnacha, who would levy this tribute. He sang this lay:—

After the battle[9] I come
To thee, Caillin of miracles.
Thy protection I implore[10]
'Gainst the demons of the angry world.

arisen from a dispute regarding it. It was always regarded with veneration by the clans of Tirconnell, particularly the O'Donnells; and was usually carried thrice, right-wise, round their armies when going to battle. See the several virtues ascribed to this relic (the name of which signifies "prœliator"), in Reeves's *Adomnan*, pp. 233, 249, 320, &c. The statement in the text, that it was given by St. Colum Cille to Caillin, is doubtless an invention, inasmuch as it seems to have been always preserved in the co. Donegal (ib. 284).

[6] *gifts*. A marg. note in A. reads, buaḋa Coluim Cille do ċomarbaib Fiodnacha, ⁊rl.; i.e. "Colum Cille's 'graces' (buaḋa; lit. victories) to the *Comarbs* of Fenagh, &c."

[7] *tanists*; i.e. tanist-abbots, or abbots-elect.

[8] *of life*. secli, for saeculi.

[9] *battle*. See p. 165.

[10] *I implore*. The words ag so ort

Is tu m'uidi is m'anmċara,
Is tu is gloine for talmain;
Mo lam derg lem chugatsa,
D'iarrad t'osuid dom anmuin.

Caillin. Mo bennacht ar do bel mbind,
Mor do maiṫ aderi rinn.
Dingebat dit breṫ chaṫa,
A Choluim go coem raṫa.

Colum Cille. Do berrsa duit ar a chenn,
A ardlegoit na hErenn,
Cuarta mo manach ga toiġ
Etir Erinn is Albain.
'S a dag trian mo ċuarta sa,
Etir Albain is Erinn,
Duit aberim ginn troscela
A Chaillin uasail glebind
A Chaillin, a ardlegoit,
A airdepscoip mo cridi,
Do ber duit go firinde,
Ferann mor gacha cilli.
Leṫ orrsa gaċ tigi oil,
Cuibrend cuigir i cedoir;
Corn gacha circaill malle,
Red ṁanchaib go dedla.
'S a chathach do scribussa;
In cethir leabar ceadna;

literally mean "here's on thee;" but the translation represents the idiomatic signification.

[1] *red;* i.e. blood-stained.

[2] *thy peace.* t'osuid, for do fosuid (*recte* fossuid).

[3] *judgment of battle.* This is in allusion to the sentence alleged to have been pronounced on St. Colum Cille, on account of his participation in the battles above referred to (p. 165), which led to his departure from Ireland. See Reeves's *Adamnan*, Int. lxxiv.

[4] *tributes.* cuarta. See note [6], p. 165.

[5] *both in.* etir=inter.

[6] *I give.* abem, A.; an error for aberim.

My tutor and soul-friend thou art;
  The purest on the earth art thou.
  My red[1] hand I bring to thee,
  Seeking thy peace[2] for my soul.

Caillin. My blessing on thy sweet mouth!
  Much of good thou say'st to us.
  I'll ward from thee the judgment of battle,[3]
  O, Colum of the mild graces.

Colum Cille. I will give to thee therefor,
  Thou arch-legate of Ireland,
  The tributes[4] of my monks at home,
  Both in[5] Ireland and Alba.

And the good third of my own tribute,
  Both in[5] Alba and Ireland,
  To thee I give,[6] by the[7] Gospel,
  Thou true, illustrious Caillin.

O, Caillin; O, arch-legate;
  Thou archbishop of my heart,
  To thee I give, with truthfulness,
  The broad land of every church.

The door-post[8] of every tavern,
  The rations of five forthwith,
  A drinking-horn for every pillow[9] also,
  Thy monks shall bravely have.

And the Cathach[10] which I wrote;
  The "Four Books"[11] besides;

[7] *by the.* The MS. has giñ, for ginn, the meaning of which is not very certain. But the translation probably conveys the sense intended.

[8] *door-post.* Leṫ orra literally signifies "half door-post," but is idiomatically used to express "one door-post," as leṫ ſúil ("half-eye") leṫ láim ("half-hand") and leṫ ċoiſ ("half-leg") are employed to express respectively an "eye," a hand, and a leg. See note [2], p. 166.

[9] *pillow.* Or *couch.* See note [3], p. 166.

[10] *Cathach.* See note [5], p. 166.

[11] *Four Books.* The Gospels. See note[4], p. 166.

Si brisfes na congala
Red manchaibsi go detla.
Eaċ gach rig 's gaċ ard abad
O Doiri go clar Corainn,
Ar chend chorcair comaidmig
Re claind crodata Conuill.
Uingi d'or gach ain tairis
Duid o chlaind Conaill ċalma;
Gaċ tres bliadna ordaigim,
Omu co laiṫi in braṫa.
Ech gach rigna romiadċa,
'S gach banntairiġi feli;
Screpall gacha ain chairchig,
Ar cend nime daib fene.
Do sil Conaill ċathcalma,
Fagbaimsi doib gan time,
Nech diultfas i n-abruimsi
Ni geba tuat na fine.

Caillin fecit.
Mois dam a ċoem daltan,
A Choluim Droma tuama,
In ticfa neċ toibechus
Mar do radius mo ċuarta.

Faitsine.
Genfid ab i Fidnacha,
Etir mathair is athair;
Nem dosom gan imresan;
Dot muintir bid tren tabuig.

[1] *it.* Viz., the "Cathach."

[2] *Corann.* See note [8], p. 97. The following note, by Thady O'Rody, is added at foot of fol. 18a, in A. As mor ant aḋbar maccaḋ a beiṫ ag eisdeacht re daoinib aimbfearaċa ag sior raḋa gur ċuir Taḋg O Rodaiġe iomad breacc san leabar Caillin so do scriobaḋ san mbliaḋain d'aois Criost, 1516. "'Tis a great cause of laughter, to be listening to ignorant people perpetually saying that Thady O'Rody put many lies into this Book of Caillin, which was written in the year of Christ's Age, 1516." Though O'Rody's annotations may escape the imputation of falsehood, they are not free from that of pedantry.

[3] *screpall.* See note [6], p. 79, *supra.*

[4] *themselves.* After this line, the scribe

'Tis it[1] that will break the battles,
Before thy monks, bravely.
The steed of each king and arch-abbot
From Derry to the plain of Corann,[2]
For the sake of glorious spoils
Attending the brave Clann-Conaill.
An ounce of gold from every chieftain
Of the race of mighty Conall,
For thee, each third year, I ordain,
From this day till the day of doom.
The steed of every proud queen,
And of every generous chieftainess;
A screpall[3] from every sheep-owner—
For the sake of Heaven for themselves.[4]
To the seed of battle-strong Conall
I award, without fear,
That whoever refuses what I say,
Shall obtain neither territory nor tribe.

Caillin fecit.

Tell me, O fair foster-son,[5]
O Colum of Druim-thuama,[6]
Will any one come who will levy,
As thou hast given, my tributes?

A Prophecy.

An Abbot will be born in Fidnacha,
Between a mother and father;
Heaven shall be his, without strife;
For thy people he will powerfully levy.

adds ıllem ın oıↄ̃ aꞇau ı bꞅecꞇꞅa; "in Leim-in-ois I am at this time." Leim-in-ois ("the stag's leap"), now "Leamanish," is a townland in the parish of Fenagh, adjoining the village of Fenagh.

[5] *foster-son.* ꝺalꞇan, dimin. of ꝺalꞇa. See note [9], p. 125.

[6] *Druim-thuama.* Drumhome, a village in the parish of the same name, bar. of Tirhugh, co. Donegal, in the church of which, said to have been founded by St. Colum Cille, was for a long time preserved the *Cathach*, or "Book of battles," above referred to. See Reeves' *Adamnan*, App. to Pref., lxiii-lxiv.

Faitpine beup. Zenpid ab i Fidnaċa,
Adepim pib gan guaa;
Gaċ duine thu tpapechup
Millfeap a chland 'pa uaa.

Faitpine beup. Genpid ab i Fidnacha,
Adepim pit gun aipde;
Gach ni in Epinn gellpa pan
Comaillpet he gan caipde.

Faitpine beup. Genpid ab i Fidnacha;
'Se tabechup do chuapta;
In aimpip Domnaill ind poip,
Ocup Conchobaip Chpuachna.

Annpin tig gall Gaidelach,
Lap a milltep do baili.
Appen biaid opt apd conach,
Ocup bid tpen do thaipi.

Gaċ duine thu pepechap,
Adepimpi tpia thuigpi,
Nem do geb o'm' tigepna,
Ocup cpedem do duitpi.

Gach duine thu tpapechap,
Adepim pit gan baegal,
Ipepn do gan impepain,
Ocup bid luath dont paegal,

[1] *who.* 'pe, for ipe, lit. "'tis he." The scribe suggests an alias reading, le, "by whom;" but the first reading accords better with the context.

[2] *Domhnall of Findross.* Domhnall Mór O'Donnell. See note [4], p. 86, and note [6], p. 87, *supra*.

[3] *Conchobhar.* This was apparently Conor O'Rourke, slain 1257. See note [4], p. 84.

[4] *Cruachan.* See note [3], p. 75.

[5] *Gall-Gaidhel;* i.e. a Foreign-Gaidhel, or, as one would say, an "English-Irishman." Thady O'Rody has added a marginal note indicating the person intended by the prophet. "Seón óg mac Raġnuill, mac Eoġuin mic Seoin, an gall-gaoidlaċ po. Ben gallda .i. Ruipelbap, a maṫaip. Fiop Gaoidal a aṫaip. Oidiop gallda puaip pop a Lundun. Ap e tug Gaill

Prophecy still. An Abbot will be born in Fidnacha.
I tell you without falsehood,
That of every man who profanes thee
The children and race destroyed shall be.

Prophecy still. An Abbot will be born in Fidnacha.
I tell thee, with a token,
That everything he promises in Ireland,
Shall be fulfilled without delay.

Prophecy still. An Abbot will be born in Fidnacha,
Who[1] will collect thy tributes,
In the time of Domhnall of Findross,[2]
And of Conchobhar[3] of Cruachan.[4]

Then will come a Gall-Gaidhel,[5]
By whom thy place[6] will be destroyed.
Thereafter thou shalt have great luck,
And thy relics shall be powerful;

Every man who obeys thee—
I say it through intelligence—
Shall obtain Heaven from my Lord,
If only he believes in thee.

Every man who thee profanes—
I tell thee, without danger—
Shall obtain Hell, without dispute;
And quick shall be [his exit] from life.

go Ḟiaḋnacha ar ttus riaṁ, iar ccogad Chromwell, A°. D°. 1652, do socrugad na tire, na raiḃ fein don arum, acht gurab ar a ċoṁairle tangadar ann; ocus dob olc leis féin sin iarttain. "This Gall-Gaidhel was John óg Mac Raghnaill, son of Eoghan, son of John. An Englishwoman, i.e., a Russell, was his mother. His father was a true Gaidhel. English tutelage he also received in London. It was he who first brought foreigners to Fidhnacha, after Cromwell's wars, A°. D°. 1652, to settle the country. He was not of the number himself; but it was by his advice, at least, they came. And he was himself sorry for it afterwards." But somebody else was meant.

[6] *thy place*; i.e. Fidnacha.

[a] fol. 18, b 2.

Fuicfet ort a chaem Chaillin,[a]
Briaṫra imda co soraib;
Buaid n-abad, buaid tanaise,
Agad go dered domuin.
Buaid comair, buaid comairċi,
Buaid crabaid ocus eniġ,
Buaid sonair, buaid comairli,
Buaid gacha dala dethinis.

[Caillin.] Is me Caillin Fidnacha;
Is me abaid Muigi rein;
O da riachtair chugamsa,
Itai it aingeal De.
A Choluim mic Fedlimid,
Mo ḃennacht ort gan erlis;
Is fagbuim dot muintirsi,
Beth ar nim ar mo deg deis. d. e. s. i. n. ch. a. t. h.

Do ro ḟas et ro forbair macni Meadba ocus ḟearguṡa fo Erinn .i. clann Conmaic ocus Cheir ocus Chuirc. Robadar dono sil Conmaic mic Fearguṡa int saindred i Condachtaiḃ .i. i Conmaicne duin moir. Ba cumung leo a forbu ocus a fearund, et ba mor leo a cinud et a comḟuiliḋi. Is airsin ro thriallsat fingail fingrandu et brisiud braithriusa inter se.[b]

[b] fol. 19, a 1.

Ro throisgseat iaram fri Dia nimi imon ċaingin sin, ar is aicci

[1] *bequests.* briaṫra; lit. "words."

[2] *tanists.* See note [7], p. 167.

[3] *grant.* fagbuim (fagbuimb, MS.); lit. "I leave."

[4] *right hand.* At the end of this line are added, in the text, the letters representing the opening words of the poem, according to the usual practice of Irish scribes.

[5] *Medbh.* Pron. *Mév.* Queen of Connacht. The Cleopatra of ancient Irish history. O'Flaherty, who describes her as "Virago potens, longæva, ac libidinibus," refers her death to *circa* A.D. 70. *Ogygia*, 276.

[6] *Fergus.* Fergus Mac Roy, ex-King of Ulster, and paramour of Queen Medbh, at whose court he sought an asylum on his departure, or expulsion, from Ulster, about A.D. 30.

To thee I leave, O gentle Caillin,
Many bequests,[1] with blessings;
The palm of abbots, palm of tanists,[2]
Have thou to th'end of the world;
The palm of power, palm of asylum;
The palm of devotion and of generosity;
The palm of happiness, and of counsel;
The palm of expedition in all affairs.

[Caillin.] I am Caillin of Fidnacha.
I am Abbot of Magh-Rein.
Since thou camest unto me,
An Angel of God thou art.
O, Colum son of Fedhlimidh,
My blessing on thee without fail.
And I grant[3] to thy people, that they
In Heaven be on my good right hand.[4]

The descendants of Medbh[5] and Fergus[6] grew and multiplied throughout Ireland, to wit, the children of Conmac,[7] of Ciar,[8] and of Corc.[9] The seed of Conmac son of Fergus, in particular, were in Connacht, viz., the Conmaicni of Dun-mor.[10] They thought their inheritance and land too confined, and their kin and blood-relations too numerous. Therefore it is that they projected a truly horrid fratricide, and breach of brotherhood, among themselves.

They fasted against[11] Heaven's God, however, regarding this affair; for

[7] *Conmac.* The descendants of this person were divided into several tribes called *Conmaicni*, each tribe being distinguished by a territorial name, as Conmaicni-Maighe-Rein (in Leitrim and Longford), Conmaicni-mara (Connemara, in Galway co.), and Conmaicni-Cuile-Toladh (the barony of Kilmaine, co. Mayo).

[8] *Ciar.* See note [8], p. 31, *supra.*

[9] *Corc.* See note [7], *ib.*

[10] *Dun-mor.* Now the bar. of Dunmore, co. Galway. An alias name for the Conmaicni of Dunmore was "Conmaicni-Cincoil-Dubhain."

[11] *against.* fri. For some curious references to the practice of fasting "against" persons, to obtain the requisite favours, see *Senchus Mór*, vol, 1. Introd.

In the Book of Fenagh, Thady O'Rody asks in the margin, fol. 18 b., cia adberad co fil litir isin aimsirsi doroisci di sin chos; "who would say that ro bai i[n] furtacht. As a haithle sin tainicc aingel o Dia dia furtacht ocus dia comairliugud imon caingin sin. Ised dono ro raidh int aingeal friu .i. fesa ocus techta do chor uathaib co Roim d'iarrad Chaillin chumachtaig .i. mac naemthan Niatach, ar is do ro ir ocus ro chettaig Dia foirithin na Conmaicnech, ocus a furtacht o a fingail, ocus faissingiugad a bferand doib, ocus fochraicc nime dia n-anmannaib ar a n-adlucad ig Cailin fodeoidh i Fidnacha Muighe fein.

Iarsodain ro chuirset Conmaicni techta co Roim ar cend Chaillin, la forcongra ocus la fulairem in aingil, et ro leicsiut faill ina fingail ocus ina mirun, co tisad in tairngertach dia soigid .i. Caillin mac Niatach. Rangatar imorro na techta co Roimh, et fo fuaratar naem Chaillin indti.

As a haitle sin doriacht Caillin mac Niatach co hErind. Do roine ferta ocus mirbaili imda indti. Ro indarb idla ocus arachta.
fol. 19, a 2. Ro bairt riga ocus ruirig, sloga ocus sochaide. Ro chuir daine i mbas ocus in oidhg, ocus in ifern co na ilpianaib iar nemcredem do Dia; et ro athbeoaig alaile o ṗein et bas iar mbit fri re ciana i mbas.

Ba fada et ba himchian, imorro, bad coir do Conmaicnib fethem ocus furnaide frisin eochair fuaislucti sin ro is Dia doib .i. Caillin, dia fertais gach maith do roine doib iar tuidecht; daig is he ro thoirmisg a fingail ocus do rat feronn doib, ocus ro congaib a n-degbraithirsi iat, ocus do bert fochraicc nime doib ar bith ag riar a chatrach; ocus air chomairchi ocus ar chaḃus do congbail di co brath, ocus ar a n-adlacad aicce iar na n-egaib.

Is amlaid forcaemnacair in ni sin.

In tan immarro doriacht Caillin dochomb nErenn i tosaig, is ann doriacht cetamus ait i raibe a chinedh ocus a chombraithre fesin .i. clanna Conmaic mic Fergusa ocus Medbi ingine Echach feidlig, do thoirmescc a fingaili ocus a fuatha. Ised em asbert friu. Ni coir,

there is now any writing (litir, "letter") that excels that above?"

[1] *messengers.* The orig., fesa, pl. of fis, "knowledge," might be, perhaps, more appropriately translated "intelligencers."

[2] *with.* The prepos. ig (written also ic, ac, oc) literally means *apud.* Caillin himself was not buried in Fenagh, although his bones were ultimately removed thither. See p. 12, *supra.* What was meant is

with Him was the power of relief. Immediately afterwards an Angel came from God to aid and counsel them respecting the matter. What the Angel then said to them was, to send off messengers[1] and emissaries to Rome, to invite powerful Caillin, to wit, the holy son of Niata; for it was to him God had granted and permitted to assist the Conmaicni, and to relieve them from their fratricide; to extend their possessions for them, and to secure Heavenly reward for their souls, on condition[2] of their being ultimately interred with[2] Caillin in Fidnacha of Magh-Rein.

Thereupon the Conmaicni sent messengers to Rome for Caillin, at the command and persuasion of the Angel, and postponed[3] their fratricide and evil intention until the prophesied one, to wit, Caillin son of Niata, should come to them. The messengers went to Rome, moreover, and found Caillin there.

Caillin son of Niata came immediately afterwards to Ireland, and wrought numerous wonders and miracles in it. He banished idols and images, and baptized kings and princes, hosts and multitudes. He sent men to death and destruction,[4] and to hell with its many torments, for disbelief in God; and he resuscitated[5] others from pain and death, after having been a long time dead.

Long, and very long, indeed, ought the Conmaicni have waited and tarried for that unlocking key God had vouchsafed to them, to wit, Caillin, if they could have known all the good that he did for them after coming; for he it was that prevented their fratricide, and that gave them land, and preserved them in good brotherhood; and that gave them the reward of Heaven on condition of being obedient to his seat, and of preserving for it [the right of] asylum, and respect, for ever; and on condition of their being buried with him after death.

How that thing happened is this wise.

When Caillin came to Ireland at first, therefore, where he first went was to the place in which were his own kin and co-brethren, to wit, the descendants

that the Conmaicni should be interred in the cemetery of Fenagh.

[3] *postponed*. The words ro leicsiut faill ina fingail signify lit. "they permitted negligence in their fratricide."

[4] *death and destruction*. The word oiḋg, translated destruction, seems a corrupt form of eg, which means "death" also.

[5] *resuscitated*. A note intimating that St. Caillin resuscitated Conall Gulban,

[a] fol. 19, b 1. em, in ni ro thriallsabair, a braithri inmaine, bar Caillin .i. fingal[a] ocus bririud braithresra; acht chena denaid an ni adersa frib. Do ġenam em, a ardlegoit ocus a ṫigerna, gidbe fon domuin ní aderasa frinn. Is hi mo chomairli-si daib, a chlanna Conmaic, ar se, anaiḋ forrna ferannaib atatai coleg. Rachatsa, em, d'iarrad ḟorba ocus ferainn daib amail bas tal do Dia. Ro molsat ocus ro oentuigset in ni sin for Chaillin. Celebraid doib iaram coleg.

Luid Caillin o Dun mor go Cruachain Ai. Fagartach .h. Cathalan ba ri forra in tan sin. Faiḋis Caillin la Fagartach in oiḋċi sin. Do ratsat em cinel Fagartaig a ser feisin do Chaillin.

Is annsin ro gellsat do screpall gaċa cairchig dia cined go braṫ do Chaillin, gach tres bliadain. Dorat Caillin doibsin iarum buaid tinolaicti ocus tabartuis, buaid marcachais ocus milraid; fer lestha righ dib do gres; buaid foṫlachta ocus fir uisce. Na buada cetna for daltaib .h. Cathalain. Acht combet do reir Chaillin is amlaid
[b] fol. 19, b 2. forbiait na buada sin.[b]

Ised do chuaid Caillin iarrodain go hard Charna, baili imbai a chara ocus a chompanach fein, co Beo Aed. Ferais Beo Aed failti

after having been more than five years dead, is added in the margin. See p. 91, *supra*.

[1] *arch-legate.* O'Rody adds the marg. note, acht nama is doig lem nar ba legoit in tan sin he, ocus ro boi ced bliadna ma ard legoit iar na idbairt do ó Patraic; "but I think that he was not a legate at that time, though he was for 100 years arch-legate after it [the legateship] had been given to him by Patrick."

[2] *at present.* coleg seems to be a corrupt form of the comp. adverb celléic, which Ebel (*Gram. Celtica*[2], 610), who thinks it comp. of the pron. *cach* (quivis) and an obsolete subst. *léic*=Armor. *lech* (locus), translates "utique," "omnino," and "semper"; but it more properly signifies "meanwhile," "at present," or "for the present."

[3] *plan.* ni; lit. "thing."

[4] *Dun-mor.* See note [10], p. 175.

[5] *Cruachan-Ai;* or Cruachan of Magh-Ai. Now represented by Croghan, or Rathcroghan, in the par. of Kilcorkey, bar. of Ballintobber, co. Roscommon; about two miles from Belanagare. Magh-Ai, the plain of Ai, extended from the town of Roscommon to the verge of the barony of Boyle, and from near Strokestown westwards to Castlerea.

[6] *Fagartach Ua Cathalain.* F. descendant of Cathalan. Fagartach was the son of Cathal, son of Muiredach Mal, son of Eoghan Sremh (see p. 113, *supra*). He is not mentioned in the usual lists of kings

of Conmac, son of Fergus, and Medbh, daughter of Eochaidh Feidlech, to prohibit their fratricide, and their enmity. This, also, is what he said to them. "That which you purposed, beloved brethren, is not right," said Caillin, "viz., fratricide and breach of brotherhood. But do what I tell you." "We shall do, truly, O arch-legate[1] and Lord, whatsoever in the world thou shalt command us." "My advice to you, sons of Connac," said he, "is that you remain on the lands on which you at present[2] are. I will go, moreover, to seek possessions and land for you, as it may be pleasing to God." They praised that plan,[3] and agreed to it for Caillin, who subsequently bade them farewell for a time.

Caillin went from Dun-mór[4] to Cruachan-Ai.[5] Fagartach Ua Cathalain[6] was king over them[7] at that time. Caillin rested that night with Fagartach. The Cinel-Fagartaigh,[8] moreover, granted his own demand to Caillin.

It was then they promised Caillin a screpall[9] from every sheep-owner of their kindred, every third year, for ever. Caillin afterwards granted them the palm of distribution and munificence, the palm of horsemanship and hunting, (and that a king's bed-fellow should be always of them); and the palm of brook-lime[10] and pure water. The same virtues [he granted] to the foster-sons of Ua Cathalain, provided they were obedient to Caillin; for thus only could these virtues prevail.

The place to which Caillin went after that was to Ard-Carna,[11] where his own friend and companion was, to Beo-Aedh.[12] Beo-Aedh bade him welcome,

of Connacht; but his son Maelcatha, Aedh son of Maelcatha, and Uada son of Aedh (whose death is recorded in the Chron. Scotorum under A.D. 592), were reckoned kings of that province.

[7] *them;* i.e. the Cinel-Faghartaigh. See next note.

[8] *Cinel-Faghartaigh;* kindred of Fagartach. This tribe was situated near Castlereagh, co. Roscommon, which is called "Caislen-riabhach-Clainne-Faghartaigh," or the "brown castle of Clann-Faghartaigh," in the Annals of Loch-Cé, at the years 1256–7. The family name was O'Cathalain.

[9] *screpall.* See note [c], p. 79, *supra.*

[10] *brook-lime.* ꝼoċlaċт. From many references in ancient historical tales, it would seem that the Irish used brook-lime for food, like water-cresses.

[11] *Ard-Carna.* Ardcarn, a village four miles eastward of Boyle, co. Roscommon, where are the ruins of an ancient church.

[12] *Beo-Aedh.* Lit. "Aedus vivus." He was bishop of Ard-Carna. His death is entered in the Chron. Scotorum under A.D.

fris, et ba subach riam. Iarsin ro chenglatar a cotach et a comchanuss. Fuair Caillin imorro ferann iarsin o Ard Charna sair.

Do luid Caillin iarsin for Sinaind co Mag Cellachain sair. Anais la Cellachan in oidchi sin, ar rob hi a n-uidi[1]. Lotar iaram co Tulaig[2] na crot. Acht ata ni chena, ro fagaibsiut Nisi (.i. mac Niatach), brathair Chaillin, iccon Bennachan[3] i Muig Nisi[4], conid ann torchair Nisi la Cellachan. Mag Cellachan imorro ainm in muigi in tan sin. Dorat imorro Cellachan in mag ocus a manchine do Chaillin, i n-eric Nisi; conid Mag Nisi o sin ale; conid aire sin is la Caillin in mag.

Anais don Caillin i Tul[aig] na crot co riacht corp a brathar (.i. Nisi) chuigi ann; conid on fuirech ocus on furnaide dorondsat na clerchi fris in corp aderar in Urnaide[5] o sin.

Ro tothlaig em Riocc Innsi bo Findi co fagbad iasc isin indbiur sin bui[a] ina farrad, et ni fuair ni di iasc. Conid in oidchi sin ro mallaigsiut in loch o na fuaratar iasg ann. Lotar iaram o'n Ornaide co Mag Rein .i. co Dun mBaili.

[a] fol. 20, a 1.

Is annsin ro fothaig Caillin roim adnaicthi na Conmaicnech .i. Fidnacha. Conid iarsuidiu ro cred Aed dub do Chaillin, ocus ro marb Fergna, ocus ro chuir na draithi i g-clochaib amail dubramar romainn. Is do na nethib[sin] ro raided in duansa sis:—

518=521. His commemoration day was March 8.

[1] *for it was their journey.* ar rob hi a n-uidi. The construction of this passage is rather rude. What the writer meant to say is, that Cellachan's residence was the end of a day's journey from Ard-Carna, whence Caillin and his companions set out.

[2] *Tulach-na-crot.* "The hill of the harps." Name obsolete.

[3] *Bennachan.* This place is no longer know by this name.

[4] *Magh-Nisi.* The plain of Nisi (pron. Nishy). In Perrot's Composition with the chieftains of Leitrim (1585), Magh-Nisi (or Moynishe) is given as an alias name for the upper (or southern) part of Muinter-Eolais (*Moynterolyshe oghtragh*), cont. 50½ quarters of land, the inheritance of the sept of Ir M'Granill, or Reynolds, and of the sept of O'Mulvey. O'Flaherty's *Iar Connaught;* App., p. 349. The residence of M'Granill of Moynishe was at Inishmurrin, in the parish of Annaghduff, bar. of Mohill; and the territory apparently extended from Kiltubbrid, on the north, to Annaghduff on the south.

[5] *the Urnaidhe.* in Urnaide. Lit.

and was glad before him. They afterwards cemented their covenant and friendship. Caillin also obtained land afterwards, eastwards from Ard-Carna.

Caillin proceeded afterwards across the Shannon eastwards, to Magh-Cellachain. He stayed that night with Cellachan, for it was their journey.[1] They went after that to Tulach-na-crot.[2] Nevertheless, they left Nisi (i.e. son of Niatach), Caillin's brother, at the Bennachan[3] in Magh-Nisi, where Nisi was slain by Cellachan. Magh-Cellachain, moreover, was the name of the plain at that time. Cellachan, however, gave the plain and its profits to Caillin, as an eric for Nisi; wherefore it has been called Magh-Nisi[4] from that time to this; and that is why the plain belongs to Caillin.

Caillin also remained in Tulach-na-crot, until his brother's (i.e. Nisi's) body arrived to him there; and hence it is, from the waiting and tarrying for the body which the clerics performed there, that the place is since called the Urnaidhe.[5]

Riocc of Inis-bo-finde[6] desired, moreover, that he might get fish in the *inbher*[7] that was near them, and he got no fish; on which account they cursed the lake that night, because they found no fish in it.[8]

They proceeded afterwards from the Ornaidhe[9] to Magh-Rein, to wit, to Dun-Baile.

Then it was that Caillin established the burial place of the Conmaicni, to wit, Fidnacha. And it was after this that Aedh believed for Caillin, and he (Caillin) killed Fergna, and turned the druids into stones, as we said before. It is of [those] things this Lay was sung.

"the waiting." This name would be Anglicised Urney, or Nurney (the latter being formed by the attraction to "Urney" of the *n* of the article, in). But there is no place in Leitrim known by this name.

[6] *Riocc of Inis-bo-finde.* See note [4], p. 82; and n. [4], p. 118.

[7] *inbher.* Usually explained as the estuary of a river; but it also signifies a pool; and the word *loch*, or "lake," is put for it in the second line following in the text.

[8] *no fish in it.* O'Rody adds in the margin, ocus nir gabad iarum iasg ann o sin ar ni biad cid beo nama air in loch sin; "and no fish was afterwards caught in it; for they (the fishes) cannot even live in that lake." He does not tell us, however, the name or site of the lake referred to, which is probably that near Kiltubbrid, in the barony of Mohill, near the road from Carrick-on-Shannon to Fenagh, which must have been Caillin's route from Ard-Carna.

[9] *Ornaidhe*=Urnaidhe (note [5]).

Fingal do triall Connmaicni
Ma ċend Duine moir,
An airdepscop oirdnide,
Caillin, nar leg doib.
Coscid do bar n-imresuin,
Do chan Caillin caid;
In cogar do rigneabair,
Legid damsa ar dail.
Is misi bar seanathair,
A sil Conmaic caoim;
D'iarrad tuillid trebthachuis
Rachaid misi daib.
Bar manċine ilerḋa
Tabraiḋ dam com chill.
Do ġenam a ṫigerna,
Gaċ ni adera frind.
Ticc ar es na caingni sin
Legoit leṫi Cuinn;
Popal uasal ainglide
Do go Cruaċuin cuir.
Fagurtaċ .h. Cathalan
Dobi i Cruacuin caim̃,
Olc re bidbad abaran
Faiscin Chaillin caim.
Cineḋ firglan Faġartaig
.h. Cathalan coeim,
Do gellsat da n-ascadaib
Riarugad in naim.
Do gellsat don naim aiḋi
I Cruaċain na cuaċ
Screpall gaċa hain ċairclig
Gaċ tres bliadain buan.[a] [a] fol. 20, a 2.

[1] *fair.* caim̃. A. has an alias reading clainn, the dat. form of clann, "proles," which seems erroneous.

[2] *sight.* faiscin, lit. "seeing." faic-sinn would be more correct.

[3] *of the cups.* na cuaċ. The word read

The Conmaicni purposed a fratricide,
    Respecting Dun-mor;
    Which the glorious arch-bishop,
    Caillin, did not allow.
"Cease from your quarrels,"
    The holy Caillin said;
    "The conspiracy which you have formed
    Submit to my decision.
"I am your old father,
    You seed of fair Conmac;
    To seek for more possessions
    For you, I will depart.
"Your numerous tributes
    Bring to me, to my church."
    "We shall do, O Lord," [said they],
    Whatever thou dost tell us."
After this agreement went
    The Legate of Leth-Chuinn,
    With a noble, angelic company,
    To Cruachan of the feasts.
Fagartach O'Cathalain
    Was then in Cruachan fair.[1]
    Hateful to a foe [would have been]
    The sight[2] of mild Caillin.
The pure-bright kin of Fagartach
    O'Cathalain, the meek,
    Promised, for the sake of gifts,
    To submit unto the Saint.
They promised their holy tutor,
    In Cruachan of the cups,[3]
    A *screpall* from each sheepfold,
    Each third succeeding year.

cuac might perhaps be also read cruac, which would signify "of the reeks," or mountains; but this reading would scarcely be topographically correct.

ISiatso na haisgeda
  Tucad doib na diaid,
  Usge findglan, fothlochta,
  Cruithnecht corcra a criaid,
Buaid tindluicti is tabartuis
  Tugad doib co fir;
  Buaid milraid is marcachuis,
  Is fir leptha rig.
Dalta gaċ ui Chaṫalan
  Acht combet da rer,
  Tug do gaċ geg glan ḟallain
  Gach buaid tug daib fein.
Teit co tech a deg carat,
  Go h-ard Carna air cuairt;
  Fuair ic Beo Aed bennachtach
  Failti soċlo suairc.
Con eclais do anustair
  Gan dol uaiṫi amaċ,
  Don leṫ thair do gabastair
  Ferand gleglan gar.
A catach do chenglatar,
  Issatharnd assin.
  Nech millfes andernsatar
  Usa thocht i ten.
Asen co mag Cellaċain
  Dar in Sinuind soir;
  Robi a n-uide tendathan,
  Anaitt isin moig.
Adaig do na comnaide
  Ic Ceallachan chass.

[1] *brook-lime.* fothlochta. See note [10], p. 179.

[2] *in clay.* a criaid. a caaid, A. caid, or caith, would mean "chaff," or husks; but criaid seems to be the reading required in order to rhyme with diaid, in the 2nd line of the stanza.

[3] *bed-fellowship.* The poet meant to say that St. Caillin conferred on the Cinel-Fagartaigh the virtue of furnishing a

These are the boons that were
    To them thereafter given:
    Pure-bright water, brook-lime;[1]
    Purple wheat in clay.[2]
The palm of distribution and donation
    Was truly to them given;
    The palm of hunting and horsemanship,
    And of bed-fellowship[3] of a king.
The foster-son of each O'Cathalain,
    If him they would obey—
    To each pure perfect scion he gave
    Every virtue he gave themselves.
To the house of his good friend he goes,
    To Ard-Carna,[4] on a visit.
    From blessed Beo-Aedh[5] he received
    A rich and joyous welcome.
At the church he there remained,
    Nor from it forth went he,
    'Till on the east side he obtained
    Convenient, fertile land.
Their covenant they ratified,
    On Saturday anon;
    Whoever nullifies what they did,
    Had much better enter fire.
From thence to Magh-Cellachan,
    'Cross the Shannon, to the east,
    Was their tedious[6] journey.
    They rested in the plain.
One night was he[7] abiding,
    With Cellachan[8] the bold.

most eligible male bed-fellow of a king.

[4] *Ard-Carna.* See note [11], p. 179.

[5] *Beo-Aedh.* See note [12], p. 179.

[6] *tedious.* This is but a conjectural translation of the word τenoαthan, which seems corrupt.

[7] *he*; i.e. St. Caillin.

[8] *Cellachan.* The pedigree of this per

Aſen do don Oṙnaiḋe,
Coṙ gab aitreb aſſ.
Fagbuit aṙ laṙ Bennaċan
Niſſi na ſuan ſaim;
Co torchaiṙ ṙe Cellachan
Bṙathaiṙ Caillin caiḋ.
O Chellaċan ċomṙamaċ
Do ḟloinnti in maġ muaḋ.
Maġ Niſſi ṙeil ṙoblaḋaċ
Aiṙ oſin anuaſ*
A bṙeṙann 'ſa mainċine
Fuaiṙ Caillin 'ſin gnim;
Gemaḋ hi tiṙ taiṙngiṙe,
Do beṙdaiſ do aṙ ſiḋ.
Niṙ gluaiſ aſ a ċomnaiḋe
Co ṙiacht chuige in coṙp;
Conid de ata in Oṙnaiḋe
Aṙ Tulaiġ na cṙot.
Mian ſiṙeiſc in inbiṙ ſin
Tic ſo Rioc ṙeil,
Ni ſuaṙataṙ impiḋig
Do ſṙomaḋ in eiſg.
Malloigṫiṙ in oiḋċi ſin
Loċ na maigṙeḋ mall.

* fol. 20, b 1.

son has not been preserved. He was probably not of the Conmaicne, or sept to which St. Caillin belonged.

[1] *Ornaidhe.* See note [5], p. 181.

[2] *Bennachan.* See note [3], p. 180.

[3] *Nissi.* Brother of St. Caillin, and the person from whom the name of Magh-Nissi ("plain of Nissi") was given to the plain previously known as Magh-Cellach-ain. See note [4], p. 180.

[4] *proud.* muaḋ. The MS. has an alias reading, moṙ; but as muaḋ, the last word in the second line of the stanza, rhymes with anuaſ, the concluding word in the last line, t has been adopted in preference to moṙ.

[5] *Is its name.* aiṙ lit. "on it", A.

[6] *for the deed;* i.e. as an eric, or fine, for the murder of Nissi. The text is 'ſin gnim; lit. "in the deed."

From that he went to the Ornaidhe,
Where he took up his abode.
In the plain of Bennachan[2] they leave
Nissi,[3] in slumber sound;
Where by Cellachan was slain
The brother of Saint Caillin.
From Cellachan the active
The proud[4] plain had been named;
Magh-Nissi, manifest, famous,
Is its name[5] from that time down.
Their land and their tributes
Caillin got for the deed[6];
Were it the land of Promise,
They'd have given it him for peace.
From his abode he moved not,
Till the corpse to him[7] was brought.
And hence the name 'Ornaidhe' is applied
To[8] Tulach-na-crot.[9]
A fancy for that *inbher's* fish[10]
Did plainly seize Riocc.
But they found no opportunity,
To make trial of the fish.
On that same night was cursed
The slow-salmon lake.[11]

[7] *to him.* chuıꝣe. chuıꝣce, A.

[8] *is applied To.* ατα . . . . αꞃ; lit. "is upon."

[9] *Tulach-na-crot.* See note [2], p. 180.

[10] *that inbher's fish*; i.e. the fish of the *inbher* which was near Ornaidhe. The word *inbher* is usually explained "estuary," or mouth of a river, and regarded as connected with Welsh *aber.* But the word *loch* (=lacus), a lake, is put for it in the second line of the next stanza. *Inbher* is frequently used in old texts to express a pool, or pond (Cf. *Book of Leinster*, 142, b. 1), which is probably its genuine meaning.

[11] *The slow-salmon lake.* In place of pointing out the situation of this lake, or *inbher*, if he knew it, O'Rody adds, for the instruction of some "William," a quatrain in praise of a Cormac Mac I Eidin (top marg. fol. 20, a).

Iasg beo ar es na coindṁi sin
Nochar gabad ann.
Rob i a n-uiḋi on Ornaide
Co sen Mag Rein ruad;
Condearna roim Conmaicni
Do. Dun mBaili mbuan.
A n-dun Chonaing beg ecluig
Do ḃi Fergna fial;
Ba freitech da freitechaib
Noem dibroig do riar.
Mac Fergna fial fregarthach,
Aed dub co n-dath n-dael,
Gebid sen ga a ṡen athar
Do dichur na naeṁ.
Rosfolluig a onfine,
Ic faicsin na naomh;
Slechtaid Aed dub doirchide
A tri coicaitt laech.
Do chuir chuca a crosana,
Da cur asin chrich;
Legga corra clochbana
Do ni in deg naom dib.
Gebid Fergna forbretaċ
In agaid na naom,
Sciath leṫan is lorgfertas
Co fann coma caom.

[1] *he*; i.e. St. Caillin.

[2] *Conaing Little-fear.* Conaing Beg-ecla, or Conangus Impavidus, from whom the *Dun* of Fidnach was anciently called Dun-Conaing. See note [3], p. 112, *supra*.

[3] *responsive.* fregarthach; i.e. responsive to his enemies, in battle.

[4] *saints.* The MS. furnishes a second reading, Aed dub co n-dath n-dael, "Black Aedh of Chafer's hue." But a marg. note intimates that the line above printed is what was isint sompla, "in the copy"; from which it would appear that the copyist of the 1516 MS. had taken

A live fish, after that billet,
Was never captured there.
Their journey from the Ornaidhe was
To noble, old Magh-Rein,
Where he[1] made a burial place for the Conmaicni
Of perpetual Dun-Baile.
In the Dún of Conaing Little-fear[2]
Was generous Fergna;
Whose vow of vows was,
Not to obey a paltry saint.
Fergna's brave, responsive[3] son,
Black Aedh of chafer's hue,
Seized his ancestor's spear
To extirpate the saints.
He suppressed his antipathy,
On beholding the saints;[4]
And dark, black Aedh bent the knee,
With his thrice fifty heroes.
He[5] sent to them his satirists,[6]
To drive them from the land.
But white, pointed, stony flags[7]
Of them the good saint made.
The prejudiced Fergna seized—
To oppose the saints—
A broad shield and club-staff,
And to fair Fan-Comha[8] went.

liberties with the text of the original, which was doubtless in the possession of Thady O'Rody, the writer of the note in question.

[5] *He;* i.e. Fergna.

[6] *satirists.* cnorana, pl. of cnoran, a buffoon, or jester; gl. "scurra." (Stokes' Ir. Gloss., p. 39). In the Cornish Vocab., printed by Zeuss (*Gram. Celt.* 1107), *mimus* vel *scurra* is explained *barth* (bard). The *crosana* were the druids above referred to (p. 115, *supra*).

[7] *flags.* See note [4], p. 116, *supra*.

[8] *Fan-Choma.* See note [1], p. 114.

Targaid Caillin comada
Don rig, ar a riar,
Co nach geb Connachta
Acht ua d'Fergna fial.
Fergna fer na fir ailli,
Ger bo arnaid og,
Ma 'ndernna do digaire
Ro folchad man fot.*

* fol. 20, b 2.

Iar fothagad imorro Fidnacha do Chaillin, ocus iar mbennachad Aeda find mic Fergna, fuair forba ocus ferand firmor o chloind Fergna, ocus o chined do chlannaib Conmaic mic Fergusa iarum.

Is airesin ro gellsat Conmaicni ciss ocus comada uatha fein ocus ó a cined co brath, do cind indernna do maith doib.

Issi so in chain ro gellsat Conmaicni do Chaillin; a n-dechmaid ocus a primitti. Uingi d'or gacha tellaig i Conmaicni .i. gach sechtmad bliadan. Screpall o gach aen duine. Tricha bo gacha belltaine o Chonmaicni Rein do Chaillin, et ech gach rig bias ar Conmaicnib. Ced chorn gacha dabcha i Conmaicne. Dechmad gach rig gebus Conmaicni ocus a indlacad co Fidnacha co Caillin. A n-adlucad i Fidnacha is Caillin, ar is he fein a mbrethium bratha.

Ro gell neam da gach aen do sil Conmaic, acht coro hadlaicthi i Fidnach[a]. Ro fagaib terci gacha maithiusa forra dia sechnaitis Fidnacha .i. terci cruid ocus cethra ocus chonaig, digal ocus duinebad, ocus cogad ocus cosnam inter se; gait ocus brait ocus fell ocus fingal; ethech ocus escuine, ocus girru saegail. Ro gell ifern doib gemad

[1] *buried*. See p. 117, *supra*.

[2] *Conmac*. Ancestor of the Conmaicni. See the Pedigree above given, p. 7.

[3] *he;* i.e. St. Caillin.

[4] *first-fruits*. primitti=primitiæ; which sounds rather modern, although the word occurs in the succeeding poem, apparently copied from the old *Book of Fenagh*.

[5] *screpall*. See note [6], p. 79, *supra*.

[6] *by Caillin*. Or by his successor.

[7] *final judge*. brethium bratha, "judge of doom." This would be encroaching on the jurisdiction of St. Patrick, who obtained, according to the Trip. Life of the Saint, the privilege of "being judge over the men of Ireland on the Last Day." *Cusack's Life of St. Patrick*, p. 417.

Caillin offered terms
To the king, for obeying him :
That none should possess Connaught,
Save a descendant of brave Fergna.
Fergna, man of excellence,
Though perfect, strong, was he,
For the violence he had done,
Was buried[1] 'neath the sod.

On the foundation of Fidnacha by Caillin, moreover, and after he had blessed Aedh Find son of Fergna, he obtained extensive possessions and land from Fergna's sons, and afterwards from his kindred of the children of Conmac[2] son of Fergus.

Therefore it is that the Conmaicni promised rent and considerations from themselves and their kindred for ever, on account of the good he[3] had done them.

This is the tribute the Conmaicni promised to Caillin; to wit, their tithes and first-fruits.[4] An ounce of gold for every hearth in Conmaicne, i.e. every seventh year. A screpall[5] from every man. Thirty cows every May from the Conmaicni-Rein for Caillin, and the steed of every king who may be over the Conmaicni. The first goblet of every vat in Conmaicne. The tithes of every king that shall possess Conmaicne. And all to be transmitted to Fidnacha, to Caillin. They should be buried in Fidnacha by Caillin;[6] for he himself is their final judge.[7]

He promised Heaven to every one of the seed of Conmac, provided they were buried in Fidnacha. He awarded[8] them scarcity of all good if they abandoned[9] Fidnacha, to wit, scarcity of stock and cattle, and of fortune; [besides] vengeance and pestilence, and war and contention among themselves; theft and robbery, and treachery, and fratricide; falsehood and malediction, and shortness of life. He promised them hell, whether it was with Cruimther-

[8] *awarded.* ro fagaib; lit. "he left."
[9] *abandoned.* dia fechnaitis; lit. "if they should avoid." From this it would appear that considerable jealousy existed between the monks of Fenagh and those of the neighbouring monastery of Cloone, regarding the burial of the dead belonging to the district.

[a]fol. 21, a 1. ag cruimthir Fraech, no gidbe maigean[a] aili i mbedis, acht i Fidnacha abain. A roga do Conmaicnib fesin, nem doib da togat i Fidnacha is Caillin; No don gach plag ocus gach teidm, gač cogad ocus gač digal dibsin forra. Saegal gairit ibus in droch betaid, ocus ifern fodeoid aca, cen bear Caillin for nim, da togat in nač ecluis oili dia huaisli.

Ni machtnad, imorro, co na beṫ roim adnaicṫi ag Conmaicaib buḋ ferr doib ina Fidnača, gen go beṫ esccaine Chaillin ocus Cholaim čille ocus na naom forra ar a sečna; ḃaili i tuc Caillin lais taisi in aon apstal déc, ocus taisi Luirint ocus Stefan, da martair; ocus baili i tuc in bret do ruide moiri og, ocus do biḋ im Crist fein iga biathad; et don baile i rabatar in commetisi do naemaib ic fognum do Dia amail foirgles in rann:—

Colum cilli fecit.

Do ḟogain runna ni breg,
Deč naim deič fichit, deič ced;
In tan do ḟuarus loġad
Dom pecṫaib in oen inaḋ.

Et don atat .ix. riga .x. do rigaib Erenn fo uir Fidnacha, amail atat isin lebar in ar ndiaid. Cait din i bfuigbetis Conmaicni roim adnaicṫi bud[b] čuibdi ocus bud ferr doib ina Fidnacha, cid ar na fathaib sin fein, gen co beth ifern aca ocus gach digal olchena ar a sečna.

[b]fol. 21, a 2.

Ced lepaid gača tigi do Chaillin ar a sindsiriučt. Ced cuib-

[1] *Cruimther-Fraech.* "Presbyter Fraech," or "Cruhir-Ree", as the name is pronounced in the locality, is the patron of the parish of Cloone, adjoining that of Fenagh. The church of Cloone, anciently called Cluain-Conmaicne, was founded by him. He was of the same sept as St. Caillin, having been the 6th in descent from Cumscrach, from whom Caillin was descended in the 4th generation (Pedig. *Leabar Brecc*, p. 16; and Ped. above printed, p. 4). The two saints were thus related; notwithstanding which, it would appear that great rivalry existed between their successors in Fenagh and Cloone. Cruimther-Fraech's day was the 20th Dec. He must have lived about the end of the 6th century. There is a tradition in the neighbourhood that a subterranean passage led from Cloone to Fenagh.

[2] *relics.* Vid. *ante*, pp. 11, 13.

[3] *place.* The word in the MS. seems like moḋ (=modus); but inad (place) would better suit both rhyme and metre.

Fraech,[1] or whatsoever other place they might be [buried] in, except Fidnacha alone. The Conmaicni themselves might have their choice—Heaven they should have if they chose [to be buried] in Fidnacha by Caillin; or else every plague and pestilence, every war and vengeance, of the foregoing to come upon them; they should have a short life in evil plight here, and hell at last whilst Caillin might be in Heaven, if they chose [to be buried] in any other church, however exalted.

'Tis no wonder, moreover, that the Conmaicni could have no place of sepulture better for them than Fidnacha, even if the curse of Caillin and Colum Cille, and of the saints, did not fall on them for forsaking it—the place to which Caillin brought the relics[2] of the eleven Apostles, and the relics of the two martyrs Laurence and Stephen; and the place whither he brought the cloth which the Virgin Mary made, and which was wont to be around Christ Himself when being fed; and the place, also, in which so many saints were serving God, as the stanza testifies:—

Colum Cille fecit.	Here served—no lie— Ten saints, ten score, ten hundred, When I obtained forgiveness Of my sins, in one place.[3]

And moreover, there are 19 kings of the kings of Ireland under the clay of Fidnacha, as they are [mentioned] in the following[4] book.

Where then could the Conmaicni find a burial place fitter or better for them than Fidnacha, for those very reasons alone, even though they should not have hell and every other retaliation for forsaking it?

The first[5] bed of every house [was awarded] to Caillin, for his seniority; the first produce[6] of every Spring; and the priority of every bath. A vessel-full

O'Rody adds the note "1210 saints together in Fenagh, as St. Colum Cille testifies, ut supra."

[4] *following.* in ar ndiaid; lit. "after us."

[5] *first*, or best. A marg. note reads cios Conṁaicnoċ Caillin; "Caillin's Conmaicne tribute."

[6] *produce.* cuibrend, lit. "portion," The word cuibrend (=com-rend, co-distribution) is put for rend (or rand), "part," or "portion," in the Irish Life of St. Brigid, Leab. Brecc, 63 a.

reind gaċa herrach. Tosaċ gaċa fotraicṫi. Lan escra as gaċ dabaig, cenmotha in ced ċorn. Do gaċa fir raiṫ, ocus screpall gaċa tigi. Ro ordaig em Caillin cathaċ uada fein do Conmaicnib do bris[iud caṫa] rompa, ar ċomallad na cana sa .i. cros ċuill do gerrad, ocus a barr tria na bolgan, iss in chathaċ sin. Is don ċanaid sin ata int arcetal sa:—

Caillin caiḋ cumachtaċ,
Epscop uasal oirdnige,
Is forbfailid fuireċair,
Ria gaċ ain do ċéin.
Ise so indligend son,
Cenn crabaid na Conmaicnech,
Do ċisaib, do dligedaib,
O Conmaicnib fein.
Dligid Caillin caemfertach
Do crechi o gaċ aon gabail,
Racus tar gaċ cet berna
Ria na airecht ard,
Dar cend choscair commaidnig,
Is madma gan contaḃairt,
Ra na crois ċaiḋ chumachtaig,
Ar gach sluag nglan ngarg.*
(* fol. 21, b 1.) Bid hi so mo chathachsai,
Ar Caillin co caem fertaib,
Mo cros chuill go cumachtaib

[1] *true rath;* i.e. every *rath*, or residence, of a man of position.

[2] *screpall.* See note [6], p. 79, *supra*.

[3] *cathach;* i.e. præliator, or battle standard; from *cath*, a battle. These relics, which, when borne round an army, with appropriate ceremony, ensured victory, were of various kinds. The *cathach* given to the Cinel-Eoghain by St. Colum Cille, now in the Royal Irish Academy, consists of a shrine containing a fragment of a Latin Psalter, alleged to be in the Saint's handwriting. The præliator given by St. Cairnech of Dulane to the Clanna-Neill was a *Misach*, or Calendar (?), from *mis*, a month. The *cathach* of the O'Kellys of Hy-Maine was the Bachall-Grellain, or Crozier of St. Grellan, their patron Saint.

out of every vat, besides the first goblet. A cow from every true *rath*;[1] and a *screpall*,[2] for every house.

Caillin also ordained, from himself, a *cathach*[3] for the Conmaicni, to break battles before them, on condition of this tribute being kept up, to wit, a hazel cross to be cut, and its top through its middle—that is the *cathach*.[3] 'Tis of that tribute this composition is [sung][4]:—

Holy, powerful Caillin;
Illustrious, noble bishop;
Joyous he and festive is
To each one from afar.
This is what is due to him,
The Conmaicni's chief of piety,
In rents, in lawful tributes,
From the Conmaicni-Rein.
Mild-virtuous Caillin is owed
A prey-cow from each capture
That through each first gap passes,
Before his august court;
In return for[5] joyous victory,
And undisputed triumph,
Thro' his holy powerful cross,
O'er every bright, fierce host.
"Let this my battle ensign[6] be,"
Quoth Caillin of the virtues mild,
"Mine hazel cross with powers great,

"or its likeness." Hazel was a curious material of which to make a sacred relic, for the hazel tree was regarded as possessing evil virtues by the ancient Irish.

[4] *sung.* The following composition is in the same metre as the poem above printed, p. 155, sq. In the translation, an attempt has been made to preserve the metre, without departing from the sense of the original. The scribe adds the marg. note i ttempul duin maili ro graiphned in let duileog; "in the church of Dun-Baile (Fenagh) this page was written."

[5] *In return for.* dar cend; lit. "over the head;" but idiomatically, "in consideration for."

[6] *battle-ensign.* cathach. See note [3], last page.

Ar na gerrad d'aon buillid,
    Itir bun is barr.
A barr tre na bolgansi,
'Sa togbail co harrachta;
Ni gebat frim manchaibsi
    Sluaig Gaideal na gall.
Dligid Caillin caimfertach
Cet lepaid do trinsiriucht;
Primit gacha ain tigi,
Cuibrend gacha h-ain errach,
    Dar cend ratha rain.
Cet tosaċ gach fotraicthi;
Cet chorn gacha h-ain dabchai;
Dligid dib an airdepscop,
    Re lan escra ain.
Nem is rath gan contabairt,
Uaimsi do gach Connaicnech,
    Ar Caillin na cell;
Ar chomet mo chaem chanai,
'S ar thogbail mo locansa,
Coscar cacha hairechta,
    Uaimsi ar a ċenn.
Nem is rath gan contabairt,
Uaimsi do gaċ Connaicnech,
Ar chomett mo chaem chisa
    Gen beat ar bith ce;
Ar chomet mo chaem chana,
Ar tocbail mo loccan sa;
Mana bett im aigidsi,
    Naḃ rathmar s' a ré.

[1] *Gael or Gall.* Irishmen or Foreigners (English).

[2] *portion.* cuibrend. See note [6], p. 193. The Church's share of Spring produce is doubtless meant.

[3] *for sake.* dar cend. See note [6], p. 195.

[4] *use.* The words of the text, cet tosaċ, mean lit., the "first beginning."

[5] *alive.* ar bith ce. An expression frequently used in old Irish to signify "in

Lopped off by a single stroke,
Between end and top.
Its top then thro' its centre passed,
And reared on high most mightily,
Against my monks shall not prevail
The hosts of Gael or Gall."[1]
To virtuous Caillin is due
The first bed for his eldership,
Of every mansion the first-fruits,
The portion[2] just of every Spring,
For sake[3] of choicest luck;
The first use[4] of every bath,
The first horn from every vat,
Is to th' archbishop due from them,
With a large vessel full.
" Heaven and grace, without dispute,
From me to each Conmaicnian,"
Said Caillin of the cells,
" If they maintain my tribute fair,
And of my place here will make choice,
Of every court the triumph they
Shall have from me therefor.
" Heaven and grace, without dispute,
From me to each Conmaicnian,
If they maintain my tribute fair
Whilst they alive[5] shall be.
If they maintain my tribute fair;
And if my place here they select;
Unless they are opposed to me,
In their time[6] they'll happy be."[7]

the world." Its exact meaning is not evident. ap is a prep. signifying "on," or "upon," and *bith* (= vita) "life;" but ce is obscure, unless it may be connected with Gr. γῆ.

[6] *In their time.* ṙ' a ṙe, for ṙe a ṙe; lit. "during their time."

[7] *they'll . . . . . be.* uaḋ, for buḋ.

* fol. 21, b 2.

Dligid Caillin caemfertach,
Dar cend ola* ard uasli,
Screpall gacha h-aen toigi,
O gaċ muintir maith.
Dligid dib an airdepscop,
Do chloind chalma Chaireda,
Bo gaċa fir raiṫ.

Otchi Caillin caimfertach
Lepaid Chruimthir chumaċtaig
Gan etec glan gle,
Tocaib let mo brecansa,
Uair Caillin co caem fertuib,
A Chruimthir ċaid ċumacttaig
Is lepaid friat re.
Misi frit laim idainsi,
Do thimthireċt altoire,
A Caillin ċaid chumaċtaig,
Gach noiḋċi is gach dia.
Dabaċ desi dagdaine,
Go furthuin a tomaltuis,
O gach fir im inadsa
Ra bithu sitsia.
M'echsa is m'erred airdepscoip
D' ḟagbail agad lepaidsi,
A Chruimthir ċaid chumachtaig.
Duitsi uair is chair;
Trian gach cuarta dligimsi,
Trian uaitsi 'ga tren tabach,

[1] *As fee for; or in return for.* dar cend. See note [5], p. 195.

[2] *screpall.* See note [6], p. 79, *supra.*

[3] *community.* muintir properly means "family," "community," or "people."

[4] *Caireda.* See note [3], p. 156.

[5] *true rath.* See note [1], p. 194.

[6] *Cruimther.* Cruimther-Fraech. See note [1], p. 192. The word *cruimther* seems cognate with the Welsh *premter;* and

To virtuous, mild Caillin is due,
As fee for[1] noble unction high,
A *screpall*[2] for each mansion,
From every good community.[3]
Due to the archbishop is,
From the brave clan of Caireda,[4]
A cow from each true *rath*.[5]

When mild, virtuous Caillin saw
The bed of powerful Cruimther,[6]
Without clean clothing white ;
"Take thou with thee this my plaid,"[7]
Said Caillin mild and virtuous,
"O, holy, pow'rful Cruimther,
Into thy bed for life."[8]
"I[9] shall be near thy pure hand,
For altar ministrations,
O, holy, mighty Caillin,
Each night and every day.
A vat for every two good men,
With their supply of nourishment,
From each man representing me,
For ever thou shalt have."
"My steed, and my archbishop's robe,
O, holy, mighty Cruimther,
Shall at thy bed presented[10] be,
To thee, since it is right.
The third of all fees due to me—
By thee the third may levied be,

both appear to be borrowed from Lat. "præsbyter."

[7] *plaid.* bɼeccan ; a speckled garment ; from bɼec, "spotted," "speckled."

[8] *for life.* ꝼɼuaꞇ ɼe ; lit. "during thy time."

[9] *I.* Cruimther Fraech here speaks.

[10] *at thy bed presented.* ꝺ'ꝼaᵹbaıl aᵹaꝺ lepaıꝺꞅı ; lit. "to be left at thy bed." The word lepaıꝺ (bed) is merely used for

A Chruimthir chaid chumachtaig,
Na teged ar cail. Caillin č.

Ro airned Caillin ní don chanaid sin Conmaicni don aingeal iar na iarfaidid de isind imacallaim .i.

Cotlad 'san imdaidsi.

a fol. 23, a 1. (fol. 22 lost).

Ro labair ar Conall ar tus, ocus ar Conmaicnib iarum.[a]

* * * * * * * *

* * * * * * * *

Aingel indisius cose,
Nirceraṫ gum riarugud
Gein marus san screbtrai. G. Gebaid.

Ro facuib em Colam cille mac Feidlimid na drochfagbala cetna do Conmaicnib dia sečnatis a cuirp ocus a cennaiğe Fidnača; ocus ro gell fos gid be nech do čloind Conmaic do ṫogfad i cill eli combiad a anam in ifern cein do biad Colum cille ocus Caillin for nim. Gid aire sin nama ba togṫa do Conmaicnib Fidnacha gach cill oile.

Colam cilli cecinit hoc.

Mo chean Caillin caid,
Mairg fris ticfa a ḟerg;
Tonn bunaid don brač;
Buinne don n-or derg.
Muir morlan gach lucht,
Ab Fidnača fír;
Mairg ticfa ra cert;
Traeṫfaid nert gač rig.

the sake of metre, instead of some word signifying house, or home.

[1] *fall not in arrear.* dol ar cail means literally "going behind." The first words of the poem, Caillin č[aid], are added in token of its completion, according to the usual practice of Irish scribes.

[2] "*Sleeping in this bed.*" The dialogue referred to, of which this is the first line, is that printed above, p. 155.

[3] *Conmaicni.* This is the last word on fol. 21, b. Fol. 22 is lost; and fol. 23 commences with the third last line of a poem, the first words of which (g. gebaid)

O, holy, mighty Cruimther,
That they fall not in arrear.[1] Caillin.

Caillin described to the Angel some of that tribute of the Conmaicni, when it was asked of him in the dialogue

"Sleeping in this bed."[2]

He first spoke of Conall, and afterwards of the Conmaicni.[3]

* * * * * * * *

* * * * * * * *

Angel that tellest so far,
They'll not cease to obey me,
Whilst it in Scripture lives.

Colum Cille son of Fedhlimidh, moreover, awarded the same evil gifts to the Conmaicni, if their bodies and bequests[4] avoided Fidnacha. And he also promised, that if any one of the children of Conmac should choose [to be buried] in another church, his soul should be in Hell, whilst Colum Cille and Caillin would be in Heaven. For which reason alone, Fidnacha was to be chosen by the Conmaicni in preference to any other church.

COLUM CILLE cecinit hoc.

My love is holy Caillin.
Woe to him who his ire encounters.
The fundamental wave of Doom;
The trumpet of red gold.
The great sea of all things full;
True Abbot of Fidnacha;
Woe to him who opposes his right.
Each king's might will he subdue.

are added to the concluding line. But the poem, if it exists in any other MS., has not been identified.

[4] *bequests*. cennaiġe. This would be the ordin. pl. form of cennaċ, which means a bargain, or condition. (*Book of Leinster*, 114, a 2; and *Leb. na h Uidhre*, 99 b). But it is probably put for cennaiṫe, which O'Donovan explains as "a gift given by last will;" (*Suppl. to O'Reilly*, voc. ceannaiṫe). But compare *cennige*, glossed "lixa"; Ebel's Zeuss, 229.

Do ſamla ni oil
Ar droing domun dein;
Mairg U Chonmaic caid
Naċ dingne do réir.
Clanna Conmaic caid
Raċtait uait bar cul;
Le deman a n-dil,
Le deman a run.
[Caillin.] Raid a Choluim ċaid
Cred bus digal doib,
Ar tochta daib uaim
Co roiſet co cluain.[1]
[C.C.] Gaċ neċ raċus uait,
fol. 23, a 2. Dot manchaib buden,
Cein rabamne ar nim
Betit ſin a pein.
[C.] Acſin orra ſein,
A Choluim na cell,
Cein beit ag tocht uaim
Sluaig diabal na cenn.
[C.C.] Gebimſi do laim
Gach aen ticfa rit,
Do gebad a olc
Ar ſcarad re corp.
Ni ardune inbain
Iſ landemin leam,
Mo manaichſi ſunn
Ar bacbail gaċ cell.
[C.] Ticfait ní da dóin,[2]
Tiachtain doib ni bet;
Bid bitamla leſ
A tiaċtain ſa ég.

[1] *Cluain.* Cloon, co. Leitrim. See note [1], p. 192.

[2] *of their will.* da dóin, for da deóin, A.

Thy like does not exist
In the vehement world's throng.
Woe to the descendant of fair Conmac
That will not thee obey.
Those children of mild Conmac
Who'll backward turn from thee—
With the demon shall be their fate,
With the demon their desire.

[Caillin]. Say, O holy Colum, what
On them shall the vengeance be,
When they from me depart
That they may go to Cluain.[1]

[Colum Cille]. Each one that forsakes thee,
Of thy own monks,
Whilst we may be in Heaven
Shall in torment be.

[Caillin]. Be it on them so,
O, Colum of the cells;
Whilst from me they are going
May hosts of demons meet them.

[Colum Cille]. I pledge thee my hand,
Whoe'er will thee oppose
Shall get his evil reward
After leaving the body.
With delightful abbacy,
Full certain to me 'tis,
That my monks shall be here,
After leaving every church.
They'll come, not of their will;[2]
No stain will coming be to them.
Immortal shall the benefit be
In their coming and their death[3]

[3] *and their death.* ꞃa éᵹ; *recte* "and his death." The original of this stanza is very corrupt.

[C.C.]

Feirrdi duitsi sin,
Lia di maiṫ id teġ
Iderasa·riu
Iar mbraṫ is mo ċean.[1] Mū.

Ro ḟaisneid ocus ro ḟoirsgleastair dono in Colum cilli sin mac Fedlimid amuil robatar Conmaicni in iarthar Connacht ar tus, ocus ro ḟobratar feall air a ċéile, ocus amuil ro ṫeguisc int aingeal doib Caillin do thabairt chuca o Roim; co torracht iarum Caillin dia cabair, ocus co fuair ferann doib o Ċloind Fergna, amail adubramar remi.[2] Conid aresin tugsat a mbeo ocus a marb[3] do Caillin co braṫ, ocus ratha[4] nime ocus talman forru im a ċomallad.

[a] fol. 23, b 1. Ro tharngir dono Caillin féin co rachtais uada Conmaicni dia n-adlucad co Cluain.[5] Conid airesin ro ḟiarfaid Caillin do Cholum ċilli agaraiḃe fios nime ocus talman, cred hi in digal do bera Dia ar Conmaicnib ar dol o Chaillin go Cluain. Ised adbert Colum cille, Bid la deman a mbas ocus a mbetha, a run ocus a cogar;[6] ocus biṫaitreb ifern doib fos, ar Colam, cein bemmi for nim. Ro ṫairngir Adamnan fos co nach gebad tuath na fine na rige in nech do ṡil Connuic nach imrobad co Caillin. Et dono ro tharngir Caillin co ticfatis Conmaicni tar anais chuige iar trill, amail ro foillsig int Aingeal do; ocus atbert na ragtais uad affiṫsi cein no marad litir i screptra ocus i scribend. Ro geall dono Colam failti hruthain uadai fein ocus flaiṫ nime iar mbrath do Conmaicnib, ar thoga doib i Fidnaċa.

Mor tra in onoir ocus in airmitin, ocus in grad dermair, tug Colam cille fein don baili uasal ainglide sin .i. Fidnacha. Atbert Colam dono, Inmuin lemsa, em, in baili si, ar se. Inmuin a aes uirtt[b] ocus crabad, a loċ ocus a usce ocus a inbera. Inmuin lem a

[b] fol. 23, b 2.

[1] *my love.* mo ċean. These are the first words of the poem, added in token of its conclusion.

[2] *before.* See above, pp. 175–181.

[3] *their living and their dead*; i.e. their living, to obey him, and their dead to be buried in Caillin's church of Fenagh.

[4] *were the pledges.* The text has forru, lit. "upon them."

[5] *Cluain.* See note [1], p. 192.

[6] *conspiracies.* cogar; lit. "whisper"; but in an extended sense, a plot or conspiracy.

[Colum Cille].   "The better for thee is that;
More good in thy house will be,"
I shall say to them,
"After judgment;" and my love.[1]

The same Colum Cille son of Fedhlimidh also related and explained how the Conmaicni were in the West of Connacht at first, and contemplated treachery against one another; and how the Angel instructed them to bring Caillin unto them from Rome; and how Caillin came afterwards to their assistance, and obtained land for them from Fergna's children, as we have said before.[2] And it was on that account they gave their living and their dead[3] for ever to Caillin; and the guarantees of Heaven and Earth were the pledges[4] for its observance.

Caillin himself, moreover, foretold that the Conmaicni would go from him to Cluain,[5] to be buried. And therefore it was that Caillin asked of Colum Cille, who had the knowledge of Heaven and Earth, what punishment would God inflict on the Conmaicni for going from Caillin to Cluain.[5] What Colum Cille said is "with the demon shall be their death and life, their secrets and conspiracies;[6] and hell shall be their everlasting abode also," said Colum, "whilst we shall be in Heaven." Adamnan likewise prophesied that any one of the seed of Conmac who would not turn[7] to Caillin should not obtain territory, or tribe, or kingship. And Caillin also foretold that the Conmaicni would return to him after a while, as the Angel manifested to him; and he said that they would not depart from him again whilst a letter lived in scripture and writing.

Colum Cille, moreover, promised to the Conmaicni eternal welcome from himself, and the kingdom of Heaven after doom, if they selected to be [buried] in Fidnacha.

Great, truly, was the honour, and the respect, and the excessive love Colum Cille himself gave to that noble, angelic place, to wit, Fidnacha. For Colum said: "Beloved to me, indeed, is this place," said he. "Beloved its men of Orders and devotion; its lake, and its waters, and its *inbhers*.[8] Beloved to

[7] *turn*. ımpobaᴅ is a corrupt form of the verb ımpoᴅ, to turn, which seems = ım-ꞅouᴅ, the p of ımpoᴅ being produced by the hardening of the m before the infected ꞅ in ım ꞅoaᴅ.

[8] *inbhers* See note [7], p. 181, *supra*,

irlann ocus a ḟaiċti ar Colam, a mag ocus a ḟerann archena. Ilmuin lem dono in lec curambi imaiṫigiḋ nan aingel. Gaċ baili i rabus cose, ar Colam, tair ocus tiar thes ocus tuaid, is dile ocus is toċa lem in roim adnaictisi na Conmaicnech, ar Colam .i. Fidnacha, oir is ann fuarus logaḋ nan uile peccad ó Chaillin. Ni maċtad, em, ar se, ce do geḃad gaċ nech a itċi ocus a esbad i Fidnacha, ar ro batar .x. naim ocus .x. xx., ocus .x. c. ic fognam do Dia isin baili sin in tan fuair Colam dilgud a ṗecad ann .i. cur in ċaṫa is na teoraib cuiluib.

Mo bennachtsa ocus bennacht in Choimded ar in inadsa, bar Colum. Bennaigim a aes uird ocus oiffrinn. Bennuigim in doirthech i cantar in celebrad, i filet na tri ced clar .i. clar fo gach clérech. Bennaigim fer gaċa cerdi ocus gacha dana genter isin bailisi do ċind a cuarta do Chaillin .i. screpall gaċ tres bliadain itir cerd ocus gaḃunn ocus in ol aes dana ocus oirfitid ocus sair. Ni roċair int aes dana fo dairsi eli araisin. Bennuigim gaċ uili ni dambia isin baili olchena, ocus in magh uili. Fagbaim ar in mbaili ta na mad archaingel co naċ raib gan celebrad ocus oifrend co dered domuin.*

* fol. 24, a 1.

Is follus do Chonmacnib conad fir gaċ indechaid ocus gaċ digal dar gell Caillin do ṫocht forra da seċnatis Fidnaċai, ar is e ant Aingel tuc gaċ fis ocus gaċ eolus do. Faṫ oili naċ etir a inchrechad .i. Colum cille do daingniugad ocus do gell[ad] gach uile dar airmius do ṫocht forra ar tregen Fidnaċai; uair ba primfaid nime ocus talman

where it has been pointed out that *inbher* (pl. *inbhera*) is put for *loch*, a lake. Here *inbhera* would seem to mean rivers, or streams. There is no river at Fenagh, unless the name may be applied to a small stream nearly closed up by the falling of a precipice which hung over it. In winter the *srath* adjoining it is often inundated. In 1688, when Ward described it, he spoke of

"Numerous fine green meadows
Along the margin of the silent river."

And the late Mr. Myles J. O'Reilly added, in a note to this description, that it was "a placid, sluggish rivulet, and the epithet silent (*ciuin*) accurately appropriate." See O'Donovan's *Breifny Letters*: Ord. Surv. Collect., R. I. Acad., p. 62.

[1] *flag-stone.* "Lec-nan-Aingel," or the "Flagstone of the Angels." See note [9], p. 121, *supra*.

[2] *the three Culs.* See p. 165, *supra*.

[3] *doirtech.* doirtech, duirtech, or dairtech, is usually explained as an "ora-

me its lawn, and its green," said Colum, "its plain, and its land besides. Beloved to me, indeed, is the flag-stone[1] which is wont to be the resort of the Angels. More dear and choice to me," said Colum, "than every place in which I have been hitherto, East and West, South and North, is this burial place of the Conmaicni, to wit, Fidnacha," said Colum; "for 'tis there I obtained the remission of all my sins from Caillin." "No wonder, truly," said he, "that every one should obtain his request and requirements in Fidnacha"; for there were ten saints, and ten score, and ten hundred, serving God in that place when Colum received pardon for his sins there, viz., the fighting of the battles in the three Culs.[2]

"My blessing, and the blessing of the Lord, on this place," said Colum. "I bless its men of Orders and Mass. I bless the *duirtech*[3] wherein is chaunted the celebration, in which are the three hundred boards,[4] to wit, a board before every cleric. I bless every man of trade and art who shall be born in this place, in consideration of his tribute [being paid] to Caillin, to wit, a *screpall*[5] every third year, by the artisan, and smith, and all the men of art and minstrelsy, and carpenters."

(He did not put[6] the men of art under any other bondage, nevertheless). "I bless everything else that may be in the place besides, and the entire plain. I grant to the place, which is the abode of Archangels, that it shall not be, until the world's end, without celebration and Mass."

It is manifest to the Conmaicni that it is true that every punishment and vengeance Caillin promised would come upon them, if they abandoned Fidnacha; for it was the Angel that gave him all knowledge and wisdom. Another reason which cannot be gainsaid is, that Colum Cille confirmed and promised that every evil I have enumerated would come upon them if they abandoned Fidnacha; for he was the chief prophet of Heaven and Earth, and never spoke

tory"; but a building furnished with 300 seats or tables, to accommodate as many celebrants, would scarcely convey the idea generally entertained of an ancient Irish oratory, which was regarded as a house of austerity or penitence. See Petrie's *Round Towers*, p. 119, sq.

[4] *boards.* clap; which also means a table. See last note.

[5] *screpall.* See note [6], p. 79, *supra*.

[6] *did not put.* ni rocair (for ni rochuir?). This clause seems parenthetical.

he, ocus ni ebert breg riam, ocus ni derna espa riam. Et dono teged gaċ dardain for nem, amail atbert fein:—

Ni eolaċ for talmain tind,
Riccim co hadbaib ifirnd.
Tegim gaċ dardain for neam,
Fo gairm rig na tri muinter.

Is credti do Conmaicnib conad fir gaċ indechaiḋ ocus gaċ digal dar gell Caillin naem mac Niataċ ocus Colum cille mac Fedlimid do ṫecht forra, da treged a roim adnaicti fein .i. Fidnacha. Et Adomnan foss da thairngiri gaċ uilc doib dia sechnati[s] Fidnacha, tertio. Colam cille do raid in rúnṫiri sís fecht nain diarabi ic celebrad do Chaillin, iar ndilgud a ċionn dau.

Celiubroim do dun mbaili,
Inad uasal ainglidi,
I fuarus caḋus fri trell,
Ic ard ṡenoir na hErenn.
Inmuin lim in baili caiḋ,
Ocus inmuin a aes graiḋ;
Inmain lim a ċloċ 's a crann;
Inmuin a loċ 's a abonn.
Inmain lium a ḟaiċṫi glan;
Inmain lim lec nan aingel;
Inmain lim gaċ inad ann;
Inmain a mag 's a feronn.
Gaċ baili da bḟacus riam,
Thuaid is tair is tes is tiar,

1 *a vain thing.* espa. The word diṁaoineas ("idleness") is added over the word, as a gloss.

2 *to Heaven.* This is probably an allusion to some alleged visions or raptures of St. Colum Cille, not mentioned in the Latin or Irish Lives of the saint.

3 *of the three peoples.* na tri muinter. A pedantic way of expressing the Trinity, perhaps.

4 *to him.* dau, for do, A. This word seems to have puzzled Thady O'Rody, a fair Irish scholar, who copies the clause in the margin, converting the words a ċionn dau ("to him of his sins") into one word, cionnta, "sins." He also observes

untruth, and never did a vain thing.[1] And, moreover, he was wont to go every Thursday to Heaven,[2] as he himself said :—

I am learned in [the affairs of] the firm Earth ;
I reach to the abodes of Hell ;
Every Thursday I go to Heaven,
At the call of the King of the three peoples.[3]

The Conmaicni should believe it to be true, that every punishment and vengeance which Saint Caillin son of Niata, and Colum Cille son of Fidhlimidh promised, will come upon them if they forsake their own burial place, to wit, Fidnacha. And Adamnan also foretold, in the third place, every evil for them, if they abandoned Fidnacha.

Colum Cille uttered this composition down here, on one occasion when he was bidding farewell to Caillin, after the pardon to him[4] of his sins :—

I bid farewell to Dun-Bailè,
  A noble, angelic place ;
  Where I found respect for a while
  With the arch-senior of Ireland.
Dear to me is the holy town,
  And dear its men of grade ;
  Dear to me its stone and tree,
  Dear its lake[5] and river.[6]
Dear to me its bright fair-green ;
  Dear to me the Angels' flag.[7]
  Dear to me each spot therein ;
  Dear its plain, and dear its land.
Than any place I've ever seen—
  North and east, south and west—

"Quia Columba pius venit ad St. Kilianum et ei confessus est peccata sua, ut patet hic et alibi in libro &c." ; and adds "lege hoc morem difficilem hanc hoc est" (sic.) Regarding the notion that St. Colum Cille had recourse to St. Caillin in his trouble, see note [5], p. 165.

[5] *lake.* Loch Salach, at Fenagh.

[6] *river.* αbonn. See note on inbher ; p. 205, note [8].

[7] *Angels' flag.* See note [9], p. 121, *supra.*

Is tocha lium dun mbaili,
Roim ro diles Connmaicni.*
Connmaicni crai buadach,
Cined bagach marcsluagach;
Do batar gu cruaidh i smacht,
In iarthar chuigid Connacht.
Do fuabair maicni Medba
Fingal mór tre domenma,
Uair nir fetsatur gan oil
Aitreb na bferann comair.
Troisgid fein fri Dia na fir,
Cia do fóired a fingail;
Gur innis int aingeal cain,
'Se Caillin gan imresain.
Do chuirsetar techta sair,
Go Roim aingliġ da iarraid,
Co tainicc in noem anair
Co Connmacnaib da cabair.
Gellsat sir co met ngosa,
Cined fialmar Fergosa,
A mbeo 's a marb cain gan feall,
Acht co tucad doib ferann.
Tig Caillin co dun mbaile,
Re cloind mairis rudraige,
Co fuair doib tir gan tacha,
O ċloind Fergna i Fidnaċa.
IAcsin tucsat slana sir,
Re Caillin mac Net narbuir

* fol. 24, a 2.

[1] *brave-hearted.* crai buadach; where crai seems wrongly written for craide ("heart"), the correct form.

[2] *messengers.* techta; from techt, going, or coming. A marginal note has ed adruimed in eolaig cur bo do uaib Congalain na techto hisin. gided ni innisit na hughair si sis na techtad. Is aire sin nachar ádilg linne a cur sis amail bud loinn le drem; i.e. "What the learned say is that those messengers were of the Ui-Congallain. These authors here,

More choice to me is Dun-Bailè,
The Conmaicni's dear burial place.
The brave-hearted[1] Conmaicni,
A martial, chivalrous race,
Were in hard subjection in
The west of the province of Connacht.
The children of Medbh essayed
Great fratricide, thro' evil mind,
Since they could not, without shame,
Abide in their narrow land.
The men themselves fasted before God,
[As to] who would save them from fratricide,
Until the mild angel told them
That 'twas Caillin, without dispute.
They sent messengers[2] to the East,
To Angelic Rome, seeking him.
And from the East the saint did come,
To the aid of the Conmaicni.
They promised him with fervour great—
The generous kin of Fergus—
Their living and dead,[3] without guile,
Provided that he gave them land,
Caillin came to Dun-Bailè,
Before Rudhraige's handsome race;
And obtained for them fruitful land,
From Fergna's clan, in Fidnacha.
Then sureties they gave to him,
To Caillin son of noble[4] Niata,[5]

however, do not specify the messengers. Therefore it is that we do not like to set them down, as would be agreeable to some." From this it would appear, (1) that the scribe was himself the composer of this poem, and (2) that he wrote it in the presence of critics.

[3] *living and dead.* See note [a], p. 204.

[4] *of noble.* narbuis. narbus (gen. narbuis) is glossed uasal maiṫ ("noble-good") in A.

[5] *Niata.* Net is put in the gen. form

Im a morad ar gaċ mud
Cein do biad muir na hinuḋ.
Isiat slana tugsat ris,
Ri Caillin co caemi cuir,
Im a riar do ṫabairt do,
Uluid uili isin oen lo.
Do gellsat duit noċa go,
Uluid uili isin oen lo.
Conmaicne con imat celg,
Co riarfatt tu gan mor mairg.
Da coimled duitsi dorus,
Mar do geallsatur do ċim,
Medeċa raṫ gaċ tigi;
Cuirfe dib annainfine.[a]
Cred im naċ fuiġbed gach nech
A itchi uait co heneċ,
Uair is duit fognuit co tenn
Urmór uarli na hErenn,
Do foġuin sunna in bres
Deich naim deich fichit deich céd,
In tan do ḟuarus logad
Dom pecthuib in oen inad.
Mo bennacht ar an inad
As a tánac co hiḃan,
Ocus bennacht Crist na ceall
Ar lucht a uird 's a aifrend.
Bennuigim in duirthech cain
Indentar ord co heinig;
Tri ced clar ta san tig,
Clar fa chomair gach cleirig.
Fear gaċ cerdi bennuigim
Aċt congene ar do baile,

[a] fol. 24, b 1.

for Iuatach, merely to avoid a metrical error.

¹ *altogether.* uili .... isin oen lo; lit. "all .... in the one day."

That every way they'd him exalt,
Whilst in its place the sea remained.
The sureties which they gave to him,
To Caillin of the fairest skin,
For giving him th' obedience due,
Were the Ulidians altogether.[1]
They promised thee, no falsehood 'tis,
By the Ulidians altogether—[1]
(The Conmaicni of many wiles)—
That they'd thee cheerfully obey.
If they again will furnish[2] thee
Thy tribute, as they promised,
'Twill of each house the luck increase;
'Twill banish from them all their foes.
Wherefore should not every one
Freely his wish from thee obtain,
Since for thee do stoutly serve
The greater part of Ireland's nobles.
Here served—no falsehood 'tis—
Ten saints, ten score, ten hundred,
When I did absolution get
For all my sins, in the one spot.
My blessing be upon the place
From which I came away so pure;
And the blessing of Christ of the Cells
On its Order-band and Mass-band.
I bless the *duirtech*[3] fair, wherein
Are celebrations nobly made.
Three hundred tables are in the house—
A table before each cleric.
The man of every trade I bless,
If he out of thy town be born.

[2] *if they furnish.* Da coimlet, for Da comailled; lit. "if they preserve."

[3] *duirtech.* Oratory. See note [3], p. 206.

Buaid gač dala dingbala
Do ar chenn chuarta dot aithne
Subdoiri is cerd is goba,
Saer is oirfidech sona;
Mo bennacht don chuiger chain,
Act co riarat do muintir.
Mo bennacht ar haes dana,
Genfer o Senchan malla,
Tabrat dot abaid cialda
Screpall oir gach tre[s] bliadna.
Bennaigim in baili reid;
Bennaigim gach ni annfein;
Is bennaigim uile in mag
Ta i farrad na cathrach.
IS misi Colam O Nell;
Facbuim do dun baile fen,
Go deired domain debrad
Noča bia gan celeabrad.
Fidnacha baili in crabaid,
Aitt i do na harčainglib.
A Criost dan denuim adrad,
Na rab si gan chelebrad.* Cet.

* fol. 24, b 2.

Ro tharrngir em Adamnan mac Tinde mic Ronain fecht oili co treiccfitis Conmaicni a roim ruidles fein fri dered domain .i. Fidnacha. Et dono ro tharrngir co ticfaitis tar a naiss aris fo deoid, dia saerad ar pein ocus ar escaine ocus ar ferg Chaillin. As ann ro tharrngir Adomnan in ni sin in tan do roine brethemnus a firi do Chaillin feisin.

[1] *will.* aithne; lit. "command."

[2] *tanner.* Subdoiri. Elsewhere written sudaire. See line[16], p. 102, *supra.*

[3] *Senchan.* The mention of this name in connexion with "men of song," or poets, suggests that the person alluded to was Senchan Torpeist, chief poet of Ireland in the early part of the 6th century, who is said to have been half-brother to St. Caillin. His name is identified with the "recovery," or composition of the *Tain Bo Cuailnge.* For some account of this

Success in every proper affair
Be his, for tribute at thy will.[1]
The tanner,[2] artisan, and smith;
The carpenter, and minstrel happy—
My blessing on the jovial five,
If they thy people will obey.
My blessing on thy men of song
Who from mild Senchan[3] may descend.
Let them give thy discreet abbot
A *screpall*[4] of gold each third year.
I bless the smooth place,
I bless every thing therein;
And I bless the entire plain
Which is near the *cahir*.[5]
I am Colum descendant of Niall.
I leave to the same Dun-Bailè,
That, 'till the end of th' oppressive world,
'Twill not be without celebration.
Fidnacha, home of devotion!
An abode 'tis for archangels!
O, Christ, whom I do adore,
May it not be without celebration.[6]

Adamnan, son of Tinde, son of Ronan, also foretold, on another occasion, that the Conmaicni would, towards the end of the world, forsake their own proper burial place, to wit, Fidnacha. And he likewise foretold that they would return at last, to save themselves from torment, and from the curse and anger of Caillin. The time that Adamnan foretold this thing was when he interpreted his vision for Caillin himself.

remarkable person, see O'Curry's *Lectures*, &c., pp. 29, 30; and *Manners and Customs*, &c., passim.

[4] *screpall*. See note [6], p. 79, *supra*.

[5] *cahir*. The *cahir*, or stone-fort, of Fenagh. See note [11], p. 125.

[6] *celebration*. The scribe adds at the end of the last line, the abbrev. for the first word of the poem, to signify that it is completed.

Fecht naon ro bui Caillin ina ċotlad co faca fis ingnad anetargnoiḋ, cotarr Adomnan chuige dia hécnaḋ do. Ro ṫinscain Caillin foillsiú-gaḋ na fisi do Adomnan, conad ann atbert :—

Atconnairc em, ar Caillin, Fidnacha do beṫ fo biastaib.[1] Atconnairc faelċoin na fed do ṫocht fo Fidnacha beus. Atconnairc muir do ṫocht tairsi. Atconnairc loċarn[2] lanfolus ar lasad im thimchell. Atconnairc riasta borba do milliud muige Rein uile. Atconnairc dui leomuin loinnmerai ic troitt ocus ic trenchomracc rim fein ocus re Fidnachu. Atconnairc me fein ag cognum ocus ag cirrbed na leomuin sin, ar Caillin, Atconnairc amail ro benn ag muchad na coindli[3] lam amail, ocus is tragad na mara. Beirsi breṫ[4] na fisi sin, a Adamnain, ar Caillin.

A primfaid[5] ocus a ardlegoitt, bar Adamnan, is i so breṫ na fisi sin[6] * * * * * * * * *
* * * * * * * * * *
* * * * * * * * * *

*Each ocus eirred rig Oilig do Chaillin gaċa sechtmad bliadain. Screball ar gach tig fo ċlannaib Eogain mic Neill. Ro fagaib Caillin ocus Cairneċ noem flaithius ocus geill o chach do chlannuib Neill.

Tug Domnall mac Aeda, ocus a chuingid ocus a chomarlig, in cis sin do Chaillin ren dol i cath Muigi Rath. Ro tharngir em Caillin riga ċlainni Conaill ocus Eogain amail tat isin duain si.

Caillin cecinit.

Berid bennacht, ergid uaim;
Innsaigid in tir fothuaid;

[1] *covered with monsters.* fo biastaib; lit. "under monsters." biastaib, abl. pl. of biast (now written piast=Lat. bestia).

[2] *torch.* loċarn=lucerna.

[3] *torch.* na coindli. coindli is the gen. sg. of coindel=Lat. candela.

[4] *interpretation.* breṫ; lit. "judgment."

[5] *primate.* primfaid. Although this word usually signifies "chief prophet" (from prim=primus, and faid=vates), it is frequently incorrectly used, as here, for "primate."

[6] *of that vision.* na fisi sin. These are the last words on fol. 24, b 2, in A, from which folios 25 and 26 are unfortunately missing. The contents of these missing leaves seem to have comprised, judging by the substance of the first paragraph of fol. 27, an account of some transactions between St. Caillin and St. Cairnech

On one occasion that Caillin was asleep, he saw a strange, incomprehensible vision, which he brought Adamnan to explain to him. Caillin began the relation of the vision to Adamnan; whereupon he said:—

"I saw then," said Caillin, "that Fidnacha was covered with monsters.[1] I saw the wolves of the forests also coming about Fidnacha. I saw the sea come over it. I saw a full-bright torch[2] flaming around me. I saw that savage monsters had destroyed all Magh-Rein. I likewise perceived furious lions contending and fighting against myself and Fidnacha. I perceived myself gnashing and hacking those lions," said Caillin. "I perceived as if I were extinguishing the torch[3] with my breath," said Caillin, "and exhausting the sea." "Do thou give the interpretation[4] of that vision, O Adamnan," said Caillin.

"O, primate[5] and arch-legate," said Adamnan, "this is the interpretation of that vision[6] * * * * * * * *

* * * * * * * * * *

* * * * * * * * * *

The steed and dress of the king of Oilech[7] to be given to Caillin every seventh year. A *screpall*[8] out of every house subject to the children of Eoghan son of Niall.

Caillin and holy Cairnech[9] granted[10] sovereignty and hostages from all to the Clanna-Neill.

Domhnall[11] son of Aedh, and his chieftains and counsellors, gave this tribute to Caillin before going into the battle of Magh-Rath.[12] Caillin foretold, moreover, the kings of the family of Conall and Eoghan, as they are in this Lay.

CAILLIN Cecinit.

Take ye a blessing. From me depart.
Invade the land towards the North.

of Tuilen (now Dulane), near Kells.

[7] *Oilech.* See note [3], p. 62, *supra.*

[8] *screpall.* See note [6], p. 79, *supra.*

[9] *Cairnech.* St. Cairnech of Dulane, near Kells. A native of Cornwall. His day in the British and Irish Calendars is 16th May. For some notices of this remarkable man, see Todd's *Irish Nennius*, App. cxi.

[10] *granted.* ꝼaᵹuıb, lit. "left."

[11] *Domhnall.* King of Ireland; ob. A.D. 639.

[12] *Magh-Rath.* The battle of Magh-Rath (Moyra, co. Down) was fought A.D. 634.

Treicfiṫi Teamair gan tlus;
Ba Emuin bias bar n-arus.
Cumcaigid ar clannuib Ir;
Aen chath daib ag dol na tir.
Na gebaid oman fo dol,
Oir bid romuib gaċ ruathor.
Do gebṫai mor d'omman and;[1]
Bar neachtra ni ba hanband.
Cuirfiṫi gleoiṫi naċ gar,
Fo iathaib ċuigid Ulad.
Mseċtait Ulaid tre ferg
Oirb uili co berna n-derg.[2]
Clofer Ulad 'sin gleo dian;
Bid cumuin leo go lan ċian.
Tosaċ tresi leṫi Cuind
Gabail Emna allus duirn;
Ar fulang gleo n-dodaing dian,
Conall Eogan is Airgiall.
Domnall is Fergus na ferg;
Da ċuingid cland Neill ni celg;
Act dias ro gab nert anair,
Co becht fothuaid ar Ultaib.
Tigernus fada co fir
[a] fol. 27, a 2. Is clannuib Neill is 'ga sil;[a]
Ar mo riar co mor 's go grib,
Bid iat cland Neill in tuaiscirt.

The ancient Irish account of the battle was published by the *Irish Archæol. Soc.*, in 1842, under the editorship of Dr. O'Donovan. This battle forms the subject of Dr. Ferguson's fine epic poem *Congal;* Dublin and London, 1872.

[1] *intimidation.* dm̄, A., which seems to be an abbrev. for d'omman; lit. "of fear."

[2] *Berna-derg.* Lit. "red gap." This is probably an allusion to Achadh-leith-derg, in Fermanagh, where the Irian race of Ulster was overpowered by the Orgallian septs in A.D. 331; in consequence of which the former were driven eastwards beyond the Bann, and their palace of Emania, near Armagh, was demolished.

Powerless Tara you must abandon.
    Emania your abode shall be.
Press ye on the sons of Ir.
    Be one body entering their land.
    Be not afraid of going;
    For every onset shall be yours.
You'll meet great intimidation[1] there.
    Your expedition will not be feeble.
    Battles not brief will be fought
    Throughout the lands of Uladh's province,
In fury the Ulidians will advance
    Against you all to Berna-derg.[2]
    Vanquished in the stern fight will the Ulidians be.
    Long shall they remember it.
The front of the battle of Leth-Chuind,
    In taking Emania by force of hands,
    After sustaining hard, stern fight,
    [Are] Conall,[3] Eoghan,[3] and the Airghialla.
Domhnall[4] and the angry Fergus[5]—
    Two heroes of the Clann-Neill—no deception—
    Are the first pair from the East, who'll obtain sway
    Northwards, over the Ultonians.
A long sovereignty, truly,
    The Clann-Neill and their seed shall have;
    By obeying me greatly, and quickly,
    They shall be the Clann-Neill of the North.

The present would therefore seem to be a retrospective prophecy, unless the expedition recommended was the one which resulted in the battle of Magh-Rath, where also the Ulidians proper were worsted.

[3] *Conall—Eoghan.* The Cinel-Conaill and Cinel-Eoghain are sometimes signified by the names of Conall and Eoghan, their respective progenitors; but neither of these persons lived at the time of the struggle between the Collas and the race of Ir, nor until a century afterwards.

[4] *Domhnall.* See note 12, p. ~~121~~. 147.

[5] *Fergus.* Son of the last-named Domhnall. His "Jugulatio" is entered in the *Chron. Scotorum* under A.D. 651.

Eogan in ardḟlaiṫius ann,
Ocus Conall na cruad land;
Genfid gan dimdaid on dreim
Rigraid imda for Erinn.
Ar scur airećas ćlann Ir
Don Erind, bid forgeall fir,
Ni cloch ilocc niġi ann
In cuir cruaid rosgab ann.
Dimbaid le Temraig na treb,
Le Cruachuin is le Caisel,
Airdrig cloindi Neill co nim
Ic fairbrig orra a hUlltaib.
Biaid a forrann ar gaċ ndaim,
No condiultat tall rem daim,
In aimsir Aeda iar cethair,
In Ard bo i lo na cetaib.
Dimiad dom chleirech, dom clog,
Ocus dom liubar co grod;
Slog dobera ṫall 'ga toig,
Mor a mela da macaib.
Biaid orra nert Danar ind;
Nert airdrig eli a hErind.
Dur gan mo reir, ceim gan chair;
Biaid a ngell i Cind ċorad.
Gebtaitt clanna Briain arsin
A ngeill uili co Cruachain,

[1] *Clann-Ir's rule.* The descendants of Ir, son of Milesius (who were better known as the Clann-Rury, from Rudbraidhe, twentieth in descent from Ir), enjoyed the chief rule over the North of Ireland down to the time of their expulsion from Western Ulster, in 334, by the Orgallian septs. The principal representatives of the Clann-Ir, or Clann-Rury, are now to be sought in the Magenis or Guinness families.

[2] *in the place.* ilocc=in loco; written as an alias reading over the words i luaig of the text, which are not correct.

[3] *Ard-bo.* Lit. the "Cows' height." Not identified. There is an Ardbo, or Arboe, in the barony of Dungannon, co. Tyrone, which was of importance in

Eoghan shall be in high sovereignty there;
    And Conall of the lances hard.
    From these shall be born, without stain,
    Numerous chieftains over Ireland.
On the cessation of Clann-Ir's rule[1]
    Of Ireland, a true saying 'twill be,
    That "not 'a stone in the place[2] of an egg' will be
    The brave knight who obtains sway there."
Woe to Tara of the tribes 'twill be—
    To Cruachan and to Cashel—
    [To see] Arch-kings of the Clann-Neill, fiercely
    Ruling over them from Uladh.
Their power shall be over every tribe,
    Until they deny my people yonder,
    In Aedh's time, according to prophecy,
    In Ard-bo,[3] in the day of the hundreds.[4]
Contempt to my cleric, to my bell,
    And actively unto my book,
    The people who offer, yonder at their houses,
    Shall cause great sorrow to their sons.
The Danars' power[5] shall be o'er them therefor;
    And the power of another arch-king of Ireland.
    How stupid, not t'obey me—a simple course[6]!
    Their hostages will be in Cenn-coraidh.[7]
The sons of Brian will after that obtain
    Their hostages all, as far as Cruachan;[8]

ancient times. But it does not seem to be the place here referred to.

[4] *of the hundreds.* This is in allusion to some great meeting, probably, in which Caillin's representative was insulted.

[5] *Danars' power;* i.e. the power of the Danes.

[6] *a simple course.* ceim cen chap; lit. "a step without error," from ceim, a step, advance, or career; and chap, acc. of cap, or capp, error, guilt.

[7] *Cenn-coraidh;* Anglicised Kincora; the residence of Brian Borumha, near Killaloe.

[8] *Cruachan.* Very probably Cruachan-O'Cuprain in the co. Cavan. See note [3], p. 75. Under the year 1008=1010 the Chron. Scotorum records a hosting by

Co ti fer aire anma
  Niba caife acht Cu chalma.
Gum lebar, gum cloc, gum scrin,
  Traiscrid Maelmara co fir;
  Tastelach gač tiri teind;
  Gebuid rigi for Erind.
Frecerid dam tuairt nach crin;
  Aitne dam aided in rig;
  Ni tuill do Temair na treb,
* fol. 27, b 1. Sluag guillbelrai da marbad.*
Gach sechtmađ bliadain re baiđ,
  Dlegaitt clanna Neill dam cáin,
  Screball derrit ar gach tig
  Eč is eirred rig Oilig.
Fagbuimsi doib is ri renn
  Luač coimeltad tar a čend,
  Da frecrat me, becht in blaid,
  Combe a nert ar a namdaib.
Bagim Brian;
  Baigim tri Aed is tri Niall;
  Fer re clod comland na cned
  Biđ e in Domnall fo dered.
Mac in leith;
  Niall in gluin ni ba tim treith;

Brian to Claenlocha of Sliabh-Fuaid (the Fews Mountains, co. Armagh), on which occasion "he carried off the hostages of the Cinel-Eoghain and of Uladh." This is possibly the proceeding hinted at in the "prophecy."

[1] *more fair.* caife; apparently for caimhe, compar. of caim, fair, and pronounced like caife.

[2] *Cu.* There were so many persons whose name began with Cu—, that it is impossible to say who was here alluded to.

[3] *Maelmara.* The Editor cannot say what person was referred to under this name, which means "servus maris."

[4] *Oilech's king.* See note [3], p. 62.

[5] *answer;* i.e. respond, in the way of paying dues.

[6] *Brian.* Probably Brian Borumha. The rest of the poem is composed in a

'Till comes a man of noble soul,
Than whom none more fair,[1] save mighty Cu.[2]
Before my book, my bell, my shrine,
Maelmara[3] will truly fast—
The traverser of each stout land,
Who over Ireland will obtain rule.
To my tribute unfailing will he respond;
To me the fate of the king is known;
To Tara of the tribes no boon 'twill be
That foreign-tongued hosts shall him slay.
Every seventh year, through love,
The Clann-Neill to me, as tribute, owe
A special *screpall* from each house,
And the steed and dress of Oilech's king.[4]
I and the King of the Stars grant them,
As sufficient reward therefor;
That if they answer[5] me, in perfect part,
Their power o'er their foes shall be.
I proclaim Brian.[6]
I proclaim three Aedhs,[7] and three Nialls.[8]
But the man to win the woundful fights
Shall, at the last, be the Domhnall.
The son of the Liath—
Niall of the knee[9] 'll not be faint-weak,

curious, but well known style, which requires that the words in the first line of every stanza should be repeated, in order to complete the line.

[7] *three Aedhs.* Five persons of the name of Aedh (or Hugh) were kings of Ireland between the sixth and tenth centuries.

[8] *three Nialls.* This is the number of persons of the name of Niall who were kings of Ireland, after St. Caillin's time.

[9] *Niall of the knee.* Niall Gluindubh, or Niall "Black-knee," King of Ireland, who was slain by the Danes, in the battle of Kilmashoge, near Rathfarnham, co. Dublin, in 917. He is here called "son of the Liath," from his father's name being Aedh Finnliath (k. of Ireland; ob. 876). From this Niall is derived the cognomen "O'Neill," or "descendant of Niall."

Ni ba deoluid dam re lind
Sil Eoguin is cland Conuill.
Derad dam,
Itir thuaide ni mo ċean;
Bid dodaing don te dobeir;
Ni mor molaim a maiḋim.
Cerram truag,
Robaḋ e mo ṡasad suan;
Subaċ me in traṫ ċanaim sailm
Ocus do nim mairb do luad.
Nirram og;
Tarrad morri ar gaċ rott;
Sochaide do chuaid rem re
Do ṡluagaiḃ fon cre is fon fot.
Tene derg
Do chlannaib Nell um amail celg;
Gach nech do bera bid nemtren;
Bid airsen celfer gaċ selg.
Conall cruaid;
Da ṡil do ḟagbur mor mbuaid;
Uair agam ta co becht
a ula 's a ḟert 'sa uaiġ.
In tarb trom;
Domnall mac Aeda nan glonn;
In cet ri do bera dam
Cach ni, romchar can a ċoll.
Longseċ lam;
Mo chen sa tan tic dommall.

[1] *it;* i.e. the treason-like "red fire"; or ardent treachery, as it may be expressed.

[2] *Domhnall.* Son of Aedh Mac Ainmirech, and king of Ireland. By him was gained the battle of Magh-Rath, over Congal Claen, prince of Ulidia. See note [12], p. 217.

[3] *Longsech.* King of Ireland. Slain in a battle in Corann (now represented by the barony of Corann, co. Sligo), by

No feeble band in his time shall be
The race of Eoghan, and Conall's clan.
Refusal to me,
In the midst of tribes, I love not;
Sad will it be for him who gives it;
Not much his success do I praise.
Though I am poor,
Sleep my satiety would be.
Joyous am I when I sing psalms,
And do commemorate the dead.
I am not young.
Many kings I've met in ev'ry way.
Great multitudes, during my time,
Have gone under the clay and sod.
A red fire
Of the Clann-Neill round me, treason-like.
Each one that offers it[1] shall be weak.
Therefore shall every chase be hidden.
Conall the brave—
To his seed great triumph I have left,
For with me certainly remains
His sepulchre, his grave, and tomb.
The heavy ox,
Domhnall[2] son of Aedh of the battles,
Is the first king who'll give me all;
Who'll love me without malice.
Longsech[3] with me.
I love the time when to my hall[4] he comes.

Cellach of Loch-Cime (now Lough Hacket, co. Galway), A.D. 701.

[4] *to my hall.* ᴅommall; which is very corrupt. The editor does not know what to make of it, unless to regard one m as redundant, and consider ᴅomall=ᴅo m' all, "to my hall;" although the use of the word all (*rectè* alla=Lat. aula), for hall, is scarcely so old as the age of the text.

* fol. 27, b 2.

Truag lem a thoirg[b] re slog somat,
Co Corann Connacht da crad.

Cara dam;
Cara do Patraicc romchar,
In dechmad mal Flaithfert[ach] find,
Riar mo mind tall in gach tan.

Rig mac rig,
Flaithfertach bid maith a dil;
Lér damsa mar forglit flaithi
Da aicnn maithi da sil.

Sil in mail,
Ocus sil Canannain choeim,
I rigi Conuill co tuillmech,
Co ti sil Luigdech in loeim.

In fer foll,
Sloindfear o muinc na nglond;
Doilig lem nach tairthenn cred;
Failid sis mo chet 's mo chonn.

Oed da ér,
In dibartach Droma les;
Do ber a ech 'sa eirred aig
Ocus mo chain dam dar m'es.

Seiser fein
Do sil Chanannain na ceil,
Uair is buidech misi dib,
Buidech in rí os gach treb.

[1] *Corann.* See note [3], p. 224.

[2] *friend to Patrick.* i.e. friend to the church and community of Armagh.

[3] *Flaithbhertach.* Son of Loingsech, king of Ireland, referred to in note [3], p. 224, and also monarch of Ireland himself. The expression, "friend to Patrick," is in allusion to his having resigned the sovereignty for a religious life. He died at Armagh in 729.

[4] *seers.* flaithi; pl. of flaith, a prince, chief, or lord; and also, in a secondary sense, a sage, or man eminent in knowledge.

[5] *Mael.* This is a puzzling abbreviation for the name of Maeldoraidh, whose descendants shared, alternately with the sept of O'Canannain, the chief power in Cinel-Conaill, or Donegal, before the rise

I grieve for his journey, with a turbulent host;
To Corann[1] of Connacht, to harry it.
A friend to me—
A friend to Patrick[2] who loved me—
The tenth prince, fair Flaithbhertach,[3]
My relics yonder will always honour.
A king and king's son—
Flaithbhertach—good will be his lot.
To me 'tis plain, as seers[4] announce,
That two good septs of his seed shall be.
The race of the Mael,[5]
And the race of Canannan the fair,
Shall opulently o'er Conall rule,
Till comes the seed of fierce Lugaidh.[6]
The mighty[7] man,
Who shall be named from *Muine nan glond.*[8]
To me 'tis sad that he reaches not earth.[9]
My sanction and sense to him are pleasing.
After him Aedh,[10]
The fugitive of Druim-les,
Who'll give me his steed and warrior-dress,
And my tribute, when I am gone.
Six are they,
Of the race of Canannan; hide it not;
For grateful towards them am I;
Grateful the King o'er every tribe.

of the Sil-Luigdech, or O'Donnells. See note [3], p. 138.

[6] *Lugaidh.* Ancestor of the Sil-Luigdech. See note [3], p. 138.

[7] *mighty.* ɼoll; most probably for ɼ̄oll (ɼoɲoll), the sign of abbrev. being omitted.

[8] *Muine na nglond.* The "thicket of evil deeds." Not identified.

[9] *reaches not earth.* This is doubtless in reference to the manner of death of Flahertach O'Canannain, chief of Cinel-Conaill, the person alluded to by the "prophet," who was drowned off the coast of Sligo, in 1153.

[10] *Aedh.* Aedh or Hugh O'Canannain, elected chief of the Cinel-Conaill in 1154.

H. Maeldoraid baigim for;
Cuiccer co nos dam romdil;
No co ti in sosar dasaigtear,
Nosmar gairther in gairm rig.
Fer in nois,
Do sil Luigdeċ detla im duais;
Egnechan corcrach nach cranna,
Roiċfed a alla in gaċ cluais.
Is a sil,
Biaid athaċ in ruathar rig;
Is ni tabrat dam derad;
Ni rammellat maith com dil.
Fear tren trom,
Mac Egneċain, Domnall donn;
Failid misi frisin fer;
Failid ri na réb co holl.
A tri mic,
Gebtaitt rigi garb a n-gleic;
Ocus in mac dib ba so
Ar is mo doberim breċ.
Ar mo riar,
[a] fol. 28, a 1. Bid corcraċ do gabail gial,[a]
Ar muir ar tir mor a threthan;
Ni gebthar fris tair na tiar.
Og 'ga riar,
Og ag dil credal is cliar.
Bid e sin in siblaċ sen
Maten na tren os druim cliaḃ
Nonbur rig,
Gebtaitt in tir tuaid da sil.

[1] *Lugaidh's race.* See note [3], p. 138.
[2] *Egnechan.* See note [5], p. 86.
[3] *Domhnall.* See note [6], p. 87.
[4] *His three sons.* Three of Domhnall Mor O'Donnell's sons became chiefs of Tir-Conaill, viz., Maelsechlainn, Godfrey,

Ua Maeldoraidh I also proclaim.
 Five of fame to me shall be true.
 Till comes the youngest, who'll enraged be,
 Formally shall the king's title be proclaimed.
The man of renown,
 Of Lugaidh's race,[1] liberal to reward,
 Is victorious Egnechan,[2] not decrepid;
 Whose fame shall reach to every ear.
With his seed
 Shall be force of the regal onset.
 And they'll not to me refusal give.
 Will not deceive me, but love me well.
A heavy strong man,
 Will Egnechan's son be, brown Domhnall.[3]
 Glad am I towards the man;
 Glad is the mighty King of things.
His three sons[4]
 Shall obtain kingship—fierce their conflicts.
 And on the youngest son of them
 Do I the most a judgment pass.
By obeying me,
 He'll be triumphant in obtaining pledges.
 On sea, on land, great his power.
 East or West he'll not be opposed.
Great at obeying;
 Great at rewarding clerics and poets,
 The prosperous traveller he will be,
 On the morn of the strong, o'er Druim-cliabh.[5]
Nine kings
 Of his race will obtain the Northern land.

and Domhnall Og.

[5] *Druim-cliabh.* Drumcliff, co. Sligo; near which Godfrey O'Donnell gained a victory over the Anglo-Norman army under Maurice Fitzgerald, the Lord Deputy, in 1247.

Bid dibsin in ball derg[1] brosnaċ
Ocus in cosraċ naċ crin.
A cland sen,
Is clann Canannain na cel,
Is clanna moelta in moeil,[2]
Bid traeta a taeib sel re sreib.
A ri raṫ,
Misi is Carnech, fir in fath,
Ro fagsam do chlannaib Neill
Flaiṫius ocus geill o chach.
'Con carnn claċ,
Tuc Domnall dam re caṫ rath,
Noeim is cuingid leṫ Cuind,
In ċuairt on tuinn[3] dam com theċ,
Co mag Rein,
Domma muintir is dam féin,
In onoir Choluim na cell,
Is in rig rodelḃ gréin.
Dol co terc,
Dom samud i criċ mac Erc,[4]
Bid moide a n-diṫ nan arus,
Lugaide a cadus co beċt.
Lor lem sein,
Mar do ċanus, is na ceil.
Is tarbach tuirem na trach
Ra beir re cach ocus beir. Beirid b.

Patraicc mac Calpuirn, primapstal hErend ocus iarthar Eorpa, ocus

[1] *Ball-derg.* ba derg; i.e. freckled, or red spotted. This epithet ultimately came to be used as a Christian name among the O'Donnells.

[2] *Mael.* An abbreviation for the name Maeldoraidh, the ancestor of the O'Maeldoraidhs, or O'Muldorys. He and Canannan, the ancestor of the O'Canannains, were sons to Flahertach king of Ireland, referred to in note [3], p. 226.

[3] *from the wave;* i.e. from the furthermost borders of Ulster.

[4] *Crich-Mac-Erc.* A name for Ulster, derived from Erc, daughter of Loarn king

Of them will be the inciting Ball-derg,[1]
And the *Coscrach* not decrepid.
His sons,
And the sons of Canannan—hide it not—
And the brave sons of the Mael,[2]
Shall be subdued, for a time, along the river.
O, King of Grace,
I and Cairnech—true the cause—
Have left unto the Clanna-Neill
Lordship and hostages from all.
At the cairn of stones,
Domhnall pledged me, 'fore the battle of Rath,
The saints and chiefs of Leth-Chuinn, that
This tribute from the wave[3] to my house should come,
Unto Magh-Rein,
For my people, and for myself,
In honour of Colum of the cells,
And of the King who shaped the sun.
If rarely go
My congregation into *Crich-Mac-Erc*,[4]
The greater[5] will be their loss at home;
Their honour certainly the less.
Enough meseems,
As I have sung; and hide it not.
Gainful 'tis to count[6] the hours.
Say this to all and TAKE. TAKE.[7]

Patrick son of Calpurnius, chief apostle of Ireland and the west of Europe,

of Scotland, and mother of Muirchertach Mac Erca, king of Ireland. Muirchertach met a strange fate, having been on the same night drowned in a vat of wine, burned in a house on fire, and then killed (!), through the machinations of a fairy, in the year 531. *Chron. Scotorum.* See Todd's *Irish Nennius*, App., p. cl.

[5] *greater.* moιꝺe. moαιꝺe, A.

[6] *to count the hours.* In other words, to observe the canonical hours.

[7] *Take.* This is the first word of the poem, repeated here, to indicate the completion of the poem. The text of MS. D

fer fuaslaicṫi gall nan Gaidel, ocus a mbreṫem braṫa. Do ratsin onoir ocus airmitin adbal do noem Chaillin mac Niatach ar a sind-
[a] fol. 28, a 2. sirecht seċ noemaib Erenn.[a] Ro bennaig a ċill ocus a chaṫruig, ocus tug ardlegoidecht Erenn do, co raibe ced bliadna ina ardlegoit. Do ratad imorro onóir adbail mor oili o Phatraicc do Chaillin, in tan robatar iar n-dichur chruim chruaiċ aird idal na hErend huile. IS iarsin do rat Patraicc a ċlog fein do Chaillin, ocus asbert Patraicc, Ro dlomus ocus ro diultus mor do noemuib Erenn im an cloccsa cus aniu, ocus ni tucus do neoch dib. Berrsi lat in clag chena, a Chaillin, et ge berar fo tri uait bid lat hé co lá in bratha.

Clog na rig nomen in cluig sin, ar is mór di rigaib Erend ro bairted as.

Du chlanuib Eogain mic Neill is duthaid in clog sin sech cach, daig is as ro baitsed da mac Muirchertaig mic Erca .i. Domnall ocus Fergus, da rig Erend. IS as ro bairted, dono, saer ċlanna hUa Neill tes ocus tuaid. Tait buada ocus fagbala maithea ar ċlanaib Neill da riarat in clog sin in tan raċus ċuca .i. sid ocus soinend, sonus ocus sobarthain, ocus raṫ rig forra. Gaċ egen ocus gaċ anforlond imbet cland Eogain, da cuirther in clog ina timchell fo tri saerfaid iat o gaċ egin. Icaid gaċ teidm ocus gaċ galar ocus gaċ
[b] fol. 28, b 1. angces, ocus gaċ[a] uili ircoit dambia forra.

IN tan naċ riarat clanna Eogain mic Neill cloc na rig ocus comarba Chaillin, iar na breṫ chuca, gorta ocus galar, terci bid ocus imad cogaid ocus creċairecht ina tir; donus ocus doċnach forra abus, ocus ifern tall.

recommences with the next sentence. See note [1], p. 166.

[1] *Cahir.* See note [11], p. 125.

[2] *Crom Cruach.* This idol, formed of gold, is said to have stood, surrounded by twelve silver idols, in the plain of Magh-Slecht, in the present county of Cavan. See the legend of their destruction by St. Patrick in Miss Cusack's Life of the Saint, p. 399.

[3] *idol.* idal. idġal, B.

[4] *name.* nō, A. noim̄, B. As to the name, see note [2], p. 140, *supra*.

[5] *that.* sin. Omitted in A.

[6] *out of it.* as. After this word, which concludes the text of p. 112 b, in B, the

and the deliverer of the hostages of the Gaedhil, and their judge of doom. He gave immense honour and respect to Caillin son of Niata, for his seniority beyond the saints of Ireland. He blessed his Church and his *Cahir*,[1] and gave him the Arch-legateship of Ireland, so that he [Caillin] was arch-legate during 100 years. Other great honour was moreover given by Patrick to Caillin, when they were after expelling Crom Cruach,[2] the chief idol[3] of all Ireland. Thereafter it was that Patrick gave his own bell to Caillin. And Patrick said, "I have refused and denied many of the saints of Ireland, unto this day, regarding this bell; and I gave it to none of them. Bear away the bell, however, O Caillin; and though it may be thrice taken from thee, it shall be thine till the day of judgment."

Clog-na-righ is the name[4] of that[5] bell, for many of the kings of Ireland were baptized out of it.

To the children of Eoghan Mac Neill the bell is appropriate beyond all others, for out of it the two sons of Muirchertach Mac Erca, to wit, Domhnall and Fergus, two kings of Ireland, were baptized.[7] Out of it were also baptized the free clanns of the Ui-Neill, South and North.

There are good virtues and bequests for[8] the sons of Niall, if they obey that bell when it comes to them; to wit, peace and fair weather, happiness and prosperity, and luck of kings, shall be theirs. Every difficulty and oppression in which the Clann-Eoghain may be—if the bell is thrice carried round them, 'twill save them from every danger. 'Twill cure every plague, and disease, and anxiety, and every evil from which they may suffer[9].

Whenever the sons of Eoghan Mac Neill shall not obey *Clog-na-righ* and Caillin's Comarb, when it is taken to them, famine and disease, scarcity of food, and much warfare and plundering, shall be in their land; misfortune and poverty shall be theirs here, and hell yonder.

following note is added; ıs aꝺbal ın scél sın Maılsecl- O bırnn ꝺo marbaꝺ a tansı; i.e. "that is awful news, Maelsechlainn O'Birnn to be slain at this time." The person referred to was probably Maelsechlainn (or Melachlainn) O'Beirne, slain by the sons of Cathal Mac Dermot, in 1536. See Ann. Loch Cé, ad ann., in which his death is much deplored.

[7] *were baptized.* ro baıtseꝺ. ro baısat, B.

[8] *for.* ar; lit. "upon."

[9] *from which they may suffer.* ꝺa mbıa forro; lit. "that may be upon them."

Dlegait sil Conuill Cremthuine a mar don clog sin na rig, daig is ar ro ḃaisted Conall Cremthainde. Dlegait clanna Conaill Gulbain mar in cetna, ar baisted Conall Gulban ass. Dlegait Oirgialla in cetna beus, ar is ar ro baisted a sindser. IS ar ro baisted clanna Briain mic Echach, im Duach ngal[ach] in ri. IS ar ro baisted Aed ocus Muiredach Muinderg rigraid hUlad. IS ar ro baisted Aongus mac Natfraiċ ri Caisil. IS ar ro baisted Branduḃ mac Echach ri Laigen. IS ar ro baisted sil Cormaic Cais mic Oilella, conid ed do rat rigi ocus oireċus doib. Cid sil ann tra aċt ni fuil in Erind ri naċ a cloc na rig ro baisted a sindser; conid de sin ro lean cloc na rig de.

Ges da gach ri atcifi clog na rig gan teacht ina dail d'ferthain failti fris ocus re a comarba; ocus mad ina suide bes, ges do gan ergi ina dail. In la atcifet hi Mailechluind[a] ni dentar olc doib. Mairg rig do rigaib Erend nach riarfaid clog na rig ocus a ċomarba co na daim .i. da fer deg. Ni coir do neoch a imchar acht fer graid nama. Gid be ri do rigaiḃ Erend for a troiscfid cliar cluig na rig co dligthech, ocus in clocc do bein ina ait choir, biaid diṫ biḋ ocus gorta ocus galar ocus teḋm ocus cogad ocus crecha ina tir, no saine ndigla for gaċ rig.

[a] fol. 28, b 2.

IS si ro cuairt cluig na rig o gaċ rig in tan raċus muinter Chaillin lais, eaċ sliarta gaċ rig co na etach; screball ar gaċ tig imbia

[1] *Conall Cremthainn.* conall crem, A. Conall Cremthainn was son to Niall Nine-Hostager. His death is recorded in the *Annals of Ulster* at A.D. 480; in the *Chron. Scotorum* at 476=480; and in the *Annals of the Four Mast.* under 475. He was the ancestor of the O'Melaghlins of Meath, the principal sept of the southern Hy-Neill, who bore the name of Clann-Colmain. The Clann-Aedh Slaine, or children of Aedh Slaine (king of Ireland, slain 604, *Chron. Scotorum*) were also descended from him. It appears from the Irish Annals that seventeen of his descendants occupied the throne of Ireland.

[2] *Brian son of Eochaidh;* i.e. son of Eochaidh Muidhmedhoin. He was the brother, therefore, of Niall Nine-Hostager; and was the ancestor of the O'Conors, O'Flahertys, Mac Dermots, and other notable families of Connaught.

[3] *Duach Galach.* King of Connacht. He lived in the time of St. Patrick, by whom he is stated to have been 'blessed' at *Dumha Selga*, which was the old name of Cairn-Fraich (now Carnfree, near Tulsk,

The descendants of Conall Cremthainn owe their obedience to this Bell of the kings, for out of it Conall Cremthainn[1] was baptized. So also do the descendants of Conall Gulban, for Conall Gulban was baptized out of it. The Oirghialla owe the same also, for it is out of it their ancestors were baptized. 'Tis out of it the sons of Brian son of Eochaidh[2] were baptized, including the king Duach Galach.[3] Out of it were baptized Aedh and Muiredach Muinderg, princes of Ulster. Out of it was baptized Aengus[4] son of Natfraech, king of Cashel. Out of it was baptized Brandubh son of Eochaidh, king of Leinster. Out of it the race of Cormac Cas son of Oilill were baptized, and it was it that gave them sovereignty and supremacy. In short, there is not in Ireland a king whose ancestor was not baptized out of *Clog-na-righ;* on which account [the name of] *Clog-na-righ* has attached to it.

It is a *ges*[5] to every king that shall see *Clog-na-righ*, not to go towards it, to bid welcome to it, and to its *comarb;* and if he be sitting, 'tis a *ges* to him not to rise to meet it. The day the O'Melachlainns shall see it, no harm shall be done to them. Woe to any king of Ireland's kings that obeys not *Clog-na-righ* and its *comarb*, with its suite, to wit, twelve men. No one should carry it about except a man in orders. Whatsoever king of the kings of Ireland against whom the attendants of *Clog-na-righ* shall legitimately fast, striking the bell in its proper place, there will be loss of food, and hunger, and sickness, and disease, and war and depredations, in his country; or some other kind of vengeance will fall on each king.

This is the fee[6] of *Clog-na-righ* from every king, when Caillin's people go with it: the steed of each king, with his clothes; a *screpall* from every house in which there shall be smoke;[7] bathing, and ablution, and

co. Roscommon), according to Mac Firbis. *Geneal.*, 196.

[4] *Aengus.* The first Christian king of Cashel, or Munster. He was baptized by St. Patrick, who, during the ceremony, incautiously thrust his crozier into the king's foot, pinning it to the ground. But Aengus never winced under the torture; and explained, when asked why he did not cry out, that he thought it was part of the baptismal ceremony!

[5] *ges;* i.e. a prohibition, or spell.

[6] *fee.* cuaiρτ. The word cuaiρτ signifies a circuit, or visitation; but it is also applied to the fees received on a visitation by a bishop or other ecclesiastic.

[7] *shall be smoke;* i.e. every occupied house.

dethaċ; fotracad ocus oraic ocus feoil ocus fledol dia ċleir; lan in ċluig o gach ri d'or no d'arget.

Mor in onóir do rat Patraicc do Chaillin, in clog sin do tabairt do seċ naemaib Erenn.

A buain in Oilech ar clannuib Eogain mic Neill, iar trosgad a cleri go dligthech. I Siṫ Aeda ruaiḋ ar Conallchaib. In Emain Maċa ar Ulltaib. A Nas ar Laignib. I Cruachan ar clannaib Duaċ. I muig Adar ar clannuib Lorcain. A buain ic Ard berna ar Mag rein ar clannaib Fergna.

Ro ḟaguib Patruig ocus Benen ocus Cairnech don ċlog sin, gid be ri do rigaib Erenn do ċluinfed faiḋ cluig na rig iar trosgad a ċleri, co nach bud indola i cliathar no a comlonn iarum, ocus maidm far i roe chatha.

Is d'onoir ocus d'airmidin cluic na riġ, ocus amail ro tindlaicc Patraic do Chaillin hé sech gac naem eli tre sinsirecht ocus onoir, ro raided in duan sa;

Beir a Chaillin clog na riġ,
Duit is dil fethal na fert.
Bennaiġsi ar clanna Neill;
Ar do riar gebaid gac neart.
Mor naem do ċuindiġ mo ċlog;
Gur anocht ni tucas uaim;
Act ge berter uait fo tri,
Is duit bus ní co lá in lúain.

[1] *Ailech.* See note [3], p. 62, *supra.*

[2] *Sidh-Aedha-Ruaidh.* The *Sidh* (pron. *shee*), or hill, of Aedh Ruadh; now Mullagh-Sidhe (or Mullaghshee), near Ballyshannon, co. Donegal. "*Sith Aedha Esa Ruaidh,*" in B.

[3] *Conallachs.* The descendants of Conall Gulban, or septs of Tir-Conaill, or Donegal.

[4] *Emain Macha.* Emania; now represented by the Navan fort, near Armagh.

[5] *children of Duach.* The O'Conors, Mac Dermots, O'Flahertys, and the other principal families of Connacht, descended from Duach Galach, king of Connacht (5th cent.), who was the youngest of the 24 sons of Brian, brother to Niall Nine-Hostager.

[6] *Magh-Adhair.* Now Moyre, a level plain near Tulla, co. Clare. Under a celebrated tree that stood in this plain

meat and drink, for its company; and the full of the bell of gold or silver from each king.

Great was the honour which Patrick conferred on Caillin, in giving him this bell in preference to all the saints of Ireland.

It should be rung in Ailech[1] against the race of Eoghan Mac Neill, after its clerics shall have fasted rightfully. In Sidh-Aedha-Ruaidh[2] [it should be rung] against the Conallachs.[3] In Emain-Macha,[4] against the Ultonians. At Naas against the Leinstermen. In Cruachan against the children of Duach.[5] In Mag-Adhair[6] against the children of Lorcan.[7] It should be rung at Ard-berna,[8] on Magh-Rein, against the children of Fergna.[9]

Patrick, and Benen, and Cairnech, left it (as a privilege) to this bell, that, whatsoever king of the kings of Ireland would hear the sound of *Clog-na-righ* after the fasting of its clerics, should not be fit to go afterwards into battle or conflict; and should be defeated in the field of battle.[10]

It is regarding the honour and reverence due to *Clog-na-righ*, and the way Patrick gave it to Caillin beyond every other saint, through seniority and honour, this lay was sung.

Take, O Caillin, *Clog-na-righ;*
To thee the wonder-working relic is due.
Bless thou, out of it, the Clanna-Neill.
By obeying thee they 'll obtain all power.
Many a saint has begged my bell.
Till to-night I gave it not away.
Though it be thrice taken from thee,
Thine own 'twill be till the Judgment Day.

the O'Briens were wont to be inaugurated as princes of Thomond.

[7] *children of Lorcan.* The O'Briens and their correlatives, descended from Lorcan, the grandfather of Brian Borumha.

[8] *Ard-berna.* "Gap-hill" (or "Gap-height"). There is no place near Fenagh known by this name; though there are two townlands in the barony of Dromahaire, co Leitrim, called Ardvarney, a name very similar.

[9] *Fergna.* The ancestor of the Breifnian families of O'Ruairc, Mac Rannell, and their correlatives.

[10] *of battle.* chatha. With this word ends fol. 28 b, in A, from which fol. 29 is missing. The contents of the missing leaf are supplied from B, in which they

Darben hé sen Chiaran sái
  Ar in rí os Tailltin uair,
  Do dichur Danmarg na tres,
  Uair nochan he a leas ro smuain.
Doben he Ruadan ar sein,
  Os dreich Tempa ar Diarmaid ndúr;
  Conaḋ de tairnid a ḟlaithius,
  Dar sging gaċ maithes on múr.
Do bi ag Cairnech re hed cian;
  Is as do riar righraid rod;
  Do bé in creaḋal firi in fath,
  Do benaḋ gaċ trath in clog.
As do bairt Cairnech gan ches
  Clann Muircertaig ṁóir nar ṁín.
  Is doiḃ do faguiḃ a tímna,
  Gomad imda uathaib righ.
Beneoin is Cairnech nar crin;
  Patraig fortaċ fir gan locht,
  Ar cathugad cruim nár lán mín,
  Tugsat do Chaillin in clog.
Do fagbatar da gaċ rig
  Atcluinfe a ḟaid gan a réir,
  Conach gebaḋ fri cleith comlaind,
  Ni mó dograind dó co pein.

occupy fol. 113 (MS. Cott., Vesp. 11.; Brit. Mus.)

[1] *rang.* darben (=do-ar-ben); lit. "struck it." See Todd's *Cogadh Gaedhel re Gallaibh*, pp. 11–13, where a somewhat different version of this stanza is given, the author being represented to be Bec Mac Dé, "poet and prophet."

[2] *Tailltiu;* gen. *Tailltenn;* now Teltown, co. Meath.

[3] *Danmargs.* Danmarkians, men of Denmark, or Danes.

[4] *Ruadan.* St. Ruadan of Lothra, (Lorrha, co. Tipperary), who quarrelled with king Diarmaid Mac Cerrbheoil, and cursed Tara, then (6th cent.) the royal residence, with tongue and bell. See the curious account of his proceedings, which are stated to have resulted in the abandonment of Tara, quoted in Petrie's Essay on Tara Hill. *Trans. R. Ir. Acad.*, vol. xviii, part II, p. 125, sq.

Old Ciaran the sage rang[1] it,
For the king, over cold Tailltiu,[2]
To banish the Danmargs[3] of the battles;
For 'twas not their good he meditated.
Ruadan[4] rang it afterwards,
O'er Tara's face, 'gainst stubborn Diarmaid;
Wherefore it was that his reign did end,
When all good vanished from the *Mur*.[5]
Cairnech had it a long time;
By it he ruled mighty kings.
He was the devotee, true the assertion,
Who used to ring the bell every hour.[6]
Out of it Cairnech, without pain, baptized
The ungentle sons of Muirchertach Mór[7].
To them he left, by testament,[8]
That from them should be many kings.
Benen[9] and Cairnech, not decrepid,
Patrick, true comforter without fault,
After warring with Crom,[10] who was not very mild,
Gave to Caillin the bell.
They awarded to every king
Who'd hear its sound without obeying it,
That he should not succeed in battle strife—
No greater anguish to him, save pain.

[5] *the Múr;* i.e. Tara, which is explained by etymologists as *Te-Mur*, or *Mur-Te*, the wall, or rampart, of a fabulous woman named Te. See Petrie's *Tara*, p. 130.

[6] *hour.* ꞇꞃαꞇh. This means time, occasion; and is here put for canonical hour, or occasion of celebration of the canonical office.

[7] *Muirchertach Mór;* i.e. Muirchertach Mac Erca, king of Ireland from 513 to 533.

[8] *testament.* See an account of St. Cairnech's legacy to the Clanna Neill, in the *Leabhar Buidhe Lecain* (MS. H. 2. 16, Trin. Coll. Dublin), col. 312, where it is stated that *Clog-Phadraig*, or Patrick's bell, was a relic which they should possess.

[9] *Benen.* St. Benignus, disciple of St. Patrick, and abbot, or bishop, of Armagh.

[10] *Crom;* i.e. Crom-Cruach, the idol alleged to have been worshipped by the pagan Irish at the coming of St. Patrick. See note [2], p. 232, *supra*.

Galur is gorta san tir,
    Terci bid cogad is crech,
    In tan nach riarat Clanna Neill
    In clog le chleir, budhi ambeṫ.
Ges da gach rig atchi in clog
    Mana ti go grod na dáil;
    Da mbett ar a ċind go fescor,
    Na seram ferund fris failtt.
In clog beg ni coir a ċleṫ,
    Berar braṫ don ti nach riar.
    Doman dochnaich do go fann,
    Is do ṡia ṫall imad pian.
Cinel Eogain doiḃ is dú
    In feathal go clú gan craḋ,
    Oir is doib dlegar co dian,
    A riar ri moradh a mail.
Beittit buaḋa for chloind Neill,
    Mo riar gach inbaid ro ria,
    Soinend, robarthan is sith,
    Ogus rath rig in gach iath.
Fagbala fire ro fear,
    Ar cinel Eogain na trear;
    Gac egin grott ambí in dream
    In clog fa tri na timċeall.
Icaid gaċ galar, gaċ teidm;
    Icaid gaċ forrand gaċ feidm;
    Dober cátuiḃ da gaċ cloind
    Mar do faguib mac Calpruind.
Fergus is Domnall nár docht,
    Bairdter artur ar in cloc.

[1] *ges.* a prohibition, or spell.

[2] *Welcome.* failtt, B., for failte, which being a word of two syllables would not suit the metre, and therefore is incorrectly written.

[3] *yonder.* In the next world.

Sickness and hunger in the land,
    Scarcity of food, war and plunder,
    When the Clanna-Neill do not obey
    The bell with its clerics, will be their lot.
It is a *ges*[1] to each king who sees the bell,
    If he come not quickly towards it;
    Were they to await it until evening,
    Standing, they must bid it welcome.[2]
The little bell—it should not be concealed—
    He that obeys it not will be judged;
    A wretched world he shall sadly find [here],
    And yonder[3] he shall reach to much torment.
To the Cinel-Eoghan doth rightly belong
    The famous relic, without anguish;
    For to them it is strenuously commanded
    That they obey it, by increasing its tribute.
The Clanna-Neill shall have privileges
    For obeying it, when it reaches them—
    Fair weather, prosperity, and peace,
    And luck of kings in every land.
True gifts are left, it is known,
    To the Cinel-Eoghain of the combats,—
    In every sudden danger in which the tribe may be,
    The bell should be borne round them thrice.
'Twill cure every sickness, every disease;
    'Twill heal all oppression, all trouble;
    'Twill give nobility to every clan,
    As the son of Calpurn decreed.
Fergus and Domnall[4], who were not niggardly,
    Were at first baptised from the bell.

[4] *Fergus and Domhnall.* The two sons of Muirchertach Mac Erca, and joint kings of Ireland, A.D. 565–566., according to the *Chron. Scot.*,=559–561, F. Mast.

Da ril bid milla gach modh;
Bet righda imda o Eoghan.
Ni uil raerclann ther na tuaidh,
Do ril Neill berers gach buaidh,
Ni cel ort gan locht ram len,
Nach ara clog ro bairted.
Dliget cinel Conaill ther
Clog-na-righ do riar romrer;
Ar do bairted an ri
Conall cuana Creamthuindi.
Ir ar ro bairtead co huain
Conall glan Gulbain atuaid;
Do fuil runna gan trena
Uadha riga ro trena.
Dlegaitt Oirgiall uile
Eirgi roime ar a ruidhi;
Uair ther, gan airder gan oil,
Ar do bairded a rinrir.
Ar do bairted clanna Briain,
Im Duach galach ar in rliab;
Ni digna drongrolt gandol
Rigraidh Connacht ar creidem.
Righraid Ulad nar clecht celg,
Aodh ir Muiredach muind derg;
Do bairdead ní brécc in dáil
Ar in clog cedna comhlán.
h. Mailechlaind a Mide,
Dleguit reir ón righrine.

[1] *Eoghan.* The son of Niall of the Nine Hostages, and great-grandfather of the two last-named kings.

[2] *Conall Cremthaind;* son of Niall of the Nine Hostages, who died A.D. 475.

[3] *Oirghialla.* See Index.

[4] *Brian.* King of Connacht; son of Eochaidh Muighmedhoin, and brother of Niall of the Nine-Hostages; and the progenitor of the principal families of Connacht.

[5] *Duach Galach.* King of Connacht,

To their race each mood shall be mellow ;
From Eoghan[1] will be numerous kings.
There is no noble clann South or North,
Of the seed of Niall that bears every triumph,
(I 'll not hide from thee, that blame may not pursue me),
Who were not baptised from the Bell.
The race of Conall in the South are bound
To obey *Clog-na-righ* ; to me 'tis known.
From it was baptised the king,
The excellent Conall Cremthaind.[2]
'Twas out of it happily was baptised
The pure Conall Gulban from the North ;
There are here, without denial,
Mighty kings from him descended.
The Oirghialla[3] are all bound
To rise before it from their seats ;
For in the South, without error, without stain,
Their ancestors were out of it baptised.
From it were baptised the sons of Brian,[4]
Together with Duach Galach,[5] on the Sliabh ;[6]
No contemptible race at marching[7]
Are the chieftains of Connacht after the Faith.
The kings of Uladh, who practised not deceit,
Aedh and Muiredach Muinderg,
Were baptised, not false the account,
Out of the same perfect Bell.
The Ui-Maelechlainn[8] of Meath—
Obedience is due from the Regal tribe ;

and son of the Brian referred to in the last note. See note [3], p. 234, *supra*.

[6] *Sliabh*. The Sliabh (or mountain) here alluded to is probably Sliabh Badhbhghna, or Slieve-Bawn, in the co. Roscommon.

[7] *marching*. The original of this line is very obscure, and the translation only conjectural.

[8] *Ui-Maelechlainn* ; i.e. the O'Melachlins, or descendants of Maelsechlainn II., king of Ireland, who died. A.D. 1022.

Ni aicfet olc, mor int aḋ,
In la atcifet in clogan.
Hi Caiseal na riġ gan gus
Is as do baisded Aongus;
Cona uaḋ gan braissi arsin,
Riġraiḋ Caisel ar creideṁ.
Branduḃ mac Echach comblad,
Is asin clog ro baistad;
Da eis co becht, gniṁraḋ gloin,
Nert riam ag riġraid Laigen.
Sil Cormaic Cais, ni brega,
Do baisted on clog cedna;
Cona finechusa feidm
Is oirechusa for Erind.
Ni uil an Erind ri reab
Nach ass do baisdead a sean;
Cona de ro lean re gairm
Clog na riġ he sech gaċ ainm.
A buain re Tailltin atuaid
Do cloind Colmain nocha buaid;
Do sil Aeda Slaine sin
Dith na daiṁe co deiṁin.
A buain ar sith Aoḋa ruaiḋ,
Fa dered ac teacht atuaiḋ;
Bid dith gach neirt beremain bind;
Snithter neart cineoil Conaill.

[1] *Aengus.* Aengus Mac Natfraich, king of Munster; slain in the year 487, by Illann, son of Dunlaing, king of Leinster. See note [4], p. 235.

[2] *Brandubh.* King of Leinster; who defeated Aedh, son of Ainmire, king of Ireland, at the battle of Dun-Bolg, co. Wicklow, in the year 598. Slain, A.D. 605.

[3] *Cormac Cas.* Ancestor of the Dal-Cais, or tribes of the O'Briens and their correlatives.

[4] *To ring it.* a buain, lit. "to strike it".

They'll not see evil—great the luck—
The day they see the little Bell.
At Cashel of the kings, without anger,
Aengus[1] was baptised out of it;
Wherefore from him, without falsehood, are
The kings of Cashel since the Faith.
Brandubh[2] the famous, Eochaidh's son,
Was out of this Bell baptised;
After him certainly, a patent fact,
The kings of Leinster have ever had power.
The race of Cormac Cas[3]—no lie—
Were baptised from the same Bell.
With their tribes [have remained] command,
And supremacy over Ireland.
There is not in Ireland an active king,
Whose ancestors were not baptised out of it;
Therefore it has followed, that it has been called
Clog-na-righ, beyond all names.
To ring it[4] to the north of Tailltiu
Is no luck to the Clann-Colmain[5];
To the race of Aedh Slaine[6] this is
The certain ruin of the sept.
To ring it on Sith-Aedha-Ruaidh,[7]
At the last, on coming from the North,
Will be the ruin of each strong sweet power.
The might of Cinel-Conaill will be cut off.

[5] *Clann-Colmain*; a branch of the Southern Hy Neill, descended from Colman Mór, second son of king Diarmaid Mac Cerbheoill, who was slain in the year 552.

[6] *Race of Aedh Slaine.* Another branch of the Southern Hy Neill, descended from Aedh Slaine, king of Ireland (ob. 600), who were settled in Meath. In later times the principal family of the race was that of O'Kelly of Bregia. See O'Flaherty's *Ogygia*, part III., cap. 93, p. 431.

[7] *Sith Aedha Ruaidh.* Now Mullaghshee, at Ballyshannon, co. Donegal. See note [2], p. 236.

A buain in Oilech co ferg,
Dith ar sil Eogain in cend;
Ni miad ni maise co han,
Da traisg[it] cliar in clogain.
A buain in Emain Macha
Ar Ulltoib bid clod ratha;
Faid in cluig bid nem co rind,
Ocus a buain co fochuind.
A buain is monar metha
Ar carn mor sleibe Betha,
Ar Airgaill; bid dith is don
Da rigaib gan a riarugad.
A buain a Nas Laigen lond,
Bid crad da cell is da cond;
Dith ar dainib, comach cruid;
Fich ag rigaib da rochtain.
A buain a Cruachuin na cet,
Ar saebaḋ sainti na set;
Biaid sil Duach a derim de,
Gan oirroim o tuaith oile.
A buain bid garb in galur,
Ar urlar Muiġi Aḋar;
Biaid sil Lorcain a lén de,
Co tren ar na timdibe.
A buain ar clannuib Fergna,
Ar maġ Rein ic Ard berna,
Bid dith as gach ard oili;
Ni fuiġbed sith na suiḋi.

[1] *Oilech* or *Ailech*. See note [3], p. 62, *supra*.

[2] *Emain Macha*. See note [4], p. 236.

[3] *Sliubh-Betha*. Now Slieve Baugh, on the confines of the counties of Monaghan and Tyrone. The cairn on the mountain is supposed to have been raised over Bith (gen. Betha), son of Ladhra, one of the first colonists of Ireland, whose death is referred to A.M. 2,242.

[4] *Nás*. Now Naas, in Kildare.

To strike it in Oilech,[1] with anger,
  Will be ruin to princely Eoghan's race.
  Nor honour, nor good, will it nobly be,
  If the clerics of the little Bell fast.
To strike it in Emain Macha[2],
  Against the Ultonians, will be destruction of luck.
  The sound of the Bell will be sharpest poison,
  If it be rung with reason just.
To strike it against the Orighialla,
  On the great cairn of Sliabh-Betha,[3]
  Is a cause of decay; loss and misfortune
  'Twill be to their kings, if they obey it not.
To strike it at Nas[4] of fierce Leinster
  Will be torment to their minds[5] and reason.
  Destruction to people, dispersion of flocks,
  Contention among kings, will its arrival produce.
If struck at Cruachan of the hundreds,
  Against the foolish lust of treasure;
  The race of Duach[6] will then be, I say,
  Without respect from another tribe.
If struck on the plain of Magh-Adhair,[7]
  Severe will the affliction be.
  Lorcan's race[8] will be in grief therefor,
  Mightily undergoing extinction.
If struck against the sons of Fergna,[9]
  On Magh-Rein, at Ard-Berna,[10]
  There will be ruin from every quarter;
  They'll not find peace in their abode.

[5] *their minds;* i.e. the minds of the Leinstermen.

[6] *Duach;* i.e. Duach Galach. See note [3], p. 234; and note [6], p. 236.

[7] *Magh-Adhair.* See note [6], p. 236.

[8] *Lorcan's race;* i.e. the O'Briens of Clare, and their kindred tribes.

[9] *sons of Fergna.* The Connaicni, or tribes of Breifne, viz., the O'Rorkes and their correlatives.

[10] *Ard-Berna.* See note [8], p. 237.

* fol. 30, a 1.

Mairg rig nach riaruig in clocc,
 Lasan* mian sith ocus socht;
 Mairg do ber dimbrig ar lo
 San ċlog ḟertaċ naċ geb ceo.
Isi ro cuairt in ċluig caid,
 O rigraid Erenn in aig;
 Eċ sliasta gaċ rig gus ruirig,
 Ocus a etaċ go grib.
Screball no set don sethal,
 Ar gaċ tig ambia dethach,
 Re ndeg ol da ċler gan col,
 Feoil fledol is fotragad.
Tabrad gaċ ri ruamnad gal
 A lan i gclog na credal,
 Cein cuarta na meallaḋ mal,
 D'or no d'airget imlan.
Fer graid da imchur ar set;
 Ni lam neċ oili co heg;
 Gid remi gan redg o tig,
 Tene derg he da ririb.
Da fer deg dlegar na daim,
 Ar fut Erenn, derb in dáil;
 Gilla graiḋinn na naem sin
 Tusa a Chaillin crin sosbein. Beir, &c.

Mag Rein cid diata. Ni. Ro foillsig Findtan mac Boċra airdsenoir ocus ardsenchaid Erenn dindsenchus Moigi Rein do Phatraic mac Calprainn. IMeolaċra, em, ar Findtan, in ní diata Mag Rein .i.

1 *whose desire.* lasan mian. lasan miaḋ, B.

2 *without fail.* co grib, "quickly."

3 *screpall.* See note 6, p. 79.

4 *set*; pron. *shéad.* The meaning of this word is rather undefined. It signified a cow, a jewel, or precious thing, as well as property or cattle of any kind. See O'Donovan's *Supplt.* to *O'Reilly*, in *voce.*

5 *beverage good.* deg ol. med ol, "mead beverage," B.

6 *tribute.* The orig. of this line is rather obscure.

Woe to the king that obeys not the Bell,
    Whose desire[1] is peace and quiet.
    Woe to whoever shows daily contempt
    To the wondrous Bell that bears not obscurity.
This is the holy Bell's tribute,
    From the valorous chiefs of Ireland:
    The riding steed of each king and prince
    And his clothing, without fail;[2]
A *screpall*[3] or *set*[4] for the relic,
    From every house in which smoke shall be,
    With beverage good[5] for its stainless clerks,
    Meat, festive drink, and bathing.
Let every king of reproving valour
    Into the bell of the faithful put,
    As a rich visitation tribute,[6]
    Its complete fill of gold or silver.
A man of grade must bear it on the road;[7]
    None else should ever[8] dare to do so;
    And if before it no gleam comes from a house,
    A red fire[9] 'twill certainly be.
Twelve men for its company are required,
    Throughout Ireland; sure is the fact.
    The beloved *gilla* of those holy men
    Art thou, old Caillin, who hast rung it. Take, &c.[10]

Magh-Rein, whence is it [so called]. Not hard to tell. Finntan, son of Bochra, arch-senior and arch-historian of Ireland, explained to Patrick, son of Calphurnius, the ancient history of Magh-Rein. "I know well the event," said Finntan, "from which [it is called] Magh-Rein. It is this."—

[7] *on the road.* ap rec. Instead of these words, A. has am, "indeed."

[8] *ever.* co heg; "till death," A, B.

[9] *red fire.* The meaning is that if the Bell and its attendants were not well received at every house visited, it would be like a devastating fire to the inmates.

[10] *Take.* This is the first word of the poem, added here in token of its completion.

daer ċís adbail mor robai ag Fomorchaib for feraib Erend fri re cian .i. da trian etha ocus blechta, ocus cet gin cecha cloinde do idlacad cuca co mag Cetni, ocus uingi d'or ar gaċ srón in Erinn.

ᵃ fol. 30, a 2. Lugaid lamfada imorro, ro fuasgail fir Erenn on daeirsi sin, amailᵃ atfiadat eoluiġ. Is e ro ḃris cath muigi Tuired for Fomorchaib. Doriacht imorro drong mor dona Fomorchaib i rian madma ocus teiċium ria Lug cus in mag ucut; conid on rian teiċmisin atberar Mag rein. Beris Lug forra i cind oirrthearach in maigi. Ro tuit, em, .ix. riga d'Fomorchaib ar Mag rein la Lug lamfada. Ro saiḋ iarum lecca lan-mora os fertaib ocus os adluictib na rigsin, conid iatsin na corrgind ar Mag rein. Aliter, Mag Rein. Bai ri amra for Erinn .i. Conaing beccelaċ. Mac sein Duaċ mic Muiredaiġ, mic Simoin bric, mic Aedain glais.

Is air in mag sa, imorro, ro caith siom, em, rigi nErenn co cend ċoicc mbliadna ndecc. Bai mac morgraḋach lais in rig .i. Cobthach mac Conaing. Do riacht Cobthach la nann do snam in loċa bui ina farrad, gur ro baided ann. Teit iarum muime Chobthaiġ, .i. Rian a hainm, dia iarmoracht fon loċ, gur ro baided ann; conad uaithe ainmnigther loċ Rein ocus Mag Rein.

ᵇ fol. 30, b 1. Noi traṫ do Chobthach fon loċ iar naᵇ bathad. Fir hErend ic a chained frisin re sin. Do ratad, imorro, Cobthach i tir iarsin ocus coland a muimi .i. Rian. Ro ferad a chluiche caine iarsin la feraib

[1] *Magh-Cetne.* A plain in the co. Donegal, between the rivers Erne and Drowse.

[2] *nose.* Hence, perhaps, the expression "paying through the nose." This exaction is not mentioned in Keating's account of the Fomorian tribute, and seems to be borrowed from the alleged exactions of the Danes, who are said to have cut off the noses of non-taxpayers. Keating adds that the tribute was paid at Allhallowtide. *See Haliday's* translation, p. 181.

[3] *Lughaidh Lamhfada.* Lughaidh (pron. Looey) of the Long Hand, thirteenth king of Ireland; slain A.M. 3330, according to the Four-Masters, but A.M. 2804, according to O'Flaherty. See *Ogygia*, p. 177.

[4] *Magh-Tuiredh;* i.e. Magh-Tuiredh, or Moy-tury, of the Fomorians; now Moytirra, par. of Kilmactranny, bar. of Tirerrill, co. Sligo. *See* O'Donovan's interesting note on the subject, Annals of the Four Masters, A.M. 3330, note[s].

[5] *Magh-Rein;* i.e. the plain of the track or path; from *Magh*, a plain, and *rein*,

"The Fomorians imposed an immense tribute on the men of Ireland for a long time, to wit, the two-thirds of their corn and milk, and the first-born of every family, to be sent to them to Magh-Cetne,[1] and an ounce of gold for every nose[2] in Ireland.

"It was Lughaidh Lamhfhada,[3] moreover, who delivered the men of Ireland from that bondage, as the learned relate. It was he that gained the battle of Magh-Tuiredh[4] over the Fomorians. A great number of the Fomorians, in their path of retreat and flight before Lughaidh, came as far as that plain; and it is from this course of retreat it is called Magh-Rein.[5] Lughaidh overtook them at the eastern head of the plain. Nine kings of the Fomorians fell, moreover, on Magh-Rein, by the hand of Lughaidh Lamhfada. Immense flags were afterwards stuck over the graves and sepulchres of those kings, and they are the *Corrginns*[6] on Magh-Rein."

Aliter, Magh-Rein. "There was an illustrious king over Ireland, viz., Conaing Bec-eclach.[7] He was the son of Duach, son of Muiredach, son of Simon Breac, son of Aedan Glas. It was on this plain, moreover, he exercised the sovereignty of Ireland during fifteen years. The king had a much loved son, to wit, Cobhthach[8] son of Conaing. Cobhthach came one day to swim in the lake that was near him; and he was drowned in it. Cobhthach's nurse, whose name was Rian, went afterwards in search of him, under the lake, and was drowned there; wherefore it is from her Loch-Rein[9] and Magh-Rein are named.

"Nine days[10] was Cobhthach under the lake after he was drowned. The men of Ireland were bewailing him during that time. Cobhthach, however, was afterwards brought ashore, together with the body of his nurse, *i.e.* Rian. His *Cluiche Caine*[11] was thereupon celebrated by the men of Ireland," said

gen. of *rian*, a path, track, course, or way.

[6] *Corrginns*; i.e. pillar stones. See the other account of the origin of these pillar stones given above, p. 117.

[7] *Conaing Bec-eclach.* See p. 26, note [3], and p. 113, note [3].

[8] *Cobhthach*; pron. "Covach."

[9] *Loch-Rein*; i.e. the Lake of Rian, from *Loch*, a lake, and *Rein*, gen. of Rian.

[10] *days.* τραth. The word τραth is used to express an indefinite period of time; but it is also used to signify a space of a day and night.

[11] *Cluiche Caine*; i.e. "game of weeping," or funeral solemnities. The word cluiċe, signifying game, sport, and pastime, is rather suggestive of the kind of exercises practised by the pagan Irish on such occasions, conspicuous among which was horse-racing.

hErond, ar Findtan, ac indisin in sgeoil-si do Patraic, ocus ba himda meic rig ocus ruirig d'feraib Erenn annsin ag caine Cobthaig.

Bamar umorro, ar Findtan, fri secht laithib na sechtmuine mar bferaib Erenn ig guba ocus ig golgaire; conad o na gairib doratsamar adearar Dun ngaire ó sin anall.

Tangatar cuccuinn don ar Findtan, bandtrochta ocus bannala Erenn do ċained Chobthaig. Iarsin ro hadlaiced Cobthach linn co nonoir moir, nai cemenai ale on ċoirrgend; fert a muime dono Reine o firt Cobthaig alle. Tictis, imorro, fir Erenn co hainteċ cus in mag sin fri ré Conuing, fri etirgleod a caingend ocus do ernad a cana ocus a ciosa; comad on rian ocus on rig s'liged do ronsat side atberar Mag Rein fós, arsinti Findtan. Ro ḟagaib, imorro, Conaing Mag rein iarum do ċumaid a mic.

Atconnarcsa diu in Mag Rein si ar Findtan, gan ait aontige de na raibe fo choill in aimsir cloinde Nemid. Atconnarc fos, a

[a] fol. 30, b 2.

Patraicc, ar Findtan[a] .ix. riga déc aga raibe rigi nErenn ar Mag R.; conad ann atat a leċtai ocus a nadnaicṫi .i. fa lec na rig.

Ba dibside Gede ollgothach, cetus, Conuing bececlaċ, ocus Eochaid Urthach in aen uaiġ; Crimthand Coscarach, Diṫorba mac Dimain, Conall gulban, Bresal bodibaid, ocus Find mac Rosa in aen uaiġ;

[1] *Finntan.* This is the celebrated Finntan, son of Bochra, otherwise called Tuan Mac Cairill, mentioned above. See p. 6, note [2].

[2] *Dun-Gaire.* Apparently another name for Dun-Conaing, or Fidnacha; comp. of *Dun*, a fortress, and *gaire*, gen. of *gair*, a cry.

[3] *women.* bandtrochta, for bantrochta, meaning a company of women. A marginal note reads "iseḋ arimit in eolaig comid uada sin ainmnigter cnoc in bantrochto," i.e. "the learned calculate that it is from them *Cnoc-in-bantrochta* ('the hill of the women') is named." See note [3]. p. 254, *infra*.

[4] *female bands.* bannala; for bandala, pl. of bandail, an assembly of women. It is from these *bannala* that Dun-ivinally, in the parish of Cloon, not far from Fenagh, is probably named.

[5] *After that.* Iarsin. Resin, A.

[6] *side.* If this part of the MS. was transcribed at Fenagh, as it probably was, the site of Cobthach's grave should be to the north of Fenagh, in the townland of Longstones. See note [4], p. 116.

[7] *track.* The gen. of *rian*, "a track," being *rein*, it is sought here to explain

Finntan,[1] relating this story to Patrick; "and many were the sons of kings and chieftains, of the men of Ireland, there bewailing Cobhthach.

"We men of Ireland," said Finntan, "were moreover engaged in sorrowing and lamenting during the seven days of the week; and it is from the cries which we uttered that *Dun Gaire*[2] is [so] called from that time to this.

"There came to us, then," said Finntan, "the women[3] and female bands[4] of Ireland, to bewail Cobhthach. After that,[5] Cobhthach was interred by us with great honour, nine paces at this side[6] of the *Corrgins*. The grave of his nurse Rian, also, is at this side of Cobhthach's. The men of Ireland used to come unitedly to that plain, during the time of Conaing, to arrange their covenants, and to pay their tributes and their rents; and perhaps it is from the track[7] and path which they made the place is still called Magh-Rein," said Finntan.[8] "Conaing afterwards abandoned Magh-Rein, through grief for his son.

"I saw this same Magh-Rein long ago," said Finntan, "in the time of Nemed's sons, when there was not in it the site of one house that was not covered with wood. I have also seen on Magh-Rein, O Patrick," said Finntan, "nineteen kings who possessed the sovereignty of Ireland; and it is there that their graves and sepulchres are, to wit, under *Lec-na-Righ*.[9]

"Of these were, firstly, Geide Ollgothach,[10] Conaing Bec-eclach,[11] and Eochaidh Opthach,[12] [who are] in one grave; Crimthand Coscrach,[13] Dithorba[14] son of Diman, Conall Gulban, Breasal Bodibhaidh,[15] and Find Mac Rossa,[16] in one

Magh-Rein as signifying the "plain of the track." But where so many attempts at explanation have been made, it may be assumed that the true etymology remains yet to be discovered.

[8] *Finntan.* ın τı ꝑınnτan, lit. "the person, Finntan."

[9] *Lec-na-Righ*; i.e. "the stone (or flag) of the kings." Not identified.

[10] *Geide Ollgothach.* "Gedius Grandivocus," king of Ireland, A.M. 3313–25, according to O'Flaherty.

[11] *Conaing Bec-eclach.* See note [3], p. 112, *supra*.

[12] *Eochaidh Opthach.* King of Ireland, A.M. 3432. See note [5], p. 25, *supra*.

[13] *Crimthand Cosgrach.* See p. 29, *supra*.

[14] *Dithorba.* King of Ireland from A.M. 3589 to 3596, according to O'Flaherty's Chronology.

[15] *Breasal Bodibhaidh.* King of Ireland, A.M. 3865–3874. See p. 32, note [2].

[16] *Find Mac Rossa.* This person is not usually included in the list of Irish kings. Finn, son of Rossa, son of Ruaidhri, is the individual referred to.

Dungal ocus Gormgal, da rig Brefne; o Leic na Lennan ale ata a fert. Cnoc in banntrochta umorro, a Patraicc, ar Finntan, .i. in cnoc alla thes don muig; .u. rigna .x. do ḟuair bas ar in maig; is de ta Cnoc in banntrochta. Do ronad, em, esbada adbbail morai oili ar Mag rein, a naem Pattraicc, ar Finntan, .i. ix. ced mor macam do maicni Partholoin, do clannuib airdrig ocus urrig, do chotar do ṡnam ar in loċ dianad ainm Loċ na pesti aniu. Focressa peist uaṫmar ċuca ar in loċ, gurobaid in macraid uili, conaċ terno naċ naen dib. Ni dernad snam ar in loċ osin anuas. IS o suidiu is Loch na pesti, ar Finntan.

Fecht naen da rabara, ar Finntan, sunn i Cnuc na rig, maraen re hEochaid Feidlech, .i. ri Erenn, tugad Cathbaid drai chuguind ann
ª fol. 31, a 1. fein. Ba faiḋ fíré in fersin,ª ar Finntan, ar ni ebairt breg riam. Deisiul dono fognid gaċ fir ocus gach fairtine, fodaig ro creided do Crist. Fiarfoiḋis in ri .i. Eochaid Feidliuċ do Cathfad draoi cinnus ro biad in mag sa fri dered domain. Frecruis Cathbad do iarum, ocus asbert, Biaid imorro in mag sa na rig, ar Cathbad, ag clerchaib fri dered aimsiri. Mit inad imorro i fil bruigen na rig is ann biass cathair ocus congbail ag Caillin noeb. Bid imda imorro guṫ cluig ocus clerech san cnocsa na rig, ar se. Biaid dono tech naided coitchenn isin cnoc sa na rig, air gaċ dam da duilgi ocus gaċ cliar ocus gaċ aidilgnech airchena da marfa biathad co dligthech fogeba ann in gaċ uile aimsir; ocus bud tellach aeidedchaire ocus feili co dered domuin in cnocsa na rig, ar Cathbad.

[1] *Dungal—Gormgal.* Not mentioned in the Irish Annals.

[2] *Lec-na-Lennan*, "the stone (or flag) of the sweethearts (or concubines)." The situation of this grave is not easily identified among the numerous sepulchres with which Fenagh abounds.

[3] *Cnoc-in-Banntrochta*; i.e. "the hill of the women." See note [3], p. 252.

[4] *Loch-na-Pesti*; i.e. the lake of the *Piast*, or water serpent. A fabulous name for Fenagh lake.

[5] *Eochaidh Feidhlech.* O'Flaherty refers the reign of Eochaidh Feidhlech, father of Queen Medbh of Connacht, to A.M. 3922. See *Ogygia*, p. 267.

[6] *Right-hand-wise.* deisiul. That is to say, he observed the old heathen practice of turning right-hand-wise, following the course of the sun, towards which his face

grave; Dungal[1] and Gormgal,[1] two kings of Breifne—on the hither side of *Lec-na-Lennan*[2] their grave is.

"*Cnoc-in-Banntrochta*,[3] moreover, O Patrick," said Finntan, "is the hill to the south of the plain; viz., fifteen queens that died on the plain—hence it is (called) *Cnoc-in-Banntrochta*.[3]

"There were other prodigious great losses suffered on Magh-Rein, O, Saint Patrick," said Finntan, "to wit; nine hundred noble youths of the descendants of Partholan, sons of arch-kings and dynasts, went to swim in the lake which is at this day called *Loch-na-Pesti*.[4]

"A horrible monster came towards them in the lake, and all the youths were drowned, so that not one of them escaped. There has been no swimming in the lake from that time to this. It is from that circumstance it is called *Loch-na-Pesti*," said Finntan.

"One time," said Finntan, "that I was here on *Cnoc-na-Righ*, along with Eochaidh Feidhlech,[5] *i.e.* the king of Ireland, the Druid Cathbadh was brought to us there. That man was a true phrophet," said Finntan, "for he never told a lie. Right-hand-wise,[6] also, he used to utter every prediction and prophesy, because he believed in Christ.[7] The king, *i.e.* Eochaidh Feidhlech, asked the Druid Cathbadh how this plain would be towards the end of the world. Cathbadh replied to him afterwards, and said, 'this plain of the kings shall belong to clerics, truly, towards the end of time. 'Tis in the place where the palace of the kings is now, moreover, that Saint Caillin's *cahir* and residence will be. Numerous, also, will be the tones of bells and clerics around this *Cnoc-na-Righ*,'[8] said he. 'There will be a general guest-house likewise on this *Cnoc-na-Righ*; for every guest however troublesome, and every poet and other needy person, that demands refection in a proper manner, will always receive it there; and this *Cnoc-na-Righ* will be a hearth of entertainment and hospitality to the end of the world,' said Cathbadh.

was turned, in performing his incantations, and uttering his predictions.

[7] *believed in Christ.* This is very improbable, in a druid; although Conor Mac Nessa, king of Ulster in the first cent., cousin-german of Cathbadh, is stated, in ancient Irish authorities, to have had information of the Passion of Our Lord. See the account of Conor's death, in O'Curry's *Lectures*, &c., App., p. 636.

[8] *Cnoc-na-Righ.* "Hill of the kings." A name for Fenagh.

Ticfa imorro naem uasal onorach sund ar Cathbad, ocus bid mann genealach do ocus damsa, aire, .i. Caillin noem; is he benneochus in baili; ocus bid la esgrib ocus a ċomarbuib in mag co brath. Mairg neċ biar na gaire isin aimsir sin .i. in dereḋ domuin, daig ni bia neam na saegal ag nech da tuillfi a escaine isin baili sin.

[a] fol. 31, a 2. Mongenar adlaicthir isin baili sin[a] ar Cathbad, uair do orduig Crist neaṁ da gaċ aen teit fo uir Caillin. Mongenar d'Ultaib na hEmna .i. do Ċlannaib Ir ocus Rudruige adluicther aga mbraṫair naom fein .i. ig Caillin, daig biaid nem aca da ċinn, ar Cathbad drai. Togaimsi isin cnocsa, ar cind Caillin ocus Patraicc ard apstal na hErend, ar Cathbad drai.

Mongenar do samaḋ ocus do muintir Chaillin fein ar Cathbad drai, ċongbas a gesa ocus a fasbala don baili da eis .i. gan diultad re dreiċ nduine o matain co fescar. IS da mbuadaib aeidi acu in gaċ aon oiḋċi co brath. Da coimlet amlaid sin biaid neam ocus saegal [fada] ag comarbaib in baili.

IS i sin faitsine in druad ar belaib Echach feidlig, a Phatraicc, ar Findtan. IS am cumainsi Eri ar da mag, ar Findtan .i. sen Mag Elta in Etar ocus Mag Rein. IS fir anddubairt Cathbad, ar Patraicc fri caċ, ocus dono fuair aen beṫa fri hainglib nimi, ar is e ro cred artus in Erinn; et dono is aingel o Dia ro fir anddubairt. Fagbuimsi fein, ar Patraicc, sonus ar in mbaili .i. nadecha aoiḋe gan riar gemad daidbir gaċ aen ann. IS annsin ro bennaig Patraicc prim apstal cnoc na rig, ocus asbert gur bo lan dainglib .i. osa cind in ar had-

[b] fol. 31, b 1. luiced[b] Caṫbad. Asbert Padruicc comad don muintir in spiruta naeṁ gach nech adnaicfithi fo uir Caillin i Fidnacha.

[1] *Sen-Magh-Elta, in Etar.* The plain lying between Dublin and Howth. In the *Chron. Scotorum*, it is stated that the plain was called *Sen Magh Elta Edair*, or *old* "Magh Elta Edair," because no tree had ever grown there. Magh Elta Edair signifies "the plain of the flocks of Edar" (a fairy king).

[2] *over-head.* The meaning is, that the air over the place of Cathbadh's grave at Fenagh teemed with the presence of Angels. But there is no authority, save the foregoing statement, to prove that the druid Cathbadh was buried in Fenagh. On the lower margin of fol. 31 a (in A), the scribe has written a stanza in very rude and incorrect language, in which Manchan, Caillin, Cairelan and Brigid are

"'A noble, honourable saint will come here, moreover,' said Cathbadh, 'and his pedigree shall be the same as mine,' said he, 'to wit, Saint Caillin. 'Tis he that will bless the place; and the plain will belong to his heirs and comharbs for ever. Woe to him who will be inimical to him in that time, *i.e.* at the end of the world; for no one will enjoy Heaven or [long] life that earns his malediction in that place.'

"'Happy are they who will be buried in that place,' said Cathbadh, 'because Christ ordained Heaven for every one that goes under Caillin's clay. Happy will it be for the Ultonians of Emania, to wit, the descendants of Ir and Rudhraigh, who shall be buried with their own holy brother, *i.e.* Caillin; for they shall have Heaven therefor' said the Druid Cathbadh. 'I elect [to be buried in] this hill, in anticipation of Caillin, and of Patrick Arch-Apostle of Ireland,' said the Druid Cathbadh.

"'Happy will it be for Caillin's own congregation and people,' said the Druid Cathbadh, 'who shall observe his prohibitions and injunctions to the place after him, to wit, not to reject the face of a man from morning until evening. It is of their privileges to have guests every night for ever. If they observe [their orders] thus, the comharbs of the place shall have Heaven and long life.' This is the druid's prophecy in the presence of Eochaidh Feidhlech, O, Patrick," said Finntan.

"I remember Ireland with only two plains," said Finntan, "viz., Sen-Magh-Elta, in Etar,[1] and Magh-Rein." "What Cathbadh stated is true," said Patrick to all; "and verily, he obtained the same life enjoyed by the Angels of Heaven; for it was he that first believed in Ireland; and it was an Angel from God, moreover, that verified what he said." "I myself," said Patrick, "bequeath happiness to the place, viz., [I decree] that no guest shall depart without being served, even though every one there be poor." Then it was that the prime apostle Patrick blessed *Cnoc-na-Righ;* and he said that the place in which Cathbadh had been interred was full of Angels (i.e. over head).[2] Patrick said that every person who should be buried under Caillin's clay[3] in Fidnacha would be of the family of the Holy Spirit.

mentioned as consuming 'very little' on an island called *Inis-dun-na-trath*, the situation of which is not easily ascertained.

[3] *Caillin's clay.* The clay of the cemetery adjoining the old church of Fenagh.

Is iatsin dinnsenchus ocus sgela Maigi Rein, ar Findtan fri Patraicc. Ro raided, em, in duansa sis ar na neithibsi, .i.

Mag Rein, ga hadbar dia bfuil;
Abair a Findtain eolaig;
In mag sin ni beg a blad;
Faguib aguinn a bunad.
Is eolach damsa budein
Int adbar dia bfuil Mag Rein;
Uair isim cuman artus
A sibal is a imthuss.
Gabail tainic in Erinn,
Mor brecht ar atainic credim;
A cis sin nir beg in snaidm;
Fine Fomra ise a comainm.
Da trian d'ith, da trian do blicht,
Tucad doib ar a mor nirt;
Fine Fomra do fuair soin
O gac rig in Erinn iathgloin.
Uingi d'or doib ar gach sroin;
D'Erinn nir damatar coir;
No gur eirig in Lug lonn,
Do rad Eri a anforlonn.
Lug lamfada tuc in maidm
Ar sil inercill, ar claind Stairn.
O rian teichmi na fer nos
Ata Mag rein na righ ros.
San chind oirrtherach don moig
Beris Lug ar in laechraid.
Fagbad na lechtaib con lin
Na corrgind, do nir dodaing.

[1] *poem*. The poem here given was probably composed by the compiler of the Book of Fenagh, as no copy of it is discoverable, save the one contained in MSS. A. and B.

[2] *Impart*. faguib; lit. "leave."

"These are the antiquities and stories of Magh-Rein," said Finntan to Patrick. This poem[1] down here was also uttered regarding these things, viz.:—

"Magh-Rein, why is it [so called]. ?
    Say, O learned Finntan;
    The fame of this plain is not small.
    Impart[2] to us its origin."
"Well known unto me myself is
    The reason why Magh-Rein is [so called].
    For I remember from the first
    Its progress[3] and its history.
"An expedition to Ireland came
    A long time ere the Faith arrived;
    Their tribute was no small oppression;[4]
    Their name is the Fomorian tribe.
"Two-thirds of the corn, two-thirds of milk,
    Were given to them for their great might.
    The Fomorian tribe received this
    From every king in bright-landed Ireland.
"An ounce of gold for every nose they got.
    To Ireland they did not grant justice;
    Until arose the fierce Lughaidh,
    Who did Ireland free from thrall.
"Lugh-Lamhfada inflicted a defeat
    On the seed of the Hercules—on the sons of Starn.
    From the line of retreat of the mighty men
    Magh-Rein is a royal road.
"At the eastern head of the plain
    Lugh overtakes the warlike band;
    In their graves, with the band, were placed
    The Corrginns—to him it was not difficult.

[3] *progress.* ṗıḃal; lit. "walking."
[4] *oppression.* ṗnaıṁ; lit. "knot;" but also signifying "difficulty," or "oppression."

Do ṡaiṫ ar fertaib na bfer
Cloċa arda mar ingnad;
O na coirrgennaib sin fuil
A lan ainm ar na laechaib.
Noi ruġa do ṫuit la Lug[aid],
a fol. 31, b 2. Ar mag rein, cóir[a] anairim
Sgela Loga sgeoil go céill;
Conid uada Mag glan Rein.
Faṫ eli fa fuil Mag Rein
Ar in mag ba riga rem;
Conuing bececlaċ combuaid
Ri Erenn ann 'sa ard ṡluag.
Do ḃi re coicc bliadnaib dec
Ar in mag Conuing na cet;
Cur baided a dag mac de,
Gur treig in mag tria tuirsi.
Dag mac ag Conuing na cuan,
Cobthach menmnaċ na marcsluag;
Do ċuaid do ṡnam ar in loċ,
Ocus do baided Cobthach,
Go tainic Rian glegel grinn,
Muimi Cobthaig mic Conuing,
Do iarad a dalta dil,
Cur baided hi na degaid.
O buime Chobtaig loċ rein
Is e derbur doib na sceoil;
O fert Chobtaig lain alle
Ata allecht is a lige.
Nai traṫ do Chobthach uan cuan.
Fir Erenn co tuirseċ truag.
In fert fa fuil sa ċuid oir,
Im eolach me cid senoir.

[1] *The names.* It may be inferred from this expression that the Corrginns, or pillar stones, had some incriptions cut on them.

"On the graves of the men he fixed
High stones, as a prodigy.
From those Corrginns the names[1]
Of the heroes are fully known.
"Nine kings fell by Lughaidh,
On Magh-Rein; to count them is right;
The tales of Lugh are tales of sense;
For from them bright Magh-Rein is [named].
"Another cause why [the name] 'Magh-Rein' is
Applied to the plain of regal sway,
Is that famed Conaing Little-fear,
King of Ireland, was there with his mighty host.
"Conaing of battles was on the plain
During the space of fifteen years;
Until his good son drownèd was,
When he through grief forsook the plain.
"Conaing of the bands had a good son,
Proud Cobhthach of the cavalry.
He went to swim upon the lake;
And Cobhthach was drowned.
"Then came the fair-bright beauteous Rian,
The nurse of Cobhthach, Conaing's son,
Seeking for her nursling sweet;
But she was drownèd after him.
"From Cobhthach's nurse is Loch-Rein named—
Such do the stories to them report;
On this side of brave Cobhthach's grave
Is her grave and resting place.
"Nine days was Cobththach under the lake.
The men of Ireland were sad and grieved.
The mound under which he and his gold[2] do lie,
I know, although a senior I.

[2] *his gold.* a ċuid oir; "his share of gold." Several of the graves at Fenagh have been examined, but no gold ornaments have been found.

Tegur a tir Cobthach cuin;
Fir Erenn toirrseċ taiduir.
Do ferad a cluichi caini
Ro riġ sluagaib fer fuiniḋ.
Dun ngairo gairther don cnoc
O terta Cobthach comnart,
Uair batar re seċtmain ann
Ag golgairi na timchell.
Tegait ċuguinn, ba scel truag,
Mna Erend ba mor in sluag;
Do ċained Cobthaig, nir ċelg,
Tainig in banntrocht belderg.
Imda ann fon nDun gairc
Mac rig ba lan d'imnaire.
Uai coim on chorrcind ale
Ata Cobthach na loiġe.
Is uime ro ṫog Conuing
In magra raidit romuinn,*
Ar med airim ann o Lug[ad],
Is ar imad a ingnad.
Do fictis cuicci fa seċ
Maiṫi Erend co haintech;
A rian sin nir beg in blad;
Conid uad ta in sen mag.
Dindsenċus in Muigi móir
Sloind ocus innis co coir;
Gaċ fert da fuil ar Mag fein,
Abair a ḟindtain esein.

* fol. 32, a 1.

[1] *game of sorrowing;* i.e. funeral games; lit. "game of lamentation."

[2] *Fir Fuinidh.* Lit. "men of the setting," or "Viri occidentales"; a metaphorical name for the men of Ireland.

[3] *Dun.* The "*dun* (or fort) of lamentation." See note [2], p. 252.

[4] *Corrginds.* The pillar stones above referred to. See note [6], p. 251, *supra.*

[5] *Lugaidh.* Either Lugaidh Lamhfada,

"Cobhthach the mild was brought ashore;
Disconsolate, sad were Irishmen.
His 'game of sorrowing'[1] was celebrated
By the kingly hosts of the *Fir Fuinidh*[2]
"Dún-gáirè[3] the hill is called,
Since mighty Cobhthach was lost;
For they were there during a week,
Engaged in loud wailing about him.
"There came to us—'twas a sad tale—
The women of Ireland, a great band.
To mourn Cobhthach, 'twas no deceit,
The red-lipped female band did come.
"Around the *Dun*[3] many were the cries
Of kings' sons, full of modesty.
Nine paces on this side of the Corrginds[4]
Is Cobhthach reposing.
"The reason why Conaing chose
This plain, which we described before,
Was from the quantity of arms there, after Lugaidh,[5]
And for the extent of its wonders.
"To him were wont in turn to come
The nobles of Ireland, unitedly.
The fame of their track[6] was not little;
And from it, therefore, the old plain is [named]."
"The Dinnsenchus[7] of the great plain,
Do thou relate, and truly tell:
Every grave that is on Magh-Rein,
Do thou describe it, O, Finntan."

(note [3], p. 250), or Lugaidh, son of Eocho Uarches, stated to have been slain by Conaing Little-fear. See p. 27, *supra*.

[6] *track*. rian; gen. rein; from which comes Magh-Rein, "the Plain of the track."

[7] *Dinnsenchus*. Ancient history, or antiquities.

Atconnairc misi Mag Rein
Gan ait aon tighi ann reid,
Acht re na adbar ḟiadaig
Ag clainn Nemid nert giallaig.
Nai riga dec ar Mag Rein,
A Patraic da credim fein;
Eri do gabsat le nert,
Ar Mag Rein ta a tiuglechtt.
Gedi ollgothach co ceill
Fa leic na rig ar Mag Rein.
Conuing bececlach combuaid,
Eochaidh orthach in en uaiġ.
Crimthann coscarach comblad,
Lan ri leṫan o Laigen;
Mor nech fuair bas o glaic gloin;
Fan leic fós ta in laech sin.
Diṫorba mac Demain dein;
Conall gulban do cland Nell;
D'Erinn domdamatar cert;
Ar Mag Rein ta a tiuglecht.
Asrin duitsi fert in rig,
Bresal bodibaid na mbrig;
Ocus Find mac Rosa ruaid
Cona ċland, tuilleḋ in aen uaiġ.
Dungal ocus Gormgal garg,
Da rig Brefne atat fon ard,
O leic na lennann ale
Ata lecht na laeċraide.

[1] *sepulchre.* tiuglechtt; lit. "last heap" (or last bed.)

[2] *Lec-na-righ.* The flag-stone of the kings. This was the name of one of the many ancient sepulchres still traceable at Fenagh; but it cannot be identified at this day.

[3] *Lec*; i.e. *Lec-na-righ,* referred to in last note.

[4] *with his sons fit in one grave.* The

"I have seen Magh-Rein
Without the site of a house there cleared;
But it was used as hunting ground
By strength-subduing Nembid's sons.

"Nineteen kings dwelt on Magh-Rein,
O, Patrick, in whom I believe.
They possessed Ireland, by their might;
On Magh-Rein their sepulchre[1] is.

"Geide Ollgothach, the wise,
Is under *Lec-na-righ*,[2] on Magh-Rein;
Conaing Beg-eclach, the famous,
And Eochaidh Opthach, are in the same grave.

"Crimhthann Coscragh the renowned,
Full, wide-ruling king, from Leinster;
Many found death by his brave hand—
Under the *Lec*,[3] also, that hero is.

"Dithorba son of fierce Deman,
Conall Gulban of the Clann-Neill,
To Ireland justice did accord—
On Magh-Rein their sepulchre is.

"Here you have the grave of the king,
Breasal Bodibhaidh the vigorous,
And of Finn son of Ross the Red,
Who with his sons fit in one grave.[4]

"Dungal and fierce Gormgal,
Two kings of Breifne, are under the height.
At this side of *Lec na Lennan*[5]
Is the grave of the warriors.

MS. A. furnishes another reading, viz.:— "no con cloich tuill iat in aen uaig .i. cloch toll oide," i.e. "or at the *cloch* they fit in one grave, i.e. *cloch toll* (hole-stone) hodie."

[5] *Lec na Lennan.* "The flag-stone of the favorites"; a fanciful name for some grave not now to be identified.

Cnoc in bantrochta ro ter,[1]
   A Patraic do reir gach geir;
Coic righna dec, raidim ruib,
   Do fuair bas ar in mor muig.
Do dechatar cus in loch
   Maicni Partholoin co moch;
Nai ced macam ba he allín,
   Do chlaind uirrig is ardrig.
Pest nime do bi san loch;
[a] fol. 32, a 2.   Do rinde riu[a] cluichi troch;
Gur ab ainm osin alle
   Don loch sin Loch na pesti.[2]
Marbais in phest sin nai ced
   Do shil Partholoin, ni breg;
Ba bronach fir Erenn de,
   Do uath[ad] a macroide.
Ni dernad snam air iarsin,
   O do baided in macraid.
In larin nir beg in sgel,
   Ersbada mora ar Mag-rein.
Do badhusa ar Cnoc-na-Rig,[3]
   Is Eochaid feidlech maraen [rim];
Dob aibind duin air in cnoc,
   Oir nir ba eguil duin do chlog.
Tegair chuiguinn Cathbad drai,
   Co hEochaidh mar ambai in rí;
Uair do adrad do Christ chaidh,
   Do righ na naingeal nimhlán.
Derial do nid Cathbad drai
   Cach faitsine, mor a gnai;

[1] *Cnoc-in-bantrochta.* "The hill of the women."

[2] *Loch-na-pesti.* The "Lake of the Serpent." The lake referred to is now known as Fenagh Lake, or Loch-Saloch.

[3] *Cnoc-na-Righ.* The "Hill of the Kings";

"Cnoc-in-bantrochta[1] is this to the South,
O, Patrick, who dissolved each spell;
Fifteen queens, I say to you,
Expired upon the great plain.
"Unto the lake did go,
At early morn, Partholan's kin.
Their number was nine hundred youths,
Of the sons of princes and arch-kings.
"A venomous serpent was in the lake,
That towards them a sad game did act.
Wherefore, from that time to this, the name
Of that lake is *Loch-na-pesti.*[2]
"That serpent killed nine hundred
Of the seed of Partholan—'tis no lie.
The men of Ireland were sad therefor—
For the drowning of their youths.
"No swimming was done in it after that—
From the time the youths were drowned.
On that day—not small the news—
Great were the losses on Magh-Rein.
"I was on *Cnoc-na-Righ.*[3]
And Eochaidh Feidlech along with me;
To us 'twas pleasant on the hill,
For thy bell we did not fear.
"Cathbad[4] the druid came to us,
To Eochaidh, where the king was;
For he did worship Holy Christ,
Of all the perfect angels King.
"Right-hand-wise[5] Cathbad used to utter
Every prophesy—great his power;

another name for the hill near Fenagh.

[4] *Cathbad.* See note [7], p. 255, *supra.*

[5] *Right-hand-wise.* Deiriul. In the performance of religious ceremonies in Pagan times, the ministers seem to have had regard to the course of the sun, whose

Coimes ni fedfad drai sir;
Bres riam ni derna d'aithris.
Do fiarfaid Eochaid feidlech
Do Cathbad drai, co demneċ;
Cindus bias in mag sa de,
In deriud na haimsire.
M mag sa ar a fuilti, a ri,
Adubairt Cathbad caem drai,
Ge ta ag rigaib, raidim ruib,
Biaid ag naemaib na degaid.
Do tairngir duinn Cathbad drai,
Ar in cnoc sa, mor a gnai,
Ait bruidni na rig abus
Combia ag Caillin ann arus.
M tulaig sa tathai, a rí,
Adubairt Caṫbad in drai,
Bud imda guṫ cluig fa cenn;
Bud binn clerig na timchell.
Biaid teċ naided coitchenn caem
Fa leth taeḃ tolċa na rig;
Riarfar ann gaċ cliar fo sech,
[a] fol. 32. b 1. Da niarfa biad co dligthech.[a]
Bendeochaid Caillin in mag,
A Eochaid is do mo chain;
Biaid in mag ga sil co brath.
Olc ni dingnet in aen traṫ.
Mongenar raċus fo uir
I relic Caillin in ruin;
Uair do ordaig Crist na cros,
Nem gaċ aen bias na arus.

movement in the Heavens they followed, by turning round on the right hand, keeping their faces to the sun. The Irish names for the cardinal points prove this: *des*, *tuaid*, *iar*, *air*, "south," "north," "west," "east," meaning respectively "right," "left," "back," "front."

[1] *race*; i.e. his successors; for it is nowhere related that St. Caillin left any other progeny, although the word sil, lit.

To equal him no druid was able ;
A falsehood never uttered he.
"Eochaidh Feidhlech did inquire
Of druid Cathbad, earnestly,
'How is it this plain will be
In the latter end of time'?
"'This plain on which you are O king,'
Said Cathbad the druid mild,
'Though kings have it, I say to you,
Saints shall have it afterwards.'
"Druid Cathbad to us foretold,
On this hill—great was his power—
That on the site of the king's mansion here,
Caillin would have a residence.
"'This hill on which you are, O king,'
Said Cathbadh the druid—
'Numerous will be the sounds of bells ;
Melodious the clerics about it.
"'A general, fair guest-house shall be
Beside the Hill of the Kings ;
Where each company will be served in turn,
If they demand food rightfully.
"'Caillin will bless the plain,
O, Eochaidh ; to him my tribute's due ;
His race[1] shall have this plain for aye :
They 'll not do evil at any time.
"'Happy he that goes under the clay
In the *relig*[2] of virtuous[3] Caillin ;
For Christ of the crosses ordained
Heaven to each one who shall be in his house.'[4]

"seed," might suggest such a supposition.

[2] *relig ;* i.e. a cemetery.

[3] *virtuous.* The MS. has in ruin, "of the secret ;" but the word ruin is merely used to rhyme with the last word of the preceding line.

[4] *in his house ;* i.e. in St. Caillin's "house of clay," or cemetery.

Buaid cleti 7 buaid catha
Ar rigaib ar dam[n]aċa;
Da mbet na loigi gan locht
Ic Caillin ina ardport.
Mairg biar ar gaire don cnoc,
In tan biar caċ uili olc;
Ni bia nem na saegul de
Ic neċ da millfe in baile.
Mand slicht dam is don naeim
Bennechur i cnoc na rig;
Biaid nem is clannuib Ir de,
Da creidet do is do baili.
Da congbad a muinter fein
A gera don naem aigbeil,
Biaid nem ocus saegul de
Is co[m]arbaib na cilli.
O matuin co traṫ luiḋi
Gan diultad re dreiċ nduine;
Do buadaib in baili de
Aiḋe ann gaċ aen oiḋċi.
Creidimsi ferta don riġ,
Adubairt Caṫbaḋ caem drai;
Biaid m'anam fa guṫ in cluig,
'San cnoc fa aticfa Patraic.
Is i sin faistine in druad,
A Patraicc da creidit sluaig.
In la sin nir bind guṫ cluig
Ar Cnoc na ri, a Patraicc.
Is misi Findtan co fir;
Is mithid dam beṫ lan crin;
Tarraid me Eri ar da mag,
Gidhe Mag rein is Sen mag. M.

[1] *ruins the town.* The word "ecce" is added in the margin, by Thady O'Rody.

[2] *Cnoc-na-Righ.* "The Hill of the Kings;" i.e. Fenagh.

[3] *sons of Ir.* See note,[1] p. 220, *supra.*

[4] *near.* fa; "around," or "under."

"'Success of conflict and of battle
Kings and royal heirs shall have,
If they be lying, without stain,
With Caillin in his chief abode.
"'Woe to him who's opposed to the hill,
The time when all shall wicked be;
For neither heaven nor long life
Shall he who ruins[1] the place enjoy.
"'Of the same race am I and the Saint
Who will bless *Cnoc-na-Righ*;[2]
The sons of Ir[3] shall have heaven thereby,
If they believe in him and [Dun-] Bailè.
"'If his own people do observe
His injunctions, for the terrible saint;
Heaven and long life therefore shall
The Comharbs of the church enjoy.
"'From morning 'till the time of rest
They must not a man's face deny;
For of the privileges of the place is,
That a guest should be there every night.
"'Henceforth I believe in The King,'
Said Cathbad, the druid mild;
'My soul shall be near[4] the sound of the bell,
On this hill to which Patrick shall come.'
"That is the druid's prophecy,
O, Patrick, in whom hosts believe.
On that day no sweet bell's sound,
O, Patrick, was on *Cnoc-na-Righ*.
"I am Finntan, truly;
'Tis time for me to be full old;
Ireland I've seen with but two plains;
Even Magh-Rein and Sen-Magh.[5]" M.

The meaning is that Cathbad's disembodied spirit would be hovering round the sound of the Christian bell.

[5] *Sen-Magh*. Sen-Magh-Elta. See note [1], p. 256.

Is fir adubairt Cathfad,
Ar Patraicc fir na maithib;
Fuair re credem in teg glan,
Imers na naingel nuasal.
Bres ni dubairt Caṫbad de,
Firfaider in fairtine;
Uair is he cet fer ro cred
In hErind he, bar Patraicc.[a]
Gaċ buaid da ndubairt Caṫbad,
Ar Mag rein cona maithib;
Is e int aingel, raidim ruiḃ,
Do ḟir comraiti Cathbaid.
Fagḃuimsi, ar Patraicc na mbuaid,
Sonus ar in mbaili mbuan;
Co fagbad ni da gaċ neoch,
Gemad daidbir gaċ clerech.
Bennaigim anos an cnoc,
Ar Patraicc, ag buain a ċlog,
Uair atat aingil nime
Uas Caṫbad na comnaide.
Fagbuimsi sin, is lor buadh,
Neam gaċ neċ ga mbia mo duan;
Uair do bi aingil nime
Des caṫbaid 'ga fairtine.
Do muintir in sbiruta naoim
Gaċ corp bias i Cnoc-na-Rig;
O ro bennaig Caillin de,
Gaċ ard ro taeb in muigi. M.
Se ced naom fa do dc.
Tainic Patraig san mbaile,

[a] fol. 32, b 2.

[1] *poor.* The sentiment expressed in this stanza conveys a pretty fair idea of the generous character of Irish hospitality, whether dispensed by ecclesiastics or laymen.

[2] *my lay;* i.e. the *Feth Fiadha*, or

"What Cathbad did relate, is true,"
Said Patrick to the chieftains.
"He obtained by faith the mansion bright
Amidst th' illustrious angels.
A lie Cathbad said not thereof;
The prophecy will be proved true;
For he the first man that believed
In Ireland was," Patrick did say.
"Every virtue Cathbadh mentioned
[Attends] on Magh Rein with its chiefs;
It is the Angel, I tell you,
That has confirmed Cathbad's sayings."
"I leave," said Patrick of the virtues,
"Prosperity to the constant place;
So that it shall provide for all,
Though every cleric should be poor.[1]
I bless the hill now,"
Said Patrick, striking his bell,
"For the angels of heaven are
Above Cathbadh, abiding.
"I leave this—and 'tis ample bliss—
Heaven to him who my lay[2] shall have;
For the angels of heaven were
Prophesying it after Cathbadh."
Of the people of the Holy Spirit shall be
Each one that is in *Cnoc-na-Righ*;
For to that end did Caillin bless
Every mound around the plain.
Six hundred saints, twice told,
Came with Patrick to the place.

Hymn alleged to have been composed by St. Patrick. See Stokes's ed., Goidelica,[2] p. 149. sq. The Hymn has also been published (amongst others) by Mr. O'Beirne Crowe, with a translation and annotations evincing much ability, and

Fuair Caillin, tria fertuib de,
A raith ar lar in maige. M. R.
Ag sin fert Chatbada drai,
Ar benaiss do chlog, a naim;
Da marad Catbad drai de,
Atfetfad sgela in maige. M. R.
A Patraig da fetuim sgel,
Is arrsuid me is nocha tren;
Ge atu anos go hanbann de,
Is eol dam sgela in moige.
M. R. ga hadbar dia fuil.

IS ferr duin hi fechtsa co ro scribam ind airchetal fesach forglide si tainig o Ard Macha illiubar naem Chaillin mic Niatach, oir ata onoir do Chaillin indti.

* * * * * *

fol 35, a 1. * * * Craig na bruigne,
Dlegar dim turim a tenna.
Domnall, Diarmaid naid tennal;
Muiredach, Murchad rinna;
Gilla na naem Feda moir;
Ni bert ann broin dam minda.
Cen corap dib fil Siadail,
Tic tri saethi da rimuib.
Genfid o mnai da naicme
Sai bara nairti o Fingin.
Amalgaid, Amlaib luaidim,
Maelbrigde foires cnedai.

acquaintance with old Irish, in the *Journal of the Hist. Soc. of Ireland*, vol. 1, 4th ser., part 8.

[1] *Magh-Rein, why is it so called.* This is a repetition of the first line of the poem, in token of its conclusion, according to the general practice of Irish scribes.

[2] *in it.* Folios 33 and 34 are missing from A., and folio 35 commences imperfectly, so that the matter or prophecy brought from Ard-Macha (Armagh) is lost, unless the scribe refers to the fore-

Caillin found, through the miracles of God,
Enough for them in the midst of the plain. Magh Rein
That is Druid Cathbad's grave,
At which thou'st rung thy bell, O saint.
If Druid Cathbad did but live,
He'd tell the stories of the plain. Magh Rein.
O Patrick, to whom I history tell,
Aged am I now, and not strong;
But though I now am weak indeed,
I know the stories of the plain.
Magh-Rein, why is it so called.[1]

It is better for us on this occasion that we should write this skilful plain poem, which came from Armagh, in the book of Saint Caillin, son of Niata, for there is honour to Caillin in it.[2]

* * * * * *

* * * the crag of the palace
I am bound to enumerate their stout ones.
Domnall, Diarmaid—not firebrands—
Muiredach, Murchadh of the Shannon;
Gilla-na-Naemh of Fidh Mór—
They'll not give offence[3] to my relics,
Though of them be not Siadal's race,[4]
Three septs[5] shall of their number come;
From a woman of their tribe will be born
A sage in their science, O'Finghin.
Amalgaidh, Amlaibh, I mention—
Maelbrighde who relieves wounds;

going poem, which is probable. In any case, the scribe's observation goes to prove that much of the contents of the present volume was derived from very old traditions.

[3] *offence*. bpoin (for bpon), lit. "sorrow."

[4] *Siadal's race.* The O'Siadail, or family of O'Sheil.

[5] *septs.* raethi (*recte* raithi), pl. of raithe, which usually signifies a "swarm," as raithe bech, a "swarm of bees."

Ꮳngnai co brath ni cromthar,
Coti Donnchad da ndela.
Donnchad dalach ni duaichnid,
For mama fir in foin nim.
Genfid uada fai famla,
Gambia adba i crich comair.
Sil Etig ollaim Elga,
Afrin nifergga a mbaga,
Bettit os legaib Banba,
No co ti alma aga.
Sil linmar do meic muirnech,
Conmac, Ciar, Corc in comair;
A Medb ractait cuiri cruaid
Fothuaid fri derer domuin.
Gebtaitt Emain a mbunad,
Cuicced Ulad re nerbert.
Bid fir i fuiglim re baig,
Ocus nocha tair for chert.
Faitsine annso beus.
Da fegad na fatha,
Tanic trath do turbroid.
Ferfaid aniu snechta,
Ni melta do Mugroin.
Do lecht ni ri loechraide,
A Tairrdelbaid[a] thar acht.
A cuingid na cetta,
Fir teca re hadart.

[a] fol. 35, a 2.

[1] *Elga.* A Bardic name for Ireland.

[2] *o'er Banba's Leeches.* In other words, the family whose fame is here extolled would be pre-eminently distinguished in medical science, beyond all others in Banba (Ireland).

[3] *Conmac—Ciar—Corc.* Sons of Queen Medbh of Connacht, by Fergus Mac Roy. See notes [7], [8], [9], pp. 31 and 175, *supra.*

[4] *Medhbh.* Queen of Connacht. See note [5], p. 174, *supra.*

[5] *Emania.* Used here for Ulster.

[6] *prophecy.* This is a distinct prophecy from the last, and is in a different metre.

Their countenances shall ne'er be humbled,
'Till, to divide them, Donnchadh comes.
Donnchadh of the assemblies; not hard to be known,
In manly deeds, is he in truth.
From him will descend a likely sage,
Who'll have a home in the neighb'ring land.
The triumphs, afterwards, of Sil-Etigh,
Ollamhs of Elga,[1] will not decay.
They will be o'er Banba's Leeches,[2]
Until valourous tribes shall come.
A numerous race of cheerful sons,
Conmac,[3] Ciar,[3] Corc[3] of Comar,
From Medhbh,[4] hardy champions, will proceed
Northwards, towards the end of the world.
They'll obtain Emania[5] as a patrimony,
Ulad's Province, by prowess.
What I assert will be famously true;
And will no blot on justice be.

A prophecy[6] here still:—

If you would observe the prophets,
The time of your trouble has come:
Snow[7] will be shed to day
That cannot deceive Mughron.[8]
Thy grave shall not be with heroes
O Toirrdhealbhach,[9] without doubt;
Thou, O leader in battles,
Shalt on thy pillow die.

[7] *Snow.* This is probably in allusion to an event recorded by the Four Mast. under A.D. 1030; namely, the death of Ruaidhri O'Canannain, on an expedition which was called the "Crech (or foray) of the snow."

[8] *Mughron.* The person so often referred to under this name in the following stanzas, has not been identified. There are several of the name mentioned in the Irish Annals, from the 8th to the 12th centuries.

[9] *Toirrdhealbhach.* Turlough O'Conor, king of Ireland; ob. 1156.

Mo na aidid Mugroin
 In dam ticfa in Erind.
 Cuiri nach ba carit;
 Nihi in barit belbind.
Mo na aidid Mugroin
 Cath na rig i Cairbriu.
 Bid coscrach slog Conaill
 Ar clod oruinn airgni.
Mo na aidid Mugroin
 Cath na Mona mori;
 Toeth leth Mogau morlond
 Re forlond na fori.
Mo na oidid Mugroin
 Muircertaċ il Letir;
 Da tuitend co homda
 Re sloġ Cnogba is Cletig.
Mo na oidid Mugroin
 Bas Conchobair Chruachna.
 Tuitfid in ri delbach
 Re teglach co fuaċda.
Mo na oidid Mugroin
 In estrechta amail,
 Mandubthar sa choirrṡliabh
 Ormain Chathail Charruig.

[1] *Barit.* This seems to have been the name of some woman, to whom the "prophet" wished to pay a compliment.

[2] *Cairbre;* i.e. Carbury, co. Sligo. It is uncertain which of the conflicts that took place in Carbury, between the O'Rorkes and O'Donnells, is here referred to.

[3] *host of Conall;* i.e. the people of Tirconnell.

[4] *battle of Móin-mór.* The celebrated battle fought at Móin-mór, near Mallow, co. Cork, in the year 1151, between the armies of Connaught and Munster, in which the Munstermen were defeated with tremendous slaughter. Four Mast.

[5] *Muircertach in Letir.* The event here alluded to, seems to be the battle of Letirluin, (a place in the par. of Newtownhamilton, co. Armagh,) fought A.D. 1166,

Greater than the fate of Mughron, is
The band that will come to Ireland;
Heroes who will not be friends;
Not like the sweet-mouth'd Barit.[1]
Greater than Mughron's death will be
The battle of the kings in Cairbre;[2]
The host of Conall[3] will triumphant be,
After inflicting slaughters upon us.
Greater than Mughron's death shall be
The battle of Moin-mór.[4]
Leth-Mogha the fierce shall fall
By the force of the pursuit.
Greater than Mughron's death, is
Muirchertach in Letir,[5]
Where he shall untimely fall
By the host of Cnoghbha[6] and Cletech.[7]
Greater than Mughron's death, is
The death of Conchobhar of Cruachan.[8]
The comely king shall fall
By his rebellious household.
Greater than Mughron's death
Is the similar catastrophe,
In which will be hacked at Corrsliabh[9]
The form of Cathal Carrach.[10]

in which Muirchertach (or Murtough) Mac Lochlainn, king of Ireland, or at least of the North of Ireland, was slain by the Oirghialla. Vid. Four Mast., *ad an.*

[6] *Cnoghbha.* Knowth, co. Meath.

[7] *Cletech;* on the Boyne, near Navan; an ancient residence of the kings of Tara, from which the men of Meath were sometimes called the "host of Cletech."

[8] *Conchobhar of Cruachan.* Conor of Croghan, or Rathcroghan, the seat of the kings of Connacht. The Conor in question was Conor O'Conor, also called Conor of Maenmagh, king of Connaught, who was slain in the year 1189, by a party of his own tribe, "at the instigation of his brother," as the Annals of Ulster state.

[9] *Corrsliabh.* The Curlieu hills, between the counties of Roscommon and Sligo.

[10] *Cathal Carragh.* Cathal Carragh

Mo na oidid Mughroin
  Oidid cretra in croibderg;
  Ocus Aed na degaid,
  Tresin mebail mordeirg.
Mo na oidid Mughroin,
  Oidid in Duinn Dabaill,
  Re cloind Neill in ortaid,
  Is re brosnaig Conuill.
Mo na oidid Mughroin
  Gach ni tarla air m'aire;
  Ni tig dim rem aimsir
  A taidbsin duit uili.
Ticfa graifnech Cruachna;
  Dith danar co dedla;
  Bid dith he ar a finne,
[a] fol. 35, b 1. Co teitt sligi ecca.[a]
Bid anbann clann Fergna
  Re a aimsir, ni chelim.
  Tares na cath coscrach
  Bid tosach do in errim.
Ticfa raman sen fir
  I tir Conuill choscraig;

O'Conor, king of Connaught, who was slain near Boyle, in the year 1201, by Cathal Crovdearg O'Conor and William De Burgho.

[1] *Crobhderg.* Cathal Crobhderg ("Red Hand") O'Conor, king of Connaught; who died A.D. 1224, in the monastery of Knockmoy, "in the habit of a Grey Friar."

[2] *Aedh*; i.e. Hugh, son of Cathal Crovderg O'Conor, and king of Connaught; murdered in 1228, by an Englishman, who was executed by the Lord Deputy for the crime. Mageoghegan states in his translation of the Annals of Clonmacnoise (A.D. 1227–8), that "the cause of killing the king of Connaught was, that after the wife of that Englishman that was so hanged by the Deputie, had so washed his head and body with sweet balls and other things, he, to gratifie her for her service, kissed her, which the Englishman seeing, for meer jealousie, and for none other cause, killed O'Conor presently at unawares."

[3] *Donn of Dabhall.* Not identified.

Greater than Mughron's death
    Is the pious end of the Crobhderg;[1]
And of Aedh[2] after him,
    Through the great red treachery.
Greater than Mughron's death
    Is the killing of Donn of Dabhall,[3]
By the steady[4] Clann-Neill
    And the rabble[5] of [Clann]-Conaill.
Greater than the fate of Mughron,
    Is each thing that has come under my notice;
My time would not suffice
    To exhibit them all to you.
The horseman of Cruachan[6] will come—
    The bold destroyer of Danars.[7]
He will be ruin to their tribe,
    Until he goes the way of death.
Clann-Fergna[8] will be feeble
    During his time, I deny not;
After the triumphant battles,
    His journey shall be quiet.
A happy man will then come
    In the land of victorious Conall,

Dabhall was the ancient name of the river Blackwater, which flows between the counties of Armagh and Tyrone, into Lough Neagh. "Donn of Dabhall" was probably the chief of some neighbouring tribe.

[4] *steady Clann-Neill.* Clann Neill in ortaid. The words in ortaid seem for in ḟortaid, "of the steadiness."

[5] *rabble.* brosn̄ for brosnaig, dat. of brosnach, "fragments," "faggots."

[6] *horseman of Cruachan.* This was probably Turlough, son of Aedh O'Conor (see note [2],), who was drowned in the Shannon, A.D. 1244.

[7] *Danars.* This word is generally applied to the Scandinavians by the Irish writers; but it is likely that the "prophet" had his eye upon the Englishmen who were appropriating to themselves, in the 13th century, the plains of Connaught.

[8] *Clann Fergna:* i.e. the septs of O'Rourke, O'Reilly, and their kindred tribes.

Bid tren ar a namit;
Mor granit re brosnaig.
Traethfaid treoin na timchell;
Imda a debtha derbam;
Re saigid co suabaċ
Ba cruadbac do i Termonn.
Tares tresa Tormuinn,
Tresa in laċa luaidim.
Rachaid cethri echtra,
Is bechta ro smuainim.
Forfear Eri uili
O nas a sar milled.
Traothfar goill na coindmed,
Ar tornem a nimel.
Domnall debthach daire;
Murchertach a Mumain;
Aed a hoileċ amra,
Re labra bid luġair.
Biaid co hanbuain Eri
Re forran na fersin;
Da tairc co raith cloentai
Ni ba moelta a mesair.
Dicerthar na danair,
Ar chaṫuib, air chredim;
Ni ba cain a costad
Ar losgad gach lebinn.

[1] *fear him.* The original of this line is very obscure, and the translation merely conjectural.

[2] *successful.* cruadbac (=crodbach), "prosperous;" from crod, stock, cattle, or property. Several words in this poem are purposely disguised in a corrupt and absurd orthography, in order to give to the "prophecy" an appearence of antiquity.

[3] *Termonn.* Probably Termon-Dabheog (or Termon-Magrath), co. Donegal, where the Cenel-Eoghain were defeated by the Cenel-Conaill, in A.D. 1043.

[4] *Lake.* Not identified.

[5] *Galls of the 'billeting.'* This is seemingly an allusion to the retaliatory massacre

He will be strong against his foes;
With terror shall they fear him.[1]
He'll subdue the mighty around him;
Many his conflicts, I assert.
By joyously advancing,
He'll successful[2] be in Termonn.[3]
After the conflict of Termonn,[3]
The battle of the Lake[4] I mention;
He will go on four expeditions,
. As I exactly think.
All Ireland will be delivered
From its state of great destruction.
The Galls of the 'billeting'[5] will be subdued,
After the humbling of their borders.
The contentious Domnall[6] of Derry;
Muirchertach[7] from Munster;
The noble Aedh[8] from Ailech,
To speak of will be sad.
Ireland will be exhausted
By the oppression of those men;
Of their expedition to Rath-Claenta[9]
Thy judgment should not be favourable.
The Danars[10] will be expelled,
After battles, after faith;
Not happy shall be their condition
After the burning of every ship.

of the foreigners billeted in Connacht, in the year 1202, as recorded in the *Annals of Loch Cé*.

[6] *Domhnall;* i.e. Domhnall MacLoughlinn (or O'Loughlin), who contested the sovereignty of Ireland with Muirchertach (or Murtough) O'Brien. See *Cambrensis Eversus*, ed. Rev. Matt. Kelly; vol. ii., p. 47, *sq.*

[7] *Muirchertach.* Great grandson of Brian Borumha. See note [6].

[8] *Aedh;* i.e. Aedh O'Neill, Lord of Oilech; ob. A.D. 1033.

[9] *Rath-Claenta.* Not identified.

[10] *Danars.* See note [7], p. 281.

A Cruaċuin, a Caisiul,
    A hOileċ nach anband,
    Tafaintear gan tlas iat
    Conas rotus marb and.
Tecait co tuaiṫ Tuirmi,
    Goill Erenn iar nimned;
    Ar torsi gaċ tartme,
    An argin 'san indread.[a] — [a] fol. 35, b 2.
Ni bia a nert a nErind
    Ohsin co brath mbechta;
    Acht turium a tamṫi,
    A lathre 'sa lechta.
Dia luain ina longaib,
    Ic degail re hElga,
    Ic seolad san chamair
    Ar fagail mor tendta.
Ar lena chind chorrbuilg
    Is and bias mo leachtra;
    Ni foetim a sena,
    Uair is it scela bechda. Da. fe. na f. am̄.

In tan iaram ba haimsiur a etsechtai do naem Chaillin mac Niataċ, et ro ba mithid la Dia a dol dochum nime; ocus dono robatar muinter nime na ressum ag furnaide etsiuchta Caillin et a dola cus in mbetha suthain; Is and ro boi Caillin in tan sin ind eclais Moċoemocc; et ro bai Manchan ina ḟarrad and. Ro gab iaram ag accallaim Manchan tria baile ocus faitsine. Ro tharrngir do dono Saxain do ṫoigeċt in Erind amail ro ḟoillsig int aingel do tria ḟis; et assert fri Manchan, ge fogabtais leṫ Chuinn uili cona gebtais a

[1] *mercy.* tlas; lit., smoothness, gentleness.

[2] *Tuath-Tuirmhi.* This was the ancient name of a district round the village of Turvey, near Donabate, co. Dublin.

[3] *ravages . . . . plunders;* i.e. the ravages and plunders to which the Danars would be subjected.

[4] *Elga;* i.e. Ireland.

[5] *fires.* The prophet meant to say, that some band of Foreigners, on their forced departure from the shores of Ireland, would

From Cruachan, from Cashel,
From Ailech not feeble,
They'll be chased without mercy,[1]
Altho' they be not slain there.
They'll come to Tuath-Tuirmhi[2]—
The Galls of Ireland, after troubles—
Fatigued from their privations,
Their ravages[3] and plunders.[3]
They'll have no sway in Ireland,
From thence to the certain Judgment;
But the enumeration of their deaths,
Their sites and graves, [shall remembered be].
On Monday in their ships,
They will depart from Elga;[4]
Sailing at daybreak,
After leaving great fires.[5]
On the meadow of Cenn-Corrbuilg[6]—
There shall my grave be—
I cannot conceal it;
For it is true history.[7]

When it was, therefore, the hour of the death of Saint Caillin son of Niata, and God thought it time that he should go to Heaven; and when also the people of Heaven were standing, awaiting the death of Caillin, and his departure to the perpetual life; where Caillin was then, was in the church of Mochoemog;[8] and Manchan[9] was there along with him. He subsequently began to converse with Manchan, through ecstasy and prophecy. He then foretold to him, that Saxons would come to Ireland, as the Angel had manifested to him through knowledge; and he said to Manchan, that though

set fire to some places which he does not indicate.

[6] *Cenn-Corrbuilg.* Not identified.

[7] *true history.* ꞅcela bechꞃa; lit., "authentic stories." But the situation of the "prophet's" grave is indeed very uncertain.

[8] *church of Mochoemhog.* *Eclais Mochaemhog*, or *Relig-Mochaemhog.* See note,[5] p. 12, *supra.*

[9] *Manchan.* See note [1], p. 12, *supra.*

[a] fol. 36, a 1. chell ocus a chathruigrium .i. Fidnacha muigi Reine muinnt Cobthaig.[a] IS mithid damsa, a Manchan, arse, dol doċom nime, daig is slan u. ced bliadan cus anocht dam. Ni uil imorro acht aen fiacal im ċinn, ocus ata ag tuitim anos. Forgillim, em, duitsi, a Manchain, et dom Dia nime et talman, na tainig breg tar mo det amos riam. Ba cosmail sium fri Patraicc on mudsin. Atberim frit, a naem Manchan, arsé, na fil naem da tarrusa do noemaib Erenn nach fuil cuairt ocus cain uada dom baili si .i. Fidnacha .m. r.

Dliġim, imorro, cetamus do Patruic Maċa, ardapstal iarthair Eorpai, a ech ocus a eirred dom ċomarbaib gach bliadain.

Dligim imorro do Brigit screpall d'or do idlacad as a cill dom chleirchib.

Dligim fo do Samtuinn, don noimoig, caċ dechmad screpall dia tabechaid.

Dligim do Ciaran, ocus d'Finnen Muigi bile, cuit tri ced ar gaċ cill.

Dligim do Ruadan Lothra, ocus do Brenuinn, ocus do Lugna, cuit tri ced in gaċ raiṫi. Cuid tri ced o gac aen don triarsa do Chaillin, o Beo Aed aird Carna, ocus o ṡesin ocus o Etuin Tuama.

Tinne airgit o Chainnech mac ui Dalon. Cuid tri ced in gaċ errach [b] fol. 36, a 2. o Berchan Cluana sosta,[b] ocus o Chaimgin Glinne da lacha. Screpall oir gaċa caṫrach o Laċtain Lugmuigi, ocus o espcop Ibar, ocus o

[1] *past my tooth.* A similar story is told of St. Mochta, of Lughmhagh, or Louth (co. Louth). See Mart. Donegal, at 19th August.

[2] *Patrick of Macha.* St. Patrick of Armagh. The same fees were of course due from his successors, if due from him.

[3] *screpall.* See note [6], p. 79, *supra.*

[4] *Samthann.* St. Samhthann, virgin, of Cluain-Bronaigh (Clonbroney), in the co. Longford, who died in the year 739.

[5] *Ciaran;* i.e. St. Ciaran of Saighir, or Seir-Keeran, in the King's county.

[6] *Finnen of Magh-Bilè.* St. Finnian of Moville (co. Down).

[7] *Lothra.* Lorrha, co. Tipperary. St. Ruadhan (or Rodanus) lived in the sixth century. In consequence of a quarrel with the then king of Ireland, he cursed Tara in 565, after which it ceased to be the seat of the Irish monarchs. See Petrie's *Tara* (Trans. R. I. Acad. vol. 18, part ii.), p. 125.

[8] *Brenainn.* St. Brendan of Clonfert.

[9] *Ard-Carna.* See note [11], p. 179.

[10] *Sesin.* In the Martyrology of Donegal, at the 31st August, Sesin, or Sessen, is said to be of Ath-omna, which was probably the old name of Kill-Sessin, or Kil-

they should obtain all Leth-Chuinn, they would not possess his church and *cahir*, viz. :—Fidnacha of the plain of Rian, Cobhthagh's nurse. "It is time for me, O Manchan," said he, "to go to Heaven; for I have completed five hundred years this night. Moreover, there is only one tooth in my head, and it is now falling. I declare truly to thee, O Manchan, and to my God of Heaven and Earth, that a falsehood has never come past my tooth[1] upwards."

He was like unto Patrick in that respect.

"I tell thee, O holy Manchan," said he, "that there is no saint whom I have met of the saints of Ireland, from whom fees and tributes are not due to my place, viz :—Fidnacha of Magh-Rein.

"I am entitled, firstly, from Patrick of Macha,[2] Arch-Apostle of the west of Europe, to his steed and his dress, [to be given] to my Comarbs every year.

"I am entitled, also, from Brigid, to a *screpall*[3] of gold, to be sent from her church to my clerics.

"I am entitled, further, from Samthann,[4] the holy Virgin, to every tenth *screpall*[3] of what she levies.

"I am entitled from Ciaran,[5] and from Finnen of Magh-Bile,[6] to the portion of three hundred [men] out of every church.

I am entitled from Ruadhan of Lothra,[7] and from Brenainn,[8] and from Lugna, to the subsistence of three hundred every quarter." The subsistence of three hundred from each of these three is due to Caillin, [viz :—] from Bec-Aedh of Ard Carna,[9] and from Sesin,[10] and from Etain of Tuaim.[11]

A bar of silver from Cainnech Mac Ui Dalon.[12] The subsistence of three hundred every spring from Berchan of Clonsost,[13] and from Caemhghen[14] of Glenn-da-locha. A screpall of gold for every mansion from Lachtain of Lugh-

teashin, in the west of the parish of Ard-carne, co. Roscommon, where the Bishops of Elphin anciently had a palace.

[11] *Etain of Tuaim;* i.e. St. Etaoin (or Modoena), of Tuaim-Naoi (now Tumna), a par. in the bar. of Boyle, co Roscommon. See the Martyrology of Donegal, at the 5th of July.

[12] *Cainnech Mac Ui Dalon.* mac ua ᴅat (MS.). St. Cainnech, or Canice, of Kilkenny; and of Aghabo, Queen's co. He had also some churches in the North of Ireland, the principal of which was Drumachose, in the barony of Keenaght, co. Londonderry, of which district he was a native.

[13] *Clonsost.* Clonsast, in the King's co.

[14] *Caemhghen;* i.e. St. Kevin of Glendaloch.

Moling a Luachair. In cetna (.i. screpall) oir gacha bliadna o Molaisi, ocus o Tigernach, ocus o Sinell (l Sincell), o Cairnech, ocus o Comgall Bennchair.

Cuairt a mainchesa gach tresar bliadain co brath o Cholam cille, ocus o [A]domnan on tir thuaid. Gach dechmad pingin go brath o Chruimthir Fraech; ocus a idlacad co Fidnacha.

Gach ab gebus i cill Iarlaidi mic Loga; a eirred do idlacad co Fidnacha.

Atlugad buidi dom Coimdid na ndula, ar naem Chaillin mac Niatach, ar ni fil in Erinn archena naem na dligim cuid tri cet de.

Ro thairngir iarum Caillin fein, co ticfad ab i Fidnacha, fri deired domuin, ro togebad in cuairtsin. Ro thairngir Caillin mor do nethib oili tria baile ocus fairtine do Manchan.

Ro thircan co ticfatis clerig fri deired domuin do fil creidme, ocus cuirfit fo dimicin ocus dimiad minna ocus bachla, ocus cluicc na naem.

Is tre dimiad ocus tre nemchadus dona naemuib millfider Eri itir mnaib ocus feraib ocus maccaib.

In tan do berait Gaidil a nonoir ocus a termannfein dona naemuib ocus da minnaib ocus da neigrib* ocus da comarbuib, conndichuirfitis Goill a hErinn, 7 congebtais Gaedel a feranna fein a frithisi.

* fol. 36, b 1.

Iscd atberim fris a Manchan, condigela mo coimdid nime ocus talman ar na Galloib sin saragad ocus airgain mo chathrach sa .i. Fidnacha.

[1] *Lughmhagh.* Louth. This is apparently a mistake for Achadh-úr, or Freshford, co. Kilkenny, of which place St. Lachtain was patron.

[2] *Bishop Ibhar*, of Beg-ere, or Begerin Island, in Wexford harbour. He was a rival of St. Patrick. A curious account of the rivalry between the saints, taken from the scholiast on Aengus's *Festology* (at 23rd April), is given in Todd's *Life of St. Patrick*, p. 216.

[3] *Moling of Luachair*; or Moling Luachra, patron and founder of Tech-Moling, or St. Mullins, in the south of the co. Carlow.

[4] *Molaise.* St. Molaise of Devenish Island, in Lough Erne.

[5] *Tighernach.* Patron and founder of Cluain-Eois, or Clones, co. Monaghan.

[6] *Sinchell.* St. Sinchell of Cill-achaidh, or Killeigh, King's co.; or St. Sinell, of Cluain-inis, in Lough Erne.

magh,[1] and from Bishop Ibhar,[2] and from Moling of Luachair[3]—the same (i.e. a *screpall* of gold) every year from Molaise,[4] and from Tighernach,[5] and from Sinell (or Sinchell),[6] from Cairnech,[7] and from Comgall of Bennchair.[8]

The dues of his emoluments every third year for ever from Colum Cille, and from Adamnan, from the northern land. Every ~~third~~ tenth penny for ever from Cruimther-Fraech[9]—and to be sent to Fidnacha.

The dress of every abbot who obtains the church of Iarlaithe[10] son of Lugh, to be sent to Fidnacha.

"Thanks be to my Lord of all things," said St. Caillin, son of Niata, "for there is not in all Ireland a saint from whom I am not entitled to the portion of 300."

Caillin himself afterwards foretold that an abbot would come in Fidnacha, towards the end of the world, who would levy that tribute. Caillin foretold a great many other things, through ecstasy and prophecy, to Manchan.

He foretold that clerics would come towards the end of the world, to disseminate religion,[11] and that they would subject the relics, croziers, and bells of the saints, to contempt and disrespect.

"It is through disrespect and irreverence for the saints that Ireland will be ruined, both women and men, and boys.

"When the Gaedhil give their proper honour and respect to the saints, and to their relics, and their heirs, and Comharbs, the Foreigners will be expelled from Ireland, and the Gaedhil shall possess their own lands again.

"What I say to thee, O Manchan, is that my Lord of Heaven and Earth will avenge on those Foreigners the violation and ravaging of my *cahir*, viz:—Fidnacha."

[7] *Cairnech.* Bishop of Tulen, or Dulane, near Kells, co. Meath. Vid. *supra*, p. 216, note [6].

[8] *Bennchair.* Bangor, co. Down; of which St. Comgall was the founder.

[9] *Cruimther Fraech.* See note [1], p. 192, *supra.*

[10] *Iarlaithe.* St. Iarlaith (or, as the name is now ignorantly written, St. Jarlath) of Tuam, who was related to St. Caillin. In Colgan's version of the life of St. Iarlaith, it is stated that he and St. Caillin were alumni of St. Benignus, the disciple of St. Patrick. *Acta Sanctorum*, p. 308.

[11] *disseminate religion.* If the Reformation is here referred to, St. Caillin, or the author of this prophecy, is certainly entitled to the character of a *vates*, as the "Old book of Fidhnacha" was written before the year 1400, and the MS. from which the R. I. Acad. copy has been taken was transcribed in 1516.

I Tig Mochaemog desgelus m'anamsa frim chorp, a Manchan, ar Caillin; ocus as ann adlecthar mo chorp fo bun in bili i reilig Moċaemog, ocus sluaig aingel imfochair. Tri ced d'ainglib ro bid imamsa ag ergi gacha maitne ocus ig luigi im imdaid; et don ni ebartur mo tratha riam co cluinid muinter nime ag celebrad.

Aiffrin ro iar Caillin for Manchan a ongad, ar robatar aingil nime ag fuirech fria a anmuin.

Is duitsin lemsa, for Manchan, a Chaillin, a ardlegoit, nach it chaṫruig ocus it chaoim chill fein ata do thaisi ocus t'esergi .i. Fidnacha M. R.

In tan, iarom, bus lom mo ċnamasai ocus mo thaisi, bar Caillin, tarrsa fein, a Manchan, ocus mo ṡamadsa om ḟidnaċ[a], ocus berid mo thaisi dom chill fein.

Ticfamait chena, bar Manchan, ocus ticfat da apstal deg na hErend linn, ocus beram do thaisi si dot chill.*

* fol. 36, b. 2.

Mo bennachtsa orrtsa, a Manchan, bar Caillin, ocus gidbe millfes ar cella araon, ni geba tuaċ na fine.

Do berra duitsi luaċ do bennachtain, ar Manċan, gidbe ni iarrfus nech dot muintir oram, fogeba uaim.

Mo ardaineri duitsi, a Manchan, co cend secht mbliadna, ar Caillin; et don beir let mo sgelasa ocus mo senchus com Fidnacha fein. Bud he Cruimther Fraech, mo chara ocus mo dalta, bus abad i Fidnacha ar tes re coicat mbliadan, co ticc Rechtus mac Naradaig. Is he adlacus cruimther [Fraech] iartain fo leic na naingel i Fidnacha.

Tria metar ocus baile ro raidh Caillin na nethisi anuas sin

[1] *Mochaemhog's relig;* or Relig-Mochaemhog. See note [5], p. 12, *supra*.

[2] *offices.* trata. The word *trath* (pl. *tratha*) properly means a time, or season, but it is also used to signify a canonical hour, and the offices or exercises appropriate thereto.

[3] *abbacy;* i.e. the successorship of St. Caillin, in the abbacy of Fidhnacha.

[4] *history;* i.e. an account of Caillin's proceedings was to be furnished to his congregation.

[5] *Cruimther-Fraech.* See note [1], p. 192, *supra*.

"In the house of Mochaemhog my soul will separate from my body, O Manchan," said Caillin, "and my body will be buried at the foot of the tree in Mochaemhog's *relig*,[1] and a host of angels near me. Three hundred angels were wont to be about me when rising every morning, and when lying in my bed; and I never said my offices[2] until I heard the people of Heaven celebrating."

Caillin afterwards requested of Manchan to anoint him, as the angels of Heaven were waiting for his soul.

"I grieve, O Caillin, O Arch Legate," said Manchan, "that it is not in thine own *cahir* and fair church thy relics and thy resurrection should be, i.e., in Fidnacha of Magh-Rein."

"When my bones and relics shall be bare," said Caillin, "do thou thyself come, O Manchan, and my congregation from my Fidnacha; and bear ye my relics to my own church."

"We shall come, truly," said Manchan, "and the twelve Apostles of Ireland shall come with us; and we will convey thy relics to thy church."

"My blessing on thee, O Manchan," said Caillin; "and whoever destroys both our churches shall not obtain territory or tribe."

"I will give thee the reward of thy blessing," said Manchan. "Whatsoever thing any one of thy people asks of me, he shall receive it from me."

"Have thou my abbacy,[3] O Manchan, to the end of seven years," said Caillin; "and also bear with thee my history[4] and my *senchus* to my own Fidnacha. Cruimther-Fraech,[5] my friend and foster-son, will be abbot in Fidnacha after thee during fifty years, until comes Rechtus,[6] son of Naradach. 'Tis he that will afterwards inter Cruimther [Fraech] under the 'flag of the angels' at Fidnacha."

Through metre and ecstacy[7] Caillin spoke the foregoing things to Manchan,

[6] *Rechtus.* ꞃecht, in A. There is no saint or ecclesiastic of this name in the Irish Calendar. The form of the name in the MS. may be an abbrev. for Rechtabra, an abbot of Liath-Mochaemhog, (and therefore a successor of St. Mochaemhog), whose death is recorded by the Four Mast., under A.D. 838. But see note [4], p. 306.

[7] *metre and ecstacy.* "Per metum [leg. metrum?) et furorem spiritualem hæc loquebatur." Marg. note, in A.

Manchan, ge ro scribamairne tria prois.[1] Ised innso in metardachtsin Caillin fein, iarna ḟoillsigud on aingel:—

A Manchan romaiccill fein,
Uair is me Caillin na cell;
Coinnisiur co dana,
Inni dambiat mor sgela.[2]
Atcondarcus fis anocht,
Do craid mo croide imam corp;
Saxuin dar sal do lethad,
Dar Erind na find fethal.
Atcondarcus fis oile,
Do craid mo conn 's m[o] croide;
Eri do beith[a] co sir,
Mo Saxain i trom daire.
Ga fad beit, a Chaillin choir,
Is hEri aca ma bron;
Innis duin a idain oig,
A uasail is a ḟireoin.
Indesat, a Manchain moir,
Mambitt aingil san chamoir;[3]
Cuicc cett, tri bliadna co becht,
In Erind ga tairmtecht.
Ge tegait in ndaim anair
'S ge gabuid leth Cuinn codail,
A deir rim int aingel tra,
Ni gabait mo bailsea.
Is misi Caillin cialda,
Ab roma do reir riagla;

[a] fol. 37, a. 1.

[1] *in prose.* tria pis; the sign of abbreviation being omitted from the p.

[2] *great accounts.* mor sgela. The rhyme is faulty in this stanza. Some critic (most likely, Thady O'Rody) observes in the margin, ni maith focerdad rind isin rannsin, a mic noemtha Niatach, ma iar nufiadnaise; "not well has a point been put in that stanza, O holy son of Niata, according to the New Testament (i.e. modern knowledge)."

[3] *present.* san chamoir; "in the

though we have written them in prose.[1] This is the metrical composition of Caillin himself, after the angel had enlightened him:—

"O, Manchan, converse with myself,
For I am Caillin of the cells;
That I may boldly relate things
Whereof shall be great accounts.[2]
"I saw a vision this night,
Which grieved my heart in my body—
The Saxons spreading across the sea,
O'er Ireland of the relics fair.
"I saw another vision,
Which grieved my head and heart
That Ireland would be for aye,
Under Saxons in great bondage."
"How long, O just Caillin,
Will they have Ireland under sorrow?
Tell us, thou perfect, pure,
Thou noble man, and true."
"I will tell, O great Manchan,
Round whom angels always present[3] are—
Five hundred and three years exactly,
They'll in Ireland be, abusing it.
"Though the host come from the East,
And though they possess all Leth-Chuinn;
The angel tells me, ne'ertheless,
That they my place will not obtain.
"I am the prudent Caillin,
Abbot of Rome[4] according to rules.[5]

camor"; but *camor* is not Irish, and is probably a loan from Lat. *camera*. Some Irish dictionaries have camhaoir, "twilight," or "dawn"; but the word is neither old nor genuine.

[4] *Abbot of Rome*. This is certainly a bounce, unless Caillin meant that he was an Abbot who had been ordained at Rome.

[5] *according to rules*. do reir riagla. The *alias* reading "ł go ro riagla," "or, very regularly," is added in the margin.

Cuicc xx.it bliadan blad bind,
Dam im legoitt air hErind.
Isfed is slan dam gan locht,
Cuicc ced bliadan cus anocht.
En fiacuil im chind gan cli,
Conas tuitenn ri baili.
Is misi Caillin gan bais;
Fada m'ais re hilar mad;
Cuicc ced bliadan cus anocht,
Oda anacc i curp criaḋ.
Noconuil naem don chuire,
Neoch do arraid me uili,
Do nach dligimm cuairt is cain,
D'Fidnacha caid Muigi Rein.
Dligim do Patraic Macha,
Do mac Calpruinn gach ratha,
A ech sa errud gan tar
Dom abaid gacha bliadna.[1]
Dligim do Brigit Banba,
D'ingin Dubthaigh co tarba,
Screball oir ar a cill cain,
'Sa innlacad dom chathruig.
Dligim do famthuinn co naib,
Don chaillig naim iduin oig,
Gach dechmad screball co fir,
Toibges in chaem do leth Cuind.
Dligim do Chiaran na cros,
Do bhi i Saighir in aruis,
Is d'Finnen Muigi bile,
Cuitt tri cett gach aen chille.

[1] *Macha;* i.e. Ard-Macha, or Armagh. The successors of St. Patrick were certainly never tributaries to the abbots of Fenagh. The statement is a pure invention of the O'Rody family.

[2] *Banba.* A bardic name for Ireland. St. Brigid was gathered to her fathers before St. Caillin was born; and her

Five score famous, pleasant years,
Have I been Legate over Ireland.
"I have faultlessly completed
Five hundred years up to this night;
In my head is one feeble tooth,
Which by good luck does not fall.
"I am Caillin, without folly;
Long is my age with honour great,
Five hundred years till to-night [have passed],
Since I came into an earthly body.
"There is not a saint of the band,
Of all those that I have met,
Who does not owe me dues and tribute,
For fair Fidhnacha of Magh-Rein.
"I exact from Patrick of Macha[1]—
From the son of Calphurn of all grace—
His steed and his garment without blemish,
For my abbot every year.
"I exact from Brigit of Banba[2]—
From the useful daughter of Dubthach—
A *screpall* of gold from her fair church;
To be delivered to my *cahir*.[3]
"I am entitled from courteous Samhthann[4]—
From the pure, perfect holy nun—
To every tenth *screpall*, truly,
That the fair one collects from Leth-Chuinn.
"I am entitled from Ciaran[5] of the crosses—
Who was abiding in Saighir[6]—
And from Finnen of Magh-Bile,[7]
To the share of three hundred from each church.

successors are therefore alluded to.

[3] *cahir.* The MS. A. adds "ɫ dom cleirchaib," "or to my clerics."

[4] *Samhthann.* See note [4], p. 286.

[5] *Ciaran;* i.e. St. Ciaran of Saighir, or Seir-Kieran, King's co.

[6] *Saighir.* See last note.

[7] *Magh-Bile* Now Moville, co. Down.

Dligim do Ruadan Lothra,
 Ar do ṡen Brenainn soċla,
 Is do Lugna na cet de,
 Cuid tri ced gaċa raithe.
Dligim do beo Aed chaem chaid,
 Is do ṫesin con oen dail,
 Is d' Etain in crabaiḋ grinn,
 Cuitt tri ċet ar gaċ aen ċill.
Dligim do mac ui Dalaich,
 O Chainneċ co caem gradaib,
 Tinni dargat congille
 O Chainneċ on ċaem dili.
Dligim do Berchan na cet,
 A Cluain ferta, nocha breg;
 'S do Chaemgin Glinde da loch,
 Cuid tri cet isin errach.
Dligim do Lachtain gan chair,
 Is do Moling a Luachair,
 Is d'espcop Ibair gech tan,
 Screpall óir gaċ aen chaṫraċ.
Dligim do Molaisi na cell,
[a] fol. 37, b. 1. Do Tigernaċ 'sdo Sinchell,[a]
 Do Chairnech 'sdo Chomgall tra,
 Screball oir gaċa bliadna.
Dligim do Cholam atuaid,
 'S d'Adomnan in chrabad cruaid,

[1] *Lothra.* Now Lorrha, a townland and parish in the barony of Lower Ormond, co. Tipperary. See note [7], p. 286.

[2] *old Brendan.* St. Brendan of Clonfert, co. Galway. There were several saints of the name, but the most notable were St. Brendan of Birra (Birr, or Parsonstown, King's co., ob. 571), and St. Brendan of Ardfert, in Kerry, and Cluain-ferta, or Clonfert, co. Galway (ob. 576). The latter is probably here referred to.

[3] *Lugna.* There were several saints called Lugna; and it is hard to say which of them is here alluded to.

[4] *Beo-Aedh.* See note [12], p. 179.

[5] *Sesin.* See note [10], p. 286.

I am entitled from Ruadhan of Lothra,[1]
And from old Brendan[2] the renowned,
And from Lugna[3] of the hundreds,
To the portion of three hundred every quarter.
I am entitled from the mild, chaste Beo-Aedh,[4]
And from Scsin,[5] at the same time,
And from Etain[6] of the joyous devotion,
To the share of three hundred from each church.
I am entitled from the son of Ua Dalaigh—
From Cainnech[7] of the mild grades—
To a bar of silver bright,
From Cainnech, the chaste friend.
I am entitled from Berchan[8] of the hundreds,
Of Cluain Sosta—'tis no lie—
And from Caemhghen[9] of Glenn-da-locha,
To the share of three hundred in the Spring,
I am entitled from stainless Lachtain,[10]
And from Moling[11] of Luachair,
And always from Bishop Ibhar,[12]
To a *screpall* of gold for every mansion.
I am entitled from Molaise[13] of the churches,
From Tigernach,[14] and from Sinchell,[15]
From Cairnech[16] and from Comgall[17] also,
To a *screpall* of gold every year.
I am entitled from Colam[18] from the North,
And from Adamnan of the rigid devotion,

[6] *Etain.* See note [11], p. 287.

[7] *Cainnech.* See note [12], p. 287.

[8] *Berchan.* Of Cluain-Sosta, or Clonsast, in the King's county.

[9] *Caemhghen;* i.e. St. Kevin of Glendalough.

[10] *Lachtain.* See note [1], p. 288.

[11] *Moling.* See note [3], p. 288.

[12] *Bishop Ibhar.* See note [2], p. 288.

[13] *Molaise.* mblaıre, A. See note [4], p. 288.

[14] *Tigernach.* See note [5], p. 288.

[15] *Sinchell.* ᴅo ꞇꞅıneall, A., which has an alias reading ꞅıncheall, apparently the more correct. See note [6], p. 288.

[16] *Cairnech.* See note [7], p. 289.

[17] *Comgall.* See note [8], p. 289.

[18] *Colam.* Colum Cille.

Cuairt a mancher is a cell,
Gach tres bliadan co coitchend.
Dligimsi do Chruimther Fraech,
Gaċ dechmad pingind co brath,
'S a idlacad dom gaire,
D' Fidnacha co coemglaine.
Dligim do deg mac Loga,
D' Iarlaithe, dom chaemchora,
Gach ab gebas a chell ċain,
A chathersed dom abuid.
Dligim do gaċ naem rem linn,
Cuid tri cet as gaċ aen chill,
Do naemaib Erenn uili,
Atlochar dom rig ruiri.
Gebuid ab ar mo chill chain,
Toibges fri deired domain,
Fri remes in Aeda uill,
Geinfes a Cruachuin chaem ċuirr,
Tig nech re sil Braide Ruairc
Fri dered domain daṫ ruairc;
Bidho a ċomainm int Aod oll,
Gebus Connachta na clann.
Togait re reimes 's re lind
Sil Fingin do mo chaem chill;
Gaċ nech dib do dol ar nem,
Gan merrugad san riċeġ.
IS andsin da icfa in fer,
Do sil Angaili na fled,

[1] *Cruimther Fraech.* See note [1], p. 192, *supra.*

[2] *Iarlaithe.* See note [10], p. 289.

[3] *Cruachan.* See note [3], p. 75.

[4] *Braide Ruairc.* Gilla-Braide O'Rourke seems here referred to, who was slain in the year 1124, according to the Four Masters.

[5] *race of Finghin.* Sil-Finghin. This was the tribe name of the family of Mac Cagadhain (now Cogan, or Mac Cogan) of Clann-Fermaidhe, or Glanfarne, in the

To the dues of their profits and churches,
Every third year in general.
"From Cruimther Fraech[1] I am entitled
To every third penny for ever;
Which must be delivered, at my call,
To Fidhnacha of mild purity.
"From Lugh's good son, Iarlaithe,[2]
My gentle friend, I do exact,
That every abbot who obtains his fair church
[Shall send] his battle dress to my abbot.
"I am entitled from each saint of my time
To the share of three hundred from every church—
From the saints of Ireland all—
Thanks be to the Lord my King.
"An abbot my fair church will obtain,
Who'll levy towards the end of time;
During the reign of the noble Aedh,
Who'll be born in fair smooth Cruachan.[3]
"One will come with the seed of Braide Ruairc,[4]
Towards the end of the bright-hued world;
His name will be the mighty Aedh;
He'll obtain Connaught of the Clans.
"In his reign and time will come
The race of Finghin[5] to my fair church;
May each one of them go to Heaven,
Without diminution, unto the Kingdom.
"Then it is the man will come,
Of the race of festive Angaile,[6]

barony of Dromahaire, co. Leitrim. See O'Donovan's ed. of O'Dugan's Topog. Poem, App., 266; and Mac Firbis's *Pedigrees*, p. 279.

[6] *Angaile.* Son of Emhin, son of roman; the common ancestor of the O'Rourkes, O'Reillys, O'Quinns, and other families of Leitrim, Longford and Cavan. He was the ninth in descent from Lughaidh Conmac, from whom the name of *Conmaicne* was derived.

Ocus bid airdirc a ainm;
Tuitfid leis mairb is biaid sel;[1]
Ri cuicc fiċitt bliadan bind;
Noconegail do eslind.
Tuitfid ri Brefni combaig
Re fear in anma comlain;
Do cliathaig Droma da dub,
Da mbiat mairb ig a nongad.
Ticfa in donn ban fingalach,
Fer in anma condeni;
A athli na comergi
Gabaid ont sliaḃ co heli.
Cadé a dil
Fir in anma a Chaillin chaeim;
Indis dúinn a fir comblaid,
A uasail a ard egnaid.
Innesat, a Manchain gloin,
A craibdig uasail idain;
A eg in oiliṫri uill,
Iar mbuaid chaṫa is comluint.
Noċa ba gili in gaeth cain,
In uair tet da oilithri;
Itir cenn is cois is láim;
Bet aingil fris ig comrad.
Maith a dil,
Uair ni ebartais acht fir;
Nem d'faġbail d'fir in anma,
A Chaillin co naem tharba.

[1] *awhile.* It would appear from the context, that some lines are here omitted.

[2] *Druim-da-dubh.* Neither the date of this battle, nor the situation of the place, has been discovered.

[3] *Donnban.* Lit. "fair prince." See next note.

[4] *of the fierce name.* This seems to refer to Ualgarg O'Ruairc (ob. A.D. 1231, *Four Mast.*); whose "Christian" name, "Ualgarg," signifies "fierce shout."

And glorious his name shall be ;
Bodies shall fall by him, and he'll be awhile ;[1]
During five score joyous years,
He need not fear neglect.
"The valorous King of Breifni will fall
By the man of the perfect name,
In the battle of Druim-da-dubh,[2]
Where dying men shall anointed be.
"The fratricidal Donnban[3] will come,
The man of the fierce name[4]—
Immediately after the rising out,
He'll obtain from the Sliabh[5] to Eli.[6]
"What is the fate, [what the fate],
Of the man 'of the name',[7] O mild Caillin ;
Tell us, thou famous man,
Thou noble, thou eminent sage ?"
"I will tell, O pure Manchan,
Thou illustrious, stainless devotee :
He shall die in a great pilgrimage,
After gaining battles and conflicts.
"Not purer is the chaste wind
[Than he], when he goes on his pilgrimage,
Both in head and foot, and hand :
Angels shall be conversing with him."
"Good is his lot, [good is his lot],
For thou hast spoken only truth ;
The 'man of the name' will obtain Heaven,
O Caillin, with holy bounty."

[5] *the Sliabh.* Slieve-an-iarainn, in the W. of the co. Leitrim.

[6] *Eli.* Some place in the eastern part of Breifne.

[7] *'of the name.'* The person referred to would seem to be Ualgharg O'Rourke, as in the second next stanza it is foretold that he would die in pilgrimage. Ualgharg O'Rourke is stated in the Irish Annals to have died, in the year 1231, on his way to the River [Jordan]. See *Ann. Four Mast.* and *Ann. of Loch-Cé*, ad an.

A Manchain ni ebart breg;
Riam ni tainig ar mo det;
Mairg do sil Fingin na ndaiṁ,
Naċ riarfa mo briaṫrasa.
Ticfaittit na crosana.
Fri dered Domain dathaig;
Beitt Gaidil go huchanach
fol. 38, a 1. Gunna meandaib tig thairiss;
Conerset na cromanaig,
Ardnaim hErenn da ċaḃair.
Clerig tig san aimsirsin,
Ri furail riagla is credmi;
Is leo dimignigther tra,
Minda is cluic, im baċla.
Treimit sin millfider tra
Fira Erend, macca is mna,
Ar dimiccin chlog is cheall,
Congeib danair a bferand.
Gaċ uair da tibred Gaidil
A termann fein do naemaib,
Cuirfear 'dib na Goill gan fell,
Is gebtait fein a bferand.
Na Gullorin raidim rib
Sairechtait minda is nemed,
Diġelaid Crist mo chara,
Ma ṡargidsin Fidnacha.
Fagbuimsi ḟagbala di,
Fidnacha con ainglidi;
ecce gairi Do neoch ṡaraigfes mo ċell,
saoġail. Gairdi saoġail is ifernn.
Fidnacha con ainglide,
Baili mo chleib 's mo chroide;

[1] *Race of Finghin.* See note [5], p. 298.
[2] *buffoons.* crosana, pl. of crosan, glossed *scurra* (Stokes's *Irish Glosses*, p. 4.) Welsh *croesan*, a "buffoon." Cf. also

"O Manchan, I have told no lie;
Never has one come past my tooth.
Woe to the race of Finghin[1] of the bands.
If they my counsels won't obey.
"The buffoons[2] will come
Towards the end of the changeful world.
The Gael will be groanful
From the troubles which will come o'er it,[3]
Until shall arise the *cromanachs*,[4]
Ireland's great saints, to aid it.[3]
"The clerics who will in that time come
To impose rules and religion—
By them shall contemnèd be
Relics and bells, with croziers.
"Through this, also, will be destroyed
The people of Ireland, men and women;
Through contempt of bells and cells,
The Danes shall obtain their land.
"Whenever the Gael shall give
Their reverence due unto the saints,
The Galls will be expelled from them, without fail,
And they, themselves, will get their land.
"Those foreigners—I say to you—
Will profane relics and sanctuaries.
Christ, my friend, will it avenge,
If they profane Fidnacha.
"I leave privileges to it—
To Fidnacha the Angelic—
BEHOLD: SHORTNESS OF LIFE.
Whosoever profanes my church,
Shall have shortness of life, and Hell.
"Fidnacha the Angelic—
Home of my bosom and my heart—

scurra (gl. barth, i.e. bard, in Welsh; Zeuss, Gram. Celt., 1107).

[3] *it;* i.e., the world.

[4] *the cromanachs.* An epithet for holy men; derived from cromad, to stoop, to bow down.

Inmuin mad ainglide,
Fagbuim ar mes gan caire.
[1] Tig Mocaemocc gan locht,
Deleochus m'anam rem ċorp
Ann adlecthar me arsoin
Ma bun in bili clotaig.
Ann adlecthar mesi fein,
A De nime seim rimcheill
Ocus sluag aingeal amra,
Imamsa im chaen adba.
Tri ced d'ainglib imamsa,
Ag ergi gaca traṫa;
Gen co faicit mo cuiri,
Bid imam sidi im loiġi
Noċo denuinn mo tratha,
Ger b' imda naoim im lathrach,
No co cluininn tuas ar nim
Muinter nime ga ndenum.*
Dena anos m'ongad a naoim,
A Manchain cus in mor main;
Uair atait muinter nimi
Na sesum com urnaide.
Do gensa hongaḋ a naim,
A mic Hiatach co ndeg aeib;
Os lomnan umuinni in tech,
D'ainglib nime as a riċeg.
Saeṫ lim
A Chaillin na naingel find,
Gan do thairi si it chill chain,
Fidnacha ċain in chrabaid.
Tan bus loma mo ċnama,
A Manchain na mordala,

* fol. 38, a 2.

[1] *Mochoemhog.* See note [5], p. 12.

[2] *offices.* tratha; i.e. canonical offices or exercises.

Delightful is the Angelic place
I leave behind me stainless.
" In the house of faultless Mochoemog[1]
My soul will separate from my body.
There I shall be buried afterwards,
At the foot of the famous tree.
" There I myself will be interred,
O God of fair Heaven, with my consent,
And a host of illustrious Angels
'Round me in my chaste abode.
" Three hundred Angels round me were,
When I got up at each canonical hour;
Though my flock see them not,
They 'll be around me when I am lying.
" I used not to perform my offices,[2]
Tho' many saints in my presence[3] might be,
Until I heard, in Heaven above,
Heaven's people performing them.
" Do thou anoint me, now, O Saint;
O Manchan of the treasure great;
For the people of Heaven are
Standing up, awaiting me."
" I will thee anoint, O Saint—
O son of Niata, of good repute—
Since the house is round us full
Of Heaven's Angels, from the Kingdom.
" 'Tis sad to me,
O Caillin of the Angels bright,
That thy relics are not in thy pure church,
Fidnacha fair of the piety."
" When my bones are bare,
O Manchan of th' assemblies great,

[3] *presence.* The poet seems to use laċṁaċ, for laṫaiṗ (presence), to suit the rhyme of the preceding line.

Tegat mo ṡam[ad] glan grind,
Combérat leo dom chaem chill.
Tairsiu fein a Manchain moir
Na nagaid dam dom onoir;
Co rabair ar mo ċind ċain,
Ag buain mo ṫaisi a talmain.
Ticfatsa is lucht in leginn,
'S da apstal déc na hErind;
Is bermait linn dot ċill ċain,
Do ṫaisi, a Chaillin ċaemglain.
Mo bennacht ar do belsa,
A Manchain chaid gan timi;
In neċ millfius ar cella
Nir gaba tuaṫ na fine.
Luaċ uaim duit do bennachtan,
A Chaillin na ced cuiri;
A itci ag gaċ aen duine
Agam dot ṁuintir huili.
Gebsi ardaine im inad
Re secht mbliadna co hidan;
Is ber co Fidnacha caid,
Let mo ṡenchus a Manchain,
Se Cruimther Fraech, mo dalta,
Gebuss ar hes Fidnacha,
Re coicat bliadain co trean,
Co tic Reċtus, a Manchan. A Manchain."

* fol. 38, b 1.

Rechtus mac Naradaig deirg,
Adlecus Cruimther gan meirg,

[1] *twelve Apostles.* For the names of the twelve Apostles of Ireland (or thirteen, as some authorities count them), see Todd's *St. Patrick*, p. 99, n. [1], and O'Donovan's ed. of *Magh-Rath*, p. 27.

[2] *Cruimther-Fraech.* See note [1], p. 192.

[3] *Rechtus.* See next note.

[4] *Rechtus, son of Naradach.* There is no mention of this Rechtus in any other authority. He was possibly the son of

Let my bright pure congregation come,
And bear them unto my fair church.
"Come thou thyself, O great Manchan,
To meet them, in honour of me;
That thou may'st be o'er my mild head,
Taking my relics from out the earth."
"I will come, and the reading band,
And the twelve Apostles[1] of Ireland;
And we will bear to thy fair church,
Thy relics, O pure, bright Caillin."
"My blessing on thy mouth,
O chaste Manchan without fear;
Whoso'er destroys our churches,
Nor territory nor tribe shall he obtain."
"The reward of thy blessing I give thee,
O Caillin of the hundred bands—
His request to every man
Of thy whole people, I shall grant."
"Take thou the abbotship in my place,
Purely, during seven years;
And to Fidnacha the holy bear
My history with thee, O Manchan.
"'Tis Cruimther-Fraech,[2] my foster-son,
That shall possess Fidhnacha after thee,
Firmly, during fifty years,
Until comes Rechtus,[3] O Manchan. O Manchan.
"Rechtus, son of red Naradach,[4]
Will bury Cruimther[5] without stain,

Naradach, who was the father of Rodaghan, *a quo* the O'Rodys, and fifteenth in descent from Lughaidh Conmhac, ancestor of the Conmaicne. But see note [6], p. 291. On the lower margin of fol. 38, b, in A, the scribe adds a note complaining that his ink had been spilled by boys, and stating that he was compelled to make more.

[5] *Cruimther*. Cruimther—Fraech. See note [1], p. 192.

Ic leic naim na naingel nan;
Foillsig do ċaċ a Manchain.

Ro conairimthir dana retlanna nime, ocus gainem in mara, et in fér ocus na huili luibi arait tria thalmain, et in druchta anus for in bfeor ocus for na luibib, ni ċoemrainn ferta Chaillin naib do airneis, manam teguscead aingel o Dia.

Fer firian tra in ferra, co nglaine aicnid amail uasalaithreċai. Fír ailithir o croid et o anmain amail Abraham. Cennais dilgadach o croidi amail Moysi. Psalmcetlaid molbthaige, amail Dauid. Estad hecna ocus eoluis amail hSolam. Lestur toga fri fogra firindi amail Pól apstal. Fer lan do rath ocus deolaidecht in spirata noib amail Eoin maccan. Lugbort cain co clannuib sualaċ. Gesca fine co toirṫigi. Tene taidlech congrus gairthe ocus teassoigechta na mac mbethad, im andud ocus im elscod deserce. Leo trian nert ocus cumachta. Colom ar chendsa ocus diniti. Naṫir ar trebaire ocus tuaichli fri ṁaith. Cendais ailgen umal inisiul fri macca bethad.* Fer dorchaide ecennais fri macca bais.

* fol. 38, b 2.

Moġ saeṫair ocus fognama do Crist. Rí ar ordan ocus cumachta, fri cuimrech et tuaslugad, fri doerad ocus soerad, fri marbad ocus bethugad.

IAris na mormirballaib si thra, iar marbad ocus bethugad daine, iar forcetal ocus baisded sochaide, IAR fothugad cell ocus congbail; iar traothad eladan ndiabul do ocus draidechta; Ro comaicsig laiṫi etsecta Caillin, ocus a thoċta do chom nime; et ro batar muintir nimi ina ferram ag a furnaide a dola doċom nime; et ro foillsiged do laiṫe a theachta do chom nime. Ro thoċaid, imorro, Caillin a bethaid, .i. 500 bliadan, in aeintib, in ernigthib, in almsanaib, i teoir i fiadnuisi in chomded. Asroet coragad na hecalsi o Manchan noeb, et ro

[1] *Manchan.* The first line of the poem is repeated, in token of its conclusion.

[2] *treasury.* estad. In the Leabhar Breacc (p. 29 a) the form is istud.

[3] *vessel.* lestur; which is glossed by soiṫioċ, a vessel, or pitcher, in the margin.

[4] *youth.* mc̄an, for maccan; the dimin. of mac, a son.

[5] *garden.* lugbort, by metathesis for lubgort, an herb-garden; from lub. an

At the holy Flag of the noble Angels—
Explain to all, O Manchan.[1]

Until then, the stars of Heaven, and the sands of the sea, and the grass and the other herbs that grow through the land—and the dew that remains on the grass and on the herbs—are reckoned, I could not relate the miracles of the Holy Caillin, unless an angel from God should instruct me.

A man of truth, however, was this man, with purity of nature, like the Patriarchs. A true pilgrim from heart and soul, like Abraham. Gentle and forgiving of heart, like Moses. A laudatory psalmist, like David. A treasury[2] of wisdom and knowledge, like Solomon. A chosen vessel[3] for the pronouncement of truth, like the Apostle Paul. A man full of virtue, and of the grace of the Holy Ghost, like the youth[4] John. A fair garden[5] to the sons of virtue. A vine branch with fruitfulness. A bright fire with the power of warming and heating the sons of life, towards promoting[6] and fostering[7] charity. A lion in strength and power. A dove in gentleness and humility. A serpent in wisdom and cunning for good. Gentle, mild, humble, lowly, towards the sons of life. A man dark and ungentle against the sons of death. A servant and labourer for Christ. A king in dignity and power, for binding and loosing, for enslaving and freeing, killing and bringing to life.

After those great miracles, moreover; after killing and reviving people; after instructing and baptising multitudes; after founding churches and establishments; after subduing the arts of demons and druidism, the day of Caillin's death and departure to Heaven drew near; and the people of Heaven were standing awaiting his going to Heaven. And the day of his going to Heaven was manifested to him. Moreover, Caillin spent his life, i.e. 500 years, in fasting, in prayers, in almsgiving, in meditation before the Lord. He received the rites[8] of the church from Saint Manchan, and bequeathed to

herb, and ᵹoꞃꞇ, a garden (Lat. hortum).

[6] *promoting.* anꝺuꝺ. This word is not found in dictionaries; but its meaning can scarcely be doubtful. Cf. ꞅꞃu anꝺuꝺ n-ane, translated "to institute hilarity" by O'Curry; Stokes's *Goidelica* [2], 176.

[7] *fostering.* elꞅcoꝺ. This word is also unknown to the glossarists; and the explanation of it above given is only conjectural.

[8] *rites.* coꞃaᵹuꝺ; lit. "arrangement," A.

timnai a foirb ocus cendas a chatrach ocus a mac necailsi do co cend uii. mbliadan, et do Cruimthir Fraech iarsin coicat bliadan.

Ro faid a spirat docom nimhe. Ocus ro hadnacht a chorp a Lia Mocoemhog, co nonoir móir ocus airmittin; conid iar lomad a chnam do ratad a thaisi co Fid[nacha], ar nir lor lais nachní comad in úr anetargnoid no hadnaicthi iar na egaib.

fol. 39, a 1. Gid mór a onóir tria na mor miorbuiluibh isin moth aboss,[a] bid mor mo a onoir in dail bratha in tan taitnigfes amail grein ind nim; in oentaid apstal ocus descipal Isai, in oentaid .ix. ngrad nimi nataiprmdecatar; in ointaid doinechta ocus diadachta mic De; in ointaid na noim trinoiti uasli .i. athar ocus mic [ocus] spiruta noib.

Alimitm, iarum, mor trocaire nDe uili chumachtaig tria impide naem Chaillin, diata lith et foraithmet in ecailsib na cristaide isin laithisi. Ro airillem, rosam, ro aitrebam ind oentaidsin in secula seculorum. Amen.

Oroit raith et toicthi ainso do Thadg O Rodaighe .i. comarbu Caillin Fidnachu; fear lan d'ecnu, et d'aithin, et d'eolus et do indicecht; et legthoir scotice; et fer doin segdu et oclachus, et fer congus buadu et gesa in baili abuil .i. tech naoided coitchend, et gan diultud re dreic nduine, acht se ina oil nemchumscuigthi andaonnacht tre bithu.

Is he in Tadg sin foderu ar muirges o maelconaire in leburs do cor indso in a sgeloigecht tre inutt a cluduin et tre romet a duthruchtu do Caillin, daig in raibi achtma dan isint senlubar.

[1] *clerics*. mac n-ecailsi; "sons of the church," A.

[2] *Lia-Mochoemhog*. Otherwise, *Relig-Mochaemhog*. See note [5], p. 12, *supra*.

[3] *strange*. anetargnoid. The way in which this word is written in the MS. puzzled Thady O'Rody, who has made an attempt to explain it, too absurd to be reproduced.

[4] *O'Rodaighe*. Over this is added ocus da chommaim .i. Onora ingen .h. Maoilmuaid; "and to his wife, Honora, daughter of O'Molloy."

[5] *seghda*. Explained in a gloss, *dan oglachuis*, or "*oglachus* poetry." *Oglachus* is a species of poetical composition which requires seven syllables in every line. See O'Donovan's *Irish Grammar*, p. 424.

[6] *oglashus*. See last note.

[7] *the place*; "i.e. Fidnacha of Magh-

him his possessions, and the government of his *cahir* and clerics,[1] during seven years; and to Cruimther-Fraech after him for fifty years.

He resigned his spirit to Heaven; and his body was interred with great honour and veneration in Lia-Mochoemhog.[2] And after his bones had become bare, his relics were brought to Fidhnacha, for he liked not at all that he should be buried in strange[3] clay after his death.

Though great his honour through his many miracles in the present life, much greater shall be his honour in the assembly of Judgment, when he will shine like the Sun in Heaven, in the union of the Apostles and Disciples of Jesus; in the union of the Nine Orders of Heaven which cannot be surpassed; in the union of the Humanity and Divinity of the Son of God; in the union of the noble Holy Trinity, the Father, Son, and Holy Ghost.

We beseech, therefore, the great mercy of Almighty God, through the intercession of Saint Caillin, whose festival and commemoration is on this day observed in the churches of Christendom. May we deserve; may we reach; may we possess that union, *in sæcula sæculorum. Amen.*

A prayer here for happiness and prosperity to Tadhg O'Rodaighe,[4] i.e., the Comharb of Caillin of Fidnacha; a man full of wisdom, and knowledge, and learning, and of jurisprudence; a reader of the Scotic; and a man who composes *seghda*[5] and *oglachus*[6]; and a man who observes the privileges and prohibitions of the place[7] in which he is, to wit, that he should keep a house of general hospitality,[8] and not deny the face of a man,[9] but be like an immoveable rock[10] in humanity for ever.

It was this Tadhg that caused Maurice O'Mulconry[11] to put this book here in a narrative form, through the extent of his learning,[12] and through the excess of his devotion to Caillin[13]; for there was only poetry in the old book.

Rein." Gloss.

[8] *hospitality.* .i. illa ocus innoiḋċi .i. ar tuathaib ocus bochtaib ocus aes gaċ dana; "i.e. day and night, for strangers and paupers, and people of every profession." Gloss.

[9] *man.* .i. do threinn na do thruaiġ; "i.e. of the great or poor." Gloss.

[10] *rock.* .i. ar aen ait bis tre bitha amail chloich nach cumscaiġter, no amail ralaig no ibar; "in one place he should be for ever, like a rock that cannot be moved, or like an oak or a yew tree." Gloss.

[11] *Maurice O'Mulconry.* The orig. of this name is added by way of gloss.

[12] *learning.* i.e. "Gaidhelic and Latin." Gloss.

[13] *Caillin.* .i. nír mhaḋ lais gan a beṫ ina sgeluiḃ; "i.e. he liked not that it should not be in narratives." Gloss.

Ro tharngair Caillin coticfad app i Fidhnacchu ro thoibeċod a ċis ar Erind fri dereth domain, et dar linne is don ti do rigni in duthracht so do bud coir sin .i. Tadg comarbu Fidnacha. Muirgius mac Paidin .h. Maelconaire ro scrib ind lebarsa do; ocus conorica Caillin sin friu aracon isin uetha hsuthain etir aingglib inne.[a]

[a] fol. 39, a 2.

Conall cuingid cloinni Neill,
Tainig a Temraig taibreid,
D'athe a [ḟ]alad is tir thuaid,
Ar ċuiccid Ulad armcruaid.
Ro bris Conall coicait cath
Ar tocht a Temraig amaċ.
Nir bris[ed] air, ba raṫ noll,
Caṫ na cliaṫach, na cómlond.
Ni dernad olc fri duine,
Do ċlannaib Neill meit bloide,
Naċ sir do ċosaitfid soin,
Re Conall nglonnmer ngulbuin.
Ni dernaḋ olc re charaid,
Conall rigda a ro tabairt,
Ise a bunad, borb a blaḋ,
Nach cend curad roricfad.
Nir dam Conall coir na cert
Do bidbaid, ba rigda in recht,
Acht sloig do ḋiṫ a doman
'Sa criċ uili d'folmugad
Nir dam cert man tir atuaid
No gur cosuin hi co cruaiḋ;
Ar na cosnum nir ceim fann,
Ronnais co feig a ferann.

[1] *Ua Maelconaire*. O'Mulconry. For some account of the scribe, Maurice O'Mulconry, see Introduction.

[2] *Conall*. Conall Gulban, son of Niall Nine-hostager. In O'Donnell's Irish Life of St. Columba (MS., Rawlinson, 514,

Caillin prophesied that an Abbot would come in Fidnacha, who would collect his tribute over Ireland towards the end of the world; and it seems to us that it is to the person who exercised this zeal towards him the duty should properly belong, to wit, Tadhg, Comharb of Fidnacha. Maurice, son of Paidin Ua Maelconaire,[1] that wrote this book for him; and may Caillin repay that to them both, in the life perpetual, amongst the Angels of Heaven.

Conall,[2] chief of the sons of Niall,
    Came from smooth-sided Tara,
    To avenge his wrongs in the northern land,
    On the province of Uladh of hard weapons.
Conall gained[3] fifty battles,
    After coming forth from Tara;
    'Gainst him was not won—'twas great luck—
    Battle, conflict, or combat.
No evil was done to a man
    Of the Clann-Neill, of great renown,
    That was not reported to him—
    To valorous Conall Gulban.
No evil was done to the friends of
    Conall, regal his great bounty,
    (Their source he is, and fierce his fame),
    That a knight's head should not repay.
Conall accorded nor justice nor right
    To an enemy—regal the rule—
    But to destroy hosts for the affront,
    And devastate his country all.
He allowed no justice to the northern land,
    Till he vigorously contested it.
    After contesting it—no weak step—
    He quickly divided its domains.

Bodleian Library, Oxford), this poem is quoted as the composition of Flann Mainistrech, (ob. 1056), although O'Reilly states that it is "by some writers attributed to Flann Mac Lonain," slain in 918. (*Trans. Iberno-Celtic Soc.*, 1820, p. lxxvii).

[3] *gained.* ro bris; lit. "broke."

Leṫ do fein ruc ar ga ċert,
Daig is leiss tangus in fecht;
Leṫ da braiṫrib gairdi gal,
Do Charpre, d'Enna, d'Eogan.
Forba Eogain ardomtha,
O Srubh Broin go glais nEnncha.
Ferann Enna siar airsin,
Co Bernas mor, co Sruthail.
Cairpri sius aniar, miad ngal;
Enna eturra is Eogan;
Fergus is Doguine balc,
Ris atuaid, a da deg mac.
Cuid is Conall fein don roind,
Teora fuind criċi Conaill;
O Fertuis co Dobar ndil;
Odta Dobar co hEidnig.*
Ota Eidnig ni sliċt cam,
Co roiċ Fodes co Cromchall;
O Bernas gan tairi threb,
Co Ros itir da inber.

* fol. 39, b 1.

[1] *Eoghan's land;* i.e. the district of Cinel-Eoghain, or Kinel-Owen, now Inishowen (the island of Eoghan), in the co. Donegal.

[2] *Srubh-Brain.* Now Struve, Shruve, or Sreeve Point, in the parish of Lower Moville, barony of Inishowen, and county of Donegal.

[3] *Glas-nEnncha.* This was probably the old name of the Errity river, which falls into the River Swilly, near Manorcunningham.

[4] *Enna's land;* otherwise Cinel-Enna. The position of this territory is described by Colgan, in a note on the life of St. Baithenus, as follows:—"Est in Tir Conalliâ inter duo maris Brachia, nempè inter sinum Loch Febhail (Lough Foyle) et sinum de Suilech (Lough Swilly), et ab hoc Enna possessam fuisse et nomen sumpsisse tradunt acta Conalli fratris ejusdem Ennæ, et aliæ passim domesticæ hystoriæ." *Acta SS.*, p. 370, note [14].

[5] *Bearnas-mor;* i.e. "the great gap," now Barnesmore, and locally called Barnas; in the N. E. of the barony of Tirhugh, co. Donegal.

[6] *Sruthail.* Now Sruell, in the parish

The half for himself he took by his right,
For with him the expedition went;
Half for his closely united brothers—
For Cairpre, Enna, and Eoghan.
Eoghan's land[1] is known to me;
From Srubh-Brain[2] to Glas-nEnnucha.[3]
Enna's land[4] from that to the west,
To Bearnas-Mor,[5] to Sruthail.[6]
Cairpre[7] to the west of him, great honour;
Enna betwixt him and Eogan.
Fergus[8] and stout Boghuine[9]—
His two good sons—to the north of him.
Conall himself had, as share of the division,
The three districts of Conall's land,
From Fertas[10] to the constant Dobhar,[11]
And from Dobhar to Eidhnech;[12]
From Eidhnech, not a crooked track,
Till it reaches southwards to Cromchall;[13]
From Bearnas without weakness of tribes,
To Ros-itir-dha-inbher.[14]

of Killyward, barony of Banagh, and co. Donegal.

[7] *Cairpre.* The descendants of this Cairpre gave name to the territory called Cairpre Droma-Cliabh (Cairpre of Drumcliff), now the barony of Carbury, in the north of the co. Sligo.

[8] *Fergus;* i.e. the son of Conall Gulban, whose territory was situated to the north-east of the barony of Banagh, co. Donegal.

[9] *Boghuine,* or Enna Boghaine, the second son of Conall Gulban, whose descendants occupied, and gave name to, the barony of Banagh, co. Donegal.

[10] *Fertas.* This is now called Farsetmore, or "the great ford," and is situated on the river Swilly, in the parish of Leck, barony of Raphoe, and co. of Donegal.

[11] *Dobhar.* The ancient name of the Gweedore (or Gaoth-Dobhair) river.

[12] *Eidhnech.* The river Enny, which flows into Inver harbour.

[13] *Cromchall;* i.e. "the bent wood," or "bent hazel." Not identified.

[14] *Ros-itir-dha-inbher;* i.e. the "Ross (or wooded point) between the two inbhers," or estuaries; one of the "Rosses," bar. of Boylagh, co. Donegal.

Ro[ind] Cairpre sair airsin floind,
 Co Faen glais a tir Chorainn.
 Amlaid sin, nir bo cranna,
 Fodlaiset a bferanna.
Ocht meic Neill ba tren a tres;
 Ceṫrar thuaid dib, cethrar thes;
 Maine thes, Laeguiri airsin;
 Conall Cremtuinne is Fiachaid.
Enna thuaid, Eogan gan ail;
 Cairpre is Conall gulbuin;
 Ge ro ḟagsatt Temraig trell,
 Nir fagsatt rigi nErend.
Des Nell ocus Daṫi thoir,
 Togthar Conall i Temraig;
 No gur breg Laeguire lonn
 Iarracht na rigi o Chonoll.
IS samlad sruic fri snaṫ
 Samlad ċloinne Neill ri cach;
 Is samlad feinned re fann,
 Samlad mac Neill re Conall.
Engnum Cuinn cedchathaiġ ċaid
 I Niall .ix. giallaig nertnair;
 Gan engnum Neill caide glonn,
 I mac aigi acht i Conall.
Lais tangatar a Temraig,
 Clanna Neill co nert menmain,

[1] *Faen-glas*; i.e. the "green slope." The alias reading *Fér-glass* ("green grass") is suggested. The place must have been situated on the southern boundary of the barony of Carbury, co. Sligo; but either name is now obsolete.

[2] *Tir-Corainn*. Now the barony of Corann, co. Sligo.

[3] *Maine*. The fourth son of Niall; ancestor of the O'Dalys of Westmeath, of the O'Catharnaighs, or Foxes, of Teffia, and of the O'Breens of Breghmhaine, or Brawney, co. Westmeath.

[4] *Laeghaire*. Monarch of Ireland; progenitor of the tribes called the Ui Laeghaire of Meath, of which O'Caindealbhain, or O'Quinlan, was the chief.

[5] *Conall Cremhthainne*. Ancestor of

Cairpre's share westwards after that, explain :
To Faen-glas,[1] in Tír-Corainn.[2]
In this manner, not by chance,
Did they parcel out their lands.
Of Niall's eight sons, strong in battle,
Four were in the North, four in the South ;
Maine[3] in the South ; then Laeghaire ;[4]
Conall Cremhthainne,[5] and Fiachadh.[6]
Enna in the North, Eoghan without stain,
Cairpre, and Conall Gulban ;
Though they abandoned Tara for a time,
They abandoned not the kingship of Ireland.
After Niall and Dathi in the East,
Conall was chosen in Tara ;[7]
Until the fierce Laeghaire coaxed
The loan of the kingship from Conall.
'Tis comparing silk[8] to yarn,
To compare the sons of Niall to any ;
'Tis comparing weaklings to heroes,
To compare the sons of Niall to Conall.
The prowess of brave Hundred-battle Conn
Was in mighty Niall Nine-hostager ;
But the valour of Niall of noble deeds
Was in no son of his, except in Conall.
Along with him[9] from Tara came
The sons of Niall, with strength of mind,

the Clann-Colmain, or O'Melaghlins, of Meath ; and seventeen kings of Ireland derived their descent from him. See O'Flaherty's *Ogygia*, part iii., p. 401.

[6] *Fiachadh.* From this chieftain are descended the O'Molloys of the King's county, and the Mac Eochagain, or Mageoghegans, of Westmeath, whose original territory, called Cinel-Fiachach from their ancestor, and Anglicised Kinelea, is now comprised in the barony of Moycashel.

[7] *chosen in Tara.* See note [6], p. 139, *supra.*

[8] *silk.* ſıpıc (siric), a loan from Lat. *sericum.*

[9] *With him ;* i.e. with Conall Gulban.

Ocus Fiachraiḃ gan laigi ;
Do digail a frithoide.
Muiredač mend luaiḋed gail,
Frithoide Conaill gulpain,
Ocus Fiachraig gan laige,
Robhe sin a ard oide.
Cana ocus a clann cnedač,
Cagad doib re Muiredach ;
Gabsatar a dun gan ḟeill ;
[a] fol. 39, b 2. Marbsad friṫoide Conuill.[a]
Rangatar na techta soir,
Dinsoiged Conuill gulbain,
Is co Fiačraig mac Echach,
Is co Niall nertchrechach.
Tainig Conall reme assin,
Ochtar doib do deg braithrib,
Ocus Fiachra co na čloind,
Co riachtatur clar Coruinn.
Targther o Ulltoib gan ḟell
Breṫ airdbrethemain Erenn,
Do Conall fein gan laige,
A naiḋiḃ a frithoide.
A dubairt Fiačaiḃ andsin,
Ard oide Conuill gulbain,
Bennačt ar mo dalta ndil,
Nar ar seoitt siṫ a einig.
Ata siṫ rogebam ind,
A Fiačruig in ḟuilt oirḟind ;

[1] *instructor.* frithoide is explained "usher" in O'Reilly's Ir. Dictionary; but it is certainly put here for oide, or teacher, the word used in the last line of the next stanza.

[2] *Muiredhach Mend.* The Four Mast., at the year 742, record the slaying of Muiredhach Mend, chief of Ui-Meith, by the Ulidians. He seems to have been the chief referred to in the text, for in the next page

 And of Fiachra without weakness,
 To avenge his instructor.[1]
Muiredach Mend,[2] whom fame reports,
 Was the instructor of Conall Gulban ;
 And Fiachra without weakness—
 His chief tutor was he.
Cana and his woundiug sons
 Were at war with Muiredach.
 They captured his fort without delay,
 And slew Conall's instructor.
The messengers went to the East,
 To seek Conall Gulban ;
 And to Fiachra,[3] Eochaidh's son,
 And to strong-plundering Niall.
Conall proceeded on after that—
 Eight good brothers were they—
 And Fiachra with his sons,
 Until they reached the plain of Corann.
By the guileless Ultonians was proffered
 The award of the chief judge of Ireland,
 To Conall himself, without weakness,
 For the death of his instructor.
Thereupon Fiacha did say,
 (Conall Gulban's chief tutor),
 "A blessing on my loved foster-son ;
 Let not treasures his condition be."[4]
"A peace there is we'll accept therefor,
 O, Fiachra of the fair golden hair,

"the host of Uladh" is represented as the party from whom Conall Gulban demanded atonement. In this case there is here a considerable anachronism, unless we understand the names of Conall and Fiachra to signify their descendants.

[3] *Fiachra ;* i.e. son of Eochaidh Muidhmhedhoin (pron. Eohy Muee-veón), and brother of Niall Nine-Hostager.

[4] *his condition be.* ꞅıṫ a enıᵹ ; lit. "be his honour's peace ;" i.e. peace for his wounded honour.

M'oide beo gan cron gan chrad,
A dun 'sa argain imlán.
Noċonfuigbe tusa sin,
Breġrech tai a Chonaill gulbain;
O ṡlog Ulad admur baig,
Noċon aigenda aḟaġbail.
Mana ḟaġar mo cert fein,
Ar Conall gulban mac Neill,
Ni uil bidbad ongebad cert,
Ar ndenam uilc rum aein fecht.
Noċo dUlltoib is nar sin,
Ar in techtairea d'Ultaib,
Acht do Niall na tuicsi tend,
D'airdrig uili na hErend.
O na rogab Conall coir,
O Ultoib collin asloig.
Araiġ Niall air a ċlainn,
Gan dol re diċeill Conaill.
Scarmid fri Conall annsoin
Conall Cremthainn a brathair,
Is Maine collin a sloig,
Is Fiaċa mac Neill nert-moir.
Fuabrit scarad frir uili,
Clanna Neill co med bloiḋi;
Acht in leoman, garg a gal,
* fol. 40, a 1. Eogan mor mac a mathar.*
Andsin atbert Eogan oll,
Tam fein lin digla ar nglonn;
Nibaṫ cesta ar ar cloind,
Misi is tusa. a Chonaill.

[1] *of comprehension strong.* na tuicsi tend. The words "no co tresi ndrend," i.e. "or with might of battle," are added as a various reading.

[2] *his mother's son.* In the tract on celebrated women, preserved in the Book of

My tutor alive, without defect or anguish,
His fort and its plunder entire."
"Thou wilt not receive that—
(Thou 'rt eloquent, Conall Gulban)—
From Uladh's host who valour boast,
It's obtainment is not natural."
"Unless my own right I obtain."
Said Conall Gulban, son of Niall,
"There's no foe from whom I'll justice take,
After doing me injury any time."
"Not to the Ultonians is that a shame,"
Said the Ultonian messenger,
"But to Niall of comprehension strong,[1]
To the chief king of Ireland all."
Since Conall justice did not accept,
From the Ultonians with all their host,
Niall commanded his children
Not to join in Conall's folly.
From Conall then did separate
His brother, Conall Cremthainne,
And Maine, with all his army,
And Fiacha, son of mighty Niall.
They all began to abandon him—
The sons of Niall of great fame—
Except the lion, fierce in valour,
Eoghan the great, his mother's son.[2]
Then the noble Eoghan said,
"We are strong enough to avenge our affronts;
We shall not be a reproach to our sons,
I and thou, O Conall."

Lecan (ff. 184–189), Indiu, daughter of Lughaidh, is stated to have been the mother of Eoghan, son of Niall, and of the two Conalls, i.e. Conall Gulban and Conall Cremthainne. The other sons of Niall were by a different woman. But other accounts differ from this. See O'Flaherty's *Ogygia*, p. 402.

Ragaid sinne liḃ annsin,
  Ar Daṫi ocus ar Fiachaidh;
  Slog somlata naċ frith faill,
  Oide is comaltai Chonaill.
Atbert Enna re Cairpri,
  Ri oide ceim gan cairde,
  Ni fuigeb Conall romchar,
  Ar smacht oide na athar.
M'ane a Enna, ar Cairbre,
  Sunn ag Conall gan chairde,
  Aisfadsa ag Eogan sunn seal;
  Mech gach seolad co sindser.
Raga misi ar iasacht let,
  Ar Laeguiri go laeċ nert;
  Danuga iasaċt gan fell,
  Uait aris ort mar iarram.
Ni tibra ar Fiacha na fled,
  Oide Conaill na corr sleg,
  Celga Laeguiri gan acht,
  Ni bi in rigi acht ar iasacht.
Cuma lem, ar Conall caid,
  Cia buss ri i Temraig Fail;
  Gidbe tir imbiusa and,
  Bid lem a rigi, ar Conall.
Indemin toiḋecht beo a caṫ,
  Ar Laegaire collan raṫ;
  Ni ro dam a Conaill ċain,
  Iasaċd bus fiaċ dom anmain.
Do rad Conall gan chaire
  A breṫir re Loeġaire;

[1] *senior.* This line seems to contain a proverb. Cairbre was the elder brother of Enna.

[2] *a loan.* The loan appears to have been the loan of the sovereignty of Tara, or Ireland, as it is explained immediately after. But Conall Gulban never was king of Ireland, and therefore could not

"We will go with you then,"
Said Dathi, and said Fiacha ;
A famous band that deserves not neglect—
The tutor and foster-brothers of Conall.
Enna said to Cairpre,
To his tutor, straight without delay,
"I'll not leave Conall who loved me,
For sake of the censure of tutor or father."
"If you, Enna," said Cairbre, "remain
Here with Conall, without respite,
I'll stay here with Eoghan awhile,
For all guidance is feeble compared to a senior."[1]
"I'll go with thee, for a loan,"[2]
Said Laeghaire of heroic strength."
"If thou fairly givest back the loan
From thee, again, when we ask it?"
"Give it not," said Fiacha of the feasts,
The tutor of Conall of the sharp spears ;
"Laeghaire will doubtless deny,
That he had the kingship only by loan."
"I care not," said Conall the brave,
"Who'll be king in Tara of Fail ;[3]
In what land soever I may be,
Its kingship shall be mine," said Conall.
"Return alive from battle 's uncertain,"
Said Laeghaire with richest grace ;
"I will not retain, O chaste Conall,
A loan which would be penal to my soul."
The stainless Conall then pledged
His word unto Laeghaire,[4]

have lent the dignity to Laeghaire. See note [6], p. 139, *supra*.

[3] *Tara of Fail.* A bardic name for Tara, which was called Temhair Fail from the stone, Lia Fail, alleged to have been brought thither by the Tuatha De Danann. *See* Petrie's Account of Tara, p. 160, *sq.*

[4] *Laeghaire.* Lcoīge, A.

Co tibred do rech gach fer,
In cet airged do ḟirfed.
Lotrat clanna Neill fothuaid,
Co hor Erau rogloin ruaid;
Gur gabradar longport ann,
Go comnart ima Chonall.[a] fol. 40, a 2.
Tinolait Ulaid a feċt,
O nar gabad uatha cert;
Co rangatur co hErr ruaid,
Do ċabair Chana clann ruaid.
Cana is Cissi na nglonn
Ocus Senach na saerchlann;
Tri rig Ulad gan laigi,
Tiagad ra na socraide.
Tri caṫa d'Ulltoib annsoin,
D'indsoigead aṫa Senaiġ;
Ocus oen chath don taeb ṫall,
Ro eirgetar ba Conall.
Comraigit uan aṫ annsoin,
Clanna Neill ocus Ulltai;
Dar aṫ Senaiġ, dar Es Ruaid,
Bui fuil co fairrgi forruaid.
Ced la Fiaċaiḃ laeċda a li,
Ocus da ċéd re Dathi;
Maine is Enna in mail,
Da cet leo san ċaṫ irgail;
Ced laeċ fri Loegaire lond,
Ocus ced re hEogan oll;
Dobherin comlann gaċ fir,
Do tren ferurib int sluaigid.

[1] *Eas-Ruaidh.* Now Assaroe, near Ballyshannon, co. Donegal. See note [7].

[2, 3] *Cana and Cissi.* These names do not appear in the authentic genealogies of the Ulidians, and are probably names of legendary personages.

That he would give him, beyond all men,
The first boon he would demand.
The Clanna-Neill went northwards,
To the margin of the bright Eas-Ruaidh;[1]
Until there they pitched their camp,
Powerfully surrounding Conall.
The Ultonians assembled their army,
Since justice was not accepted from them;
And then proceeded to Eas-Ruaidh,[1]
To protect Cana of the noble clanns.
Cana[2] and Cissi[3] of the valorous deeds,
And Senach[4] of the noble race—
Three kings of Uladh without weakness—
Came with their multitudes.
Three battalions were the Ultonians then,
Going towards Ath-Senaigh;[5]
And one battalion on the other side
Rose up around Conall.
They then fought around the ford[6]—
The Clann-Neill and the Ultonians.
Over Ath-Senaigh,[5] o'er Eas-Ruaidh,[7]
Blood flowed unto the crimson sea.
A hundred fell by Fiacha, warlike his look,
And two hundred Dathi slew;
By Maine, and the chief Enna,
Two hundred fell in the battle-strife.
A hundred heroes fell by fierce Laeghaire,
And one hundred by the famous Eoghan.
Such were the deeds of each man,
Of the heroes of the host.

[4] *Senach.* *See* note [1], next page.
[5] *Ath-Senaigh.* *See* note [1], next page.
[6] *the ford*; i.e. Ath-Senaigh, or the ford at Ballyshannon.
[7] *Eas-Ruaidh*; or Eas-Aedha-Ruaidh. The Salmon Leap at Assaroe, near Ballyshannon. The name signifies, literally, the "cataract of Red Hugh."

Gnimrada Conuill co ngail,
Nir beg a erba d'Ulltaib;
Cana srimach, cona claind,
Do roċair do laim Conuill.
Torchair for ri Conall soin
Senach o bfuil aṫ Senaiġ,
Ocus tri ced, sloindti sin,
D'Ultoib rian dol don laṫair.
Cisi ri Carbroiġi cruaid,
O doċoid on ath fothuaid,
Torchair le Conall gnim ngle,
Conid uada sid Cisi.
A ċaṫreim osin amaċ,
A airneis is cran folaċ,
On chaṫ sin aṫa Senaiġ
Co scainnir ndeirc ndegenaiġ[a]
Caṫ Bernais, caṫ Dobair duinn;
Caṫ Locha Febail foruill;
Caṫ Gairgi, caṫ Srubai Broin;
Ocus caṫ airdi Eogain.
Caṫ Boirni, caṫ Inbir uill,
Ocus caṫ Comair chrualoinn.
Caṫ Line co forni fuil,
Caṫ Boirni ocus caṫ Belaig.

[a] fol. 40, b 1.

[1] *Ath-Senaigh.* Now Ballyshannon, co. Donegal; properly Bel-Atha-Senaigh, the "mouth of the ford of Senach."

[2] *Cisi.* Pron. *Kishy.* A fabulous character. See note [4].

[3] *Carbroighi.* Corbraige was the name of a sept anciently located in Fanad, in the north of the present co. of Donegal, from one of whom St. Colum Cille's mother was descended. See *Mac Firbis's* Geneal., 151.

[4] *Sidh-Cisi;* pron. "Shee-Kishy," and now Sheegys, a townland to the north of Ballyshannon, in the parish of Kilbarron, barony of Tirhugh, co. Donegal.

[5] *Bearnas.* The "Gap;" probably Barnismore, in the barony of Tirhugh, co. Donegal.

[6] *Dobhar.* Or Gaeth-Dobhair (?); the Gweedore river, co. Donegal.

[7] *Loch-Febhail.* Lough Foyle.

The achievements of valorous Conall
To th' Ultonians caused no small loss.
The grumbling Cana, with his sons,
Fell by the hand of Conall.
By the same Conall still was slain
Senach, *a quo* Ath-Senaigh,[1]
And three hundred, be this noted,
Of the Ultonians, before leaving the place.
Brave Cisi,[2] king of Carbroighi,[3]
When he went northwards from the ford,
Fell by Conall, a glorious deed;
So that from him Sidh-Cisi[4] is [named].
His battle-career from thenceforth
To relate, superfluous is,
From that battle of Ath-Senaigh,
To his latest crimson fight.
The battle of Bearnas;[5] the battle of brown Dobhar,[6]
The battle of the famous Loch-Febhail,[7]
The battle of Gairig;[8] the battle of Srubh-Brain,[9]
And the battle of Ard-Eoghain.[10]
The battle of Boiren;[11] the battle of great Inbher;[12]
And the battle of Comar[13] of the fierce valour;
The battle of Linè,[14] where blood was shed;
The battle of Boiren,[15] and the battle of Belach.[16]

[8] *Gairig.* Not identified.

[9] *Srubh-Brain.* See note [2], p. 314.

[10] *Ard-Eoghain.* "Eoghan's Height." Not identified. The alias reading ɫ c. cairgi ennuig, is written over the name arda eogain.

[11] *Boiren.* Anglicè "Burren." There are several places called "Burren" in Ireland; and it is uncertain which of them is here referred to.

[12] *Inbher.* Inver, in the bar. of Banagh, co. Donegal.

[13] *Comar.* Probably Comber, co. Down, which is an anglicised form of the Irish *Comar* ("a confluence"), also written "Comer" and "Cummer."

[14] *Linè.* Magh-Linè, or Moglinny; in the bar. of Upper Antrim, and co. of Antrim.

[15] *Boiren.* See note [11].

[16] *Belach.* Belach means a "pass." But there are so many places in Ireland called *Belach* (or "Ballagh"), that it would be hard to determine which is here meant.

Caṫ Cloċair, cat Cnuċa cruaiḋ;
Caṫ Maċa, caṫ Emna uair;
Caṫ Delgan dal condemne;
Caṫ Daen is caṫ Muirthemne.
Caṫ Carad is caṫ Greini,
Caṫ Cruaċan, caṫ Corrsléḃi;
Caṫ Cera, caṫ Gallmi gloin,
Caṫ Aidni is caṫ Umaill.
Caṫ Luimniġ, caṫ Luachra airrin;
Caṫ Claenratha, caṫ Caisil;
Caṫ Cliach, caṫ Claire, caṫ Rois,
Caṫ Eni, caṫ Argetrois.
Mairti, Liamain, Liṗi lonn,
Siuir Beoir Berba, Alma oll;
Edar ath in derca daill,
Laiṫri sin caṫa Conaill.
Deich caṫa dib illaignib,
In ndigail Neill nertadbail,
Deich caṫa i Mumain martair,
Is ocht caṫa ar Connachta.

[1] *Clochar.* Probably Clogher, co. Tyrone, anciently called "Clochar-mac-Daimheine," or the "Stony-place of Damhein's sons."

[2] *Cnucha.* Now known as Castleknock, near Dublin.

[3] *Macha;* or Ard-Macha ("Macha's height"); Armagh.

[4] *Emania.* The seat of the Ulidian monarchs; the site of which is now known as the Navan Fort, near Armagh.

[5] *Delga.* Or Dun-Delgan, Dundalk.

[6] *Daen.* Not identified.

[7] *Murthemne.* This was the name of a district comprising the greater part of the county of Louth. Some of the battles recorded in the *Tain Bo Cualnge* were fought in it.

[8] *Caradh.* This was the name of a place in Roscommon, and the northern boundary of the O'Kellys' country (Hy-Maine). See O'Donovan's *Tribes and Customs of Hy-Many*, pp. 66, 134.

[9] *Grian.* A river that falls into Lough-Grany, in the barony of Tullagh, co. Clare, and that anciently formed the southern boundary of Hy-Many, *Ib.* p. 134, note.

[10] *Cruachan.* Rathcroghan, in Roscommon; the ancient seat of the kings of Connaught.

[11] *Corrsliabh.* Now the Curlew Hills, between Roscommon and Sligo.

[12] *Cera.* The barony of Carra, co. Mayo.

[13] *Gallimh.* Galway. The MS. A. furnishes the alias reading no glinde in gluind or "of the Glen of the deed," the

The battle of Clochar;[1] the hard battle of Cnucha;[2]
The battle of Macha;[3] battle of noble Emania;[4]
The battle of Delga,[5] a vehement meeting;
The battle of Daen,[6] and the battle of Murthemne.[7]
The battle of Caradh;[8] the battle of Grian;[9]
The battle of Cruachan;[10] the battle of Corrsliabh;[11]
The battle of Cera;[12] the battle of bright Gallimh;[13]
The battle of Aidhne,[14] and the battle of Umhall.[15]
The battle of Luimnech;[16] the battle of Luachair[17] thereafter;
The battle of Claenrath;[18] the battle of Cashel;
The battle of Cliach;[19] battle of Claire;[20] battle of Ross,
The battle of Eni,[21] battle of Airgetross.[22]
Maistiu,[23] Liamhain,[24] the rapid Liffey,
The Suir, Nore, Barrow; noble Alma;[25]
Etar,[26] the ford of blind Derc[27]—
These are the battle-fields of Conall.
Ten battles of them were in Leinster fought,
In revenge of Niall[28] of the mighty strength.
Ten battles in Western Mumha,[29]
And eight battles over Connachtmen.

situation of which is uncertain.

[14] *Aidhne.* Or Ui-Fiachrach-Aidhne; now represented by the diocese of Kilmacduagh, co. Galway.

[15] *Umhall.* Now represented by the bar. of Burrishoole, co. Mayo.

[16] *Luimnech.* Limerick.

[17] *Luachair.* The hilly district of Sliabh-Luachra, between Limerick and Kerry.

[18] *Claenrath.* One of the residences in ancient Tara was called *Claenrath* (or "sloping rath"); but the place here alluded to seems to have been in Munster.

[19] *Cliach.* A district in the co. Limerick, lying around Knocklong, in the barony of Coshlea.

[20] *Claire.* The ancient name of the hill near Duntrileague, co. Limerick.

[21] *Eni.* Not identified.

[22] *Airgetross.* The old name of a district in the barony of Fassadining, co. Kilkenny.

[23] *Maistiu.* The Hill of Mullaghmast, co. Kildare.

[24] *Liamhain.* A district containing Dun-Liamhna (now Dunlavin), co. Wicklow.

[25] *Alma.* The Hill of Allen, co. Kildare.

[26] *Etar.* Howth.

[27] *Derc.* The situation of *ath-in-dercadaill* has not been discovered.

[28] *In revenge for Niall;* i.e. Niall Nine-Hostager, who was slain by Eochaidh, son of Enna Cennselach, a Leinster prince. See Chron. Scotorum, ad an. 411.

[29] *Mumha.* Munster.

Da caṫ .x. leis ar Ulltoib,
Mar indisit na hugdair;
Ro ba fecht flaṫa ar fianaib.
A secht caṫa air Oirgiallaib.
Caṫ Temra, caṫ Tailten thair,
Ocus caṫ Tlachtga taebglain,
Ro bris ar fearaib Mide,
Fris ni ragaib Laegaire.
Deich caṫa ocus da cet sin,
Ar na rim a Manistir,
D'Oengus maraen is do ḟlann,
Ro chom in gres do Chonall. Conall Cuingi.[a]

[a] fol. 40, b 2.

ENNA dalta Cairpri cruaid,
Ro gab ṫir nEnna armruaid;
Fagbais in cuingid a ċloind,
I forcad cenecoil Conaill.
Ga ra ḟagaib Enna a ċloind
I forcad ċineoil Conaill,
Ro treged iat 's ni ar laige,
Go re Asla is Tipraide.
Clann Eirci is Fergus gan faill,
Do treicset sil nEnna uill,

[1] *Airghialla*, or Oirghialla. The descendants of the "Three Collas," who conquered the ancient Ultonians, and wrested from them the greater part of Ulster.

[2] *Temhair;* i.e. Tara, co. Meath.

[3] *Tuilltiu.* Now Teltown, in the co. Meath.

[4] *Tlachtgha.* Now the hill of Ward, near Athboy, co. Meath.

[5] *two hundred.* da cet. As the battles mentioned amount to about fifty, for *da cet*, we should read da ficet, "forty."

[6] *Manister.* Manister-Buite, or Monasterboice, co. Louth.

[7] *Flann.* Flann Mainistrech, or Flann of the Monastery (Monasterboice). See note [8], p. 123.

[8] *Conall.* The first two words of the poem, *Conall Cuingi*, are added in token of its completion; after which the scribe

Twelve battles he gained over the Ulidians,
As the authors do relate.
A prince's expedition 'gainst heroes seemed
His seven battles over the Airghialla.[1]
The battle of Temhair;[2] the battle of Tailltiu[3] in the east,
And the battle of fair-sided Tlachtgha,[4]
He gained over the men of Midhe,
For Laeghaire did not him oppose.
Ten battles and two hundred[5] are these,
As counted in Manister,[6]
By Oengus, together with Flann,[7]
Who composed the work for Conall.[8]

ENNA,[9] foster-son of hardy Cairbre,
Occupied Tir-Enna[10] of the bright weapons.
The warrior left his descendants
Under the protection of the Cinel-Conaill.
Though Enna his descendants left
Under the protection of the Cinel Conaill,
They were forsaken, and not through weakness,
Till the time of Asal and Tipraide.
The sons of Erc[11] and guileless Fergus[12]
Abandoned the race of noble Enna,

writes ro cuirris rein lebar ronacha me, ardaig ir clerech do rcrib rompla na bloidiri de; "the Old Book of Fenagh has tired me, for it was a cleric that wrote the exemplar of this part of it."

[9] *Enna.* This poem is quoted in O'Donnell's original Life of St. Colum Cille, in the Bodleian Library, as the composition of Flann Mainistrech. There are various copies of the poem in the MS. collection of the Royal Irish Academy; but none of them very good.

[10] *Tir-Enna*, or Cinel-Enna. *See* note [4], p. 314.

[11] *Erc*, or Earc, daughter of Loarn Mór, king of Alba, or Scotland; who was first married to Muiredhach, son of Eoghan, and after Muiredhach's death to Fergus, son of Conall Gulban.

[12] *Fergus.* *See* last note.

Do maccaib a mathar mban,
Do Muirchertach 's do Moan.
Ga ra gab Enna gan ail
Tir nEnna gan uiresbaid,
Nir gab nech orin alle,
Da sil gur gab Tirraitti.
Sesca bliadna truag in dáil,
Dares Enna eneċnair,
Gan nert ga sil na tir tall,
Acht Eogan air is Conall.
Ni bai cosruchus ris sin
Ag sil Conaill ná Eogain,
Im ṫir nEnna ba mor muirnn,
Ar baiḋ ingine Louirnd.
Erc ingen Loairn gan len,
Maṫair na nocht mac mortren,
Is a sil is treorach ṫall
Itir Eogan is Conall.
Tigernaċ ba tren a rig,
Is Feradach co flaitheṁail;
Muirchertaċ, Moan co raṫ,
Clann Erci re Muirodaċ.
Clann Tigernaig o taib te
Sil Tigernaig mic Erce,
Feradaċ fein flaiṫ amuig,
O dat cenel Feradaig.

[1] *Muircertach and Moan.* These were two of the sons of Earc, by Muiredhach, cousin of Fergus. This Muircertach, or Muircertach Mac Erca, was king of Ireland from A.D. 513 to 533. Moan was the ancestor of the Cinel-Moen, the chiefs of which were the Ui Gairmledhaigh, or O'Gormleys; whose original territory was comprised in the present barony of Raphoe; but they were driven across the Foyle by the O'Donnells.

[2] *since.* orin alle. The words "no da sil, no dar dail," i.e. "of his race, or across Dail (the river Deel, or Dale-burn)," are added over orin alle. But the next line commences with the words da sil.

[3] *Eoghan.* The race of Eoghan, or Cinel-Eoghain.

[4] *Conall.* The Cinel-Conaill, or race of Conall, are here meant, the name of

For the sons of their fair mother,
For Muircertach[1] and Moan.[1]
Though Enna the stainless possessed
Tir-Enna, without deficiency ;
None of his seed possessed it since,[2]
Till Tipraide did it obtain.
For sixty years, pitiful the case,
After Enna of honour great,
His sons had no power in their land yonder ;
But Eoghan[3] and Conall[4] ruled it.
There were no 'mearings' during that time,
Between the race of Conall or Eoghan,
Regarding the land of Enna of great mirth,
Out of love for Loarn's daughter.
Erc, daughter of Loarn without woe,
The mother of the eight valiant sons ;[5]
'Tis her seed that is powerful yonder,
Between Eoghan and Conall.
Tigernach, whose rule was strong,
And Feradach of princely sway,
Muirchertach and lucky Moan,
Were Erc's sons by Muiredach.
The Clann-Tigernaigh from the warm side
Are the race of Tigernach, son of Erc ;
Feradach, too, was a full ripe[6] prince,
From whom are the Cinel-Feradhaigh.[7]

their ancestor being frequently used to represent the tribe.

[5] *eight valiant sons.* The four sons of Erc, by Muiredhach, son of Eoghan, son of Niall, were Muirchertach Mac Erca, king of Ireland, Feradhach, Tighernach, and Moan. Her four sons by Fergus, son of Conall Gulban, were Sedna, Fedhlim (father of St. Colum Cille), Brendan, and Loarn.

[6] *ripe.* amuig, which means "within", A. But in other copies of the poem the word is abaiḋ, "ripe."

[7] *Cinel-Feradhaigh.* The Cinel-Feradhaigh were seated in the barony of Clogher, co. Tyrone. The chief family name was Mac Cathmhail, a name which has been anglicised "Caulfield, and Campbell."

Cenel Moain co medaib,
O Moain mac Muiredaig;
Muirchertaċ co meḋair mir,
*fol. 41, a 1. IS uadh airdrigrad Oiligh.[a]
Sil sin na cethri mac min
Ro bai ag Eirc a nEogan tir;
Sloindfet anos sluaig co rind,
Sil mac nEirc i criċ Conuill.
INd Erc is a clanna soin,
Ingen Loairn a hAlbain,
Tuc Fergus mac Conaill chain,
A crui des Muiredaig.
Setna Feidlimid ro fer,
Brenain is Loairn lain des,
Clann Erci delbgora in droing,
Is Fergusa mic Conaill.
Ni bai ag Fedlimid do cloind,
Acht Eogan bec is Coluim (.i. C[ille]).
Nir ḟag Brenuinn, rem co raṫ,
Cland aċt Baithin bithmaith.
Loorn ba laidir a glac,
Rop uasal primgeine a mac,
Ronan athair na mac mend,
Colman, Fingin, is Laissend.
Na tri meic sin ro fag Erc,
Gan sil aċt naob co naemnert;
Setna, aicci ro silad
Tuath chairech is tren riga.

[1] *Cenel-Moan.* gĩl moaĩ, A.

[2] *Ailech.* See note [3], p. 62, *supra.*

[3] *Had.* robai. Other copies of the poem have ro fag, "left."

[4] *A weapon'd host.* sluag co rind. Other copies read gan faill, "without fail," a more correct expression. See Todd's *Nennius*, App. cv.

[5] *Baithin.* He was first cousin of St. Columba, his successor in the abbacy of Hy (or Iona), and the founder of the church of Tech-Baithin (or Taughboyne),

The Cenel-Moan[1] the powerful are
From Moan, son of Muiredach;
From Muircertach of the merry mind
Are the chief kings of Ailech.[2]
These are descendants of the four gentle sons
Whom Erc had[3] in Tir-Eoghain.
Now I shall name to you a weapon'd host,[4]
The race of Erc's sons in Tir-Conaill.
The Erc, whose sons these are,
Was daughter of Loarn of Alba;
Whom Fergus, son of mild Conall, took
For a dowry, after Muiredach.
Sedna, Fedhlimidh, it is known,
Brenainn and Loarn fully fair,
Were the sons of Erc (nobly formed the band),
And of Fergus, son of Conall.
Fedhlimidh no children had
Save little Eoghan and Columkill.
Brenainn of happy career left
No child, save Baithin[5] ever-good.
Loarn[6]—strong was his hand—
Great was the first born of his sons,
Ronan, father of the noble men,
Colman,[7] Finghin[8] and Laisrenn.[9]
Those three sons[10] whom Erc left
Had no issue save saints of holy grace;
But from Setna did descend
Territorial chiefs, and mighty kings.

co. Donegal. He died on the 9th of June, A.D. 600, three years after St. Columba.

[6] *Loarn*; i.e. the son of Fergus Cennfoda, by Erc, daughter of Loarn Mór.

[7] *Colman*; or Columbanus. See Colgan's *Trias Thaumat.*, p. 480, note [k].

[8] *Finghin*. The copy in the O'Conor Don's MS. has "Seighin." See Todd's *Nennius*, App., p. cvi., *n.* [s].

[9] *Laisrenn*. See Colgan, *Tr. Thaum.*, p. 481, note [26].

[10] *Those three sons*. It should be "three of the sons."

Sedna mac Fergusa fáil,
  O fuil sil Sedna saer nair,
  Cenel Lugdaċ thair sa bos,
  Sluag Fanad co fir follus.
Cland Chiarain, cland Crunnmail ċain,
  Is clann Loingsig co rigaib;
  Is iatsin co ngnim ngora,
  Sil Sedna mic Fergusa.
Sil mac Erci sin gan ail,
  Itir Conall is Eogan.
  Agsin a gcairdes bai la,
  Do sil Cormaic mic Enna.
Do ċuindig Erc cumaid caith
  Ar a hoċt maccaib mor blath,
  Ferann foiṫi na friċ faill,
  O maccuib i crich Conaill.
A heiċ a hor a hetaċ,
  A tidnacal trentretaċ.
fol. 41, a 2. A frestal fós co fleḋaib,
  Uaitho ar maccuib Muireḋaiġ.
Do rinne a timna ra nos
  Erc ocus ni himar bros;
  A criċ do Chairneċ miad ngal,
  Do deg mac a derbrethar.

[1] *Fail;* i.e. Ireland.

[2] *In the East and here;* i.e. in Scotland and in Ireland.

[3] *Fanad.* A territory in the north of the co. Donegal, extending from Lough Swilly to Mulroy Lough, and from the sea to Rathmelton.

[4] *Conall.* Put for Tir-Conaill, or Donegal.

[5] *Eoghan.* For Tir-Eoghain, or the country of the descendants of Eoghan, son of Niall Nine-Hostager.

[6] *noble.* cath, A.; but caid in the copy of the poem in the O'Conor Don's MS.

[7] *in fee simple.* na friċ faill. Dr. Todd observes that this is a Brehon law term, nearly equivalent to "our *fee simple.*" See *Irish Nennius*, Appendix, p. cvii., *n.*[b].

[8] *her sons.* The copy in the O'Conor

Setna, son of Fergus of Fail,[1]
From whom are the noble, brave Sil-Setna,
The Cenel Lughdech, in the East[2] and here,
And the host of Fanad[3] manifestly.
The Clann-Ciarain, fair Clann-Crunnmail,
And the Clann-Loingsigh with their kings—
They are, with valorous deeds,
The race Setna, son of Fergus.
These are the stainless seed of Erc's sons,
Both in Conall[4] and Eoghan.[5]
Behold their relationship once
To the seed of Cormac, Enna's son.
Erc besought a noble[6] gift
From her eight sons of great renown;
Land for her maintenance, in fee simple,[7]
From her sons[8] in Conall's land.
Her horses,[9] her gold, her clothes,
To be furnished in full measure,[10]
And also to be supplied with banquets,
She exacted from the sons of Muiredach.
She made her will before her death,
Did Erc—and no falsehood 'tis.
Her land (she gave) to Cairnech of great fame,
To the good son of her sister.[11]

Don's MS. has o ṗıl mac Eıṗc," from the seed of Erc's sons."

[9] *horses.* This stanza does not occupy the same place in the MS. A., as in the O'Conor Don's MS., in which it follows the next stanza but one.

[10] *full measure.* ꞇṅ ꞇ̄ꞇac, for ꞇꞃen ꞇꞃeꞇaċ; lit. "flock-heavy." ꞇꞃom ceꝺac, O'Conor Don's MS.; the meaning of which is nearly similar.

[11] *sister;* i.e. Pompa, or Bebona, daughter of Loarn Mór; and wife of Saran. St. Cairnech was the founder of Tulen, now Dulane, near Kells, co. Meath, and died about the year 539. See *Irish Nennius*, p. 178, and App., p. ci. For his genealogy, see the Geneal. Table in Reeves's ed. of *Adamnan*, pp. 438–9.

A hoirrod gaċa bliadna,
Mar do boċ beo rem riagla,
Is ced do gaċ cruid arsin
Do Chairneċ o sil Eogain.
Tucsat meic Fergusa di
Druim Ligen ar a huaisli;
Ar a comdosi is tir thall,
Itir Eogan is Conall.
Tucsat sil Eogain a cis
Fri re Chairnig gan naċ scis;
Ocus do ratsat miad ngal,
Da os re fichit bliadan.
Massan is Casan arsin,
Da comarba deis Charnig;
Tucsat Druim Ligen gan chain,
Ar chis Charnig do congbail.
Tucsat d'oib Neill co rath
Gan chis gan fecht, gan sluagad;
Gid cia no ċongbaḋ gaċ sol
Cis Carnig a Druim Ligen.
Fergus mac Muirchertaig moir,
Cona cloinn uasal ardmóir,
Gabsat in Druim sa ċis de
Fir Droma Ligen laigco.
Ro bai in ferand amlaid sin
Fri re seisir genealuig,

[1] *Druim-Lighen;* or Cruachan-Lighen, now Drumleene, on the western bank of Lough Foyle, near Lifford, co. Donegal. This stanza follows the one beginning "Erc besought," in O'Conor Don's MS.

[2] *Between Eoghan and Conall;* i.e. between Tir-Eoghain and Tir-Conaill.

[3] *race.* mic, sons, A., in which the word sil, race, or seed, is added as a various reading over mic.

[4] *Massan and Cassan.* Colgan says that Massan was the St. Assan (Massan=Mo-Assan, my Assan) commemorated in Martyrologies on the 27th of April; and that Cassan was the St. of the same name whose festival was observed on the 20th

Her suit of apparel every year,
As if she were alive—a regular act—
And an hundred of every kind of stock,
To Cairnech from Eoghan's race should be given.
The sons of Fergus gave to her
Druim-Lighen,[1] for her excellence;
Because of its fitness in the land yonder,
Between Eoghan and Conall.[2]
The race[3] of Eoghan paid their tribute
During Cairnech's time, without murmur.
And they gave it, great the fame,
For twenty years after him.
Massan[4] and Cassan[4] subsequently,
Two comharbs after Cairnech,
Gave Druim-Lighen, without tribute,
For the maintenance of Cairnech's rent.
To the prosperous Ui-Neill they gave it,
Free from rent, expedition, or hosting,
If they would maintain, for all time,
Cairnech's tribute in Druim-Lighen.
Fergus, son of great Muirchertach,
And his mighty, noble sons,
Took the Druim,[5] subject to this tribute,
[And hence] were called *Fir-Droma-Lighen*.[6]
The land was in this manner,
During the time of six generations,

of June. See *Acta Sanctorum*, p. 783, note [8]. They are mentioned as contemporaries of St. Cairnech in the ancient tale called aıdeꝺ Muıṗceṗꞇaıᵹ mıc Eṗca, or "the tragic death of Muircertach Mac Erca," a copy of which is preserved in the MS. H. 2. 16, Trinity Coll., Dublin.

[5] *Druim*. Druim-Lighen.

[6] *Fir-Droma-Lighen*; i.e. "men of Druim-Lighen." The particular sept known by this name was that of O'Donnelly. See O'Donovan's pedigree of this respectable family, Appendix to *Four Masters*, p. 2426.

O Enna anuas gan laige,
Go ro in trenfir Tipraidi.
Tipraidi mac Tnuthaig tric
Mic Luigdeċ is mic Cormaic
Mic Conchobair[1] * *
* * * * *

Tanaic Tipraitti o Themraig
Ma ṫogairm Arla engaig;
Tangatar ann dias blathaċ,
Ronan ocus Uargalaċ.[a]
Domnall mac Aeda na nos,[2]
He ro chuir Tipraitti andes,
Do ċosnam in tiri teinn
Do Tipraitti a nirt Conaill.
Tinolais Tipraite tren,
Clanda Luigdech na laemsgel,
Cormac * * *
Ciaran ocus Tigernach.
Comergit cenel Eogain
Ma Maelfitrig nar deolaid,
Ma Connalaċ cain gan cradh,
Ma Dalbaċ is ma Conmal.
Torchair Maelfitrig ferrda,
Do laim Tipraide Tempa;
Ri garb mac Ronain co raṫ,
Taeṫ Conmal is Connalach.
Torchair Arla, garg a gail,
Do laim Dalbaig puirt Comair;
Torchair Dalbaċ san debaid,
Do laim Fingin na degaid.

[a] fol. 41, b 1.

[1] *Conchobhar.* The rest of this stanza is wanting in the MS. A. It is also wanting from the copy in the O'Conor Don's MS.

[2] *Domhnall, son of Aedh.* King of Ireland; ob. A.D. 640. *Chron. Scotorum.*

Down from Enna who was not feeble,
'Till the time of powerful Tipraidè.
Tipraidè, son of active Tuathach,
Son of Lughaidh, son of Cormac,
Son of Conchobhar[1] * *
* * * * *

Tipraidè from Tara came,
At the call of valiant Asal.
There also came a famous pair;
Ronan and Uargalach.
'Twas Domhnall, son of Aedh[2] of the cascades
That sent Tipraidè from the south,
To contend for the stout land,
For Tipraidè, with Conall's might.[3]
The powerful Tipraidè collects
The Clann-Luighdech, famous in story,
Cormac[4] * * * *
Ciaran and Tigernach.
The Cinel-Eoghain arise,
With Maelfitrigh who was not mean,
With mild Connalach without anguish,
With Dalbach, and with Conmal.
The manly Maelfitrigh fell
By the hand of Tipraidè of Tara.
By Garbh, Ronan's lucky son,
Conmal and Connalach fell.
Asal, fierce his valour, fell
By the hand of Dalbach of Port-Comair;
Dalbach in the fray was slain,
After that, by Finghin's hand.

[3] *Conall's might;* i.e. the power of the Cinel-Conaill.

[4] *Cormac.* The rest of the line is wanting in A.

Uargalaċ is Ronan rann,
  Torcratar le Forannan;
  Torchair Forannan Febail,[1]
  Do laim croda Caibdenaig.
Brister[2] tri caṫa sin muig,
  Ra Tipraiti mac Tnuthaig;
  Sil Eogain ma meala i maig,
  Is tir Enna ina duthaig.
Do rad Tipraite gan tor,
  Don triar tanaicc na tinol,
  O glais na nenach[3] nedig,
  Co Druim marthar[4] nduibedig.
Rudless Tipraide foin tair,
  O tha Dail[5] co Finn[6] formir,
  O lec Tamlacha co tenn
  Co Cruaċan is go Leṫglenn.
Rudless Asla dair delbus,
  O Sruthail is o Bernus,
  Onnus omail andar,
  Go dail ro ardgaib Assal.
Gabsat don taeb oili im Dail
  Ronan, Uargalaċ armchair.
  Mac d'Uargalaig gluair greḋaċ,
  In cuingid cruaid Coldenach.
Mac do Ronan Uargus oll,
  Dar bo mac Bresal borb lonn;
  Mac d'Asla Fingen co seb,
  Senathair ċloinde Fingin.

[1] *Febhail;* i.e. the Foyle, or Lough Foyle.

[2] *were won.* brister, lit. "are broken."

[3] *Glas-na-Nenach.* See note, [3], p. 314.

[4] *Druim-Iarthar.* This was the name of some place on the western boundary of Tir-Enna, co. Donegal. But it has not been identified.

[5] *Dail:* i.e. The river Dale, now called Burndaley, which flows from Lough Dale to the Foyle, and joins that river to the north of Lifford.

[6] *Finn.* The Finn river, which flows nearly parallel to the Dale, on the south.

Uargalach and Ronan bold
Were slain in fight by Forannan ;
Forannan of Fobhail[1] fell
By the brave hand of Coibdenach.
Three battles on the plain were won[2]
By Tipraidè, son of Tnuthach ;
Eoghan's race was mocked in the plain,
And Tir-Enna became his (Tipraidè's) own.
The stainless Tipraidè gave,
To the three who in his muster came,
From bright Glas-na-Nenach,[3]
To the dark-surfaced Druim-Iarthar.[4]
Tipraidè's own estate in the East
Was from the Dail[5] to the rapid Finn ;[6]
From Lec-Tamlacha[7], stoutly,
To Cruachan,[8] and to Leth-glenn.[9]
The patrimony of Asal, the fair formed, was
From Sruthail,[10] and from Bernas,[11]
* * * * *[12]
To the Dail,[13] Asal nobly possessed.
On the other side of the Dail did settle
Ronan, and Uargalach of the straight weapons ;
Inciting, brave Uargalach's son
Was the bold champion, Coibdenach.
Ronan's son was famed Nargus,
Whose son was haughty, fierce Bresal ;
Asal's son was good Finghin,
The ancestor of Clann-Finghin.

[7] *Lec-Tamlacha.* The "flag-stone of Tamlach." Not identified.

[8] *Cruachan.* Now Croaghan, barony of Raphoe, co. Donegal.

[9] *Leth-glenn.* Somewhere near Croaghan, referred to in the last note.

[10] *From Sruthail.* opputhail, A. See note [6], p. 314.

[11] *Bernas.* See note [5], p. 314.

[12] The original of this line is so corrupt, that the Editor does not venture to translate it.

[13] *Dail.* The river Dale, or Burndaley. See note [5].

Siol Enna ar a rab a raṫ,
  Tucsad do ċinel Lugdaċ,
  Gaċ darna rot na tir thall,
  Da ndin in agaid echdrann.
Tugsat cinel Luigdech luinn
  Soċar mór don Enna ċloind;
  In tres baili in gaċ tuaiṫ theinn,
  Doib in uair bud crinill.
Ro cenel nEnna gan ḟaill
  Drechta rig cenel Conaill.
  Leosom ro deṫber na recht,
  A ḟeṫim a cġairechd.
Milċoin ċineil Conaill ċaid
  Cenel nEnna heinechnair;
  Cenel Lugdaċ co lin nga,
  Muni roċair sil nEnna.   Enna d. cā.

A eolċa Conaill ceoling,
  Sloinnid duin, dail naċ deolaid,
  Ga cuis mar gab Dalaċ dil,
  Forlamus for a briathrib.
Fiarfoigit eli uil ann,
  Do ċleirċib Conaill cet ceall,
  Ga naeb ro rac brethir mbuain
  Do ċlannuib Dalaig drech ruaiḋ.
Mar e Colum cille caid
  Ro racc in mbreṫir tre baid,

[1] *his luck;* i.e. the luck of Enna, progenitor of the Sil-Enna, or Cinel-Enna.

[2] *descendants.* ḡn, A. This is a loose form of abbrev. for cinel, "family," or "kindred."

[3] *the support are.* The first words of the poem are repeated in token of its conclusion.

[4] *YE jovial learned.* This poem is quoted in O'Donnell's life of St. Colum Cille, as

Enna's race, who enjoyed his luck,[1]
    Granted to the Cinel-Luighdech,
    Each second sod in their land yonder,
    For defending them against strangers.
The descendants[2] of fierce Lughaidh gave
    Great favours to Enna's sons—
    The third town in each stout district
    [Should be] theirs, when they were unprepared.
To the Cinel-Enna, without doubt, belong
    The offices of the king of Cinel-Conaill;
    With them by right of law doth rest,
    To attend him, and to guard him.
The watchdogs of the brave Cinel-Conaill
    Are the Cinel-Enna of honour great;
    The Cinel-Luighdech of many spears
    Of Sil-Enna the support are.[3]

YE jovial learned[4] of [Tir-] Conaill,
    Explain to us—no subject mean—
    The reason why belovèd Dalach[5]
    Over his brethren rule obtained.
Ask, all of you who are there,
    Of the clerics of Conall of the hundred cells,
    What saint left a lasting blessing[6]
    To the sons of ruddy-visaged Dalach.
If 'twas the holy Colum Cille
    Who, thro' love, the blessing left;

the composition of Flann Mainistrech. Copies of it are contained in MSS. in the Library of Trinity College, Dublin, and in the R. I. Acad.; but none so old or accurate as the present.

[5] *Dalach.* See note [1], p. 352.

[6] *blessing.* bреτhιр (brethir), lit. "a word."

Cinnus ro ac, coluib gall,
'S nač inann re i rabatar.
Gid cia ro ḟireḋ gan crad
Lebar čilli mic nEnan,
Ro geabtha ar a lar co lom
Fir gača dala i Conoll.[a]

[a] fol. 42, a 1.

Is ann do ḟuarusa fein
Senčus dremi dib co réid;
Otha Lugaid do Lachtmuig,
Co Dalač mac Muirchertaig.
Lugaid mac Setna na srian;
Do ba mac Ronan rigḟial;
Mac do Ronan Garb congal;
Mac do Garb cet Cennfaolad.
Fiamain fuilech, ferda a gail,
Cet mac Cinnfaelad fleda;
Athair na slogh sunn co sal,
Or genetar clanna Fiamain.
Mac oili Cindfaolad sin,
Maelduin athair Airnelaig;
Tri meic d'Airnel[ach] miad ngal;
Snedġal, Fiangus, Cendfaelad.
Cennfaelad segainn sercač,
Do roba mac Muirchertač;
Muircertach saidbir some,
Cona raignib ra čloinne.
Maelfothbil, Maelgaethe ger,
Ocus Cernačan corrtren;

[1] *Cill-mic-nEnain.* Now Kilmacrenan, co. Donegal. The Book of Kilmacrenan has totally disappeared.

[2] *in its pages.* ar a lar; lit. "on its surface." A.

[3] *Conall.* Put for Cinel-Conaill, or Tirconnell. Some doggerel is written on the lower margin of fol. 41, b.

[4] *Lughaidh.* Ancestor of the Cinel-Luighdech.

How did he leave it—wondrous fact—
Since they lived not at the same time.
But if, without much pain, you searched
The book of Cill-mic-nEnain,[1]
There in its pages[2] you'd plainly find
The knowledge of each event in Conall.[3]
'Twas there I plainly found, myself,
The history of a branch of them,
From the time of Lughaidh[4] of Lachtmagh,
To Dalach,[5] son of Muircertach.
Lughaidh, son of Setna[6] of the bridles,
Had a son, generous Ronan.
The son of Ronan was the valorous Garbh;
Garbh's son was the first Cennfaeladh.
The wounding Fiaman, of manly might,
Was festive Cennfaeladh's first son;
Parent of the hosts from this to the sea,
From whom are derived the Clann-Fiamain.[7]
Another son this Cennfaeladh had,
Maelduin, father of Airnelach.
Three sons had famous Airnelach,
Snedgal, Fiangus, Cennfaeladh.
Cennfaeladh, the loving chief—
Muircertach was son to him;
Muircertach, the rich and happy,
With his cluster of great sons.
Maelfothbil, Maelgaethe the keen,
And strong-bodied Cernachan,

[5] *Dalach.* The eighth in descent from Lughaidh, and ancestor of the O'Donnells.

[6] *Setna.* See the pedigree compiled by Dr. Reeves, *Adamnan*, p. 342, with which this poem completely agrees.

[7] *Clann Fiamain.* A tribe name of the O'Dogherty's of Inishowen, co. Donegal. Dochartach, *a quo* the name of O'Dogherty, was the grandson of Fiaman, who was the seventh in descent from Conall Gulban.

Dalaċ, Bradagan comluid,
Coic meic maithi Muircertuig.
Bradagan is Dalaċ dian,
A mathair acu ar aon rian.
Aen mathair con triar eli;
Ba comlan a cairdine.
Ar neg Muirċertaig, ni go,
Roindseat in clann sin a ċro;
I coicc rannaib, rigda in roind;
Coic puirt gaċ fir don comroind.
Seacht mbliadna Dalaiġ ba slan
Ar neg a athar do tham;
Fobarrsiut gan ni do de,
Do ċru a athar re a oige.
Gid og libsi Dalaċ donn,
Atbert Bradagan med nglonn,
Dligid cuid don chro ċabraid
fol. 42, a 2. Ar a ḃeṫ og anarraid.
Atbert Maelfothbil fergach,
Is Cernachan cruaid celgach,
Ni miad linne liṫ gan acht,
Beṫ ar urcod re og mac.
Na hindirid da bar maccaib,
Atbert Bradagan tre baid.
Misi coisenus gart glan,
A ċuid do mac mo mathar.
Annsinn atbert Dalaċ des,
Nir ḃfuiġell olc anairċes,
Berid mo ċuid don chro ċain,
Do cind ḟorlamais oruib.
Sanntach na brathair man crod;
Tainig foċaib a denam.

[1] *They;* i.e. his elder brethren.

[2] *submit.* The literal translation of the original is "for the sake of supremacy over you."

Dalach, and famous Bradagan,
Were the five good sons of Muircertach.
Bradagan and Dalach bold
Had the same mother, as it chanced.
One mother had the other three;
Their relationship was thus complete.
After Muircertach's death—no lie—
These sons divided his property,
Into five parts—regal the division.
Five forts had each man for his share.
Dalach's years were only seven,
At his father's death from pestilence.
They[1] attempted to give him none
Of his father's wealth, on account of his youth.
"Though young you deem the brown Dalach,"
Said Bradagan of many deeds,
"A share of the stock is due to him
Because he's young and immature."
The angry Maelfothbil said,
And hard, deceitful Cernachan,
"We like not, certainly, that we
Should have but the same as a young lad."
"Tell not that unto your sons,"
Through friendship, Bradagan did say;
"'Tis I that will rightfully defend
His portion for my mother's son."
The comely Dalach then did say—
'Twas not a bad, unripe decision—
"Take ye my share of the fair stock,
If ye will to my rule submit."[2]
The brothers, greedy for the wealth,
Agreed the compact to fulfil.[3]

[3] *fulfil.* The original, closely translated, would read "it occurred to them to do it" [i.e. to agree to the condition imposed by Dalach].

Ro fegsat huili co becht
Ar Bradagan in aeinfecht.
Tabraid do cendaċt gan crad,
Adubairt riu Bradagan.
Rigi do Dalach 's da chloind
Do thairngir daibsi Coluim.
Is amlaid do thairngir sin
Mac fialbreṫaċ Feidlimid;
Mac ar a mbiad Dalaċ des,
Clanna Luigdech ga mor leass.
INdesatsa daib tre threoir,
A ebdoide og an uirsgeoil,
Mar do tairngired co tenn
Dalaċ ga mbiad in deg clann.
Merlech do chuaid gan tsena,
Do ṡil Tipraidi is Enna,
Do merli ar groid Ronain ruaid,
Dar gabad he co hanuain.
Dubenach a ainm in ḟir,
O fuil muinter Duibenaig.
Ar do cetgabad can crad
Cadaċ conige Adamnan.
Triallter a chrochad co tend,
Co tanig Colam na ċend;
Foillsigter do sin miad ngal,
In fer caidaiġ ga chrochad.*
INdails[in] ga triallter lib,
Adubairt Colam caemdil,

* fol. 42, b 1.

[1] *tale.* The original is rather obscure; and the editor cannot make a better attempt at rendering it. In a copy of the poem in the MS. 23, C, 33, in the R. I. Acad., the line is represented by *bud aobda an fath ursgeoil:* "'twould be a famous subject of a tale."

[2] *Enna.* Ancestor of Cinel-Enna.

[3] *Dubhenach.* dubenaig, MS.

[4] *Muinter-Duibhenaigh.* O'Devany, now Devany, without the O'. Of this family was Conor O'Devany, bishop of

They all then looked fixedly,
Together, upon Bradagan.
"Give him supremacy, without anguish,"
Unto them said Bradagan
"'Kingship to Dalach and his children'
Colum-Cille to you foretold."
"In this wise such did prophesy
The true-judging son of Fedhlimidh:
'The son who's comely Dalach called,
Him shall Clann-Luigdech fully serve.'"
"I will tell you, for your guidance,
You young men, the famous tale,[1]
How powerfully was prophesied
Dalach, who shall have the good sons.
"A robber went, without denial,
Of the race of Tipraide and Enna,[2]
To rob the stud of Ronan the red;
When he untimely captured was.
Dubhenach[3] was the man's name,
From whom are Muinter-Duibhenaigh;[4]
For at first a *cadach*[5] was pris'ner ta'en,
Without remorse, until[6] Adamnan.
To hang him 'twas strongly sought,
Till to oppose it Colum came;
For to him wondrously 'twas shown,
That a Cadach-man[7] was about being hung.
"Why is this deed attempted by you,"
Said Colum the beloved and meek;

Down and Connor, put to death in Dublin in 1614.

[5] *cadach;* i.e. a person under the protection of a covenant.

[6] *until.* conige. The MS. has coigē, which would usually represent *coingen.*

[7] *Cadach-man.* A man under protection. See note [5]. The orig. of these two lines is very loosely constructed The poet meant to say that until Adamnan's time no guarantee could prevent the arrest of a person for certain offences.

Gen go fetabar cose,
Bar naenta ar nim is naiscthe.
Adais Colam a lama,
Man crochaire co dana;
O thapla na ċenn gan on,
Ro bo teand int anacol.
Ni dailsin ba doilig lem,
Adubairt Ronan ro thend;
Beir lat a Cholaimb ua Chuind
Mar aen 's gaċ dail biar etraind.
Mar do leigis lium gaċ dail,
Do raid Colam cille cáid,
Genfid dod síl, rigḋa in raṫ,
Mac damba comainm Dalach.
Fagbaim do is da chloind,
Coscur caṫa is comluind,
Buaid mbrethri, buaid mbrige afos,
Buaid rigi le hairechurs.
Genfer cethrar uad do ċloind;
Gebaid dias dib ár leṫ Cuind;
Is gebaid in diass oile
Rigi Fodla fondgloine.
Egneċan, Caṫbar da chloind,
Gebtaitt airdrigi ar leṫ Chuind;
Conn ocus Caṫbarr oili,
Bid leo in Fodla ḟoltbuide.
Agsin senchus na breṫri
Chloinde Domnaill ċind chlethi,

[1] *Dalach.* Ancestor of the O'Donnells. This Dalach was the seventh in descent from Ronan, who was son of Lugaid, son of Setna, son of Fergus Long-head, son of Conall Gulban.

[2] *From him;* that is to say, four sons would be born of his stock.

[3] *Leth-Chuinn;* i.e. Conn's half, or the Northern half of Ireland.

[4] *bright-landed—yellow-haired—Fodhla.* Fodhla was a bardic name for Ireland. The epithet "yellow-haired" is probably

"For though you knew it not hitherto,
Your covenant in Heaven is bound."
Colum closed his hands,
Boldly, around the hangman grim;
And when Colum opposed the deed,
Strong the protection truly was.
"This affair were sad to me,"
The mighty Ronan then did say.
"Have thy way, O, Colum Ua Cuinn,
As in all things that 'twixt us may be."
"As thou hast granted me every thing,"
The holy Colum Cille said,
"Of thy seed shall be born, by royal grace,
A son whose name shall be Dalach.[1]
"I leave to him, and to his sons,
Triumph of battle and conflict;
The palm of eloquence, and of vigour here;
The palm of kingship, with supreme rule.
"From him[2] shall descend four sons,
Of whom two o'er Leth-Chuinn shall reign.[3]
And the two other shall obtain
The kingship of bright-landed Fodhla.[4]
"Egnechan[5] and Cathbarr,[6] of his sons,
Shall have the chief kingship of Leth-Chuinn;[3]
Conn,[7] and another Cathbarr,[8]
Yellow-haired Fodhla[4] shall possess."
That is the history of the prophecies
Of the Clann-Domhnaill, head of battles,

in allusion to the colour of the ripe corn fields.

[5] *Egnechan.* Chief of Tirconnell; ob. 901.

[6] *Cathbarr.* Son of Domhnall Mór, progenitor of the O'Donnells.

[7] *Conn.* The fourth in descent from Domhnall Mór.

[8] *Cathbarr.* Doubtless, Cathbarr O'Donnell, father of the last-named; but neither of them was King of Fodhla, or, Ireland.

Mar fuarus i Cill mic nEoin,
Illebraib, ni hord aineoil.

ATA sunn senchus naċ suaill,
Do rig Esa roglain ruaid,
Gaċ ni dliġes ni duaiṫnid,
Is beres o prim ṫuaṫaib.
Da dabach .x. do linn maiṫ;
A tri ordáil do lan braiċ;
Ced muc, ced mart ar na mes,*
Ced brat, ced matal mordess;
Tri ced bairgen co ma ṫri,
Cis Cairbri sin don airdrig,
Gaċa bliadna, liṫ gan locht,
'Sa idlacad co a ardḟort.
Dlegait Cinel nEnna uill
An cedna do rig Conaill;
Andlig sil nEnna uile,
Dleagaitt Cinel mBogaine.
Dartroige is Tuaṫ Raṫa,
Fir Luirg co nilar fatha,
Do rig Erni ruaṫar ngle,
Dlegait biathad gaċ raiṫe.
Cinel Luigdeaċ, ni dleghd dib
Acht comaidechd a nairdrig.

* fol. 42, b 2.

[1] *Cill-mic-nEoin.* Properly Cill-mic-nEnain, now Kilmacrenan, co. Donegal.

[2] *not mean.* This poem is in the style of the poems contained in the "Book of Rights," and claims for the chief of Tirconnell privileges not allowed to him in that compilation. There are a few modern copies of this poem in the Libraries of Trinity College and the R. Ir. Acad.

[3] *King of bright Es-Ruaidh;* i.e. the king of Cinel-Conaill.

[4] *Cinel-Enna.* See note [4], p.314, *supra.*

[5] *king of Conall;* or of Cinel-Conaill.

[6] *Cinel-Boghaine.* The descendants of

As I found it in Cill-mic-nEoin,[1]
In books. 'Tis no unknown tale.

HERE is a history, not mean,[2]
For the king of bright Es-Ruaidh;[3]
What he's bound to give is not unknown,
And what he receives from his chief tribes.
Twelve vats of good ale,
And thrice the measure of good malt,
A hundred pigs, a hundred fat beeves,
A hundred garments, a hundred fine cloaks,
Three times three hundred cakes,
Is the tribute of Cairbre to the arch-king,
Every year, a choice without fault;
And to be conveyed to his chief abode.
The great Cinel-Enna[4] are bound to give
The same, to the king of Conall;[5]
And what the Cinel-Enna owe,
Cinel-Boghaine[6] are bound to pay.
The men of Dartraighe[7] and Tuath-Ratha,[8]
The Feara-Luirg,[9] for many reasons,
To the king of Erne[10] of brave routs,
Owe refection every three months.
Cinel-Luighdech are not bound to supply
But the guardianship of their arch-king;

Enna Boghaine, second son of Conall Gulban, who gave name to the present barony of Banagh, co. Donegal.

[7] *Dartraighe.* Now the barony of Rossclogher, co. Leitrim.

[8] *Tuath-Ratha*; i.e. "the district of the fort," anglicised Toorah; in the bar. of Magheraboy, co. Fermanagh.

[9] *Feara-Luirg*; or "men of Lurg," who were seated in the present barony of Lurg, co. Fermanagh.

[10] *King of Erne.* An alias name for the king of Cinel-Conaill, borrowed from the river Erne.

A triaṫ chuca ar cuairt arsin,
Gan biad d'idlacad uathaib.
Ised fodera doibsin,
Gan biad d' idlacad uathaib,
A linmaire thuaid ga toig,
Is burba int sluaig a Temraig.
Eol dam tri tuaṫa na ṫir;
Cis na cain ni dlegar dib;
Clann Murchada in lamaig luinn,
Clann Dalaig, is clann Domnuill.
Is uime naċ dlegait sin
Cis na cain do righ uathaib;
Daib is duthaid in rige;
Ni chraid caċ a comdine.
Ni uair naċ leis Temair tenn,
Ocus airdrigi nErenn,
Do rig Era ruaid ni dlecht
Cis na cain, na comaidecht.
Ge deċ ri Conuill i cein,
I sluaiged rig Temrach trein;
Ni heigen beres o ṫoiġaidecht,
Acht do ṫuilled thuarusdail.
Ge digset i caṫ cenn i cenn,
Sluaig Conuill re rig Erenn;
Gach a marbthar dibh san ċaṫ,
Dligat a ic ri Temrach.*
Ni dlegait lon leo bar sed,
Laeċraid Chonaill na caemchet;
Acht in cein ra buid i muiġ,
Ri hErenn ga fritholaim.

* fol. 43, a 1.

[1] *rudeness.* bba. The poet evidently entertained some grudge against his contemporaries of Tara (or Meath); the reason assigned for the exemption of the Cinel-Enna from tribute, being not only unlikely, but libellous.

[2] *his land;* i.e. the country of the king of Cinel-Conaill.

Their chief may come on a visit to them,
Without their being bound to give him food.
The reason why they are not bound
To furnish food from themselves,
Is their numbers at home in the North,
And the rudeness[1] of Tara's host.
I know three tribes in his land,[2]
Who do not owe rent or tribute ;
Clann-Murchadha of fierce exploits,
Clann-Dalaigh, and Clann-Domhnaill.
The reason why they are not bound
To give rent or tribute to any king,
Is because the kingship is their due ;
And none his kindred should aggrieve.
When strong Tara to him does not belong,
And the arch-kingship of Ireland,
The king of Es-Ruaidh is not entitled
To rent or tribute, or attendance.[3]
Though the king of Conall goes afar,
In the hosting of great of Tara's king ;
'Tis not compulsion that takes him from home,
But to earn recompense.
If together into battle go
The host of Conall with the king of Ireland ;
The king of Tara is bound to pay
For all of them in the battle slain.
The warriors of fair-trooped Conall
Are not bound to take food on the march ;
But whilst they may be in the field,
The king of Ireland must them supply.

[3] *attendance.* The poet meant to say, probably, that when the king of Cinel-Conaill was not supreme Monarch of Ireland, he was not entitled to tribute from the three septs mentioned in the second stanza preceding.

Gid mor do mac for conair,
Ni dleċd a agra oraib.
Tuarusdal rig cuiccid cruaid
Dlegar do riġ Era Ruaiḋ.
Tuarusdol tri nurriġ noll
Da gaċ urrig i Conall,
No go tegait slan da tig,
Gan ḟeall gan agrai oraibh.
Tuarustal urrig eli
Gaċa taisig a treibe;
Tuarustal taisig arsin
Gaċa haen brugad uathaib.
IS aire dlegait sium soin,
Clanna Conaill gulbain gloin,
Ar thecht sloiged nar dlecht dib,
Uaisli is crodacht a ċatġnim.
Patraicc do ḟaguib doibsin;
Uad ro scribad illebraib;
Gach ni dlegaitt linaib la,
Crist ga comed mar ata.

A liubair ta ar do lar
Senchus comuaige comlan,
Do rig echtach Oilig uill,
Is do riġ ċinid Chonaill.
Dlestir sin onoir ndeolaid,
Duit a liubair lantreoruig.
Agat ata fis gaċ cert
Do rigaib tenna in tuaiscert.
IN tan bus ri ri Oilig
Ar sluag Conaill cet guinid,

¹ *pages.* lar, lit. "middle," or "surface." There are a few modern copies of this

Though great [the wrong] they commit on the march,
It must not be against them charged.
The stipend of a brave provincial king
Is due to the king of Assaroe.
The stipend of three noble dynasts
Is due to each dynast in Conall,
Until they come safe to their homes,
Without deceit, or charge against them.
The stipend of another dynast
Is due to each leader of a tribe;
The stipend of a leader then
Is due to each *brughaidh* of them.
The reason why to this are entitled
The clans of Conall Gulban brave,
Is for going on hostings not due from them,
And the greatness and valour of their battle-deeds.
Patrick bequeathed it to them;
By him it was written in books.
What they are entitled to, for all time
May Christ preserve it, as it is.

O BOOK in thy pages[1] is
A complete, perfect history,
For the mighty king of Oilech great,
And for the king of Conall's race.
Bound are they to pay rich honour
To thee, O fully guiding book;
Thou hast knowledge of each right
For the mighty kings of the North.
When the king of Oilech is king
O'er the battle-wounding host of Conall,

poem in Dublin; but none so good as the present text.

Dlegaitt tuarastal gaċ ain,
  Ota brugaid co hairdriġ.
IN tan bus ri ri Conuill,
  Ar sil nEogain ni dodaing;
  Dliged in cedna dib sin,
  O bus airdri hé úastaib.[a]
fol. 43, a 2.
Coicait eċ is coicait bo,
  Coicait cloiḋim, coicait go,
  Coicait sciath, coicait con ngle,
  O gaċ righ dib daroile.
Se sceiṫ, se cloideṁ, se coin,
  Se heich, se mogaid, se doim;
  Tuarastal gaċ urrig sin,
  On riġ bus airdri uastaib.
Cutrama a leithi sin thall,
  Gaċa tairis, ni breṫ ċam;
  A leṫ sin cian bus cuman,
  Tuarastal gaċ ard brugaid.
Ni dliged airecht dib amne,
  Tar a cheann sin da cheli,
  Acht sloiged co reim ratha,
  Is comergi cruad chaṫa.
Sluaig dib re beodacht comblaid,
  Re haġ is he hindsaiged;
  Sluag eli re costad caṫ,
  Ocus re coscur cliaṫaċ.
INtan bus ri ar Erinn uill
  Ri Eogain, no ri Conaill,
  Ced da gach crud, ba ginn ngle,
  O gach rig dib daroile.

1 *Conall.* Put for Cinel-Conaill.

2 *to them;* i.e. to the Cinel-Eoghain.

3 *to the other.* That is to say, when the king of Cinel-Eoghain exercises supremacy over Cinel-Conaill, he is bound to give the stipend to the king of the Cinel-Conaill,

Each man to stipend is entitled,
From the *brughaidh* to the arch-king.
When the king of Conall[1] is king
O'er the formidable race of Eoghan,
He is bound to give the same to them,[2]
Since he is over them arch-king.
Fifty steeds, fifty cows;
Fifty swords, fifty spears;
Fifty shields, fifty fine hounds,
From each king of them to the other.[3]
Six shields, six swords, six hounds,
Six steeds, six slaves, six oxen—
This is the stipend of each chieftain,
From the king who is arch-king over them.
The value of the half of that
Is due to each captain—'tis no false award.—
The half of this (long be it remembered),
Is the stipend of each *brughaidh* great.
No party of them thus is bound,
In consideration therefor, to the other;
Save as to hostings, with great dispatch,
And "rising out" for hard battle.
A host of them for famous courage,
For valiant deeds, and for attack;
Another host to maintain the fight,
And to take the battle spoils.
When the king of Eoghan,[4] or of Conall,[5]
Is king over Ireland great,
A hundred of each flock, plain fact, [is due]
From each king of them to the other.

and *vice versa*.

[4] *king of Eoghan;* i.e. the king of the Cinel-Eoghain.

[5] *of Conall.* Put for Cinel-Conaill.

En ċogur leo andis artus,
No co cumad a caemrus,
Ri Cruachna, ri Cearna adċiam
Cucu assin, is ri Airgiall.
Mar ċumaid a mbreṫ do breṫ,
Rigrad chloinde Chuind ar leṫ;
Rigrad Ulad chuca assin,
Is rigrad mor gaċa cuigid.
Fir Erenn o ṫuinn co tuinn,
Ar breṫ Eogain is Conaill;
Re rigi no gan riġi,
Is he sin a sen dine.
En dliged doib sunn ro ḟes,
D' Oilech is d' Ear ruaid na nes.
En ainmniugad orra assin,
Ar sloġ Conaill is Eogain.*
INann briaṫra doib ga tig,
O re Patraicc is Chairnig.
In da ḃrathair, gruaid fri gruaid,
Inann buaid inann dimbuaid.
Ni mo is raiḃte sluaig Oilig
Re sloġ Eogain armdoilig,
Na fri slog Conall gan chrad,
O re Chairnig mic ḟarain.
Air ainmnigther iat huile
O Oileċ co mét gaili,
Oir is he Oileċ gan ḟell
Inat rig tuaiscert hErenn.

* fol. 43, b 1.

[1] *Cearna.* In the Dinnsenchus, Cearna is described as situated in Meath; the king of which territory would, therefore, be called king of Cearna, according to the custom which anciently prevailed of designating Irish kings from some remarkable places within their dominions.

[2] *province.* cuigid; lit. "fifth." Ireland being anciently divided into five provinces, each province was known as a cuigid, or "fifth." Thady O'Rody adds in the margin: nir b'ecno dun in cetroimi sin acht congbalaċ do cur fris in ni rompu: "that quatrain was not plain to

One secret council both first should have,
Until their compact they conclude.
The kings of Cruachan, and of Cearna,[1] we see
Come to them then, and the king of Airghiall.
As they prepare to give their award,
The chiefs of Conn's clann should be apart;
The chieftains of Uladh should then approach them,
And the great chiefs of every Province.[2]
The men of Ireland from wave to wave,
Are under the award of Eoghan and Conall;
With kingship, or without kingship,
That is their ancient right.
One law obtains for them, here 'tis known—
For Oilech and Eas-Ruaidh of the cascades.
One appellation therefore have they—
The host of Conall and Eoghan.[3]
The same blessings[4] had they at their homes,
From the time of Patrick and Cairnech,
The two brothers[5]—cheek to cheek—
Equal their luck; their misfortunes equal.
The 'host of Oilech' is not more applied
To the host of Eoghan of weapons hard,
Than to the host of griefless Conall,
From the time of Cairnech, Saran's son.
The reason why they all are named
From Oilech, home of valour, is
Because Oilech is, without guile,
The Royal seat of the north of Ireland.

us, but as supporting the thing preceding." It is no wonder the construction should have puzzled the worthy antiquary.

[3] *Eoghan.* The note "ir mor ḟeronn ind roinn sin," i.e. "great is the inheritance of this party," is added in the margin.

[4] *blessings.* briathra, lit. "words."

[5] *the two brothers.* In da brathair. The *alias* reading don da brathair, "to the two brothers," is added over the words in the text.

Ni sin do ṡenchus int sluaiġ
Conaill is Eogain armchruaid.
Is he Fland gan crad gan ċair
Ro scriḃ it lár a libair.

IN cert for chloind na Colla,
For sluag Luċair Liathdroma,
Cindus a tuarustail tall
Ic rig Fuait na find ḟerann.
Ata sund, sloindfider daib,
Senċus cloinde Carbri chain.
Cluinid, a sluag Fail na fian,
Tuarusla aili Airgiall.
Dliged ri Airgaill co naeib,
O rig Erenn abradċain,
Saer gellsine, saire cor,
Tuarustal is tidnacal.
Nai ngeill do rig Fodlo ar feċt,
Do deoin rig Airgiall aenfecht,
Illaim rig Tlachtga na tor,
Gan ċaċt ocus gan ċengol.
Eirred a ndingbala doib,
Each, cloidiṁ coneltaib óir;

[1] *Collas.* Colla Uais, Colla Menn, and Colla Dachrich. See O'Flaherty's *Ogygia*, pars. III. cap. lxxv., lxxvi. Copies of this poem (ascribed to St. Benen, or Benignus), are preserved in the Books of *Ballymote* and *Lecan*, from which it has been printed by Dr. O'Donovan, in his edition of the *Book of Rights*, p. 144, sq.

[2] *Liathdruim*; or the "ridge of Liath," son of Laighen-Leathan-Ghlas; a name for Tara.

[3] *of what kind.* Cindus. The Books of *Ballymote* and *Lecan* read can fis, "without the knowledge," which is less correct.

[4] *king of Fuait.* A bardic name for the King of Airghiall. Fuait or Fuaid, otherwise Sliabh-Fuaid, is the highest of the "Fews" mountains, in the co. Armagh.

[5] *shall be told.* sloindfider. sloind-fead-sa, "I shall tell," Books of *Ballymote* and *Lecan*.

This is some of the history of the host
Of Conall and Eoghan of hard weapons.
It was Flann, without grief, without stain,
That wrote it in thy middle, O Book.

THE question with the sons of the Collas,[1]
With the bright host of Liathdruim,[2]
(Is) of what kind[3] are their stipends yonder,
From the king of Fuait[4] of the fair lands.
Here it is: to you shall be told,[5]
The history of the sons of fair Cairbre[6]—
Hear! ye hosts of the Fenian Fail,[7]
The grand stipends of the Airghialla.
To the majestic king of Airghiall is due,
From the fair-browed[8] king of Ireland,
Free companionship, freedom of contracts,[9]
Stipend and presents.
Nine hostages to the king of Fodhla,[10] on a journey,
With the consent of the king of Airghiall, together [are given],
Into the hand of the king of bushy Tlachtga,[11]
Without confinement,[12] and without restraint.
A suitable attire for them;
A steed, a sword with studs of gold;

[6] *Cairbre;* i.e. Cairbre Lifechair, king of Ireland, A.D. 277, from whom the Orighialla were descended, through his grandsons, the three Collas.

[7] *Fenian Fail.* A bardic name for Ireland.

[8] *Fair-browed.* ábradcain. aigeadchain, "fair-faced," *Ballymote* and *Lecan.*

[9] *freedom of contracts.* saire cor. saer a chor, "noble his engagement," *Ballym.* and *Lecan.*

[10] *king of Fodhla.* Another name for the king of Ireland.

[11] *bushy Tlachtga.* Tlachtga na tor. Tlachtga tair, "Tlachtgha in the East," *Ballymote* and *Lecan.* The king of Ireland was sometimes called king of Tlachtgha. The hill of Tlachtgha, now the "Hill of Ward," is a small hill near Athboy, co. Meath.

[12] *confinement.* cacht. carcra, prisons, *Ballym.* and *Lecan.*

Cogar cumaid cumthaig nam,
Do feruib aili Oirgiall.[a]

[a] fol. 43 b 2.

Meṫ orra danelat as,
Meṫ don riġ ros ċuir fo glas;
[Acht sin] ni dluig duni de,
Do rig Oirgiall oirnide.
Gid be ard port aidbli drend,
Imbe airdrigi nErend,
Do flaiṫ Oirgiall gan astar,
Is uad dliges tuarastal.
Tricha sciaṫ scellbuide sceinb,
Tricha brat corcra is coemselb,
Tricha cloidim cruaid hi caṫ,
Tricha gobar luaṫ leimnech;
Gaċ tres bliadain buan in drenn,
Do rig Fuait na find ferann,
O ard ḟlaith Tailltem na tor,
Is e sin a tuarustol.
Dlegait riga a tuaṫ na ṫir,
O flaiṫ Maċa na mor gnim,
O iarla in ċairn cruaid i caṫ
Eich is arm is etach.
Tri mna, tri mogaid mora,
Tri heich diana delbċora,
Do rig O Nuallan on loch,
O rig Emna na nuarboṫ.

[1] *men.* feraib, abl. pl. of fer, a man. aitirib, abl. pl. of aitire, a hostage, *Ballym.* and *Lecan.*

[2] *Decay.* meṫ. mesa, "worse," *Ballym.* and *Lecan.*

[3] [*save that*]. The corresponding words within brackets in the text are supplied from *Ballymote* and *Lecan*, being erased in the MS. A.

[4] *whatever.* This and the three next stanzas are not in the copy of the poem in the Books of *Ballymote* and *Lecan.*

[5] *king of Fuait.* See note [4], p. 364.

[6] *prince of Tailltiu;* i.e. the king of Ireland; so called from Tailltiu, or Telltown, co. Meath, a place much celebrated in

Secret confidence, fine buildings,
For the noble men[1] of Oirghiall.
Decay upon them if they elope thence;
Decay[2] on the king that puts them in fetters.
[Save that[3]], no man is entitled to aught
From the illustrious king of Oirghiall.
In whatever[4] high abode of great contests,
The arch-king of Ireland may be—
To the chief of Oirghiall, without journeying,
He's bound to give stipend therefrom.
Thirty beauteous, bossy shields;
Thirty purple cloaks of fair shape;
Thirty swords hard in battle;
Thirty swift, prancing horses.
Every third year, lasting the condition,
To the king of Fuait[5] of the fair lands—
From the high prince of Tailltiu[6] of the bushes—
That is the stipend.
The kings in his country, his land, are entitled,
From the lord of Macha[7] of the great deeds,
From the earl of the Cairn, brave in battle,
To steeds, and arms, and raiment.
Three women,[8] three bondmen big;
Three swift, fair shaped steeds,
To the king of Ui-Niallain from the lake,[9]
From the king of Emania[10] of the cold huts [are due].

ancient times.

[7] *lord of Macha;* or of Ard-Macha (Armagh); another name for the king of Airghiall, or Oriel, the ancient limits of which embraced Armagh.

[8] *Three women.* The rights of the king of Ui-Niallain are differently stated in the poem in *Ballym.* and *Lecan.*

[9] *Ui-Niallain from the lake;* Ui-Niallain, now the baronies of Oneilland, co. Armagh, adjoining Lough-Neagh.

[10] *king of Emania.* An alias name for the king of Airghiall; from Emania, now the Navan fort, near Armagh, the ancient residence of the kings of Ulster of the Rudrician line.

Dligid ri hua mBresail mblaiṫ,
  Coic eiċ donna do do raṫh,
  Coic bruit, coic cuirn cuirther do,
  Coic matail aili ind aen lo.
Dligid ri Ua nEchaċ áib,
  Coic bruit corcra co caemlaeib,
  Coic sceiṫ, coic cloidim, cuicc cuirnn,
  Coic eich glana gabalguirm,
Dligid ri Ua Meṫ na ndal,
  O rig Maċa na mordal,
  Ceṫri claidib, ceṫri cuirnn,
  Ceṫri heich, ceṫri bruit guirmm.
Tuarustal ri Ua Tortain,
  Tri bruit corcra co corthair;
  Tri sceith, tri cloidme catha,
[a] fol 44, a 1. Tri heich donna deg datha.[a]
Dligid ri Ua mBriuin Archaill
  Secht neich, tri cuirnn re tagraim,
  Secht mogaid naċ cela in chain,
  Ocus secht mna da ndingbail.
Dligid ri tri tuaṫ ar tir
  Tuarastal eli don rig,

[1] *Ui-Breasail.* Otherwise called Ui-Breasail-Macha, and Clann-Breasail. It was the name of a district in the present barony of O'Neilland East, co. Armagh. The stipends of the king of Ui-Breasail are differently stated in the poem in *Ballym.* and *Lecan.*

[2] *Ui-Echach.* Iveagh, co. Down; the patrimony of the family of Magennis.

[3] *Ui-Meith;* or Ui-Meith-Macha, a district comprising the present parishes of Tullycorbet, Kilmore, and Tehallan, in the barony and co. of Monaghan. The sept from which it took its name was descended from Muiredhach *Meith*, or "the fat," son of Imchadh, son of Colla Dachrich. See Colgan's *Trias Thaumat.*, p. 184, *n* [16].

[4] *Ui-Tortain;* or Ui-Dortain, i.e. the descendants of Tortan, or Dortan, son of Fiach, son of Feidhlim, son of Fiachra, son of Colla Dachrioch; who were seated

To the famous king of Ui-Breasail[1] is due
Five brown steeds, as a reward;
Five garments, five goblets are given to him,
Five beauteous mantles on the same day.
To the noble king of Ui-Echach[2] is due
Five purple, fair-bordered garments,
Five shields, five swords, five drinking horns,
Five pure, iron-gray, riding steeds.
To the king of Ui-Meith[3] of the meetings is due,
From the king of Macha of the great assemblies,
Four swords, four drinking horns,
Four steeds, four blue garments.
The stipend of the king of Ui-Tortain[4] is,
Three purple garments with borders,
Three shields, three swords of battle,
Three brown, well coloured steeds.
To the king of Ui-Briuin-Archaill[5] is due,
Seven steeds, three cups, to be demanded;
Seven bondmen—let not the tribute be denied—
And seven women suited to them.
To the king of Tri-Tuatha[6] in his land is due
Another stipend from the king;

in the north of the present co. of Meath, about Ardbraccan.

[5] *Ui-Briuin-Archaill.* A district in the barony of Dungannon, co. Tyrone, the name of which was derived from the descendants of Brian of Archoill, son of Muiredhach Meith, ancestor of the Ui-Meith. The stipends of the king of Ui-Briuin-Archaill are given somewhat differently in *Ballym.* and *Lecan.*

[6] *Tri-Tuatha;* i.e. "three territories." The poem in *Ballym.* and *Lecan* reads "Ui-Tuirtre," a district situated on the east side of the Bann and Lough Neagh, in Antrim. As "Ui-Tuirtre," was also called the "Tuatha of Tort," the tribe that gave it name being descended from Fiachra Tort, grandson of king Colla Uais, the name "Tri-Tuatha" probably refers to it, unless it applies to the three tribes mentioned in the same stanza. See notes [1], [2], [3], next page.

Fir Lemna, Ua Cremthainde chair,
Sil Dubṫiri aiṫ amnais.
Ceṫri heiċ dingbala do,
Ceṫri bruit corcra im ċaem lo,
Ceṫri cloidim, ceṫri cuirnn,
Ceṫri sceiṫ troma tulguirm.
Dligid ri Dartroige im aig
Ceṫri mogaid mor aistir;
Cethri cloidim cruaid i cleiṫ,
Ceṫri heich, cethri h-or sceiṫ.
Dligid ri bFer Manaċ mor
Coic bruit co cortharaib oir,
Coic sceiṫ, coic cloidim chaṫa,
Coic longa, coic luirechai.
Dligid ri bFernmaigi in fuinn
Ceṫri cuirnd lorglana im loinn,
Coic sceith, se cloidim chaṫa,
Se mna ocus se fiḋċella.
Dligid flaith Mugdorn is Rois,
Se mogaid gan mordatos,
Se heich, se cloidiṁ, se cuirnn,
Se bruit ċorcra, se bruit guirm.
Ata sund senċus na slog
Dia tard grad go braṫ Beineon;

[1] *Fir Lemhna*, or "men of Lemhain;" a sept anciently located in the plain of Magh-Lemhna, which comprised the parish of Clogher, and part of Errigal-Keeroge, co. Tyrone. See Reeves's *Colton's Visitation*, p. 126.

[2] *Ui-Cremthainne.* A tribe of this name was anciently located in the present barony of Slane, co. Meath.

[3] *Dubhthir.* The situation of the "race of Dubhthir" has not been satisfactorily identified; but they were probably located about Clogher, co. Tyrone; for O'Dubhagain states that O'Duibhthire was chief of the race of Daimhin, from whose sons Clogher was called *Clochar mac Daimhin.*

[4] *Dartraighi;* i.e. Dartraighe-Coininnsi; now the barony of Dartry, co. Monaghan, over which O'Baeighcallain

Fir-Lemhua,[1] fair Ui-Cremthainne,[2]
[And] the quick, sharp, race of Dubhthir.[3]
Four befitting steeds for him ;
Four purple cloaks of texture fine ;
Four swords, four drinking horns,
Four heavy, blue-bordered shields.
To the brave king of Dartraighi[4] is due,
Four bondmen of great travail.
Four swords hard in battle,
Four steeds, four golden shields.
To the great king of Fera-Manach[5] is due,
Five garments with borders of gold ;
Five shields, five swords of battle ;
Five ships, and five coats of mail.
To the king of Fern-Mhagh[6] of delight is due,
Four fair-shanked cups for enjoyment,[7]
Five shields, six swords of battle,
Six women, and six chess boards.
To the lord of Mughdhorn and Ross[8] is due,
Six bondmen without pride ;
Six steeds, six swords, six drinking cups,
Six purple garments, six blue cloaks.
Here is the history of the host
To whom Benen[9] gave perpetual love,

(O'Boylan) was chieftain, in the time of the topographer O'Dubhagain.

[5] *Fera-Manach.* A tribe which has given name to the present county of Fermanagh. The name in the *Ballymote* and *Lecan* copies is *Lethrind,* which would therefore seem to be an alias name for Fermanagh.

[6] *Fern-Mhagh.* Now the barony of Farney, co. Monaghan.

[7] *for enjoyment.* im loinn. im lind, "for ale." *Ballym.* and *Lecan.*

[8] *Mughdhorn and Ross.* Mughdhorn is now the barony of Cremorne, co. Monaghan. The territory of Ross, or Fera-Rois, comprised the present parishes of Carrickmacross and Clonany, co. Monaghan, and parts of the adjoining counties of Louth and Meath. But its exact limits have not been defined.

[9] *Benen.* St. Benignus, disciple and successor of St. Patrick, and the person to

Acht in ti bus treorach test,
Ar gach neolach is ard cest. In cest.

Do bi imorro duan isint sen liubar Chaillin i Fidnacha roba ṡompla duin, naċ fagaim a tus; ocus ag so in mbloid fuaramar di, daig ni hail las in comarba Caillin fodruair in lebar do graipned duinne cen a scribad, ge ni fuil a remtus ann. Hoc est,[a]

[a] fol. 44, a. 2.

Oed in cet fer craides me;
Nuċaticabra re ré;
Benfaid scor na scol dom druim,
Ocus da trian a ferainn.
Acht go ḟeithear athaig doib
In druimm fodeiri dom deoin,
Ticfat riu ni breg a mbraṫ,
Doibrium bid egen m'atach.
Ticfa ingnaṫ,
Ocus ni chelim ar chach;
Ocus ni ticfa ar muig siuir
A leṫét dO Bruin co brath.
Tigernan ainm in rig reil;
Tigernaċ m'ainmsi budein;
Innisit na psailm sunna,
Adar nainm sat ionna.
IS letsa a mathair gan ail,
Is ra Maodog a athair,

whom the compilation of the "Book of Rights" has been attributed. See O'Donovan's ed. of the *Book of Rights*, Introd., p. 111 *sq*.

[1] *Hoc est.* Tadhg O'Rody adds a note, expressing his opinion that the beginning of the poem will never be found. The Editor has not been able to find a copy in any MS. collection that he has examined. It must have commenced with the words abair frim, "Tell me."

[2] *Druim;* or ridge. The imperfect state of the poem renders it difficult to identify either the persons, or places, mentioned in it. But by the *Druim*, the poet seems to have meant the "ridge" of Fenagh.

[3] *A prodigy.* ingnaṫ, for ingnad: lit. "unusual." Apparently an epithet. A fanciful name for the Tighernan mentioned in the next stanza.

[4] *plain of Siuir.* The text is very uncertain. It looks like muig siuir, "on

Save the person of guiding knowledge,
To every sage 'tis a great question. The question.

There was also a poem in the Old Book of Caillin at Fidnacha which was our examplar, the beginning of which we cannot find. And here is the fragment we have found of it; because the Comharb of Caillin who caused us to write the book, does not wish that we should not write it, though its beginning is not forthcoming. Hoc est.[1]

Aedh is the first man who'll me torment;
But I will not come in his time.
He'll take the school bands from my Druim,[2]
And two-thirds of its possessions.
But though they be quiet for a time,
In Druim,[2] at length, by my will,
Their deceit shall on them recoil—no lie—
To implore me they'll be compelled.
A prodigy[3] will come;
And I hide it not from all.
And never on the plain of Siuir[4]
Will come his like of the Ui-Briuin.
Tigernan[5] is name of the manifest king;
Tigernach is my own name;
The Psalms do here relate,
That our names are identical.
To you[6] belongs his stainless mother,
And his father to Maedhog,[7]

the plain of Siuir" (which would be nonsense, for *Siuir* is the Irish name of the river Suir, with which the Hy-Briuin of Breifne had no connexion), or like ni uiᵹ ꞅiuiꞃ, which seems quite unintelligible.

[5] *Tigernan.* The person here referred to was probably Tighernan O'Rourke, king of Breifne, slain by Hugo De Lacy in 1172.

[6] *To you.* The poet was apparently addressing some one of the clann to which the mother of Tighernan O'Rourke belonged.

[7] *to Maedhog.* St. Maedhog was abbot of Drumlaine, in the co. Cavan, which in the 12th cent. was included in the territory ruled by the O'Rourkes.

Do berthar d'fer na cét part,
Nem ocus bas in airechd.
Loisgfither orra as gaċ aird,
Betitt huili fo muiċ marb,
Bid bechd brig Brefnech na mbraṫ,
In traṫ erges Aed engaċ.
Bid he in duinebad co nim,
Int Oed Engaċ a Cruaċuin;
Cuirfid fo doeri in drem dil,
Co dia dardain sin Luaċair.
Ni Luaċair co luine léin,
Is terc nech thuiccer fo gréin;
Luacair ard i toeṫrat fir,
Ḟuiṫi ata alt in buanfir.
Ni mo ċin don chomdail cruaid,
Dambet fir na fuiglib fuait;
Diṫ ar danaraib co becht,
Scarfuidther Oed re ard nert.
Gid doirb dluig,
Aed sin ċaṫ do geba a guin;
Biaid a lecht co demin de
fol. 44, b. 1. 'Sa fert re Colum Cille.
Sin ard uar,
Do geba mac uge duad;
Noconaincenn e in sluag menn;
Biaid a ċend fo chasaib cuan.

[1] *in an assembly.* An allusion, probably, to the death of Tighernan O'Rourke. The Annals of the Four Masters state that he was slain at Tlachtgha (the Hill of Ward, near Athboy, co. Meath), which Cambrensis calls "O'Roric's hill." *Hib. Expug.* Lib. I, cap. xl.

[2] *Aedh Engach.* "Aedh the valiant." A person mentioned in Irish prophecies as destined to free Ireland from thrall. See *Annals of Loch-Ce*, ad an. 1537. See note [1], p. 376.

[3] *pestilence.* duinebad: lit. mortality.

[4] *Luachair;* or "heath." There are many places of this name in Ireland. The place here referred to has not been identified. It is evidently not the real name, as the "prophet" says that "few under the

To the man of the hundred parts will be given,
Heaven; and death in an assembly.[1]
They'll be oppressed from every point;
Will all in mortal sadness be.
The power of the deceitful Breifnians will be short,
When Aedh Engach[2] shall arise.
He'll be the poisonous pestilence[3]—
This Aedh Engach from Cruachan—
He'll put the faithful band in bondage,
Until the Thursday in Luachair.[4]
The Luachair of misfortune fierce;
Few under the sun comprehend it;
The high Luachair[4] where men shall fall—
Under it is the form of the lasting man.
My love is not for the combat fierce,
Where men shall be on gory biers.
Ruin shall on the Danars[5] fall;
His high power shall from Aedh depart.
Though hard the parting,[6]
Aedh in the fight shall receive his death-wound;
His grave will therefore surely be,
And his tomb, with Colum Cille.
In the cold Ard,[7]
Hugo's son[8] will hardship meet.
The great host cannot protect him—
His head shall be under the feet of troops.

sun comprehend it." The poet has indeed made it incomprehensible.

[5] *Danars.* Lit. "Danes;" but sometimes applied to Foreigners generally.

[6] *parting.* ɒluɪɣ. Only half the line is given in the orig., by which it is to be understood that the half given should be repeated.

[7] *Ard.* This clause should be repeated, to complete the line. The situation of the "Ard" has not been identified. The names of persons and places have been purposely mystified by the poet, or prophet.

[8] *Hugo's son.* This may be a reference to "William Gorm," son to Hugo De Lasci. See note [5], p. 72, *supra*.

[1]Mac in duind do geba braṫ,
Is lais do berthar in cath;
Do geba geognad is guin
O Aed engaċ sin irgail.
Biaid gair garb ma loċ ngabair;
Faoicfer fadb san beirn lemain,
Tuarsena timṫi don ar
Bet ma imlaib in lochan.
In caṫ sin is atai rad,
A Tigernaig na nai ngraḋ
Ca fad uainne d' aimsir sin,
Faillsig do chach a deimin.
Bliadain, da ḟicet, cuicc ced,
Eaḋ atchither dam, ni breg,
Co tabraid mac in Duinn cath,
Is na Goill don Aed engach.
Indered in mi marta,
Im traṫ teirti, san traṫsa,
Do berthar in cath acruim,
Dambia mor cleth tre ċoluinn.
Srainfid in saṫi sa thuaid;
Bid meḋon laiṫi don uair;
Lingfid bran do ċurp annsin,
I ngurt sreb i cnuc meadair.
Gid mor cath acruim cnesta,
Do beraid Gaidel festa,

[1] *Mac in Duinn.* "The son of the Donn (or chief)." If this was the "son of the Donn" referred to supra, p. 151 (i.e. Domhnall Og, son of Domhnall Mór O'Donnell), the battle of which the "prophet" speaks was the battle of Disert-da-chrich (now Desertcreaght), in the barony of Dungannon, co. Tyrone; fought in A.D. 1281, between the Kinel-Conaill and Kinel-Eoghain, in which Domhnall Og was slain. His opponent was Aedh Buidhe O'Donnell, son of Domhnall Og, son of Aedh Meith (or the Fat), who would therefore seem to be the person alluded to as "Aedh Engach." See note [2], p. 374.

Mac in Duinn[1] will be betrayed.
By him the battle will be fought.
He'll wounds and injuries receive
From Aedh Engach,[2] in the fight.
A fierce wail shall be round Loch-gabhair,[3]
Weapons will be left in the lion's gap;
Relics of the cruel slaughter,
That round the borders of the lake shall be."
"This battle of which thou speakest,
O Tigernach[4] of the nine grades—
How long is that time from us?
Explain to all the certainty."
"A year, forty, five hundred,
Is the time manifested to me, no lie,
Until *Mac in Duinn*[1] gives battle,
And the Galls, to Aedh Engach.[2]
In the end of the month of March,
At the hour of tierce, at this hour,
The battle will be fought, which I proclaim,
Where lances large shall through bodies be.
The men[5] will succeed towards the North;[6]
The hour will be the middle of day;
Ravens will perch on bodies then,
In a course field on Cnoc-Medhair.[7]
Though many the battles, I mildly proclaim,
The Gaeidhel shall thenceforward fight;

[2] *Aedh Engach.* See last note.

[3] *Loch-Gabhair.* This is the name of the lake of Lagore, co. Meath. But some northern lake of the same name must be intended.

[4] *Tigernach.* From the allusion to the "nine grades," it would seem that Tigernach was an ecclesiastic; but nothing is known regarding him. He could not have been the same as the annalist Tigernach.

[5] *men.* ꞅaṫi, a multitude (lit. "swarm.")

[6] *towards the North.* ꞅa ꞇhuaıꝺ. Apparently for ꝼa ꞇhuaıꝺ; "northwards."

[7] *Cnoc-Medhair.* Not identified.

Is he in caṫ sin lerr leod
 Mo do ber Eri ar aneol.
Mairg do Cruaċuin dar cinned;
 Biaid gair huaṫmar ma Oilech;
 Biaid Eri ar tuitim annsin,
 Acht gid cian uain, a Cruimthir.
Biaid nert Brefnech fo ṫemair,
 Areir ċaṫa cnuic Medair;
[a] fol. 44, b. 2. Ni demaitt[a] cert man tir thair,
 Is gebtait nert air Chruachain.
Gebtait Conmaicni gan crad
 Ferann foda re farrann;
 Gebtait in grinde mor mer,
 Gan chlod co Bile ṫened.
Risin fingalaċ naċ fann,
 Bed a mnai co hutmall,
 Ma fer lonncraiti ar gaċ leṫ,
 Biaid Conmaicne co coscrach.
Cuirfid gleo garb re Gall,
 Ni ba fer fann re fedain;
 Ni maiti da bidbadaib band;
 Re a imguin noċon anand.
Tres na crandċa, tres in chluid,
 Ocus tres na mona amuig;
 Tres timdibech Muigi Treg,
 Lasin fingalach fertar.

[1] *Cruachan.* Rathcroghan, co. Roscommon.

[2] *Ailech.* See note [3], p. 62.

[3] *Cruimther.* This poem, of whose authorship we know nothing, seems to have been addressed to Cruimther-Fraech, patron of Cluain-Fraich (or Cloonfree), co. Leitrim, already referred to. See note [1], p. 192.

[4] *eastern land;* i.e. the country about Tara.

[5] *Bile-Tenedh.* Lit. "Fire-tree." Said to be the place now called Billywood, par. of Moynalty, bar. of Lower Kells, co. Meath.

[6] *Fingalach.* An epithet signifying "fratricidal." The individual to whom it was applied has not been identified; but

That fatal, wounding battle 'tis
That Ireland will distract the most.
Woe to Cruachan,[1] for which it was destined.
Round Ailech[2] will be a fearful wail.
Ireland will be a-falling then;
But still it is far from us, O Cruimther.[3]
The Brefnian power shall be over Tara,
After the battle of Cnoc-Medhair.
They'll not observe right tow'rds the eastern land,[4]
And will obtain sway over Cruachan.
The Conmaicne without anguish will get
Extensive lands, by violence;
The great, cheerful band shall get,
Without defeat, to Bile-Tenedh.[5]
By the Fingalach[6] not weak
Their battle dresses will be kept busy;
'Gainst angry men on every side,
The Conmaicne will triumphant be.
He'll wage fierce battle against the Galls;
No weak man he to bear command.
Before his foes he budges not;
Nor waits he to receive the wound.
The battle of the Crannach,[7] the battle of Clud;[8]
And the fight of the Moin[9] outside;
The destructive battle of Magh-Tregh,[10]
Will by the Fingalach be fought.

he was probably Ualgharg O'Rourke, ob. A.D. 1231. *Vid. supra*, p. 68, n [1].

[7] *Crannach.* This seems to be the place elsewhere called Crandchain. See notes [6], [7], p. 77, *supra.*

[8] *Clud.* Not identified.

[9] *Moin.* "Moin" means a bog. In the reference above made (p. 77) to the battle of Crannagh, or Crandchain, the field of battle is stated to have extended "from the Moin (bog) unto the river."

[10] *Magh-Tregh.* A plain in the co. Longford, called Moytra in Anglo-Norman documents. The extent of Moytra is defined in an Inquisition taken at Ardagh on the 10th of April, in the 10th year of the reign of James I. It included the parish of Clongesh, bar. of Longford.

Brised brosnach mor amach,
Ar na Galloib re clod crech;
Brath nach cinntig do cach tig
A cath impir a nessbaid.
Biaid mongar mor is braisi
Alla thes do Chill glaisi,
In la bid cletmar na fir,
Ma echraid bid ain imguin.
Ni Fingalach for na fras,
Do ber ar Galloib garb tress,
Ma buaib ar fud in feda,
Ni ba huain na hinnreda.
Soscel do gach anmuin truaig,
Dliges dilgad co la in luain.
Rig inallaid os gach muig,
Tig sir na Galloib, abair.[3]

* fol. 45, a. 1.

Teoru clandu Fergusa for a longus co Mumnecha .i. Mod Taeth, or chinset Ciarraighe Luachra ocus Cuirche, ocus hui Choindend, ocus Conmaicni uili. Cland Fir doichet, Corcumruad. Fertlachtga, or chinset na cethre hArad .i. .h. Monan, ocus .h. Fidmuine, ocus Artroigi, ocus Teochraide. Do cloind Fergusa dono fir Muigi Feine, ocus fir olechd fiac dontair conarrad side.

[1] *Imper.* The place now called Emper, in the barony of Rathconrath, co. Westmeath. The details of the battle are not known to the Editor.

[2] *Cill-glaisi.* Probably the place now called Kilglass, in the co. Longford.

[3] *say.* The words abair frim ("Say to me,") with which the poem commenced, are added here, in token of its conclusion. But the earlier portion is unfortunately missing; and the Editor has not discovered a perfect copy of it. Some lines unconnected with the subject of the poem are added at the end of fol. 44, b 2, which are not worth reproducing.

[4] *Fergus.* See notes [7], [8], p. 31, and note [6], p. 174.

[5] *Modh Taeth.* This was an *alias* name for Ciar, son of Fergus, by Queen Medhbh, and ancestor of the septs called Ciarraidhe.

[6] *Ciarraighe-Luachra.* The ancient inhabitants of the northern part of the co. Kerry.

[7] *Ciarraighe-Chuirche.* The tribe that gave name to the present barony of Kerricurrihy, co. Cork.

A scattering rout will he inflict
On the Galls, with loss of preys.
A doom unknown to all shall come—
Their loss in the battle of Imper.[1]
There will be great shouting and excitement,
To the south of Cill-glaisi,[2]
The day the men shall warlike be,
In mortal strife about their steeds.
The Fingalach of the showers, still,
Will o'er the Galls a fierce battle gain;
About their kine, along the wood,
Not slow shall the plunderings be.
May the Gospel reach to each poor soul
Deserving forgiveness, to the day of doom.
May the glorious King over every land
Oppose the foreigners, and say.[3]

The three sons of Fergus[4] exiled to the Munstermen were, Modh Taeth,[5] from whom descended the Ciarraighe-Luachra,[6] and the [Ciarraighe]-Cuirche,[7] and the Ui-Choinnend,[8] and all the Conmaicne.[9] The Corcomruadh are the descendants of Fer Doichet;[10] Fer Tlachtgha, from whom the Four Aradhs[11] are descended, to wit, the Ui Monan, and Ui Fidhmuine, and the Artroighi, and Teochraide. Of the descendants of Fergus, also, are the Fir-Muighe-Feine,[12] and Fir Dlechd;[13] from Fiach Dontair they are called.

[8] *Ui-Choinnend*, or Ciarraighe-Choinnend. *See* O'Flaherty's Ogygia, part III., cap. xlvi.

[9] *Conmaicne*. There is some error here; for the Conmaicne were the descendants of Conmac, son of Fergus.

[10] *Fer Doichet*. An *alias* name for Corc, son of Fergus Mac Roy.

[11] *Aradhs*. These tribes were seated in the present counties of Limerick and Tipperary. See O'Donovan's ed. of the Book of Rights, p. 46, note [e].

[12] *Fir-Muighe-Feine;* i.e. the tribes anciently inhabiting the present baronies of Fermoy, and Condons and Clongibbons, co. Cork.

[13] *Fir-Dlechd*. There is apparently some error here. In Mac Firbis's genealog. work this clause reads, "Fer-Dechead, or Fiach, son of Fergus—from him these are."

Clann Medba la Fergus .i. Ciar ocus Corc ocus Conmac, ocus Ulland ocus Elim, Corru ocus Corp ulumb.

D'oen breith ructha Ulaim ocus Corru, da mac Fergusa; ocus is amlaid rucṫa Corru ocus cluas Ulaim ina beolu, iar na tesgad de.

Genealach Conmaicni ainso.

Coicc meic Cumscraig mic Cechta mic Eirc mic Erdail mic Cechta mic Duib mic Medruaid, mic Nerta mic Fornerta, mic Cechta, mic Uisle, mic Beirri, mic Beidbi [mic Doilbri] mic Luigdech Conmaic, (a quo Conmaicni), mic Oirbsin mair (a quo loch nOirbsin), mic Sethenoin, mic Segda, mic Aitri, mic Alta, mic Ogamuin, mic Fidchuire, mic Doilbri, mic Eona, mic Calusaig, mic Mochta, mic Mesamuin, mic Moġa taeth, mic Conmaic, mic Fergusa, .i. Fraech, Findfer, Findchaemh, Corchar, Ciri. Clann Findfir mic Cumscraig .i. Conmaicni rein isin
fol. 45, a. 2. Bresni. Clann Findchaim, Conmaicni Chuili ocus Conmaicni mara. Clann Corcair, Conmaicne bec Mide. Ciri is uad cinel Cirend i crich mac nErci. Clann Fraich mic Cumscraig, Cas a quo cenel Cais; Lugna, a quo cenel Lugna; Duban, a quo cenel Dubain.

Genealach .h. Crechain ainso.

Crechan, mac Angaili mic Fadaluiġ, mic Findtain, mic Aeda, mic Luigdech mic na hoidċi, mic Dubain, mic Fraiċ, mic Cumscraig.

Findchaem, imorro, aen mac lais .i. Cairid. Ceṫra mic Caireda .i. Brug, Erc, Enna, Ainli.

Cenel nEnna; Maelbrenaind dall, mac Fechtgaile, mic Moċan, mic Indercait, mic Forraeda, mic Congen mic Congaeith, mic Cuanscrein, mic Carthainn, mic Enna, mic Caireda, mic Findchaeim, mic Cumscraig.

[1] *Cecht.* mc̄ cechta, MS.

[2] *Medhruadh.* "Maghruadh," supra, p. 4.

[3] *Loch-Oirbsen.* Lough Corrib, co. Galway.

[4] *Sethnon.* "Ethedon," *supra*, p. 4.

[5] *Atri.* "Art," *supra*, p. 4.

[6] *Conmaicni-Rein*; or Conmaicni of Moy-Rein, in the co. Leitrim.

[7] *Conmaicni-Chuile*; or Conmaicni-Cuile-Toladh, in the barony of Kilmaine, co. Mayo.

[8] *Conmaicni-Mara.* The people of Connemara, co. Galway.

[9] *Crich-mac-Erci.* Otherwise called Conel-mac-Ercc. See note [4], p. 230.

[10] *Cinel-Cais.* A sub-section of the

The children of Medhbh by Fergus were, viz.:—Ciar, and Corc, and Conmac, and Illand, and Elim, and Conri, and Corb Uluim.

At one birth [Corb-]Uluim and Conri, two sons of Fergus, were born; and the way Conri was born was, with Uluim's ear in his mouth, after having been cut off from him.

The Genealogy of the Conmaicni here.

The five sons of Cumscrach—son of Cecht,[1] son of Erc, son of Erdail, son of Cecht,[1] son of Dubh, son of Medhruadh,[2] son of Nert, son of Fornert, son of Cecht[1] son of Uisel, son of Beiri, son of Beidhbe, [son of Doilbhre], son of Lughaidh Conmac (*a quo* Conmaicni), son of Oirbsen the Great (*a quo* Loch-Oirbsen)[3], son of Sethnon,[4] son of Seghda, son of Atri,[5] son of Alta, son of Ogamun, son of Fidhchar, son of Doilbhre, son of Eon, son of Calusach, son of Mochta, son of Mesamun, son of Mogh Taeth, son of Conmac, son of Fergus—were Fraech, Findfer, Findchaemh, Copchas, and Ciri. The descendants of Findfer, son of Cumscrach, were the Conmaicni-Rein[6] in Breifni. The descendants of Findchaemh were the Conmaicni-Chuile,[7] and the Conmaicni-Mara.[8] The race of Copcas were the Conmaicni-Bec of Meath. Ciri; from him are the Cenel-Cirend in Crich-mac-Erci.[9] The sons of Fraech, son of Cumscrach, were Cas, *a quo* Cinel-Cais;[10] Lugna, *a quo* Cinel-Lugna;[11] Dubhan, *a quo* Cinel Dubhain.[12]

The Genealogy of O'Crechan[13] here.

Crechan, son of Angaile, son of Fadalach, son of Findtan, son of Aedh, son of Lughaidh-Mac-na-haidchi,[14] son of Dubhan, son of Fraech, son of Cumscrach.

Findchaemh, also, had one son, viz:—Cairid. The four sons of Cairid were Brug, Erc, Enna, Ainle.

The Cenel-Enna: Maelbrenainn the blind, son of Fechtgal, son of Mochan, son of Indescat, son of Forsaedh, son of Congen, son of Congaeth, son of Cuanscremh, son of Carthann, son of Enna, son of Cairid, son of Findchaemh, son of Cumscrach.

Conmaicne.

[11] *Cinel-Lugna.* Another section of the same family.

[12] *Cinel-Dubhain.* A branch of the Conmaicne seated in the barony of Dunmore, in the N. of the co. Galway.

[13] *O'Crechan.* The situation of this family is uncertain; but they probably belonged to the Cinel-Dubhain.

[14] *Mac-na-haidchi;* lit. "son of the night." But a marg. note suggests mic Naidech, "son of Naidech."

Genealach Commaicni Cuila Tola.[1]

Mughron mac Loingsig mic Cellaig, mic Adamnain, mic Clothachtaig, mic Lugdech, mic Ruadrach, mic Faelain, mic Aignighe, mic Findtain, mic Trena, mic Andlend, mic Brugad, mic Caireda, (is he ro slecht do Patraicc i Temraig),[2] mic Findchaeim, mic Cuimscraig. Item, Ferchar mac Conmaige mic Ailgile, mic Degail, mic Lugdach, mic Ruadrach. Item, Sochlachan mac Clotgaib, mic Oichi, mic Clothachtaig,[a] mic Lugdach, mic Ruadrach.

[a] fol. 45, b 1.

Maenach, mac Gaibredan mic Domgnaraich mic Suair, mic Selbaig mic Indellaig mic Bricine, mic Carnain, (diata cairthe Carnain),[3] mic Tail, mic Aindli, mic Caireda, mic Findchaim.

Genealach Commaicni Rein

TRI meic Onchon, mic Findloga, mic Findfir, mic Cuimscraig, .i. Nédi ocus Filled ocus Luachan. Se mic Neide, .i. Fingin, a quo sil Fingin; Findellach, a quo sil Findollaig; Fithrech, a quo sil Mailfithrich; Faelchu, a quo clann Faelchon; Maeltolla, a quo h. Baithir, ocus .h. Chorra; Fidlin a quo muintir Fidlin ocus muintir Macniad; ocus Carthach a quo Cruimther Fraech mac Carthaig.[4]

Coicc mic Fingine, mic Neide .i. Fibrainn, Maeldabrac, Mochan, Rechtabrand, Rindellach.

Coicc mic Fibraind mic Fingine, Maerne, Faelgus, Faall, Goll, Calbrann. Mac do Mairne Croman, a quo Clann-Cromain.

Tri mic Croman, Emin, Bibrach, Gillga, a quo muintir Gillgain .i. Tellach nGormgaili ocus Tellach Connucan ocus Tellach Maeilciarain. Emin mac Croman; mac do fein Angaili a quo muintir Angaili, .i. Tellach Congalain, ocus Tellach Finnachan,[b] ocus Tellach Floinn, ocus Tellach Scalaige. Bibrach, imorro, mac do sin Eolus a quo muintir

[b] fol. 45, b 2.

[1] *Cuil-Tola.* Now Kilmaine bar., co. Mayo.

[2] *Cairid.* See p. 157 *ante*, where Caillin is addressed as the descendant of Cairid, as a ua caid Caireda. The name of Cairid is not found in the pedigree of the saint given at the beginning of this volume; and if a descendant of Cairid's, he must have been so in the female line.

[3] *Cairthe-Carnain*; i.e. the pillar stone of Carnan. Not identified.

[4] *Cruimther-Fraech.* See note [1], p. 192.

The Genealogy of the Conmaicni of Cuil-Tola.[1]

Mughron, son of Loingsech, son of Cellach, son of Adamnan, son of Clothachtach, son of Lughaidh, son of Ruadhra, son of Faelan, son of Aignech, son of Findtan, son of Tren, son of Aindliu, son of Brugad, son of Cairid,[2] (who bent the knee to Patrick at Tara), son of Findchaemh, son of Cumscrach. *Item*, Ferchar, son of Cumaighe, son of Ailgil, son of Degal, son of Lughaidh, son of Ruadhra. *Item*, Sochlachan, son of Clothgabh, son of Oiche, son of Clothachtach, son of Lughaidh, son of Ruadhra.

Maenach, son of Gadredan, son of Domgnasach, son of Suar, son of Selbhach, son of Indellach, son of Bricin, son of Carnan, (from whom is the Cairthe-Carnain),[3] son of Tal, son of Ainle, son of Cairid, son of Findchaemh.

The Genealogy of Conmaicni-Rein.

The three sons of Onchu, son of Findlugh, son of Findfer, son of Cumscrach, were Neidhe, and Filledh, and Luachan. Neidhe had six sons, to wit, Finghin, *a quo* Sil-Finghin; Findellach, *a quo* Sil-Findellaigh; Fithrech, *a quo* Sil-Mailfithrigh; Faelchu, *a quo* Clann-Faelchon; Maeltolla, *a quo* Ui-Baithir and Ui-Chorra; Fidlin, *a quo* Muintir-Fidlin and Muintir-Maeniadh; and Carrthach, *a quo* Cruimther-Fraech,[4] son of Carrthach.

The five sons of Finghin, son of Neidhe, were Fibrainn, Maeldabhrach, Mochan, Rechtabrand, Rindellach.

The five sons of Fibrainn, son of Finghin, were Maerne, Faelgus, Faall, Goll, Calbrann. Maerne had a son, Croman, *a quo* Clann-Cromain.

The three sons of Croman were Emin, Bibhsach, Gillgan (*a quo* Muintir-Gillgain,[5] to wit, Tellach-Gormghaili, and Tellach-Connucan, and Tellach-Maelciarain). Emin, son of Croman, had a son Angaile, *a quo* Muintir-Anghaile,[6] to wit, the Tellach-Congalain, and Tellach-Finachan, and Tellach-Floinn, and Tellach-Scalaighe. Bibsach, also, had a son Eolus, *a quo* Muintir-Eolais,[7]

[5] *Muintir-Gillgain.* The tribe-name of the families of O'Quin and their correlatives, who occupied a large territory in the present co. Longford.

[6] *Muintir-Anghaile.* The tribe-name of the O'Farrells of Longford.

[7] *Muintir-Eolais.* The tribe name of the Mag Rannell (or Reynolds) family, co. Leitrim, and their immediate connections.

Eolais, .i. tellach Mailmuiri, ocus tellaċ Mailmartain, ocus tellaċ Cennetig, ocus tellaċ Cerballain, ocus tellaċ nOdrainn, et tellaċ nAinfeith, ocus tellaċ mBroagain.

Maeldabrac mac Fingin, mic Neide, a quo muinter Geradain .i. tellaċ Tanaide, ocus tellach Finnoigi, ocus tellach nGabaḋain.

Sirten mac Maildabrac, a quo muinter Siriten, .i. tellach Mailduin, ocus tellaċ Mailmiadaig.

Calbrann mac Fibrainn, a quo clann Calbruinn .i. Clann Martain, ocus cland Maildulige, ocus cland Bradain, ocus clann Arcain, ocus tellaċ nUanan.

Faal mac Fibraind, a quo muinter Eothaid .i. Cuachan a ainm .i. tellach Maengaili, ocus tellach Mailbelltaine; ocus Cainiḋe, a quo muinter Chainide.

Faelgus mac Fibraind, da mac lais .i. Maelconaill a quo muinter Conaill, .i. tellach Ciaragan, ocus tellaċ Cenddubain; Dubindri a quo .h. Brosgaid. Goll mac Fibrainn a quo .h. Brangusa. Mochan mac Fibrainn, no Fingin mē Neidi, a quo muinter Moran, ocus hi Chluman.

Rechtabrand mac Fingin, a quo .h. Mailtuili. Rindellach mac Fingin, a quo .h. Balban, ocus .h. Blosgaid, ocus .h. Derlaid.

[a] fol. 46, a 1.

Ite andso sil Findellaig,[a] mic Neide, .i. clann Fermaige, .i. na mna .i. clann Cellachan, ocus clann Mailtsamna, ocus clann Taeḃachain, ocus clann Uban, ocus clann Luġann, ocus clann Uanán.

ITE annso clann Findicci .i. na mna oili .i. clann Telline, ocus clann Cronan, et clann Ainnsin, ocus clann Chirdubain, ocus clann Finn, ocus clann Ciaracan, ocus clann Ibill.

Ite annso clann Faelgusai .i. clann Chorrdercain, ocus clann Gemain, ocus clann Chathusaig, ocus clann Dinnaċain, ocus clann Birin, ocus clann Anaire, ocus .h. Conbuide, ocus .h. Gellustain, ocus

[1] *Muintir-Geradhain.* Anglicè, Muntergeran. This tribe was situated in, and gave name to, a district in the north of the co. Longford, on the west side of Lough Gowna. The family name was Mac Finnbhairr (or Maginver), sometimes Anglicised Gaynor.

[2] *Muintir-Siriten.* The family (or sept)

to wit, Tellach-Maelmuiri, and Tellach-Maelmartain, and Tellach-Cendetigh, and Tellach-Cerbhallain, and Tellach-Odhrain, and Tellach-Ainfeth, and Tellach-Brogain.

Maeldabhrach, son of Finghin, son of Neidhe, *a quo* Muintir-Geradhain,[1] to wit, Tellach-Tanaidhe, and Tellach-Finnoigi, and Tellach-Gabhadhain.

Sirten, son of Maeldabhrach, *a quo* Muintir-Siriten,[2] to wit, Tellach-Maelduin, and Tellach-Maelmiadaigh.

Calbrann, son of Fibrainn, *a quo* Clann-Calbrainn; to wit, Clann-Martain, and Clann-Maelduilighe, and Clann-Bradain, and Clann-Arcain, and Tellach-Uanan.

Faal, son of Fibrainn, from whom are the race of Eothaidh (whose name was Cuachan); to wit, Tellach-Maenghaili, and Tellach-Maelbelltaine; and Cainidhe, *a quo* Muintir-Chainidhe.

Faelgus, son of Fibrainn, had two sons, viz:—Maelconaill, *a quo* Muintir-[Mael]Conaill, i.e., Tellach-Ciaragain, and Tellach-Cendubhain; Dubhindsi, *a quo* Ui Brosgaid. Goll, son of Fibrainn, *a quo* Ui Brangusa. Mochàn, son of Fibrainn (or of Finghin son of Neidhe), *a quo* Muintir-Moran, and Ui-Chlumhain.

Rechtabhrand, son of Finghin, *a quo* Ui Maeltuili. Rindellach, son of Finghin, *a quo* Ui Balban, and Ui Blosgaidh, and Ui Deslaidh.

Here are the descendants of Findellach, son of Neidhe; to wit, the Clann-Fermaighe, i.e. *na mna*,[3] viz:—the Clann-Cellachain, and Clann-Maelsamhna, and Clann-Taebhachain, and Clann-Ubhan, and Clann-Lughann, and Clann-Uanan.

These are the descendants of Finoice (i.e. the other wife); to wit, the Clann-Telline, and Clann-Cronan, and Clann-Ainnsin, and Clann-Chirdubhain, and Clann-Finn, and Clann-Ciaracan, and Clann-Ibill.

These are the descendants of Faelghus, viz:—the Clann-Corrdercain, and Clann-Gemain, and Clann-Cathusaigh, and Clann-Dinnachain, and Clann-Birn, and Clann-Anaire, and Ui Conbhuidhe, and Ui Gellustain, and Ui Riaglachain.

of Sheridan of Leitrim co.

[3] *na mna.* The meaning of this is not clear. *Na mna* is the nom. pl. and gen. sg. of *ind ben*, "the woman." For *na mna* we should probably read *na ced mna*, "of the first wife."

.h. Riaglachain. Ithe fil Mailifithrig mic Neide .i. clann Clothachtaig, ocus clann Oirechtaig. Ithe clann Micniad mic Fidlin mic Neide .i. Maenachan ocus Cuaille, ocus Maelagan, ocus Conmael ocus Cellachan. Ite clann Faelchon mic Neidi .i. Bradagan ocus Doraiden, ocus Ceirin ocus Maelenaig.

Luachan mac Onchon, a quo cinel Luachan; da mac lais .i. Dub ocus Find. Find, imorro, aen mac lais, .i. Maelgenn. Maeilgenn imorro, cethri mic lais .i. Tormadan, ocus Cuagan, ocus Cailti, ocus Maelpatraig. Aen mathair ag Maelpatraicc ocus ic Tormadan, ocus aen mathair con dias oili. Tormadan, imorro, .u. mic lais .i. Uarursci ocus in Cleirech, ocus Tanaide, Maelfinnen, ocus Maelmuadog. Da mac ac Uarursgi .i. Cu buide, ó bfuilet .h. Conbuide, ocus Gillasinaig,
fol. 46, a 2. o fuilet mic Gillasinaig. Tanaide o bfuil tellach Tanaidhe .i. mic Cuinn et mic Fachtnain. Tellach Maelfinden .i. meg Muiredaig ocus .h. Dimusaig. Tellach Cleirig .i. mic Gilli riabaig ocus mic in Crosain, ocus meg Donngaili. Cuacan, imorro, ocht mic lais .i. Orchad o fuilid meg Orchada; Maelfabuill, o fuilid muinter Maelfabuill; Sluagachan ó bfuilid meg Sluagachain; Caeman, o bfuilid meg Caoman; Cul re casan, ó bfuilid mic Cuil re casan; Cobthach o fuil meg Cobthaigh; Ceirr ciaban, o fuilit mic Cirr ciabain; Duban ó fuilid i Duban, o indri doiri Dubain.

Cailti mac Mailgind o fuilit .h. Chailti. Maelpatraicc mac Mailgind, o fuilid i Mailpatraicc.

Dub mac Luachain, tri mic deg lais .i. Eturran, o fuilid .h. Eturrain; Maelmocheirgi, o fuilit muinter Maelmocheirgi; Gabadan

¹ *Ui-Conbhuidhe*. This name would be Anglicised O'Conway, or Conway without the O'.

² *Mac Muiredaigh*. Or Mac Murray.

³ *Ui Dimusaigh*. Anglicè, O'Dempsey.

⁴ *Mac-in-Crosain*. This was the Irish form of the name of the present families of Crosbie of Kerry, and M'Crossan of Tyrone.

⁵ *Mac Donnghaile*. Anglicè, Mac Donnelly.

⁶ *Muintir - Maelfabhaill*. A family named O'Maelfabhaill furnished chiefs to the Lordship of Carraig-Brachaide, in Inishowen, in the 11th and 12th centuries. But they were not of the Conmaicne race.

⁷ *Mac Caemhains*. This name would be Anglicised M'Keevan; or Keevan,

The descendants of Maeltitrech, son of Neidhe, were the Clann-Clothachtaigh, and Clann-Oirechtaigh. The sons of Maeniadh, son of Fidhlin, son of Neidhe, were Maenachan, and Cuaille, and Maelagan, and Connael, and Cellachan. The sons of Faelchu, son of Neidhe, were Bradagan, and Doraidhen, and Ceirin, and Maelenaigh.

Luachan, son of Onchu, *a quo* Cinel-Luachain, had two sons, viz:—Dubh and Find. Find, moreover, had one son, viz:—Maelgenn. Maelgenn, however, had four sons, viz:—Tormadan, and Cuagan, and Cailti, and Maelpatraig. Maelpatraig and Tormadan had one mother; and the other two had one mother. Tormadan, also, had five sons, viz:—Uarusci, and "The Clerech," and Tanaidhe, Maelfinnen, and Maelmoedhog. Uarusci had two sons, viz:—Cubuidhe, from whom are the Ui Conbhuidhe,[1] and Gilla-Sinaigh, from whom are the Mac Gilla-Sinaighs. Tanaidhe: from him are descended Tellach-Tanaidhe, viz:—the Mac Cuinns, and Mac Fachtnains. Tellach-Maelfinnen, viz:—Mac Muiredaigh,[2] and Ui Dimusaigh.[3] Tellach-Cleirigh, viz:—Mac Gilla-Riabhaich, and Mac-in-Crosain,[4] and Mac Donnghaile.[5] Cuacan, moreover, had eight sons, viz:—Orchad, from whom the Mac Orchadas are descended; Maelfabhaill, from whom are Muintir-Maelfabhaill;[6] Sluagachan, from whom are the Mac Sluagachains; Caemhan, from whom are the MacCaemhains;[7] Cul-re-Casan,[8] from whom are the Mac Cuil-re-Casans; Cobhthach, from whom are the Mac Cobhthaighs;[9] Ceirr-Ciabhan, from whom are the Mac Cirr-Ciabhains; Dubhan, from whom are the Ui Dubhain,[10] from Inis-Doiri-Dubhain.[11]

Cailti, son of Maelgenn; from him are the Ui Chailti.[12] Maelpatraig, son of Maelgenn; from him are the Ui Maelpatraig.

Dubh, son of Luachan, had thirteen sons, viz:—Eturran, from whom are the Ui Eturrain; Maelmocherghi, from whom are Muintir-Maelmocherghi;[13]

without the "Mac."

[8] *Cul-re-Casan.* Lit., "back to the path."

[9] *Mac Cobhthaighs.* Mac Coffeys, or Coffeys.

[10] *Ui Dubhain.* O'Dubhains, O'Duanes, or Duanes.

[11] *Inis-Doiri-Dubhain.* The "Island of Dubhan's Oak-wood." Not identified.

[12] *Ui Chailti.* O'Keeltys, or Keeltys.

[13] *Muintir-Maelmocherghi.* The name of O'Maelmocherghi (from Maelmocherghi, "servant of the early rising") is now generally Anglicised "Early."

o fuilit i Gaḃadain; Damach o fuilit .h. Damaig; Eralb a quo .h. Erailb; Bathbarr a quo .h. Bathbarr; Muineċan a quo .h. Muinechain; Maelfuthain, a quo .h. Maelfuthain; Cianacan, a quo .h. Cianacain; Búiḃin a quo .h. Baiḃin; Braici a quo .h. Braici; Maelcain a quo .h. Maelċain; Treodmann a quo .h. Treodmainn.

* fol. 46, b 1. Filleḋ mac Onċon, aen mac lair .i. Naradaċ. Se mic Naradaig .i.* Rodachae, ocus Ailḃi; aonmathair occa .i. Beḃinn ingen Cernachain, mic Duiḃdothra; ocus is orrarin forasaigh Aḋomnan gan chlannugad fria a cheli co brath; Duinċine a quo .h. Duinchinne; Molt a quo .h. Muilt. Cu Ulad o fuil mic Conulad; Tormaḋ a quo .h. Tormaiḋ. IS iad sin mic na mban taide, ocus raidit foirenn conad dalta in Tormaḋ sin.

Ailbe a quo .h. Ailbe, ocus mac do Duḃroda a quo .h. Duḃroda. Rodachae, imorro, is do ro tiḋnaic Aḋamnan abdaine Fidnacha do gres, ocus da sil co brath. Fer leṫlama ocus lertha rig ocus tairis dib. Buaid comairci ocus nenig, ocus fad saegail do gach abad ina inad.

Tri mic Roidaichae .i. Maengal, a quo .h. Maengaili, ocus Maeileoin donn, ocus Maeileoin finn; aen mathair acu. O Maeileoin finn atat mic Gilla Chair ocus mic Goill in Farais, ocus mic Mailḟeichin ocus mic Inairgiġ, ocus mic Sprengaluig, ocus mic in Chleirig. IS o maccaib in Chleirig gabthar abḋaine ocus óirchinnecht i Fidnacha do gres. Alaxandar ainm in Chleirig o a thurtidib. O Maileoin donn atat mic Gillachirr, ocus mic Gillacharraig, ocus mic Gilla find, ocus mic Gilla Muire.

[1] *Ui Muinechain.* O'Moynahan, or Moynahan.

[2] *Ui Cianacain.* O'Kenegan, or Kenegan.

[3] *Rodachae.* Ancestor of the family of O'Rody.

[4] *Dubhdothra.* The descent of this man is continued in the margin thus: son of Donnchadh, s. of Baethin, s. of Blathmac, s. of Felim, s. of Crimthan, s. of Scannlan, s. of Aedh Finn, s. of Fergna.

[5] *on these.* Or rather, on the children and descendants of Rodacha and Ailbe.

[6] *companion.* Fer leṫlama; lit. a "hand-man," or in common phrase, a right-hand-man. A marg. note has et

Gabadhan, from whom are the Ui Gabhadhain; Damach, from whom are the Ui Damaigh; Eralb, *a quo* Ui Erailb; Bathbarr, *a quo* Ui Bathbairr; Muinechan, *a quo* Ui Muinechain;[1] Maelsuthan, *a quo* Ui Maelsuthain; Cianacan, *a quo* Ui Cianacain;[2] Buibhin, *a quo* Ui Buibhin; Braici, *a quo* Ui Braici; Maelcain, *a quo* Ui Maelcain; Tredinan, *a quo* Ui Tredmain.

Filledh, son of Onchu, had one son, viz., Naradach. Naradach had six sons, viz:—Rodachae[3] and Ailbe, who had the same mother, to wit, Bebhinn daughter of Cernachan, son of Dubhdothra[4] (and it was on these[5] Adamnan imposed a command never to intermarry with each other); Duinchine, *a quo* Ui Duinchinne; Molt, *a quo* Ui Muilt; Cu-Uladh, *a quo* Mac Conuladh; Tormadh, *a quo* Ui Tormaidh. These are the sons of the concubines; and some persons say that this Tormadh was a foster-son.

Ailbe, *a quo* Ui Ailbhe: Dubhroda, *a quo* Ui Dubhroda, was son to him. To Rodachae it was, moreover, that Adamnan presented the abbacy of Fidnacha in perpetuity, and to his race for ever. Of them shall always be a companion[6] and bed-fellow of a king and chieftain. Every abbot in his [Caillin's] place shall have the palm of protection and honour, and length of life.

Rodachae had three sons, to wit, Maengal, *a quo* Ui Maenghaili, and Macleoin the Brown, and Macleoin the Fair. They had the same mother. From Macleoin the Fair are [the families of] Mac Gilla-Chais, and Mac Goill-in-Fasaigh, and Mac Maelfeichin, and Mac Inairgigh, and Mac Srengalaigh, and Mac-in-Chlerigh. From the sons of "the Clerech" the abbotship and herenachship in Fidnacha are always filled. (Alexander was the Cleric's name from his parents). From Macleoin the Brown are (descended) the Mac Gilla-Chirrs, and Mac Gilla-Charraighs, and the Mac Gilla-Finds, and Mac Gilla-Muires.

coṁairle et cogair rig dib, ocus caḋais ocus oirechtais, ocus buaiḋ n-oilithre for gach abad in inad Caillin tre bithu beṫa; "and of them shall be royal counsellors and confidants, and [men] of honour and authority; and the palm of pilgrimage shall belong to every abbot in Caillin's place for ever and ever." This note should probably be included in the text; but the copyist left no mark to indicate where it should be inserted.

a fol. 46, b. 2. Genealaċ .h. Rodaichae sunna in bfechtsa .i. comarba Fidnacha Muigi Rein mu fiadnuse.a

Genealach abaḋ Fiḋnacha.

TADG,[1] imorro, ainm in chomarba ḟollaṁnaiġes Fiḋnacha in tan-sa. IS he fodruair in leḃar sa do lesuġaḋ ocus do núaḋorúgaḋ do, daiġ ro arsaig ocus ro urchraid in chairt i raibe fein leabar Caillin ria sunn, ocus dono ni raibe acht tra metar abain cus anos; ocus ta ina sgelaib ocus drechtaib budesto.

Brian imorro, et Uilliam, a da derbrathair an Taidg sin, ag forcongra choraigṫi in liubair sos.

Dar mo debrod ni uilid tri naitni chothaigti a cuingi fein .i. aeḋeḋchairi choitchenn d'feraib Erenn, et gan diultad re dreich nduine itir lo ocus oiḋċi, i cill na i congbail in Erinn, iar na mbreṫ d'aen lanaṁuin, is ferr ina in triarsa .i. Tadg .i. in comarba, et Brian ocus Uilliam .i. tri mic Taidg.

mic Uilliam,
mic Matha,
mic Robet,

mic Seaain,
„ Lucais,
„ Ele,
„ Gilla na naem,
„ Egnig,
„ Gilla muire,
„ Gilla beraig,
„ Domnaill,
„ Aeda,
„ Mailmichil,
„ Mail muire,
„ Gilla Isa,
„ Mailmichil,

mic Feichin,
„ Mail Isa,
„ Gilla crist,
„ Gormgaile,
„ Gilla Manchain (.i. in Caillinech),
„ Argail,
„ Alaxandair .i. in clerech,
„ Maileoin find,
„ Rodiachae,
„ Uaradaiċ,
„ Fillid,
„ Onċon.

[1] *Tadhg.* The following genealogy has been printed, from MS. A, by O'Donovan,

The genealogy of O'Rody here now, to wit, the Comharb of Fidnacha of Magh-Rein, in new testimony.

The Genealogy of the Abbot of Fidnacha.

Tadhg, then, is the name of the Comharb who governs Fidnacha at this time. It was he who caused this book to be amended, and newly arranged for him, because the vellum in which Caillin's Old Book was before this time had grown old and decayed; and, moreover, it was only in metre until now; and it is in stories and poems from henceforth.

Brian then, and William, the two brothers of this Tadhg, were also commanding the arrangement of the Book.

By my God of judgment there are not, in church or house in Ireland, born of the same couple, three better props than these three, for maintaining their own obligation, to wit, to dispense general hospitality, without offering refusal to the countenance of man, both day and night, viz., Tadhg,[1] i.e. the Comharb, and Brian, and William, viz.:—three sons of Tadhg,

son of William,
son of Matthew,
son of Robert,

Son of John,
,, Luke,
,, Ele,
,, Gilla-na-Naemh,
,, Egnech,
,, Gilla-Murry,
,, Gilla-Beraigh,
,, Domhnall,
,, Aedh,
,, Maelmichil,
,, Mael-Murry,
,, Gilla-Isa,
,, Maelmichil,

Son of Feichin,
,, Mael-Isa,
,, Gilla-Christ,
,, Gormgal,
,, Gilla-Manchan (i.e. the Caillinech),
,, Ardgal,
,, Alexander (i.e. the Cleric),
,, Maeleoin the Fair,
,, Rodachae,
,, Naradach,
,, Filledh,
,, Onchu,

in the *Miscellany of the Celt. Soc.*, vol. I., p. 113; but not with his usual accuracy.

mic Finnloga,
" Finnfir,
" Cumsgraich,
" Ceuchd,
" Eairc,
" Earcbair,
" Echd,
" Duib,
" Meadhruaid,
" Nearta,
" Foirnearta,
" Eacht,
" Uisle,
" Beurra,
" Beidbe,
" Luighdioch Conmaic a quo Conmhaicne,
" Oirbrean mair,

*fol. 47, a 1.

mic Eitheanoin,
" Seghdo,
" Roighno,
" Aithre,
" Alta,
" Oghamain,
" Fiochaire,
" Doirbre,
" Eona,
" Cheudguine-calasaigh,
" Measamhain,
" Mogha taoith .i. mhogha doid,
" Conmhaic,
" Feargusa,
" Rosa,
" Rudhraighe,
" Sitrighe, 7c.[1]

CAIRBRE, Eogan, Enna eim,
Ocus Conall mor mac Neill;
Is misi is eolach don droing,
Roinn a triucha 'sa torainn.

[1] *Sitrech;* or Sithrigh. At the end of the foregoing genealogy, fol. 46, b., Thady O'Rody has furnished the links between himself and the Tadhg with whom the genealogy begins, thus:—

Mise Taidg O Rόdaige, mac Gearoid oig, mic Taidg, mic Gearόid, mic Taidg, mic Taidg, mic Uilliam, ut supra, 1688. "I am Tadhg O'Rody, son of Gerald junior, son of Tadhg, son of Gerald, son of Tadhg, son of Tadhg, son of William, *ut supra*. 1688."

In the foregoing pedigree, which differs but slightly from the pedigree of St. Caillin above printed (pp. 4—7)—the number of generations being the same in both from Cumscrach, the common ancestor of St. Caillin and Tadhg O'Rody,

Son of Findlugh,	Son of Eithedon,
" Findfer,	" Seghda,
" Cumscrach,	" Roighne,
" Cecht,	" Aithre,
" Erc,	" Alta,
" Eredar,	" Ogaman,
" Echt,	" Fidchar,
" Dubh,	" Doirbre,
" Medhruadh,	" Eon,
" Nert,	" Cedguine-Calasagh,
" Fornert,	" Mesamhan,
" Echt,	" Mogh Taeth, i.e. Mogh Doid,
" Uisel,	" Conmac,
" Berra,	" Fergus,
" Beidbhe,	" Ros,
" Lughaidh Conmaic, *a quo* Conmaicne,	" Rudhraighe,
" Orbsen Mór,	" Sithrech, &c.[1]

CAIRBRE,[2] Eoghan, active Enna,
And great Conall, son Niall—
'Tis I that am learned [in regard] to the band,
The division of their cantreds, and their mearings.

to Rudhraighe son of Sithrech—there are altogether sixty-six generations between Tadhg O'Rody, (*ob. circa* 1704), and Rudhraighe son of Sithrech. Allowing thirty years as the average length of a generation, this would refer Sithrech's period to about 280 years B. C. His great grandson Fergus Mac Rosa (or Fergus Mac Roy) is generally stated, however, to have lived in the early part of the first cent. of the Christian Era; and if this be so, the chronology of the pedigree is about 160 years astray.

[2] *Cairbre.* There is no other copy of this poem, as far as the Editor is aware, to be found in any other Irish MS. In O'Donnell's Life of St. Columba, Rawlinson, 514 (Bodleian Library, Oxford), where it is referred to, the poem is quoted as from "Caillin's Old Book."

Tri triucha Conuill na cath,
Is a tri con triar menmnach;
Gur tsinsed uaithib amach
Cland Eogain mic Neill neimnech.
Tricha Cairbri mic in rig,
O abuind móir go Call crín.
O Chall crin osin alle,
Gus in call cain i foithre.
Tricha Esa ruaid re baig,
Maigrich iasgaich inberaich,
O chall cháin na crobang cas
Co hEdnich torainn dtrenglais.
Triucha Bagune mblechta,
Eolchai de lucht na quesda;
O Ednič co Dobar ndil,
Silius as na garb sleibtib.
On Dobar dirsgir cedna,
Tricha Luigḋech mic sedna,
Cus in abainn is glan li,
Danap comainm Suilidi.
Tricha Enna siar arrin,
Co Bernus mór, co Sruthair,
Tarbach tir Enna na ngread,
Soir co Fernach na feinneḋ.

[1] *Trichas.* For the contents of the Irish *Tricha-ced*, or cantred, see Dr. Reeves's paper on the *Townland Distribution of Ireland;* Proceedings of the R. I. Academy, vol. 7, p. 474, *sq.*

[2] *Abhain-mor;* i.e. "the great river;" the Avonmore, a river which rises in Templehouse lake, and joins the Coolany river between Collooney and Ballysadare, co. Sligo.

[3] *Call-crin;* i.e. "the withered hazel." Its position has not been indentified. But it must have been near Ballyshannon.

[4] *Call-cain in Foithre,* or the "fair hazel in Foithre." "Foithre" means a wood. The position of this *Call-cain* has not been ascertained, but it was probably in the northern extremity of the present barony of Carbury, co. Sligo.

[5] *Tricha of Es-Ruaidh;* or cantred of Assaroe; corresponding to the present barony of Tirhugh, co. Donegal.

Three *Trichas*[1] had Conall of the battles,
And three the spirited trio had;
And out from them did spread
The vigorous clann of Eoghan MacNeill.
The *Tricha* of Cairbre, the king's son,
Was from Abhain-mor[2] to Call-crin;[3]
From Call-crin thence hither,
To the Call-cain in Foithre.[4]
The *Tricha* of Es-Ruaidh[5] the famous,
Salmony, fishy, full of pools,
Was from Call-cain of the fair nut-clusters,
To the green, loud-sounding Edhnech.[6]
The *Tricha* of Boghuine[7] of the kine,
As the inquiring people know,
Was from Edhnech to the deluging Dobhar,[8]
That from the rugged mountains flows.
From the same impetuous Dobhar,
The *Tricha* of Lughaidh, son of Setna,
Extends to the river of clear aspect,
The name of which is Suilidhi.[9]
Enna's *Tricha*[10] then westward spreads,
To Bernas-Mor,[11] and to Sruthair.[12]
The rich land of Enna of the studs extends
Eastwards, to Fernach[13] of the Fians.

[6] *Edhnech.* The river Enny, which falls into the bay of Donegal.

[7] *Tricha of Boghuine.* Corresponding to the present barony of Boylagh and Banagh, co. Donegal.

[8] *Dobhar.* The Gaeth-Dobhair, or Gweedore river, co. Donegal.

[9] *Suilidhi.* The river Swilly. Fuilidh (for Suilidh), MS. From this it would appear that the territory of Cinel-Luigdech nearly comprised the present barony of Kilmacrenan.

[10] *Enna's Tricha;* otherwise called Cinel-Enna. See note [4], p. 314.

[11] *Bernas-Mór;* or the great gap. See note [5], p. 314.

[12] *Sruthair.* Written Sruthail *supra*, p. 314. See note [6], *ib.*

[13] *Fernach.* Now Farnagh, parish of Aughnish, barony of Kilmacrenan, co. Donegal.

Triucha Eogain moir na rend,
A tonngairi ina timchell;
On tuinn brisius risin sruib,
Co tarbhan charda in chomthnuiḋ.
Nir miad la sil Eogain uill
Beṫ ar én triucha ferainn;
Sinit a narma catha,
Co riachdar Ard mor Macha.
Ard Macha ag sil Eogain uill,
Ocus Doiri ac sil Conuill[a]; [a] fol. 47, a 2.
Druim chliab ac sil Cairbre chain,
Gen gur miad le Connachtaib.
A buidi sa benidecht,
Curap sosad dom anmuin;
Is truag̃ lem mo deg̃ oirecht,
Mar do luid orra Cairbre.
Eogan agmar innsaig̃thech,
Rochlecht ruathar is airgne;
Ge ro sgailit a clanna,
Rob hi a chuid ranna Cairbri.

ESTID re Conall calma,
Ocus re hEogan ampa;
Mar do rinnedar an ndail
I mullach droma Cruachain.

[1] *Srubh;* i.e. Srubh-Brain, for the situation of which see note [2], p. 314.

[2] *Tarbhan.* The scribe first wrote tarrcham, but added a b over the c, as if he desired to correct the name to Tarbhan. *Tarbhan* would signify a "little bull"; and was probably the name of some whirlpool, or rapid, on the Foyle near Derry.

[3] *Ard-Macha.* Armagh.

[4] *Druim-Cliabh.* Drumcliffe, co. Sligo; here put for the barony of Carbury, in which it is situated.

[5] *pressed.* The writer here seems to imply that the descendants of Cairbre

The *Tricha* of great Eoghan of the spears,
Surrounded by its roaring wave,
Was from the wave that breaks against the Srubh,[1]
To the curling, envious Tarbhan.[2]
The race of great Eoghan did not like
To be confined to one cantred of land;
So they extended their arms of battle,
Until they reached great Ard-Macha.[3]
Ard-Macha[3] belongs to Eoghan's race,
And Derry to the race of Conall;
The seed of mild Cairbre have Druim-Cliabh,[4]
Though the Connacians like it not.
May their thanks, and their blessings,
Conduce unto my soul's quiet.
But I grieve for my good people,
How Cairbre upon them pressed.[5]
The valorous, assaulting Eoghan,
Practised routs and plunders.
Though his children have separated,
His share of the division was Cairbre.[6]

LIST[7] ye to the mighty Conall,
And to illustrious Eoghan—
How they effected their arrangement
On the top of Cruachan's ridge.[8]

seized upon a part of the territory now forming the county of Leitrim.

[6] *Cairbre.* The last word is repeated, to signify the conclusion of the poem; but the sense of the last line is not very clear.

[7] *List.* This poem is quoted from "Caillin's Old Book," in O'Donnell's Irish Life of St. Columba, already referred to.

[8] *Cruachan's ridge.* Previously called Cruachan-Lighen, or Druim-Lighen. See note [1], p. 338.

Adubairt Eogan gan feill,
  Dena a roind duin a Conaill,
  Cairbre sluagbuidnech na crech,
  Ocus Enna irgalach.
Mad misi randus na fir,
  A derim rit a Eogain,
  Nach bfuiġbe caem na cara,
  Raġa uaimsi des ranna.
Noċon aitech duitsi soin;
  Ised atber re a brathair,
  [ ]at ar los chloidim chuirr
  O Eas Ruaid co Rus Irguill.
Da ċuinngi tu orrsa soin,
  Scaoilfid ar conne a Eogain;
  Biaiḋ agamsa sin rim gus,
[a] fol. 47, b 1. Na se triucha ro chosnuss.[a]
Adubairt Eogan co ceill,
  Fer reiḋigthe chloinne Neill,
  In te rus tangamar fecht,
  Tabramni do ar trindsirecht,
Do genfa fein roind daeibsi,
  'S do Chairbre beinne baeisi;
  Do ragtha duit he don roinn,
  No in naide Enna aluinn.
Leig dam Enna ar a oigi;
  Fail mo lama is mo doitti;
  Ni biasom mairc re la,
  Dar ab mo ssraicsi uasa.
Torċair let Cairpre de soin,
  Oir is let Enna amlaid;
  Da mera dam re nert nga,
  Saigfet ar chlannaib Colla.

[1] *Since thine.* The whole of the first, and a part of the second, of the corresponding words in the text have been obliterated.

The guileless Eoghan said,
"Make a division for us, O Conall;
'Twixt troopful Cairbre of the preys,
And the warlike Enna."
"If 'tis I that divides the men,
I say to thee, O Eoghan,
That nor companion nor friend shall get
A choice from me, after the division."
"Thou shouldst not insist on that,"
He (Eoghan) to his brother said,
"Since thine,[1] by virtue of the sharp sword,
Is from Es-Ruaidh to Ros-Irguill.[2]
"If thou askest this of me,
Our meeting must end, O Eoghan;
I shall have, by my valour,
The six cantreds which I have won."
Then said the sensible Eoghan,
The pacificator of Clann-Neill,
"To him with whom we a-hosting came,
Let us give seniority.
"I myself will make a division for you,
And for Cairbre the most simple;
He in the division shall be yours,
Or the youthful, handsome Enna."
"Leave me Enna, for his youth;
[By] my hand ring and finger ring,
He 'll not be sorrowful in his time,
Over whom my power shall be."
"Take with thee Cairbre, therefore,
Since Enna is also thine;
If I am able, by the power of spears,
I'll advance upon the clanns of Colla."

[2] *Ros-Irguill.* Now the district of Ross-Guill, in the parish of Mevagh, in the north of the co. Donegal.

Iarsin sgailit clanna Neill
A coimde Chruachain colleir,
Go menmnach ba mer a muirn,
Gaċ fer dib ċom a ḟeruinn.
Adubairt Enna in fer fial,
Ra Conoll, ra ndola siar,
Ro lucht chland Colla na crech,
Sunna is ail lem in ḟuirech.
Ac, a Enna, na cagair,
In ail dithai na habair,
Ergri co Doiri na ndam;
Faidfetsa anoir co Cruachan.
Gabas Enna a nDoiri dil,
Dun Chalgaich mic Aithemuin;
Gabais Conall cona droing
Siar co hEss ruaid mic Badoirn.
Desid Eogan co hOilech,
[a] fol. 47, b 2. In leoman[a] gan imḟuirech,
Ocas gabas Cairbri in aiġ
Siar co glend ndirech nDallain.
Ar faicsi Enna da ṫig,
Daig Eogan ag a áithigid;
Ger mac athar air do fell,
On ló rainic do Chonall.
Cuiris Enna techta siar,
Go Conall nGulban nglan fiall,
Da innisin tiar ga thoig,
Eogan air ig anáiġiḋ.
IS olc int adbar tnutha,
Ar Enna i cind in triucha;

[1] *Doire.* Derry, or Londonderry.

[2] *Cruachan;* or Cruachan-Lighen, now Drumleene, near Lifford.

[3] *fort of Calgach;* or Doire-Calgaigh, the ancient name of Derry.

[4] *Es-Ruaidh-mic-Badhuirn.* The Es (or Cataract) of Aedh Ruadh, son of Badhurn. See note [7], p. 325.

The Clann-Neill after that dispersed,
Altogether, from the Cruachan meeting—
Joyously—sprightly was their mirth—
Each man of them to his own land.
Enna, the generous man, did say
To Conall, before going westwards,
Against the plundering Clann-Colla,
"Here it is I fain would rest."
"No, Enna; say not so;
Utter not the sinful wish.
Go thou to Doire[1] of the troops;
I will stretch eastwards to Cruachan.[2]"
Enna settled in faithful Doire,[1]
The fort of Calgach,[3] Aitheman's son.
Conall with his band possessed
Westwards to Es-Ruaidh-mic-Badhuirn.[4]
The lion, Eoghan, proceeded
To Oilech,[5] without much delay;
And the valorous Cairbre possessed
Westwards, to straight Glenn-Dallain.[6]
On Enna's approach to his house,[7]
He found Eoghan occupying it;
Though his father's son, him he deceived,
From the day he (Enna) joined Conall.
Enna sends messengers westwards,
To generous, pure Conall Gulban,
To relate in the west, in his house,
That Eoghan was opposing them in the east.
"'Tis a bad cause of jealousy,"
Said Enna, anent the cantred;

[5] *Oilech.* Or Ailech. See note [3], p. 62, *supra*.

[6] *Glenn-Dallain.* A remarkable valley, situated partly in the co. of Sligo, and partly in Leitrim. The Church of Cill-Osnata, or Killasnet, in the barony of Rossclogher, is in it.

[7] *his house*; i.e. Derry.

Is in phurt na dóiġ d'ḟaġail
A longaiḃ do danaruiḃ.
Mois do mac mo mathar,
Mise ni lesc mo lathar;
Ersed amach mar do gell,
No fuirġed ṫall in Oilech.
Doiri longpurt Baedain binn
Ua Ainmirech mic Chonuill,
Remi ri bliadain gan fell,
Ar ngabail rige nErend.
Ba longpurt he d'Aed na mbend,
Doiri Chailgich na ngeben,
Gur ċuit ri Colam na cell,
Ar crabud ar crosfigell.
Tri riġ a Conall na cath,
Tainic re Colam craibdech;
Ised tucsadar a ngeill,
Co Doiri nuasal naigbeil.
Me air ċomairci in moir choimded,
Lo brisfidther na slebte;
Illo bratha na dreċan
Bid lethan lucht a essi.
Cominmain lem arsinde
Conall Eogan is Carbre
Ocas Enna fial malle,
Gar bé deired a nessi.

[1] *my mother's son;* i.e. Eoghan, who had the same mother as Conall Gulban, the speaker.

[2] *out.* amach. The scribe has written a b over the m; but abach, the alias reading suggested, meaning "dwarf," seems unsuitable.

[3] *Oilech.* See note [3], p. 62, *supra.*

[4] *Ainmire.* Rectè Fergus. Baedan, king of Ireland, who was slain in 571, was the son of Ninnidh, son of Fergus Cennfoda, (son of Conall Gulban). Ainmire was also a grandson of Fergus, by his son Sedna.

[5] *Aedh-na-mBenn;* i.e. Aedh, or Hugh, son of Ainmire, Monarch of Ireland; who was slain A.D. 594.

[6] *cros-figells.* Cros-figell is explained in O'Clery's glossary as "urnaigte, no

"'The place most likely to be taken,
From their ships, by the Danars."
"Say unto my mother's son,[1]
That my valour is not slothful;
Let him go out,[2] as he promised,
Or remain yonder in Oilech.[3]"
Derry was the seat of pleasant Baedan,
Grandson of Ainmire,[4] Conall's son,
Before, and for a year without fault,
After assuming the kingship of Ireland.
It was the seat of Aedh-na-mBenn[5]—
Was Doire-Chalgaigh of the fetters—
Till it fell to Colum of the Cells,
Thro' devotion, thro' *cros-figells.*[6]
Three kings,[7] from Conall of the battles,
Came before Colum the devout.
The place to which they their pledges brought,
Was formidable, noble Derry.
May I be under the great Lord's safeguard,
The day the hills shall sundered be;
On the sounding judgment day,
Great will be the number of his people.[8]
Equally dear to me, however,
Are Conall, Eoghan, and Cairbre,
And generous Enna likewise,
Though he is the last of the band,[9]

faire, do ní duine ar a glúinibh, ocus a lamha sínte a gcrois," i.e. "prayers, or vigils, which a man performs on his knees, and his hands stretched out in [the form of] a cross."

[7] *Three kings.* The three kings in question were—1, Ainmire, son of Sedna, slain 565; 2, Baedan, son of Ninnidh, slain 571; and 3, Aedh, son of Ainmire, slain in 594. The latter is stated to have presented Derry to St. Colum Cille.

[8] *his people.* Lucht a erri; the members of Colum Cille's company, whom he will have saved from perdition.

[9] *the last of the band.* Enna was the youngest of the sons of Niall Nine-hostager. The first line of the poem is here repeated, in token of conclusion.

AILLIN caid cumachtach,
Epscop uasal oirdnide,
Do rinde mor d'ḟir ḟertaib
  Ar gach tir ar nuair.
Tainic Caillin caemḟertach,
Is aingel ga forċongra,
Gurab and do suidestair,
  Ag dun mBaili mic Buain.
Do ṡir Caillin caemḟertach,
In tir ar ar suidestair,
No go ḃfuair in adnacal,
  Ina ḟarrad thall.
Conall mac Neill naigiallaig,
Cuig bliadan co leṫ fa mor ṫalmain,
Do faeth do laim Conachtaig,
  Isé do ḃui ann.
Atċuala clann chaem Conaill
Caillin caid cumachtach,
Nas lebaid a nard athar,
  Ar Muig roglan Rein;
Do sirset da ṡindsirechd,
Sen Chaillin do ṫathbeoaġ(ad),
  Chaem Chonuill mic Neill.
Tancatur clann chaem Chonuill
Co Caillin caid cumachtach,
  Co Fidnacha fir;
Tucsatar do Chailline,
A ċuairt is a cennaige,
  Ar dursad a riġ.

¹ *Caillin.* This is a very rare poem, no other copy of it being known to the Editor. It is in the same metre as the poems printed, pp. 154, sq., and 194, sq. That the metre is pretty old is plain from the fact that a poem in the same style, in praise of St. Colum Cille, is contained in *Lebor na hUidhre*, 15, a.

THE HOLY, powerful Caillin,[1]
The illustrious noble bishop,
Wrought many true miracles,
By turns in each land.
Fair wonder-working Caillin came,
An angel commanding him,
And the place where he settled was
At Dun-Baile-mic-Buain.[2]
Fair wonder-working Caillin searched,
The land that he had fixed upon,
Until he found the sepulchre,[3]
Near him yonder placed.
Conall, son of Niall Niaghallagh,
Who five and a half years buried lay,
Who fell by the hands of a Connachtman[4]—
'Twas he that was there.
When the clann of mild Conall heard
That holy, powerful, Caillin
Was over their great father's bed,
On sparkling Magh-Rein ;
They begged, for his seniority,
That old Caillin would resuscitate
Mild Conall Mac Neill.
The clann of mild Conall came
To holy, powerful Caillin,
To righteous Fenagh.
Unto Caillin they did give
His tribute and conditions,
For awaking their king.

[2] *Dun-Baile-mic-Buain* ; i.e. the fort of Baile, son of Buan. See note [10], p. 125.

[3] *sepulchre*. The grave of Conall Gulban. See note [1], p. 140.

[4] *Connachtman*. See above, pp. 89 and 139, where Conall Gulban is said to have been slain by the 'Masraidhe,' a Firbolg tribe who were seated in the neighbourhood of Fenagh.

Annsin ro sir Cailline,
Ar in coimde cumachtach,
    Anam Conaill cruaid.
Atracht Conall cornamach,
Tria ḟertuib in aird espcoip,
I fiadnuise in oirechta,
    Suas as in uaiġ.
[1]Assin tainig Adomnan,
Co Caillin caid cumachtach,
    Co fidnacha fein;
Dindsoiged in ardespcoip,
Gu ro leg a ḟoirsgela,
    Go rabat da reir.
Ann ro bennaig Cailline
Clanna Conaill cumrumaig,
    Ar nergi don riġ;
Rath cagad, rath comairli,
Rath riġi, rath nairechais,
    Rath cloinde, rath bid.[a]
[a] fol. 48, a 2.
Senais aris Cailline
Cenel Conaill cornamaig,
    Ar nergi dond rig;
Grain ced ar gach aen nonbar,
Grain nonbair ar aen duine,
Ag gabail daib airdrige,
    Ar gach tir do thir.
Assin tucad legaitecht
Innsi Erend ardmoire,
Do Chaillin chaid chumachtach,
    · Ar nergi dond rig.
Do chuaid Caillin cumachtach,
Air cuairt Erend ardmóiri,

[1] *him;* i.e. St. Caillin.

[2] *Caillin.* Cailline, MS.; the e being

Thereupon Caillin besought,
From the powerful Sovereign,
Hardy Conall's soul.
The vigorous Conall then arose,
Through the powers of th' archbishop
In presence of th' assembly,
Up from the tomb.
Afterwards came Adamnan,
To holy, powerful Caillin,
To Fidnacha itself;
To visit the archbishop,
Until he read his gospels all,
And all did him[1] obey.
Thereupon Caillin[2] did bless
The clanns of vigorous Conall,
After the king arose.
Luck of war and counsel [he gave them],
Of kingship and supremacy,
Of children, and of food.
Then Caillin again did bless
The vigorous Cenel-Conaill,
After the king arose;
"The strength[3] of a hundred in every nine,
The strength of nine in each man be,
When assuming arch-sovereignty,
From land unto land."
Then was given the legateship
Of Ireland's isle, exalted, great,
To holy, powerful Caillin,
After the king arose.
The powerful Caillin did go
On a circuit of great Ireland,

added to complete the number of syllables required by the metre.

[3] *strength.* ꝺ̄ꞃaın. This word properly signifies fear; but in a secondary sense the power to inspire fear.

Go raibe 'ga forcetal,
    Ar gach tir do thir.
Do ċuaid Caillin caemfertach,
I criċ Connacht chaom aluinn,
    Go rainig co Muaid.
Ua Fiachra is ua Amalgaid,
Do leigset do Chaillinc,
Co tarat leic Adamnan,
    Uair is he forfuair.
IS ann fagbuis Adomnan
Do chatraig chaoim Chaillini,
    Adrad ar a lar.
Bireċ ar do chathraigsi,
Uinge d'or da thabartur
Innti ar inad aen tige
    Co mac alla ann.
IAsrin tainig Caillini,
Iar cuairt Erenn ardmoire,
    Co Fidnaċa ar cul;
Gur ċuir uada Adamnan,
Co na srinn ċaid ċumdaiġthi,
I tir Fiachrach is Amalgaid,
    No gur gab in mur.
Cairnech, Cridan, Cairedan;

[1] *Ui-Fiachrach.* The descendants of Fiachra son of Eochaidh Muigh-medhoin, who gave name to the barony of Tir-Fiachrach, or Tireragh, co. Sligo.

[2] *Ui-Amalghaidh.* The descendants of Amhalgadh, or Awley, son of the foregoing Fiachra, who inhabited the territory now called Tirawley (Tir-Amhalghaidh), in the co. Mayo.

[3] *Lec-Adamnain;* i.e. Adamnan's flag. There is no reference to this flag in any of the tracts relating to Adamnan, unless it was the large flag forming the rude bridge called *Drehid-Awnan*, or "Adamnan's Bridge," near the old church of Skreen (Scrin-Adamnain), bar. of Tireragh. See Reeves' *Columba;* Introd., p. lxii.

[4] *floor.* This line is very loosely constructed, it being left in doubt whether Adamnan sanctioned the practice of worship in Caillin's church; or the use of his

So that he was instructing it,
    From land unto land.
Mild, wonder-working, Caillin went
To the fair, fine land of Connaught,
    Till he came to the Moy.
The Ui-Fiachrach,[1] the Ui-Amhalghaidh,[2]
Permission unto Caillin gave,
So that he brought Lec-Adamnain,[3]
    For 'twas he it that found.
'Twas then that Adamnan did leave
Unto mild Caillin's residence,
    Worship on its floor:[4]
Increase unto thy city be:
An ounce of gold, as tribute,
It shall have from every house-site,
    Wherein an echo[5] is."
Afterwards Caillin did come,
From visiting great Ireland,
    To Fenagh back again;
When he away sent Adamnan,
With his holy, covered shrine,[6]
To Tir-Fiachrach and [Tir]-Amhalghaidh,
    Until he reached the main.[7]
Cairnech,[8] Cridan,[9] Cairedan,[10]

flag-stone on occasions of worshipping.

[5] *echo.* m̄c alla, for mac alla. As an echo is rarely heard in any occupied house, the tribute here promised to Caillin could hardly have produced much.

[6] *shrine.* This shrine, or ſcpın, was preserved in the church founded by Adamnan in Tir-Fiachrach (or barony of Tireragh), co. Sligo, which obtained the name of "Skreen" from this circumstance. See Reeves' *Columba*; Introd., p. lxii.

[7] *main.* muıp, for muıpı, "the sea." The church of Skreen is not far from the bay of Sligo.

[8] *Cairnech.* See note [9], p. 217.

[9] *Cridan.* There were several Irish saints of the name of Critan, or Cridan. It is not easy to say which of them is here referred to.

[10] *Cairedan*; or Cairiotan, of Druim-Lara; whose festival was on the 7th of March, according to the Mart. Donegal.

Bricin, Iarlaithe co mbaid,
Feidlim, Deaga in deg ordain,
Mochaemog caid cumachtach,
Cruimther Fraech co mor fertaib,
Ocus Manchan* mirbailech;
Rob iatsin in mor muinter,
Popal Caillin caid.
Mo dub diglach degfertach,
Bid agat a Adomnain,
Bind a guth ra bein.
Bidh e in clagan Adomnain,
D'Uib Fiachrach, d'Uib Amalgaid,
'S do shil Chonuill Corcraig,
Mairg airech gus ricfasan
Mana beth da reir.
Gabais tnuth is mor formatt
Popal Caillin cumachtaig,
Ri hAdamnan adamru,
Gura chlaechlo a li.
Gurro cuirret Adomnan,
O a manchaib, o a mancheraib,
Andiaid Choluim chumahtaigh,
Ro go riachd co hI.
Ansin atbert Adomnan,
Ri Caillin caid cumachtach,
Bid agut mo manaigsi,
I bfagus, i cein.

* fol. 48, b 1.

[1] *Bricin.* Of Tuaim-drecain, or Tomregan, near the village of Ballyconnell, and on the frontiers of the counties of Cavan and Fermanagh. See O'Donovan's ed. of the *Battle of Magh Rath*, p. 283.

[2] *Iarlaithe.* St. Iarlath, patron of Tuam, co. Galway; ob. 481.

[3] *Feidhlim.* There are several persons of this name in the catalogue of Irish saints; but the individual here referred to was probably Feidhlimidh of Cill-mor-Dithraibh, or Kilmore, in the bar. of Boyle.

[4] *Deagha.* Bishop, and founder of Inis-Caoin-Deagha, now Inishkeen; a church near which are the remains of a round tower, giving name to a parish lying

Bricin,[1] friendly Iarlaithe,[2]
Feidhlim,[3] Deagha[4] of good degree,
Powerful, holy Mochaemhog,[5]
Cruimther-Fraech[6] of virtues great,
And Manchan[7] the miraculous—
These were the great company,
  Holy Caillin's band.[8]
"My wondrous, good *Dubh-diglach*[9]
Thou may'st have, O Adamnan;
  Sweet its tone to sound.
"Be it the Clogan-Adamnain,[10]
For Ui-Fiachrach and Ui-Amhalghaidh,
And for victorious Conall's race—
Woe to the chief whom it shall reach,
  Unless he it obey."
Jealousy and great envy seized
Mighty Caillin's family,
Against illustrious Adamnan,
  So that his glory changed;
And they did send off Adamnan,
From his monks, from his perquisites,
After powerful Colum,[11]
  Until he reached to Hi.[12]
Thereupon said Adamnan,
To holy, powerful Caillin,
"Thou may'st have all my monks,
  Both anear and afar."

partly in the co. of Monaghan, and partly in the co. of Louth. See Shirley's *Account of Farney*, pp. 180, 181.

[5] *Mochaemhog.* See note [5], p. 12, *supra.*

[6] *Cruimther Fraech.* See note [1], p. 192, *supra.*

[7] *Manchan.* See note [4], p. 12, *supra.*

[8] *band.* popal=Lat. populus.

[9] *Dubh-diglach;* i.e. "black-revenging"; apparently a different bell from Clog-na-righ, for which see note [2], p. 140.

[10] *Clogan-Adamnain;* i.e. "Adamnan's little Bell."

[11] *Colum.* St. Colum Cille.

[12] *Hi;* i.e. Iona, or Hy Colum-Cille, in Scotland.

Bennacht ar do manchaibsi,
Ar sil Fiachra is Amalgaid,
'S ar sil Conaill chorcruiġ,
Da ndenat mo réir.
IS ann atbert Cailline,
Ri hAdamnan adamra,
Ro bad medair suairc.
Biḋsi sunn im inadsa.
Is comed mo loccan sa,
'S na dilsiġ mo mancharsa,
Cein beosa ar mo cuairt.
Ro scrib Colam caemfertach,
Ina lebar isisi,
In sencus co caiḋ;
Sencus Caillin cumachtaiġ,
Ocus Conuill ċomramaiġ,
Da marthain da noirechtaib,
Comad moidi a cail. CAILLIN CAID.

Dliged Caillin on tir thuaid,
Do sil Conaill cloidemruaid,
Co Fidnacha na cet cros,
Lan a lerge ar a ċomos.

Finit don med fuaramar do sen liubair Caillin,
A°. D¹. M°. 500. r. C°.

[1] *blessing.* This blessing would seem to have been uttered by St. Caillin.

[2] *remain here:* i.e. at Fenagh. This stanza is probably misplaced, and should come before the 5th stanza preceding, in which Adamnan's expulsion by St. Caillin's community is related.

[3] *history.* There is no account of this

"A blessing[1] be upon thy monks,
On the seed of Fiachra and Amhalgaidh,
And on victorious Conall's race,
    If they do me obey."
Then it was that Caillin said,
Unto illustrious Adamnan,
    That pleasant it would be.
"Do thou remain here[2] in my stead,
And keep thou my little place,
And do not alienate my dues,
    Whilst I am on my tour."
Fair, wonder-working Colum wrote,
In his book of history,[3]
    The *senchus* holily;
The *senchus* of Caillin great,
And of triumphant Conall,
To preserve it for their assemblies,
    That the higher might be their fame. HOLY CAILLIN.[4]

Caillin's dues from the northern land,
From the race of red-sword Conall;
To [be sent to] Fenagh of the hundred crosses,
(Whose plain full is at his command).[5]

Finit of all we found of Caillin's Old Book.
A.D. 1516.

history alleged to have been written by St. Colum Cille. The statement probably alludes to the portion of the present work ascribed to that saint. Vid. *supra*, p. 201.

[4] *Holy Caillin.* These are the first words of the foregoing poem, added here in token of its conclusion.

[5] *command.* This stanza is written in a curious zig-zag fashion at the end of the work (fol. 48, b.)

INDEX.

www.ingramcontent.com/pod-product-compliance
Lightning Source LLC
Chambersburg PA
CBHW022139300426
44115CB00006B/256
* 9 7 8 3 3 3 7 1 4 7 7 3 0 *